KT-471-157

岸本斉史

2016 ...er going for f...r
...years ...... And if I do say so
myself, I think I've worked pretty
hard... So I thought to myself,
feeling pretty good about it out
on the porch. I'll keep giving it my
best in year five!

—*Masashi Kishimoto, 2003*

Author/artist Masashi Kishimoto was born in 1974 in rural
Okayama Prefecture, Japan. After spending time in art college,
he won the Hop Step Award for new manga artists with his
manga **Karakuri** (Mechanism). Kishimoto decided to base his
next story on traditional Japanese culture. His first version of
Naruto, drawn in 1997, was a one-shot story about fox spirits;
his final version, which debuted in **Weekly Shonen Jump** in
1999, quickly became the most popular ninja manga in Japan.

30131 04502157 0

London Borough of Barnet

NARUTO VOL. 19
The SHONEN JUMP Manga Edition

STORY AND ART BY MASASHI KISHIMOTO

Translation/Kyoko Shapiro, HC Language Solutions, Inc.
English Adaptation/Ian Reid, HC Language Solutions, Inc.
Touch-up Art & Lettering/Gia Cam Luc
Design/Yvonne Cai
Editor/Joel Enos

Editor in Chief, Books/Alvin Lu
Editor in Chief, Magazines/Marc Weidenbaum
VP of Publishing Licensing/Rika Inouye
VP of Sales/Gonzalo Ferreyra
Sr. VP of Marketing/Liza Coppola
Publisher/Hyoe Narita

NARUTO © 1999 by Masashi Kishimoto. All rights reserved.
First published in Japan in 1999 by SHUEISHA Inc., Tokyo.
English translation rights in the United States of America and
Canada arranged by SHUEISHA Inc. The stories, characters and
incidents mentioned in this publication are entirely fictional.

No portion of this book may be reproduced or transmitted
in any form or by any means without written permission
from the copyright holders.

Printed in Canada

Published by VIZ Media, LLC
P.O. Box 77010
San Francisco, CA 94107

SHONEN JUMP Manga Edition
10 9 8 7 6 5 4 3 2 1
First printing, October 2007

BARNET LIBRARIES

GOSH   2011

PARENTAL ADVISORY
NARUTO is rated T for Teen and is recommended
for ages 13 and up. This volume contains realistic
and fantasy violence.
ratings.viz.com

www.viz.com

THE WORLD'S
MOST POPULAR MANGA

www.shonenjump.com

SHONEN JUMP MANGA EDITION

NARUTO™

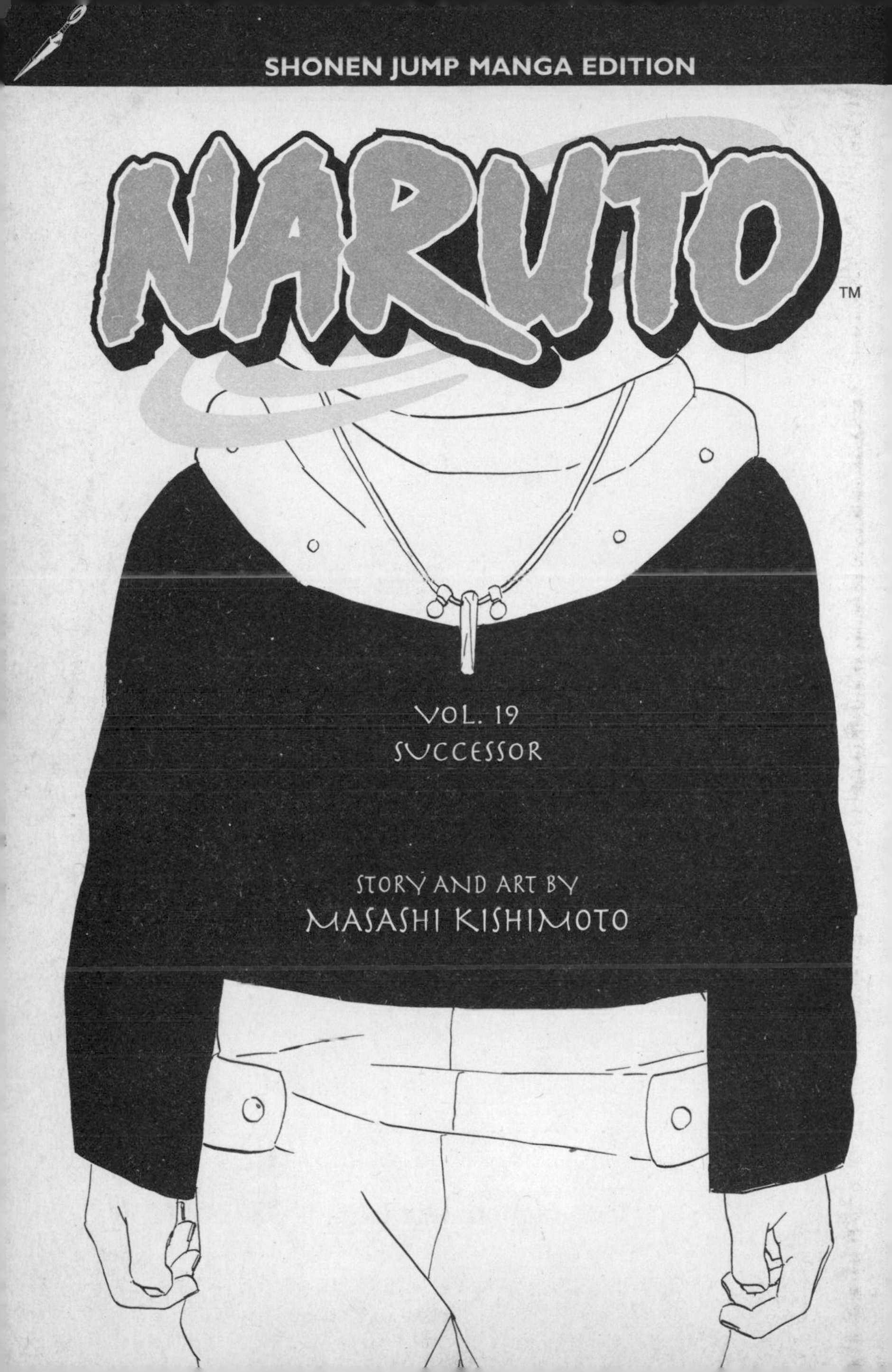

VOL. 19
SUCCESSOR

STORY AND ART BY
MASASHI KISHIMOTO

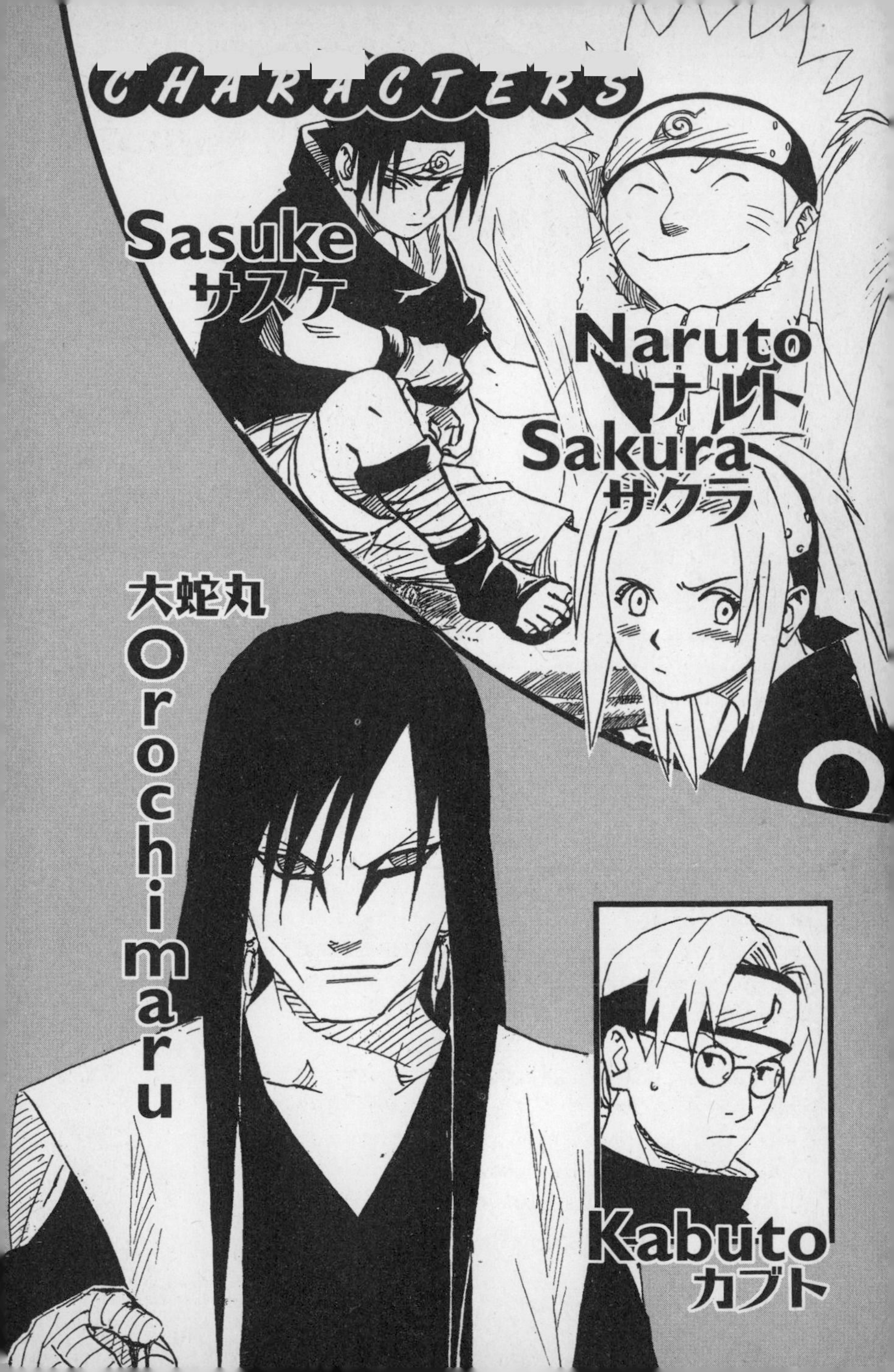
CHARACTERS
Naruto
ナルト
Sakura
サクラ
Sasuke
サスケ
Kabuto
カブト
大蛇丸
Orochimaru

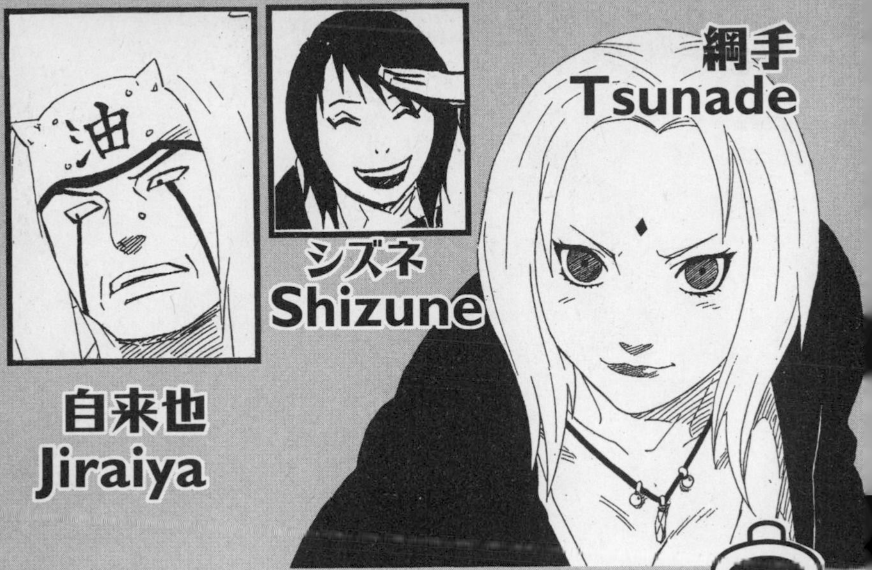
網手
Tsunade
シズネ
Shizune
自来也
Jiraiya

The Story So Far...

Twelve years ago a destructive nine-tailed fox spirit attacked the ninja village of Konohagakure. The Hokage, or village champion, defeated the fox by sealing its soul into the body of a baby boy. Now that boy, Uzumaki Naruto, has grown up to be a ninja-in-training, learning the art of ninjutsu with his teammates Sakura and Sasuke.

Naruto and company take on the Chûnin Selection Exams but suffer a sudden attack from Orochimaru in the Forest of Death. Orochimaru leaves a curse mark on Sasuke's body and vanishes, only to return during the final round to launch *Operation Destroy Konoha!* While Naruto battles Gaara, the Third Hokage falls to Orochimaru.

Jiraiya, taking Naruto along for training, sets out on a journey to find the Fifth Hokage, Tsunade. Meanwhile, Orochimaru makes Tsunade a proposition: in exchange for healing his arms, he would revive her deceased loved ones. As Tsunade struggles to decide, Jiraiya and Naruto arrive on the scene. What will Tsunade choose...?!

NARUTO

VOL. 19
SUCCESSOR

CONTENTS

Number 163: Undecayed...!!

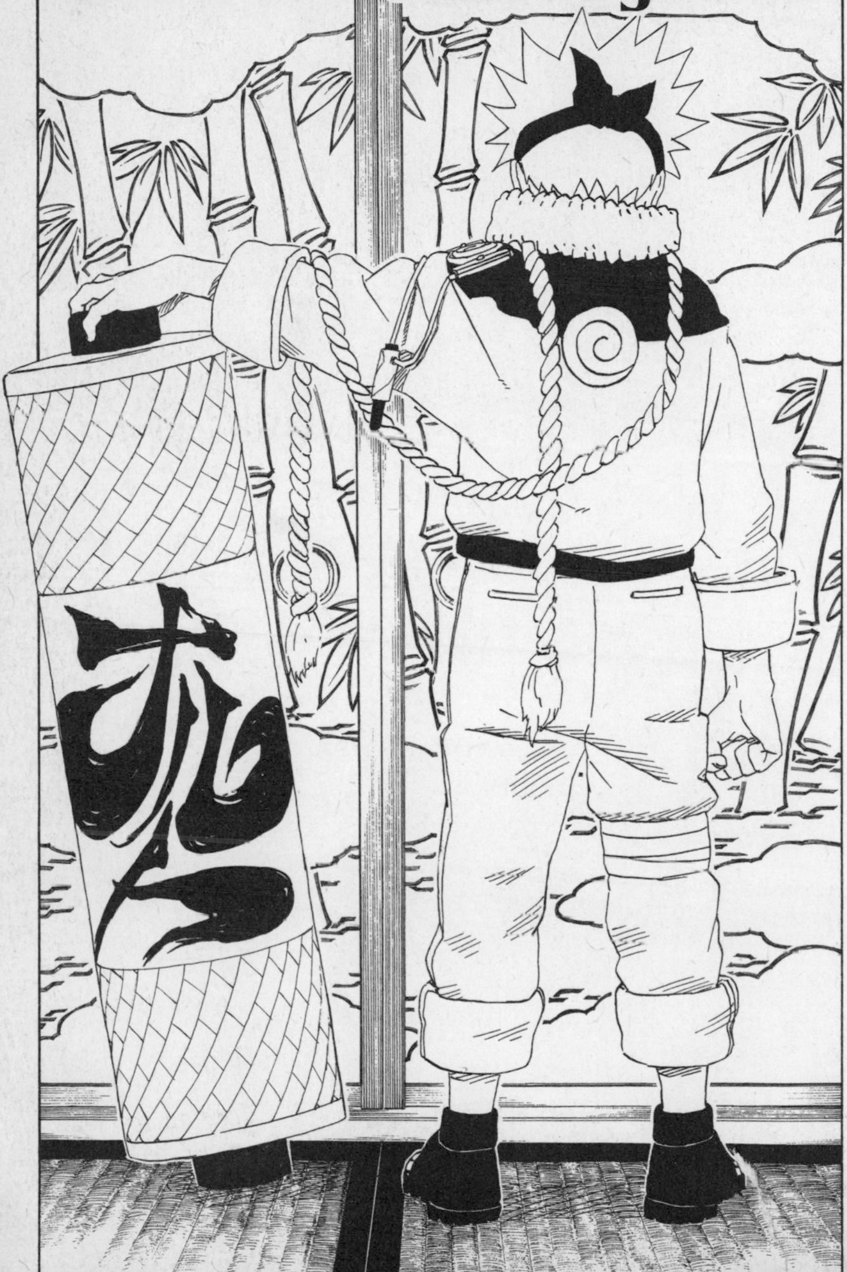

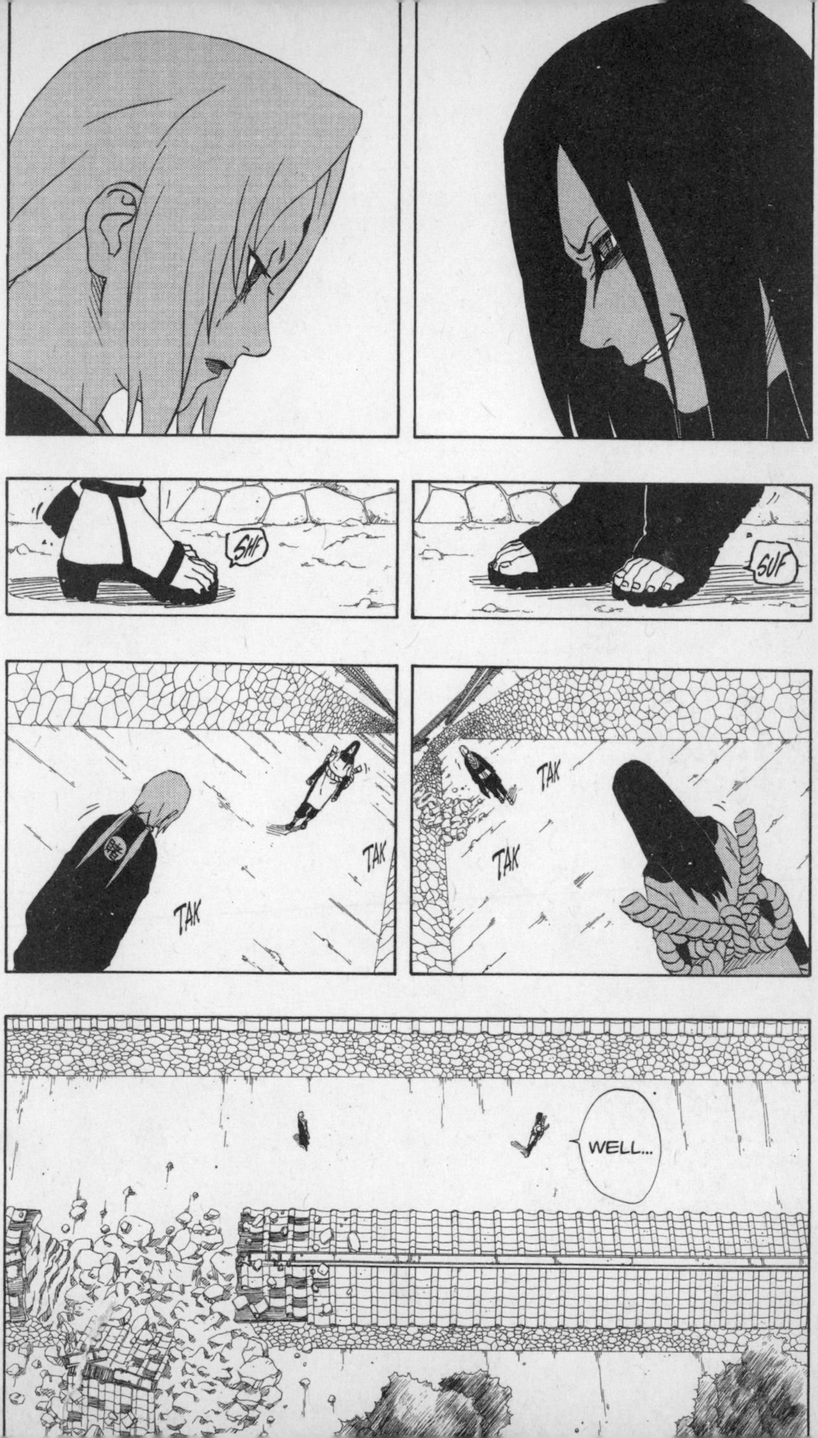
SUF
SHF
TAK
TAK
TAK
TAK
WELL...

READ THIS WAY

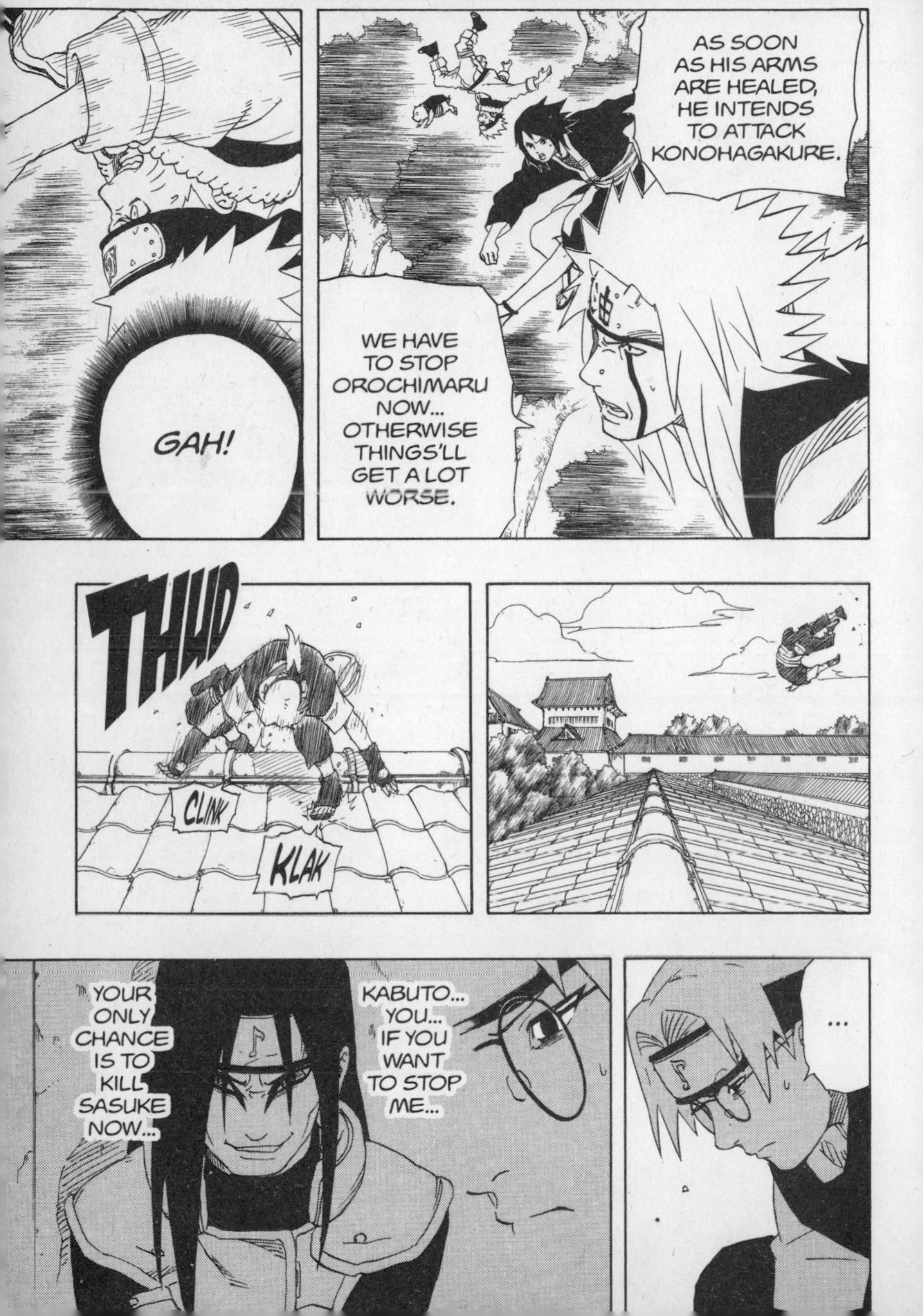
AS SOON AS HIS ARMS ARE HEALED, HE INTENDS TO ATTACK KONOHAGAKURE.
WE HAVE TO STOP OROCHIMARU NOW... OTHERWISE THINGS'LL GET A LOT WORSE.
GAH!
THUD
CLINK
KLAK
...
KABUTO... YOU... IF YOU WANT TO STOP ME...
YOUR ONLY CHANCE IS TO KILL SASUKE NOW...

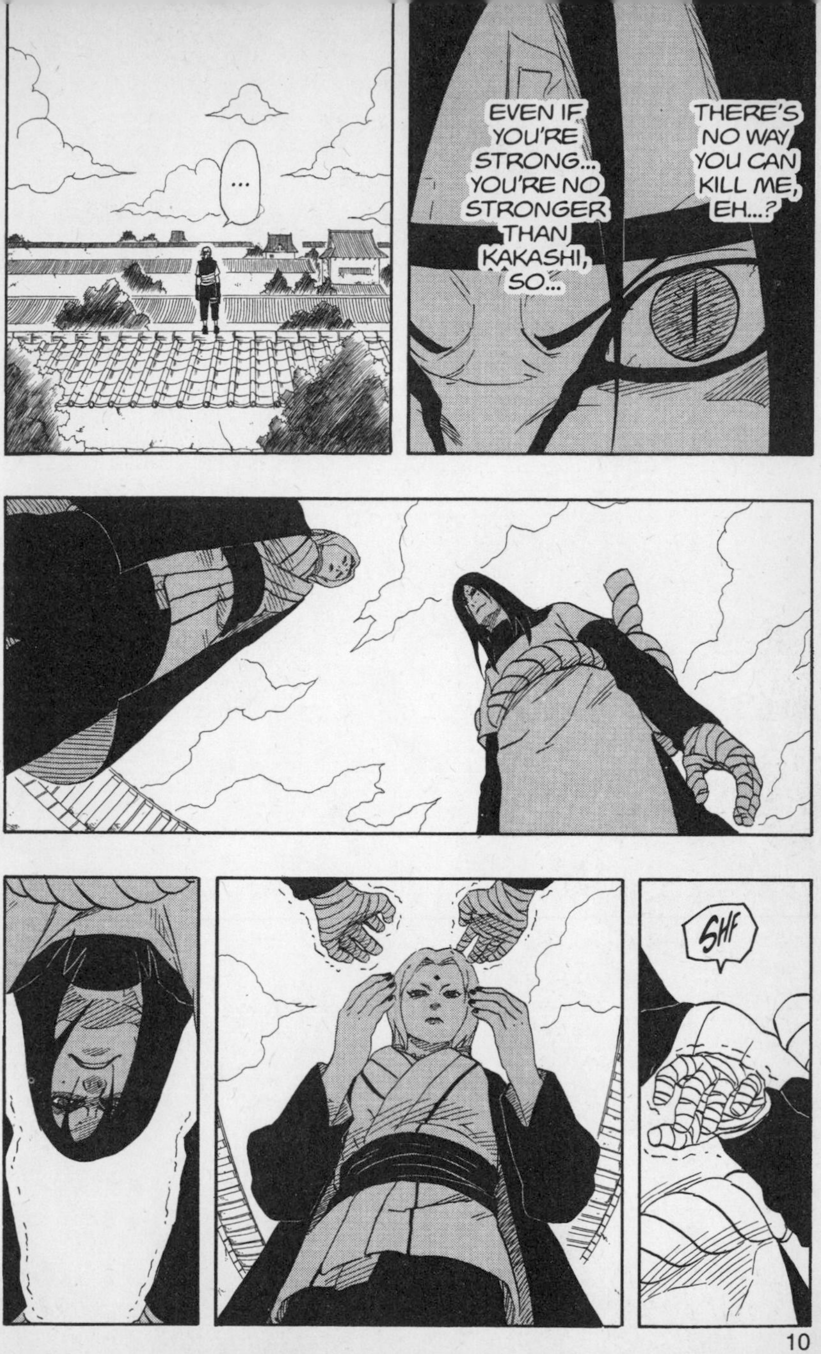
THERE'S NO WAY YOU CAN KILL ME, EH...?
EVEN IF YOU'RE STRONG... YOU'RE NO STRONGER THAN KAKASHI, SO...
...
SHF

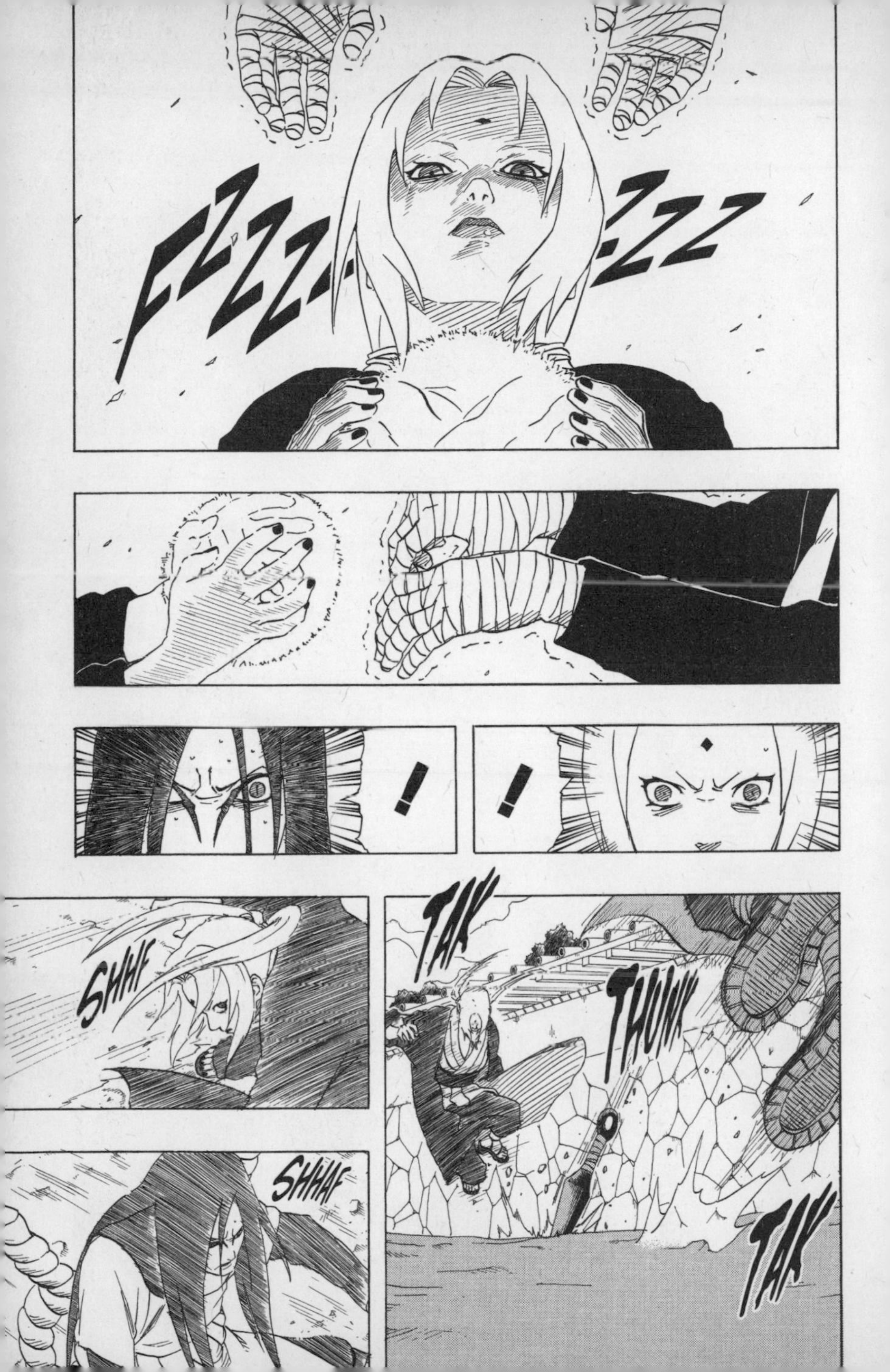
FZZZ...
...ZZZ
!
!
TAK
THUNK
TAK
SHHF
SHHAF

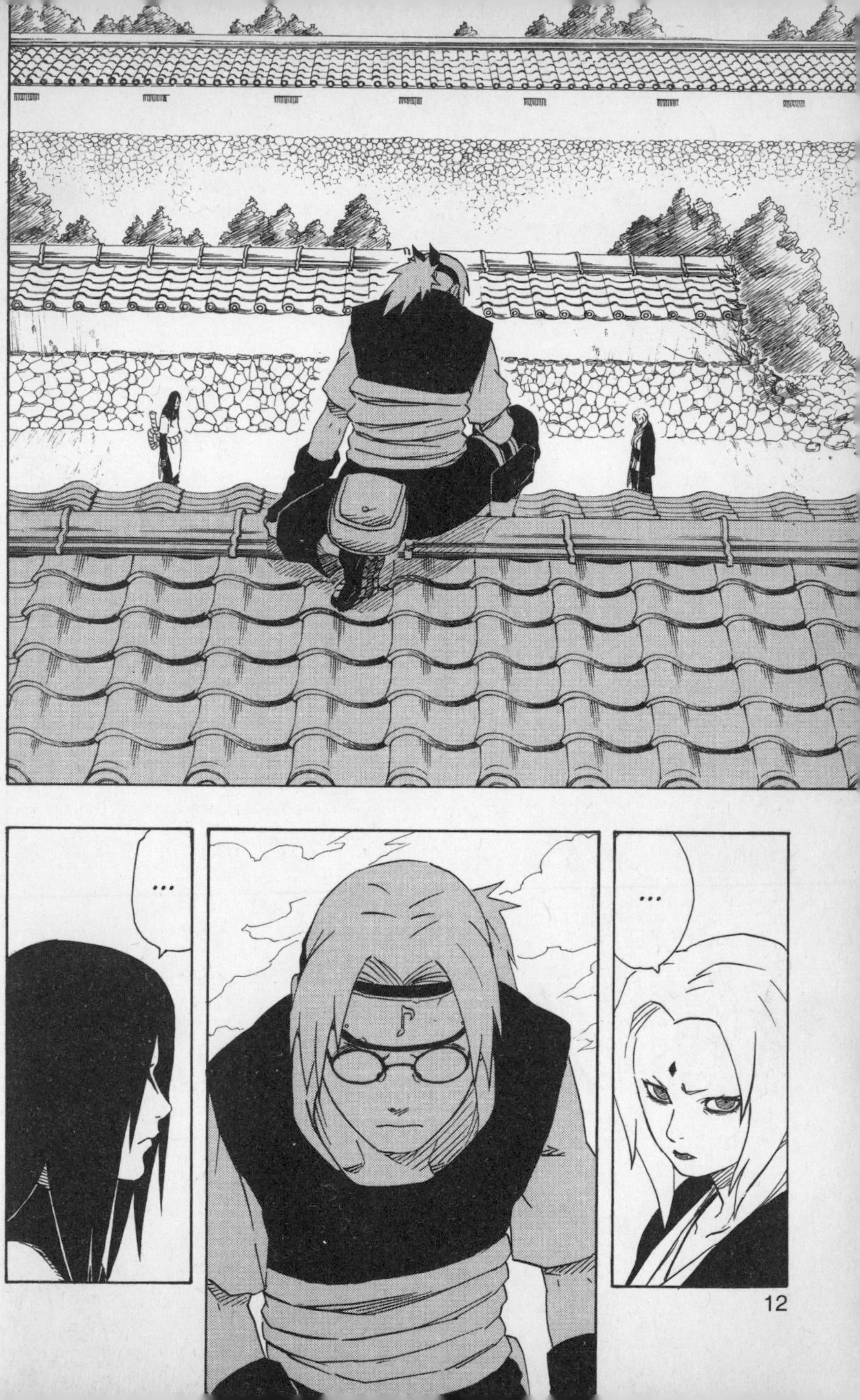
...
...

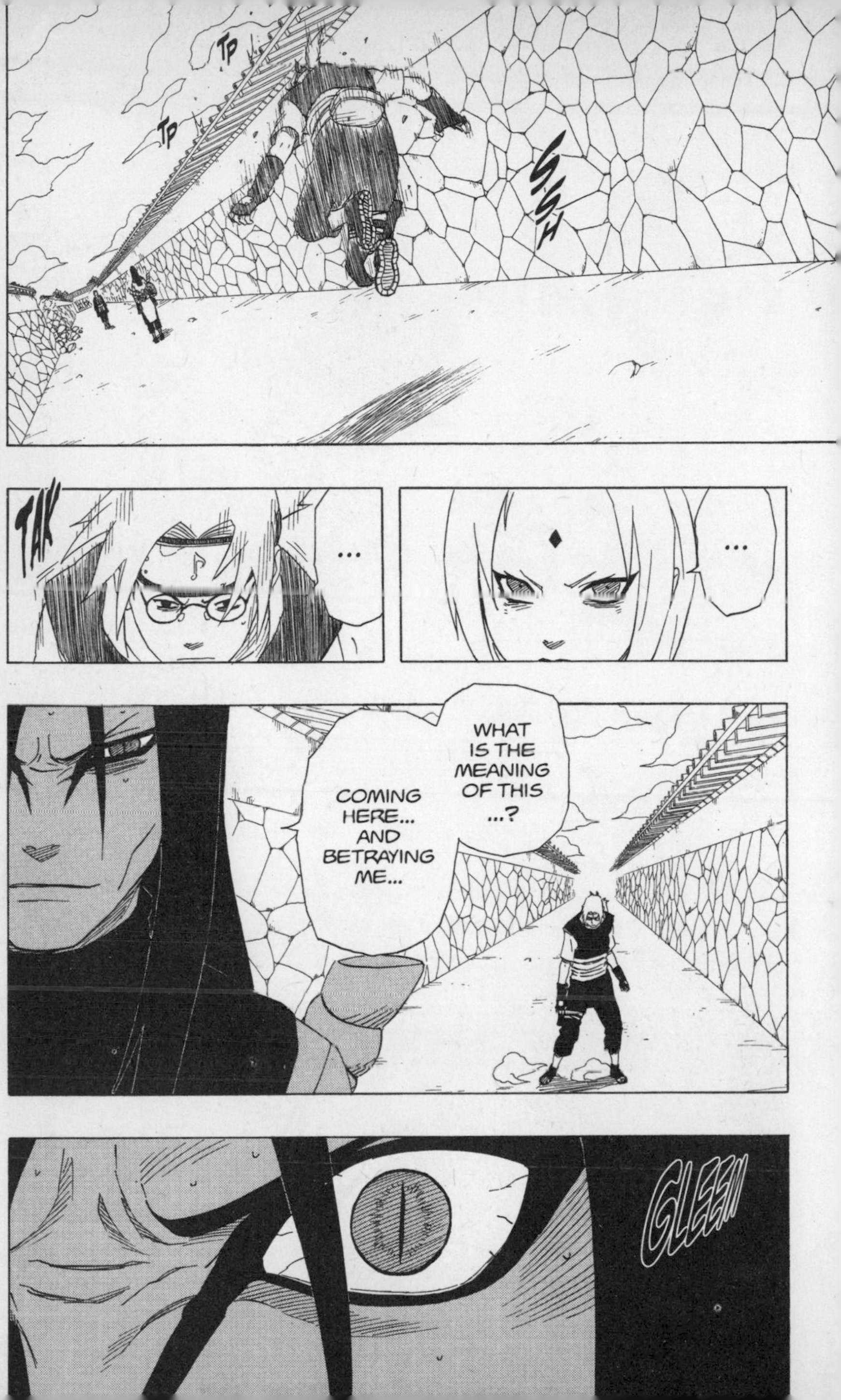
TP
TP
SWSH
...
TAK
...
WHAT IS THE MEANING OF THIS ...?
COMING HERE... AND BETRAYING ME...
GLEEM

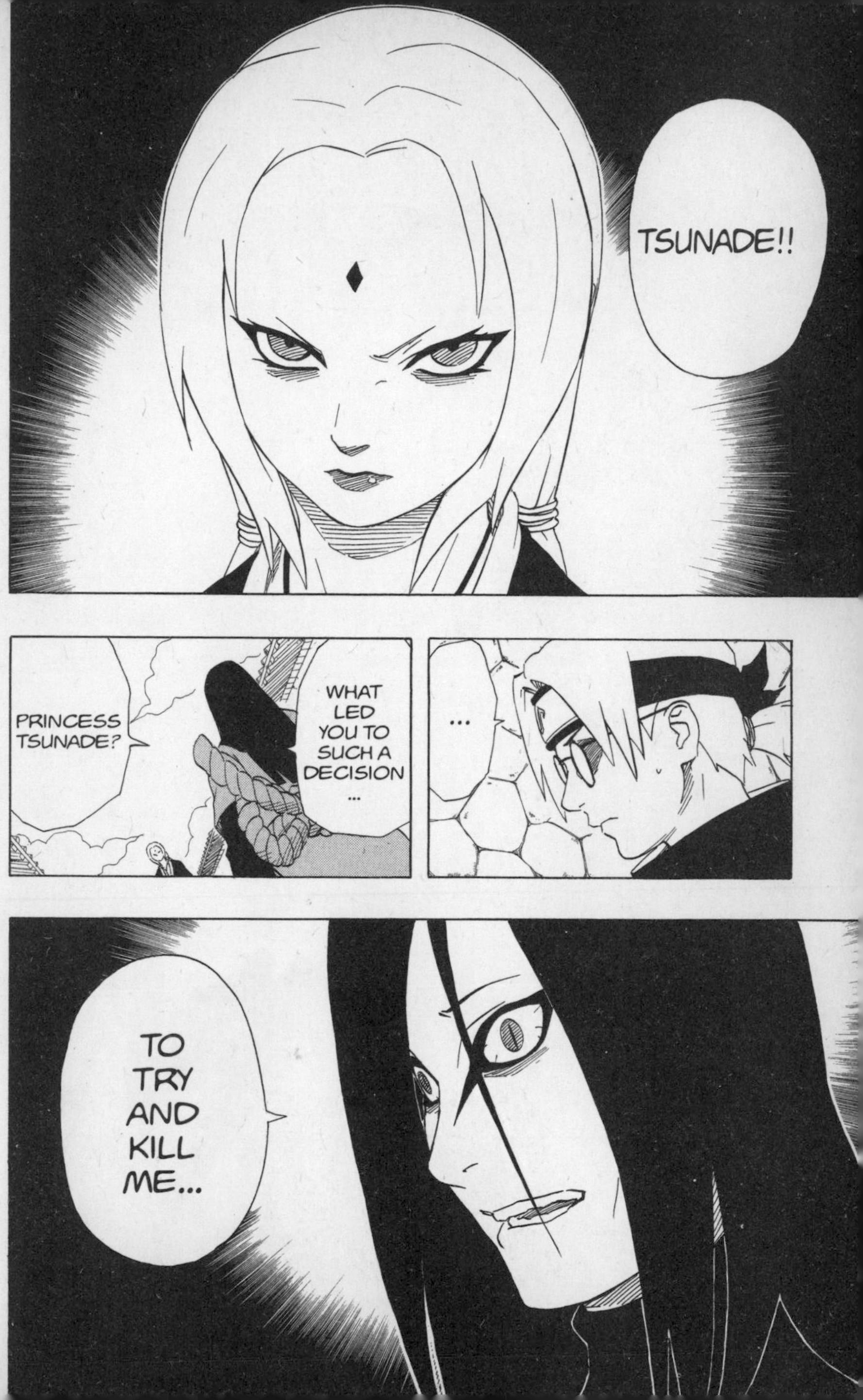
TSUNADE!!
...
WHAT LED YOU TO SUCH A DECISION ...
PRINCESS TSUNADE?
TO TRY AND KILL ME...

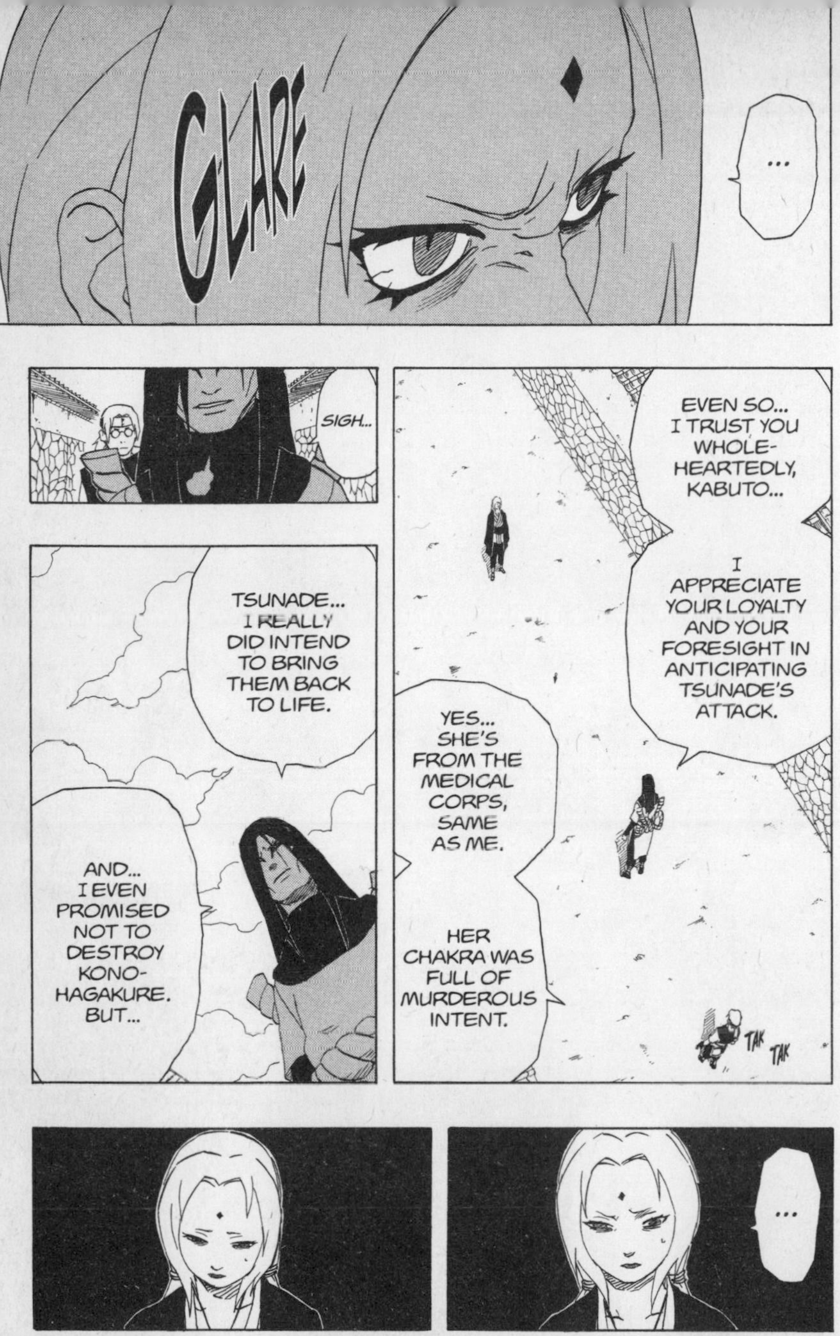
...
GLARE
EVEN SO... I TRUST YOU WHOLE-HEARTEDLY, KABUTO...
I APPRECIATE YOUR LOYALTY AND YOUR FORESIGHT IN ANTICIPATING TSUNADE'S ATTACK.
YES... SHE'S FROM THE MEDICAL CORPS, SAME AS ME.
HER CHAKRA WAS FULL OF MURDEROUS INTENT.
TAK TAK
SIGH...
TSUNADE... I REALLY DID INTEND TO BRING THEM BACK TO LIFE.
AND... I EVEN PROMISED NOT TO DESTROY KONO-HAGAKURE. BUT...
...

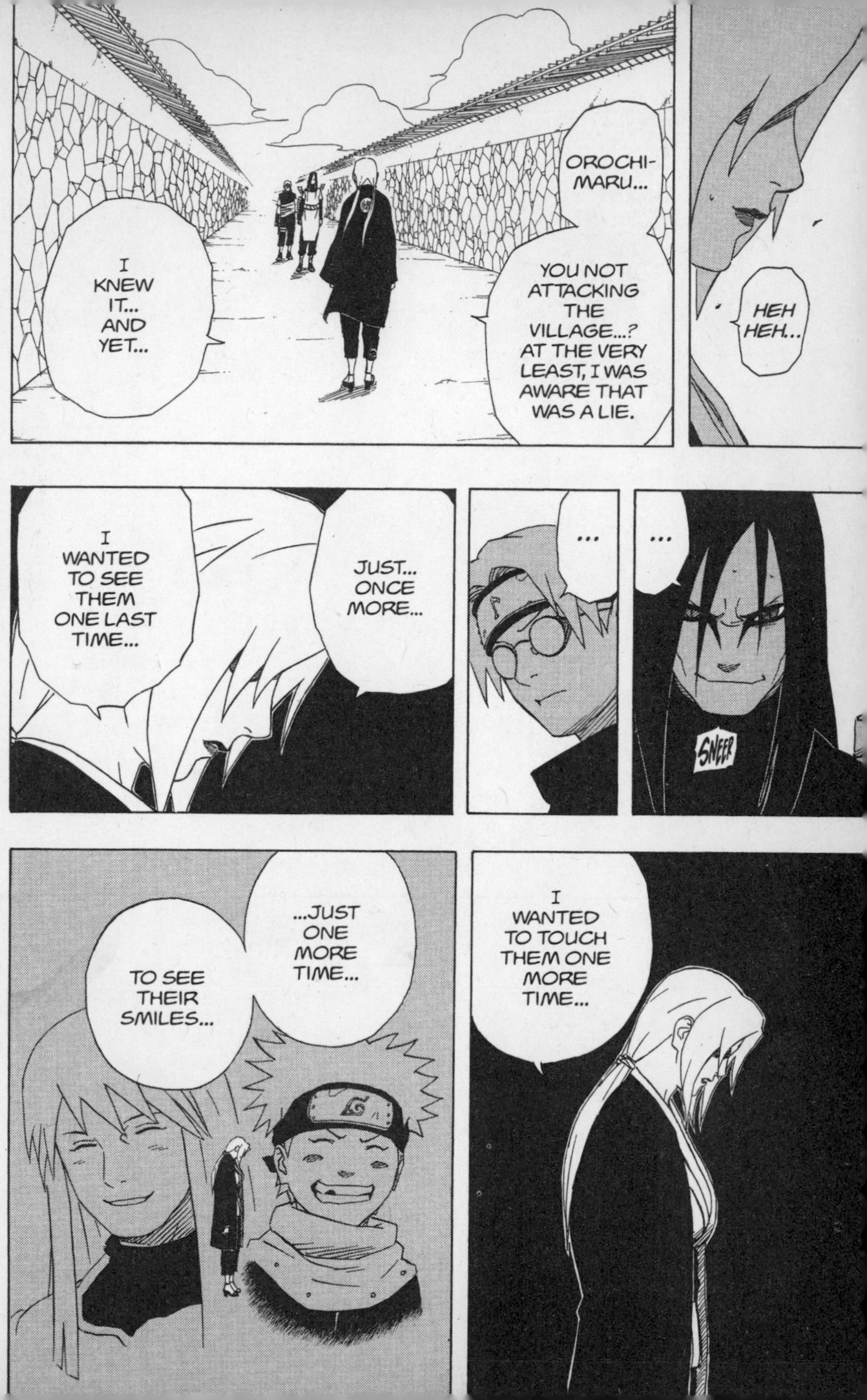
HEH HEH...
OROCHI-MARU...
YOU NOT ATTACKING THE VILLAGE...? AT THE VERY LEAST, I WAS AWARE THAT WAS A LIE.
I KNEW IT... AND YET...
...
SNEER
...
JUST... ONCE MORE...
I WANTED TO SEE THEM ONE LAST TIME...
I WANTED TO TOUCH THEM ONE MORE TIME...
...JUST ONE MORE TIME...
TO SEE THEIR SMILES...

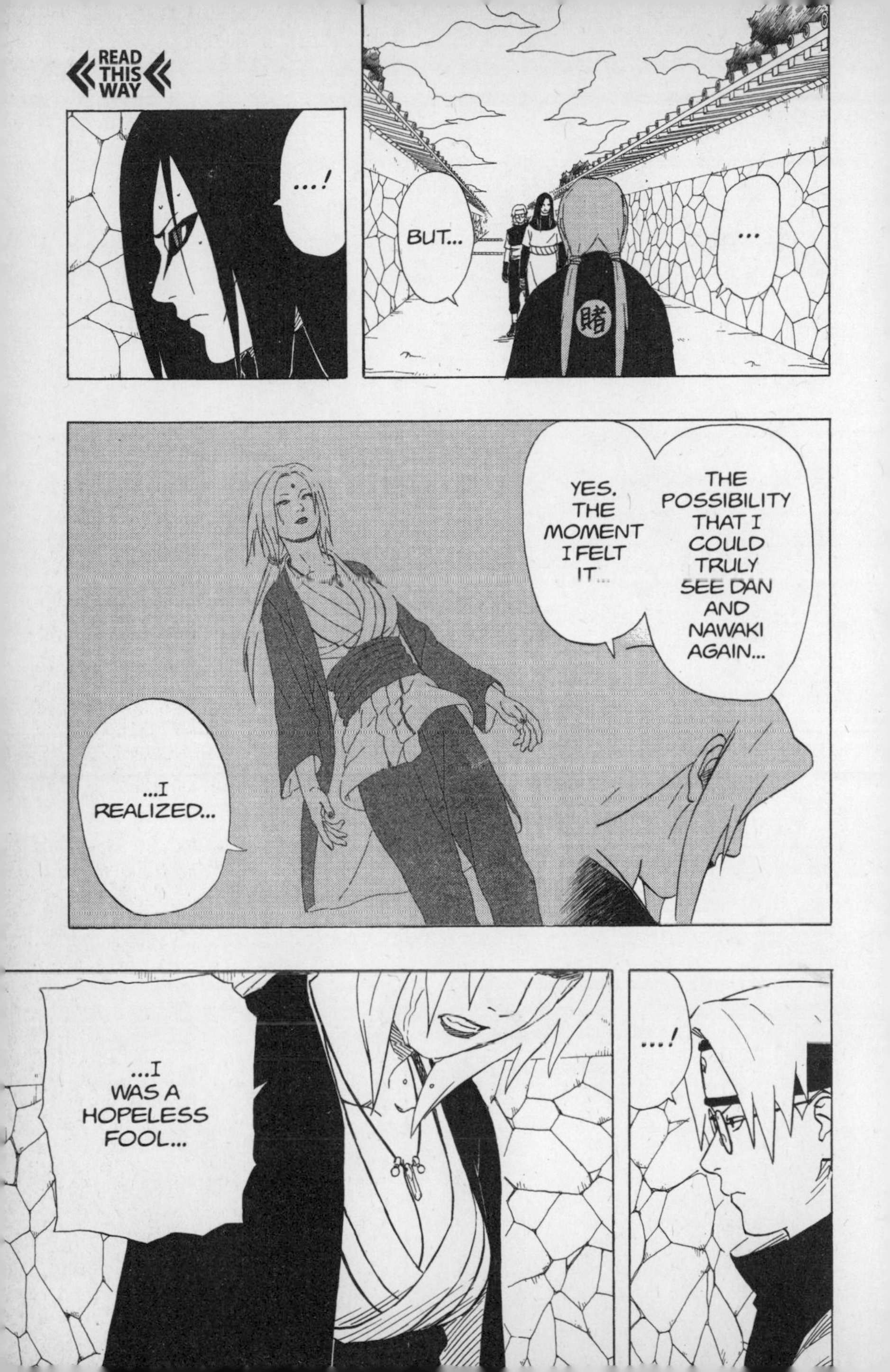
READ THIS WAY
...
BUT...
...!
THE POSSIBILITY THAT I COULD TRULY SEE DAN AND NAWAKI AGAIN...
YES. THE MOMENT I FELT IT...
...I REALIZED...
...!
...I WAS A HOPELESS FOOL...

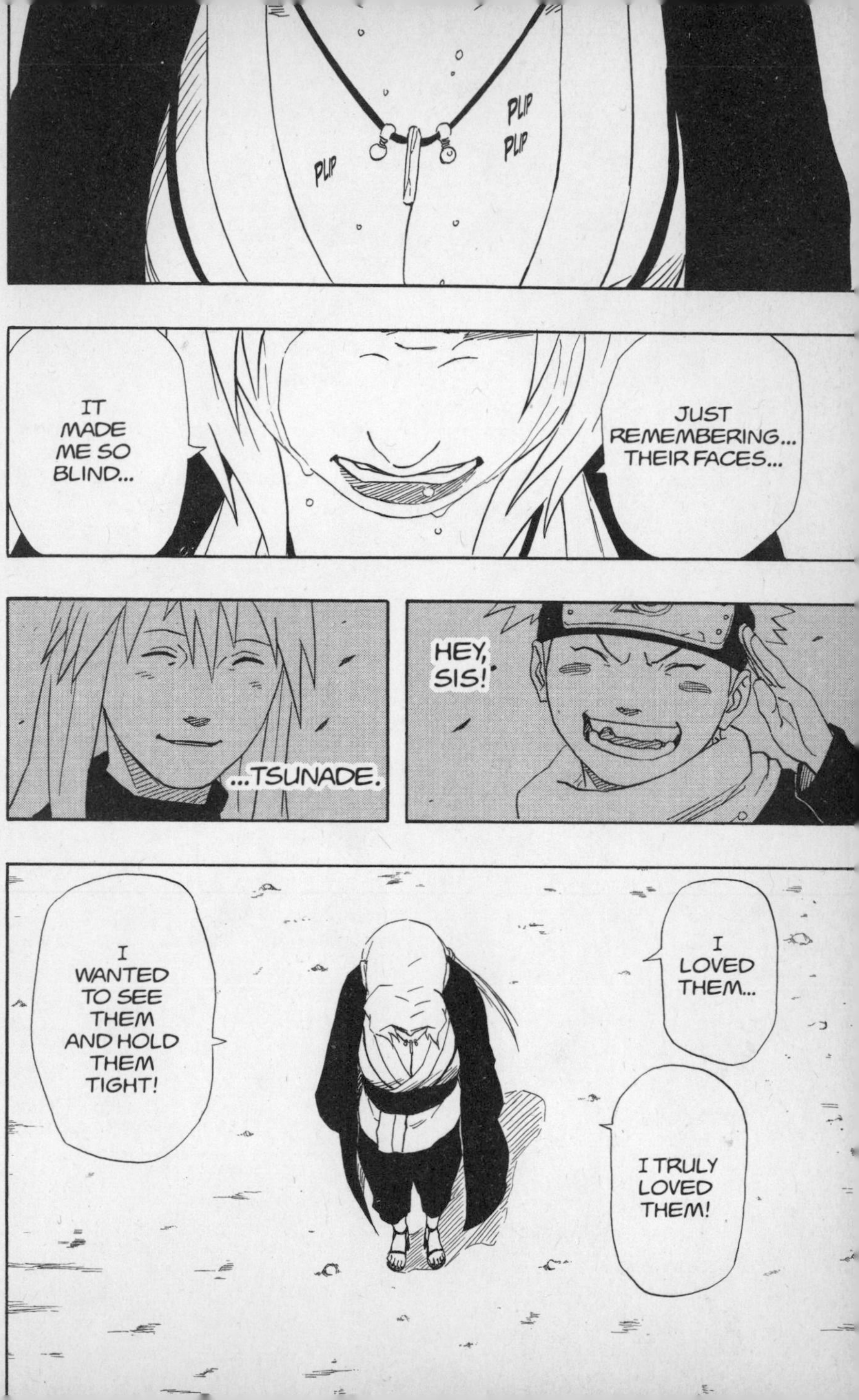
PLIP
PLIP
PLIP
JUST REMEMBERING... THEIR FACES...
IT MADE ME SO BLIND...
HEY, SIS!
...TSUNADE.
I LOVED THEM...
I TRULY LOVED THEM!
I WANTED TO SEE THEM AND HOLD THEM TIGHT!

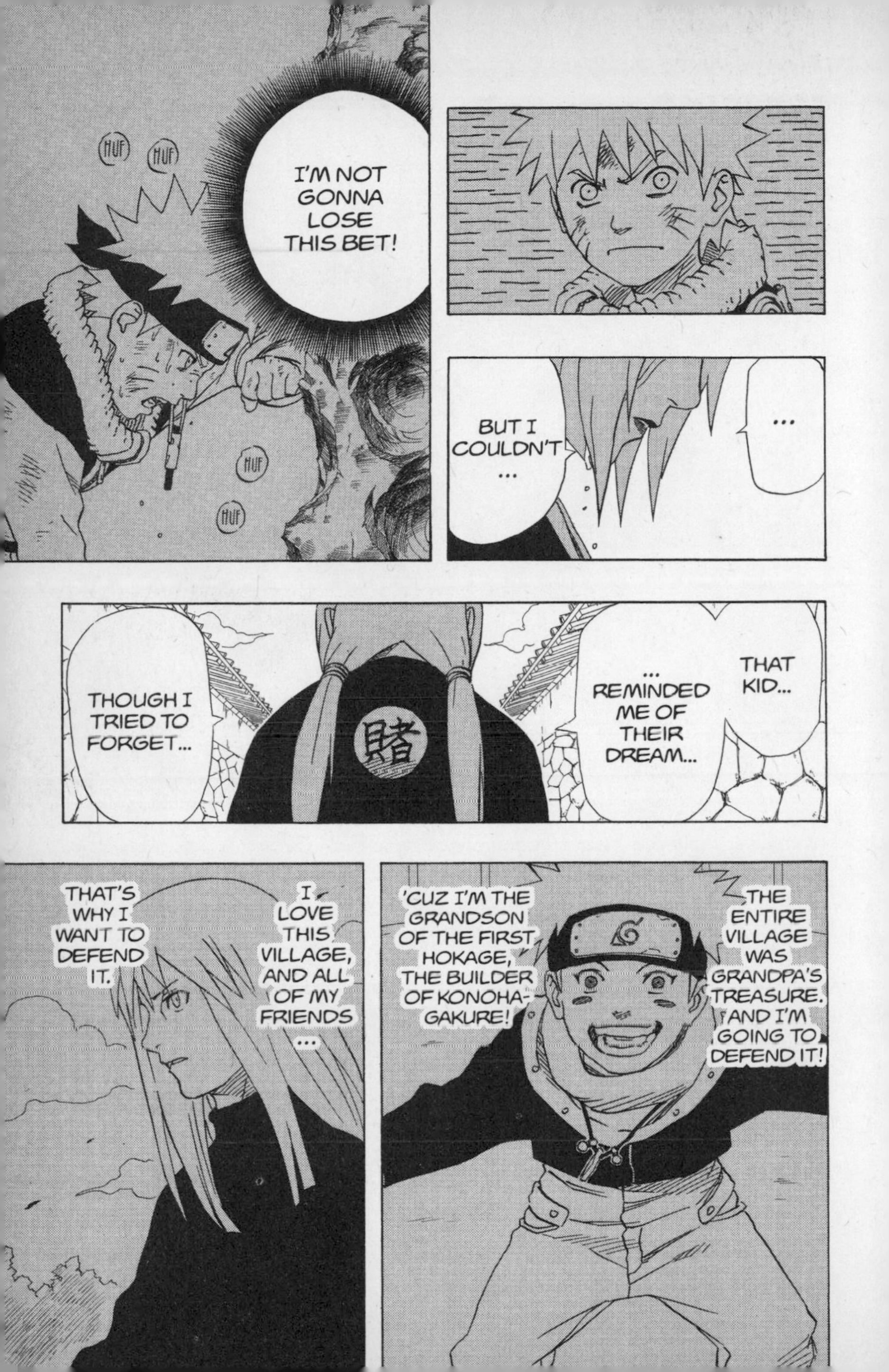
...
BUT I COULDN'T ...
HUF
HUF
I'M NOT GONNA LOSE THIS BET!
HUF
HUF
THAT KID...
... REMINDED ME OF THEIR DREAM...
THOUGH I TRIED TO FORGET...
賭
THE ENTIRE VILLAGE WAS GRANDPA'S TREASURE. AND I'M GOING TO DEFEND IT!
'CUZ I'M THE GRANDSON OF THE FIRST HOKAGE, THE BUILDER OF KONOHA-GAKURE!
I LOVE THIS VILLAGE, AND ALL OF MY FRIENDS ...
THAT'S WHY I WANT TO DEFEND IT.

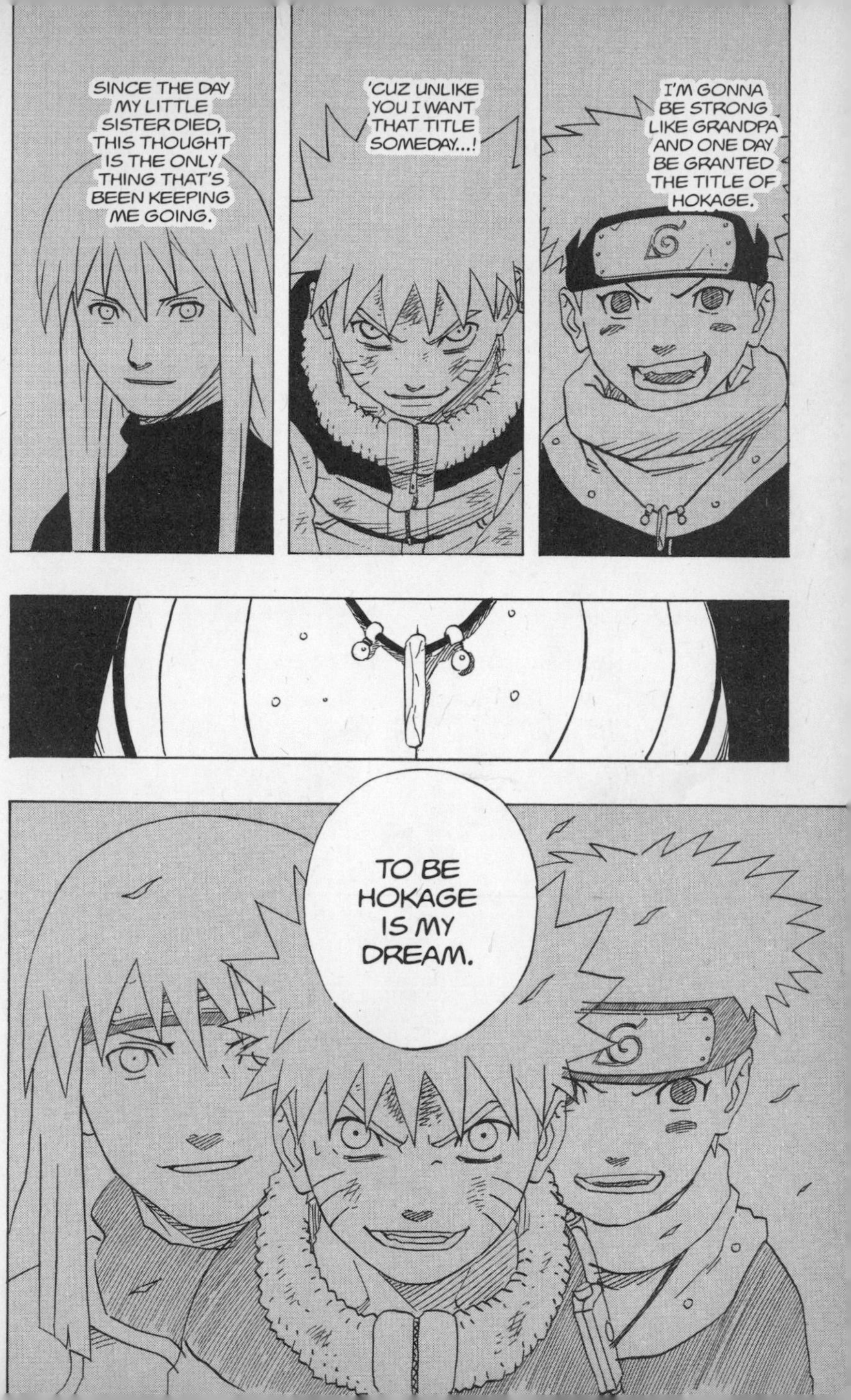
I'M GONNA BE STRONG LIKE GRANDPA AND ONE DAY BE GRANTED THE TITLE OF HOKAGE.
'CUZ UNLIKE YOU I WANT THAT TITLE SOMEDAY...!
SINCE THE DAY MY LITTLE SISTER DIED, THIS THOUGHT IS THE ONLY THING THAT'S BEEN KEEPING ME GOING.
TO BE HOKAGE IS MY DREAM.

READ THIS WAY

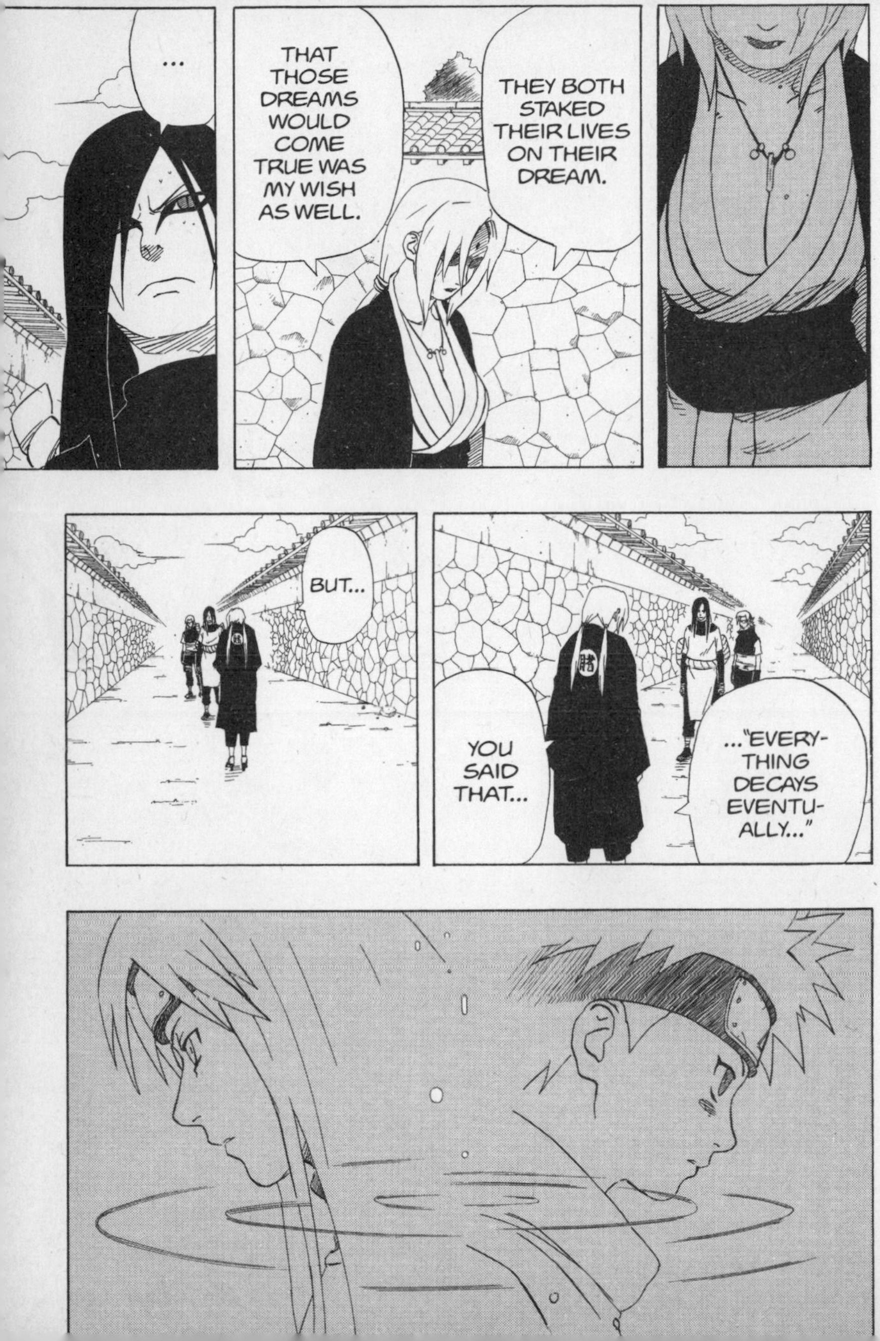
THEY BOTH STAKED THEIR LIVES ON THEIR DREAM.
THAT THOSE DREAMS WOULD COME TRUE WAS MY WISH AS WELL.
...
YOU SAID THAT...
..."EVERYTHING DECAYS EVENTUALLY..."
BUT...

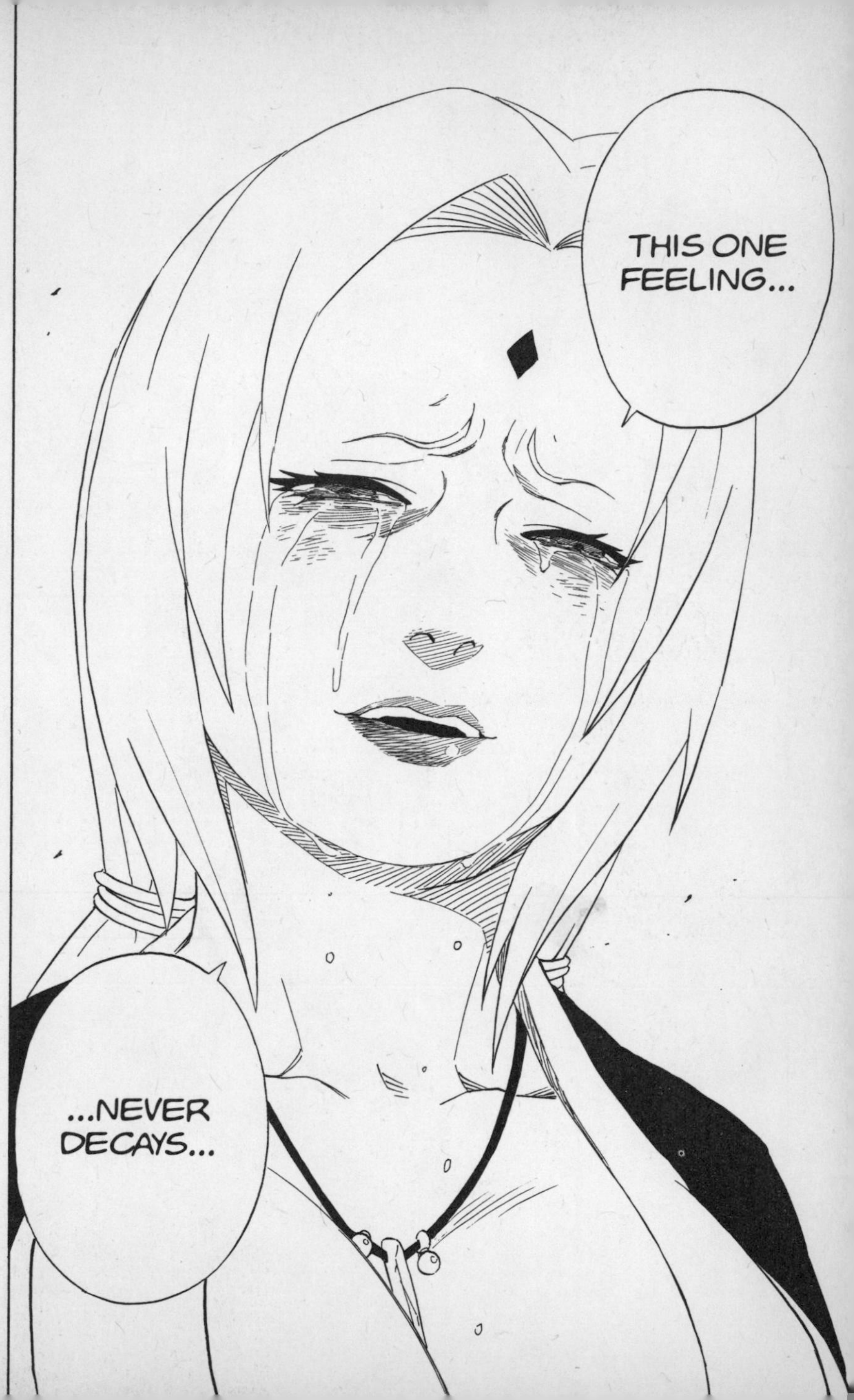
THIS ONE FEELING...
...NEVER DECAYS...

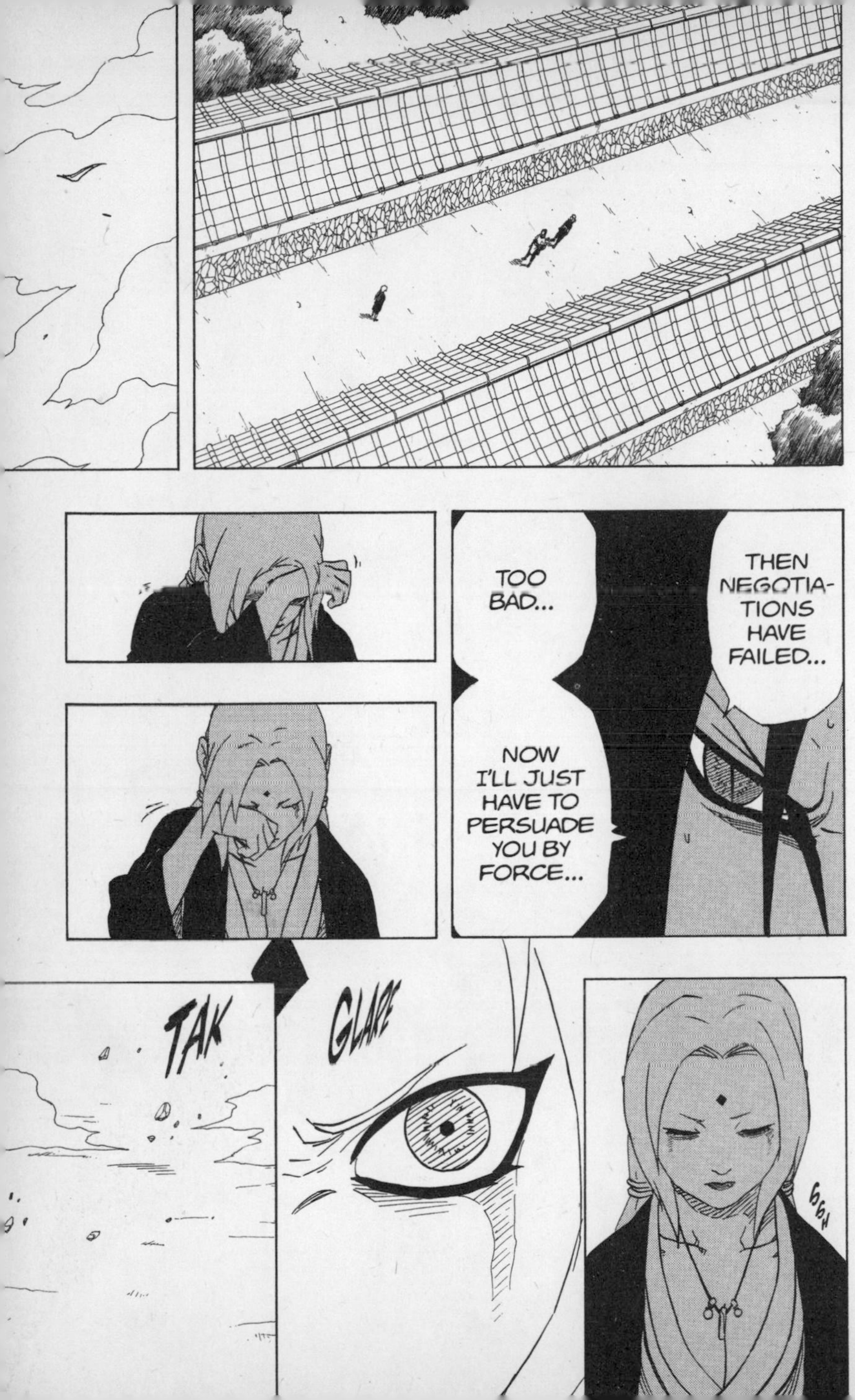
THEN NEGOTIATIONS HAVE FAILED...
TOO BAD...
NOW I'LL JUST HAVE TO PERSUADE YOU BY FORCE...
GGH
GLARE
TAK

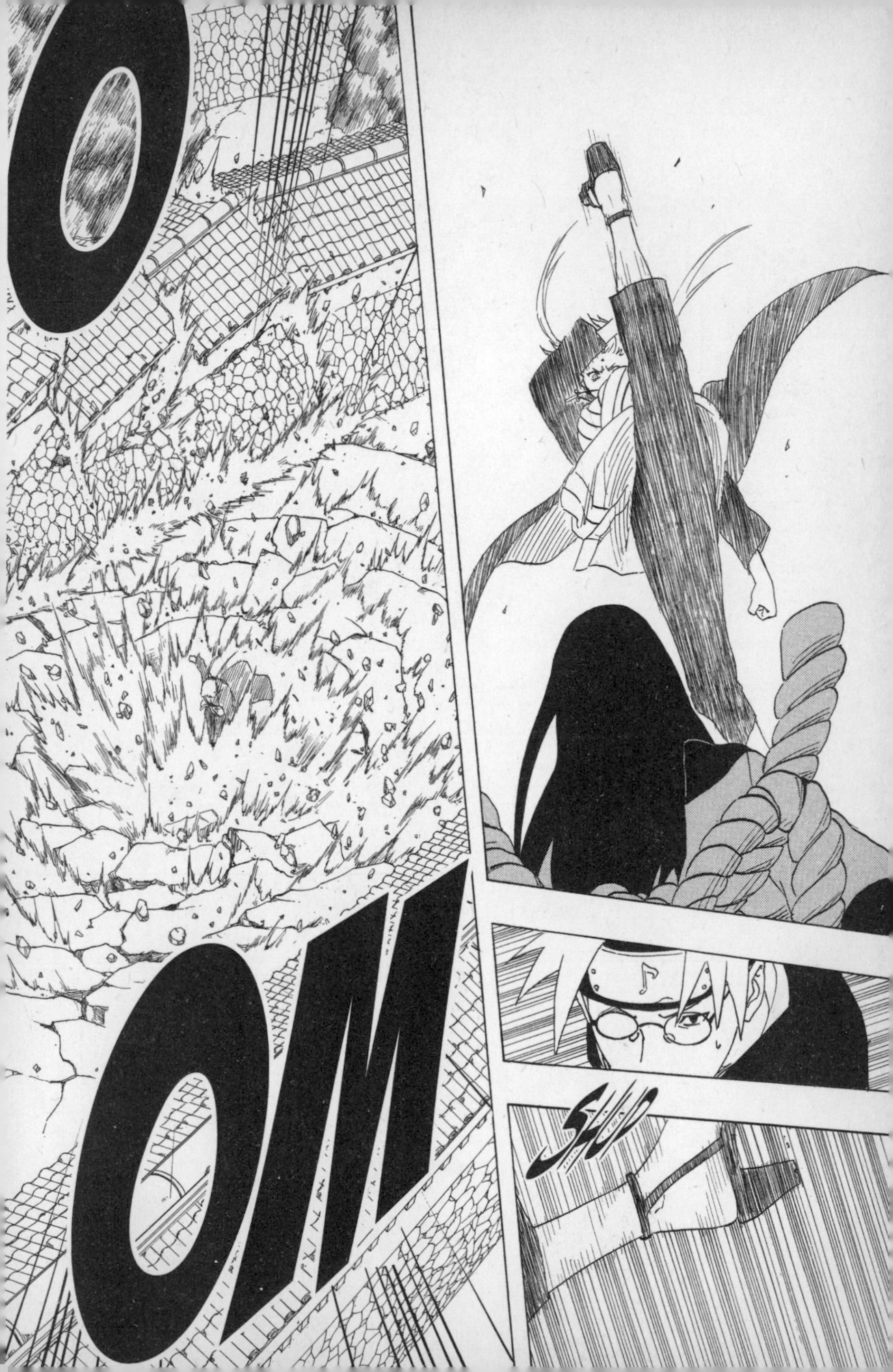
OOM

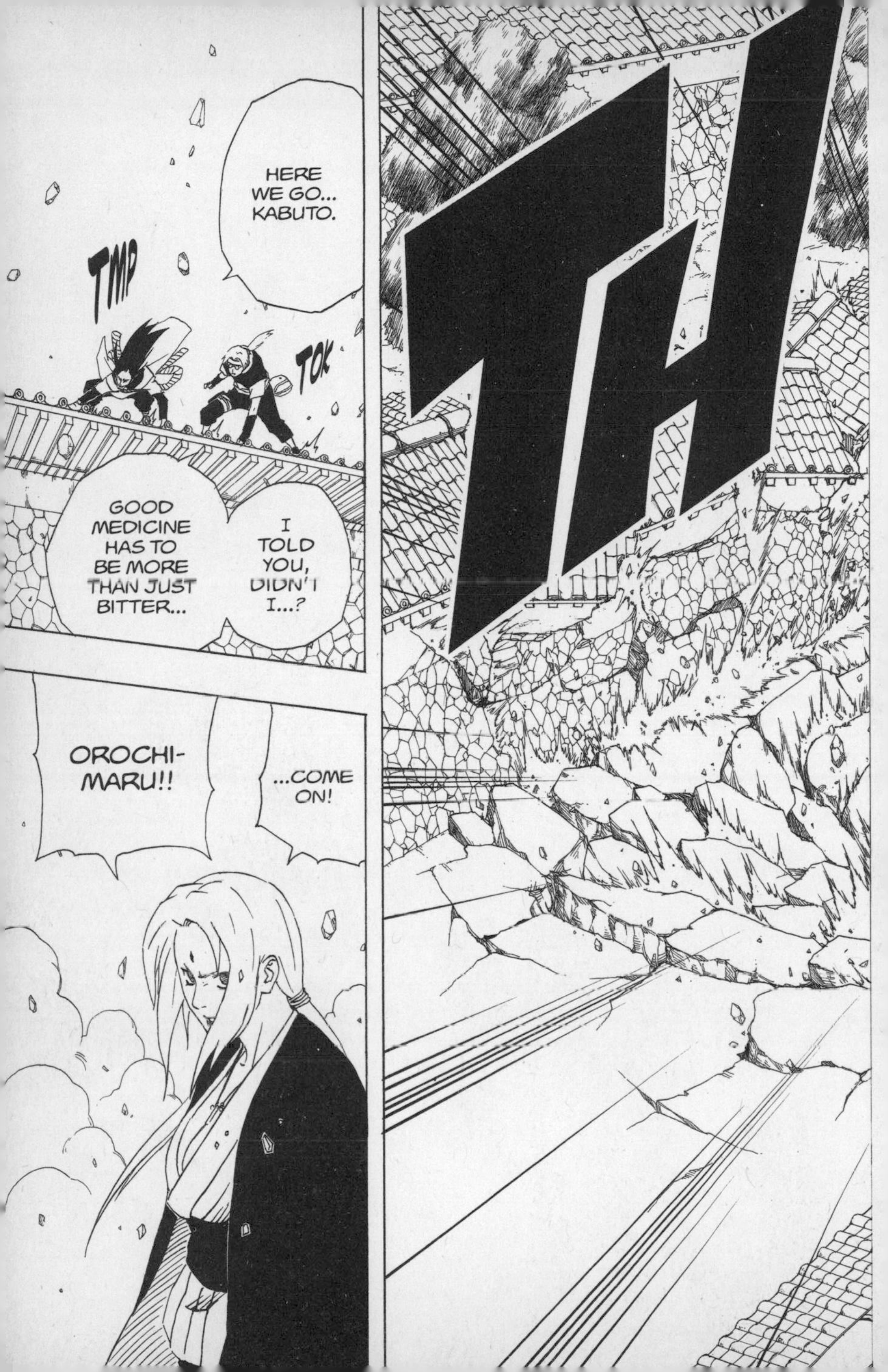
TH
HERE WE GO... KABUTO.
TOK
TMP
I TOLD YOU, DIDN'T I...?
GOOD MEDICINE HAS TO BE MORE THAN JUST BITTER...
...COME ON!
OROCHI-MARU!!

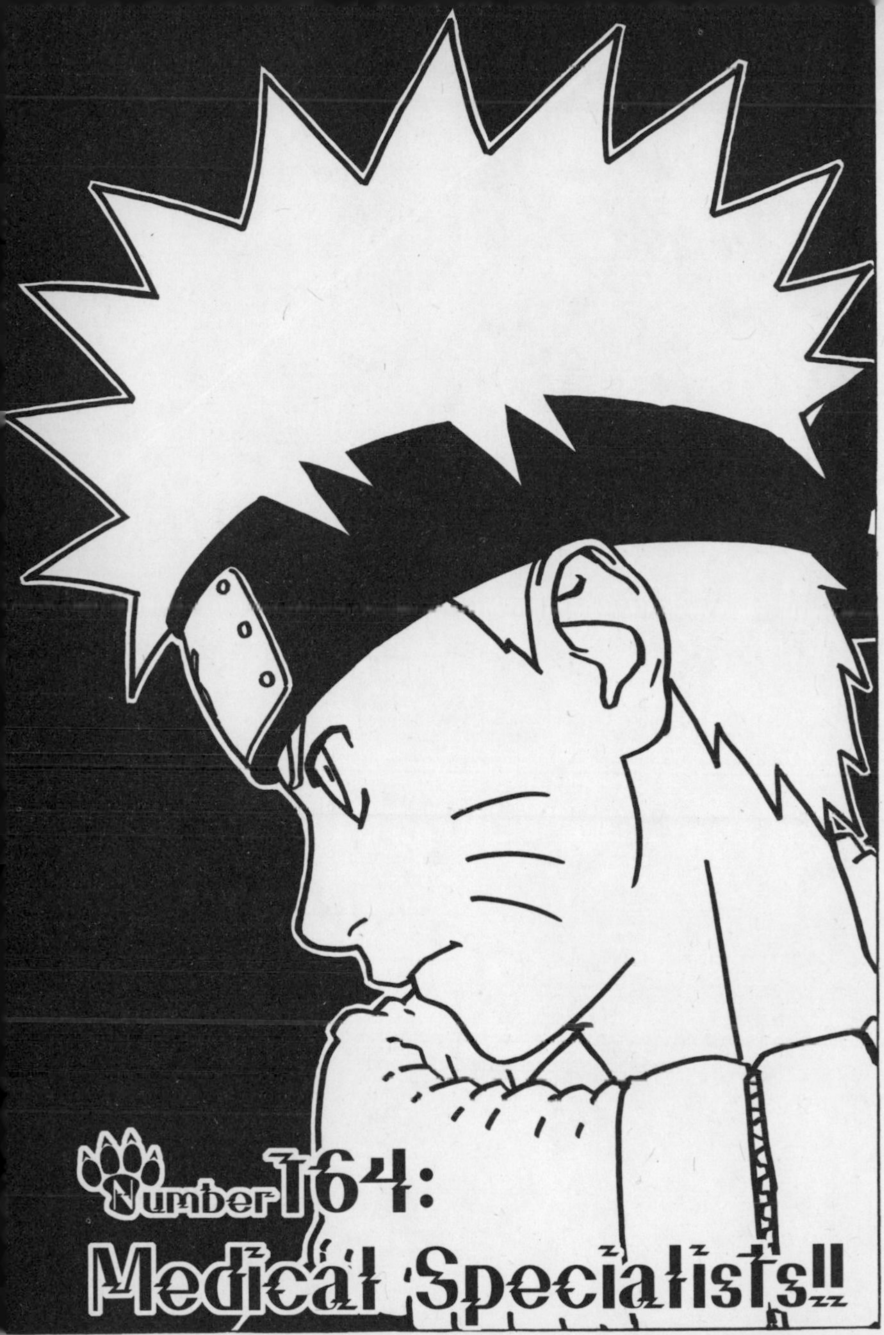
Number 164:
Medical Specialists!!

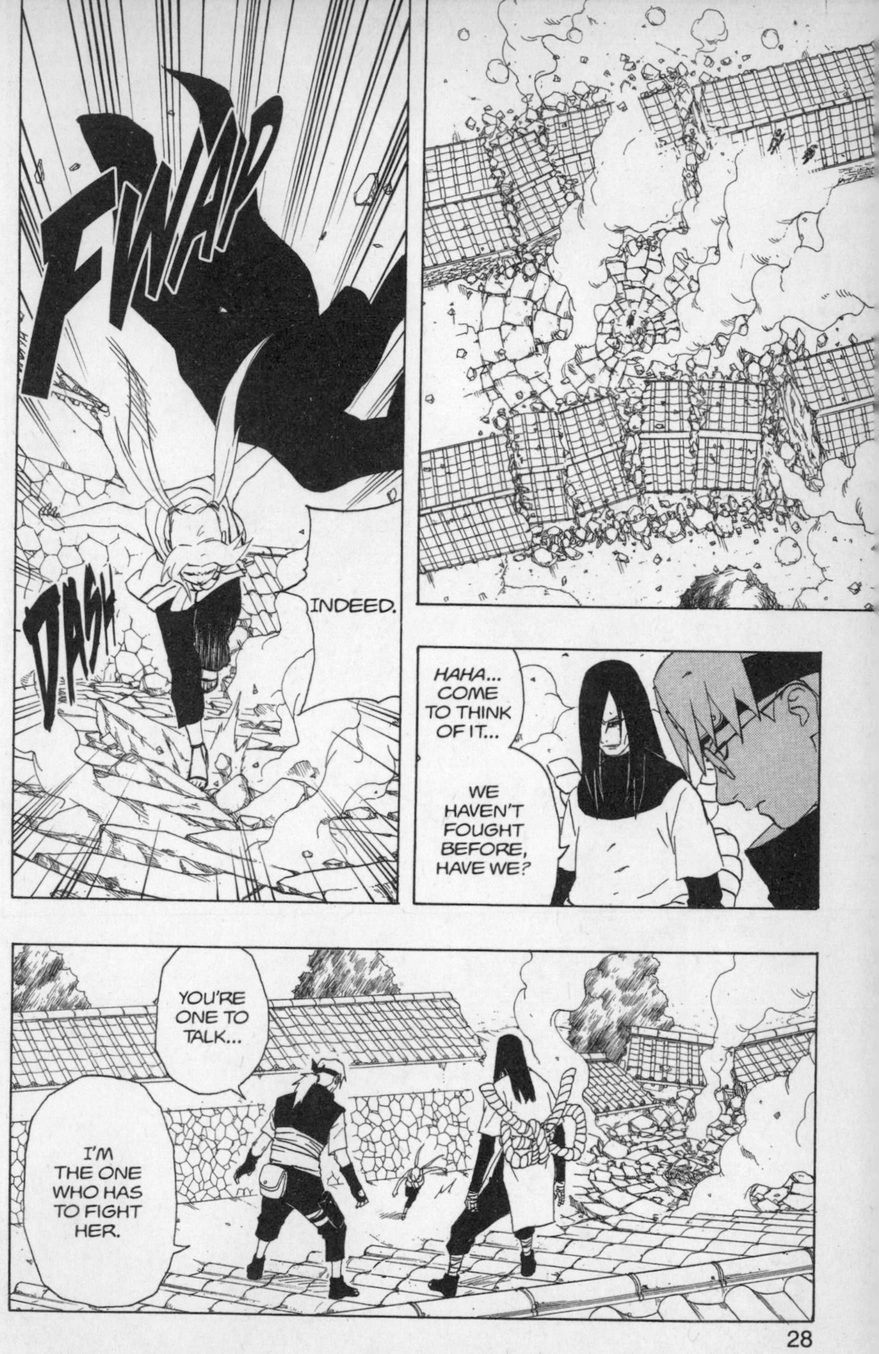
HAHA... COME TO THINK OF IT...
WE HAVEN'T FOUGHT BEFORE, HAVE WE?
FWAP
INDEED.
DASH
YOU'RE ONE TO TALK...
I'M THE ONE WHO HAS TO FIGHT HER.

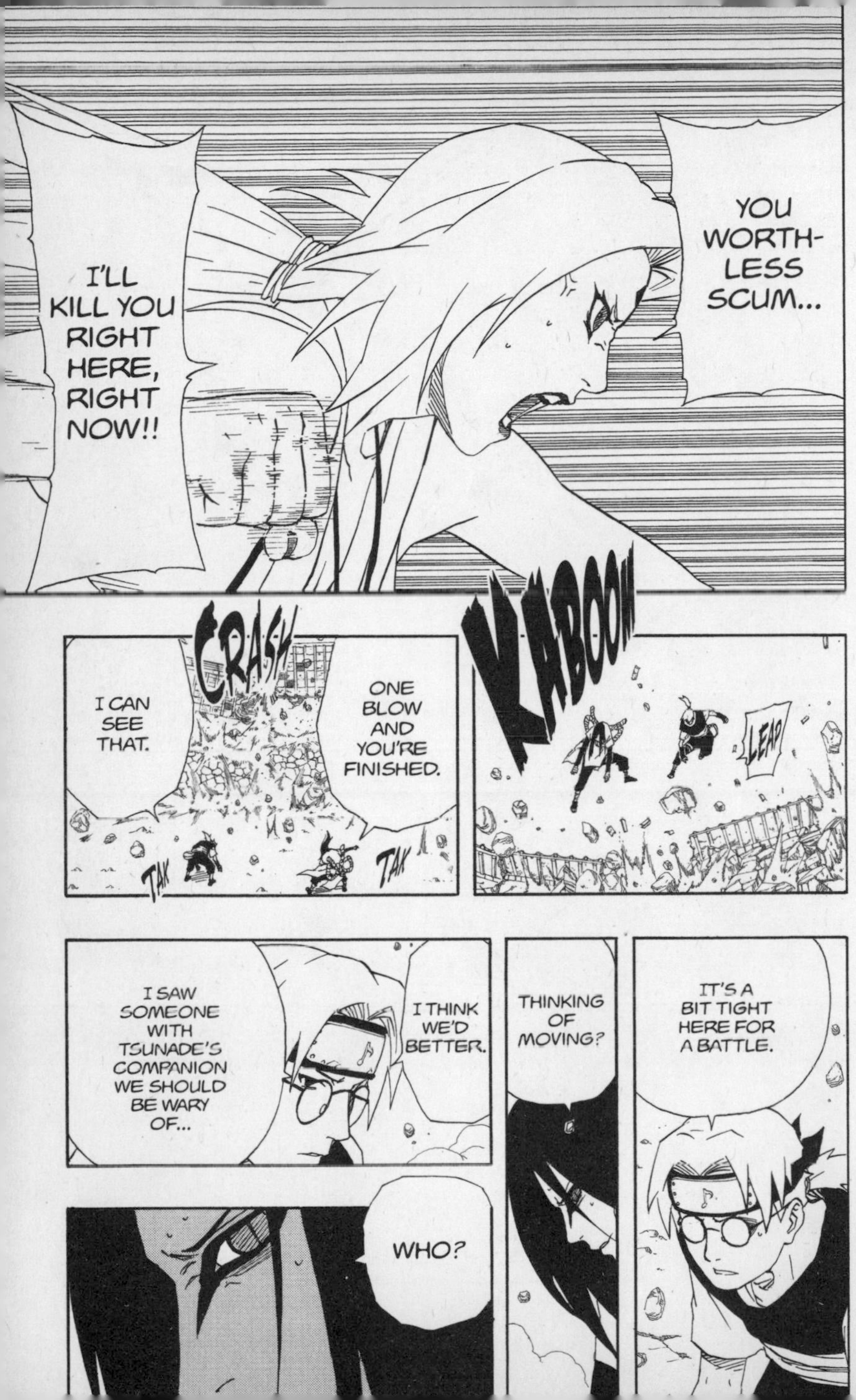
YOU WORTHLESS SCUM...
I'LL KILL YOU RIGHT HERE, RIGHT NOW!!
KABOOM
LEAP
CRASH
ONE BLOW AND YOU'RE FINISHED.
I CAN SEE THAT.
TAK
TAK
IT'S A BIT TIGHT HERE FOR A BATTLE.
THINKING OF MOVING?
I THINK WE'D BETTER.
I SAW SOMEONE WITH TSUNADE'S COMPANION WE SHOULD BE WARY OF...
WHO?

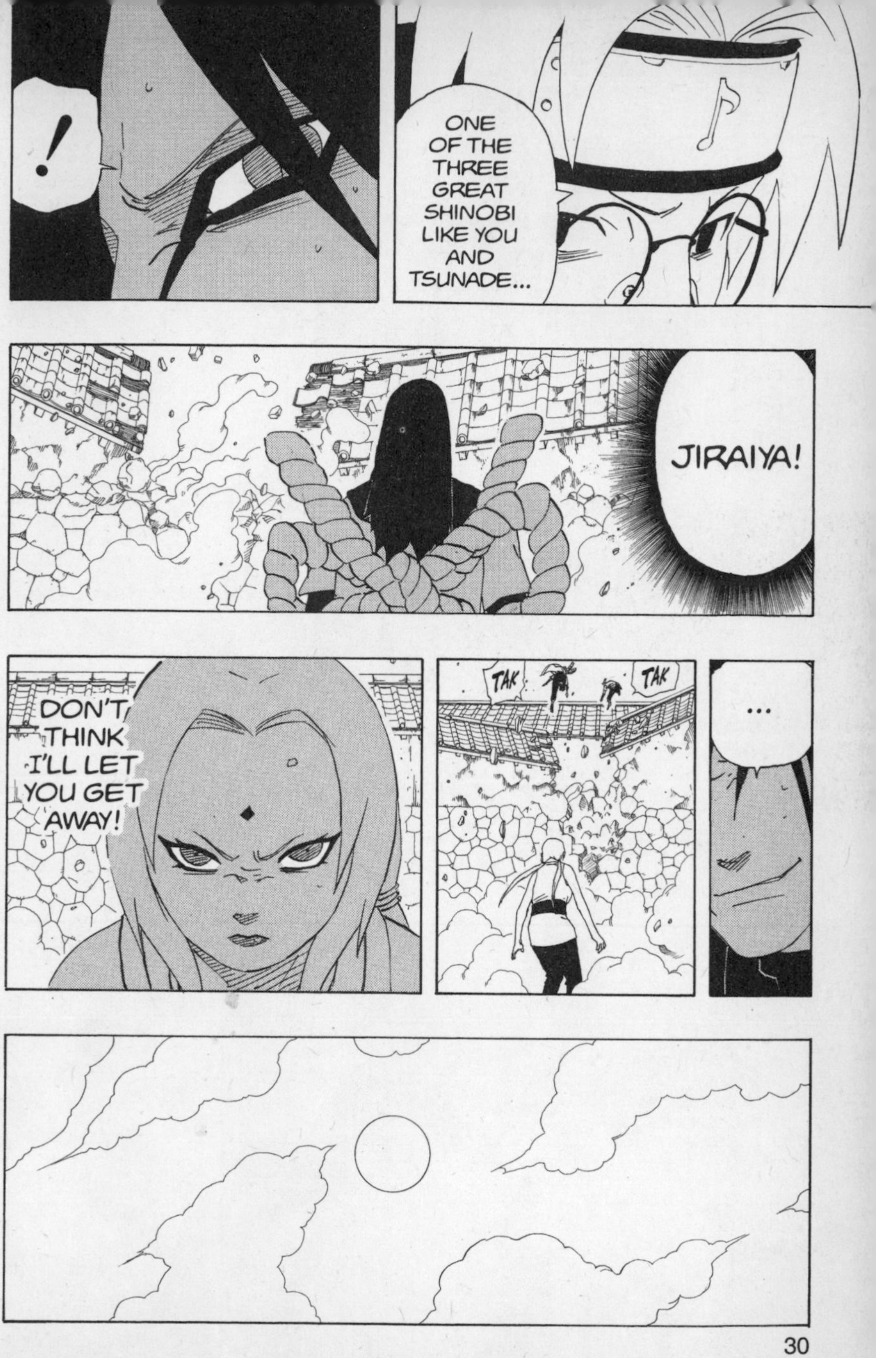
ONE OF THE THREE GREAT SHINOBI LIKE YOU AND TSUNADE...
!
JIRAIYA!
...
TAK
TAK
DON'T THINK I'LL LET YOU GET AWAY!

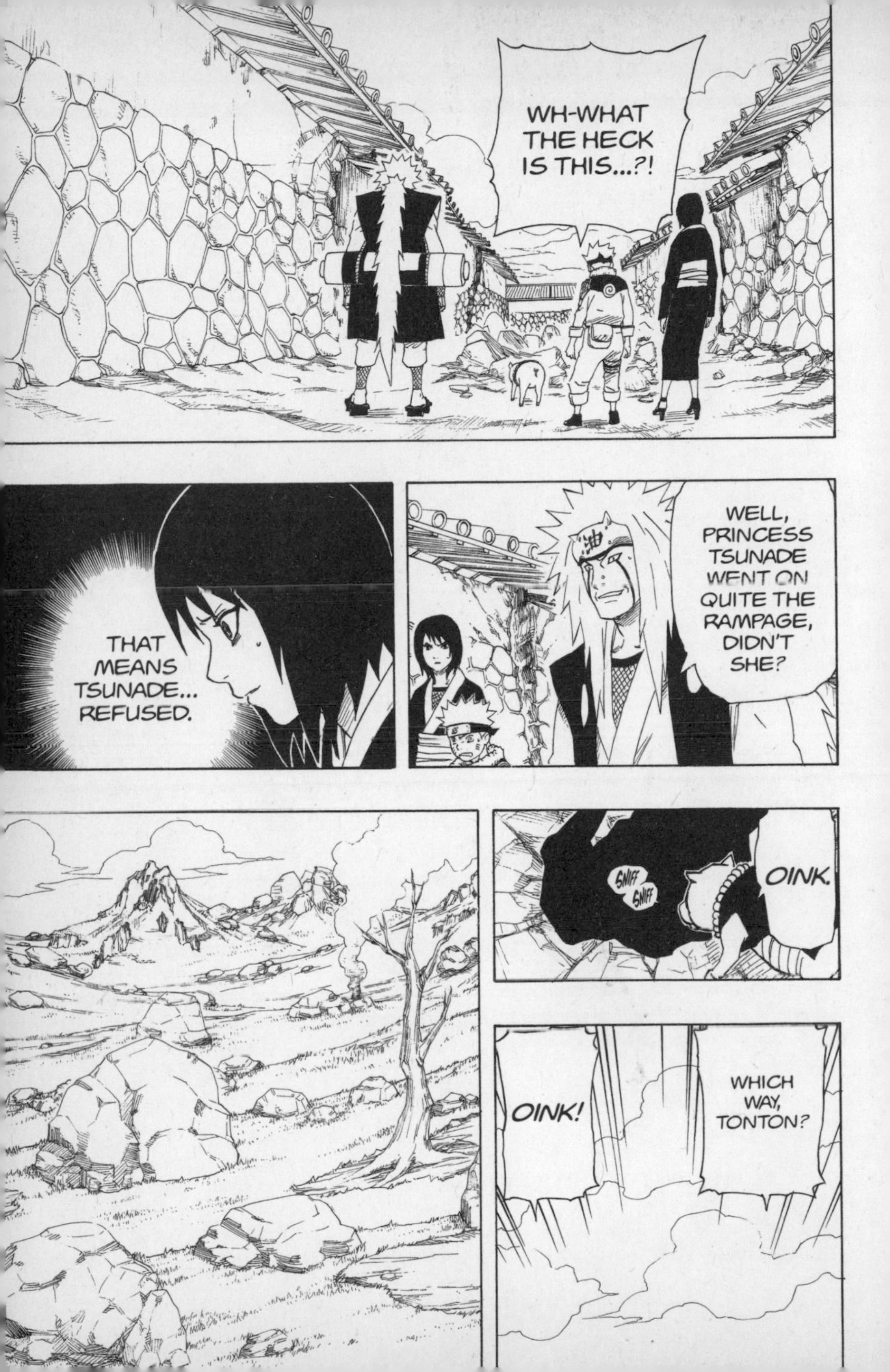
WH-WHAT THE HECK IS THIS...?!
WELL, PRINCESS TSUNADE WENT ON QUITE THE RAMPAGE, DIDN'T SHE?
THAT MEANS TSUNADE... REFUSED.
OINK.
SNIFF SNIFF
WHICH WAY, TONTON?
OINK!

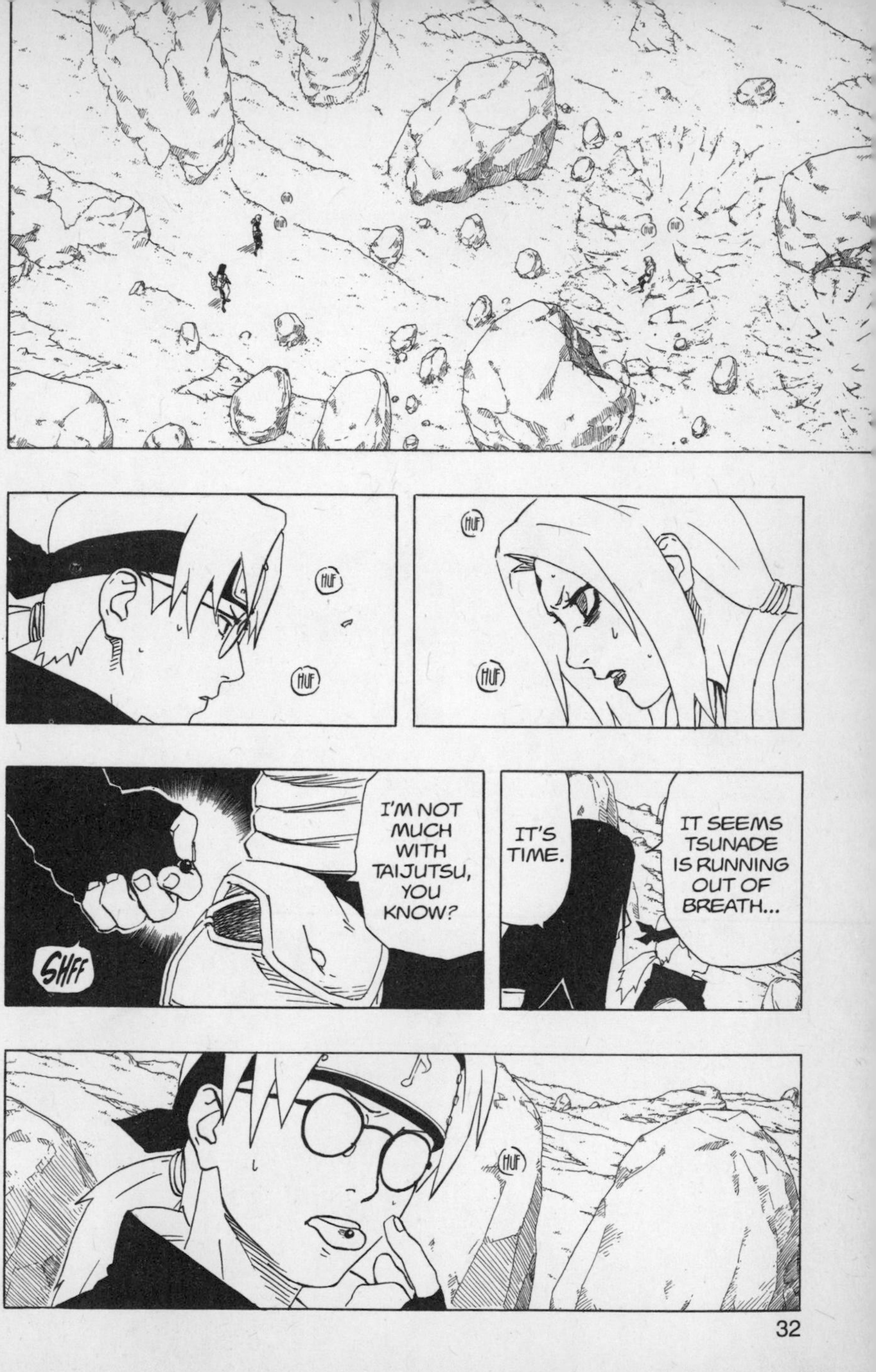
HUF
HUF
HUF
HUF
HUF
HUF
HUF
HUF
IT SEEMS TSUNADE IS RUNNING OUT OF BREATH...
IT'S TIME.
I'M NOT MUCH WITH TAIJUTSU, YOU KNOW?
SHFF
HUF

READ THIS WAY

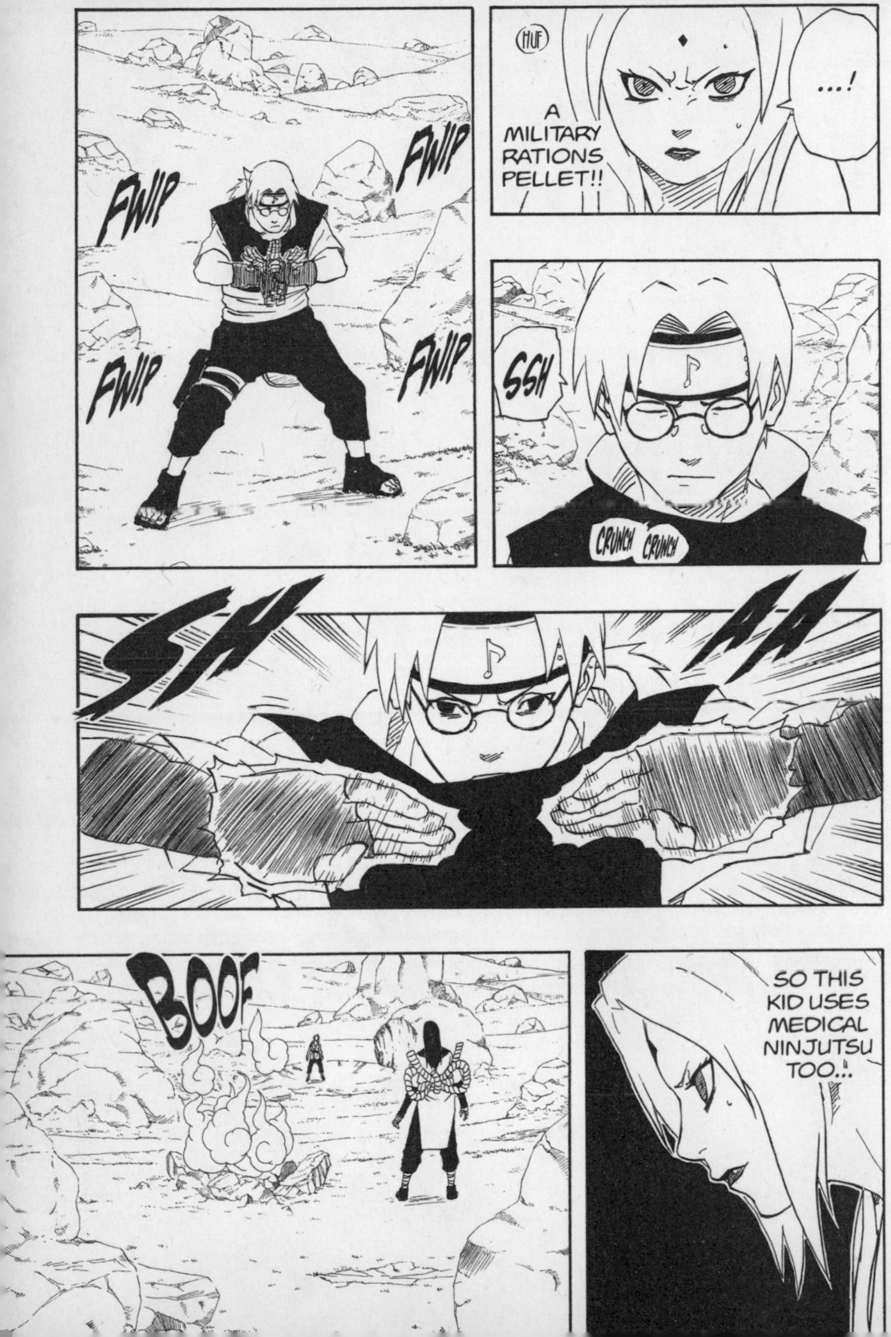

...!
HUF
A MILITARY RATIONS PELLET!!
SSH
CRUNCH CRUNCH
FWIP
FWIP
FWIP
FWIP
SHAA
SO THIS KID USES MEDICAL NINJUTSU TOO..!!
BOOF

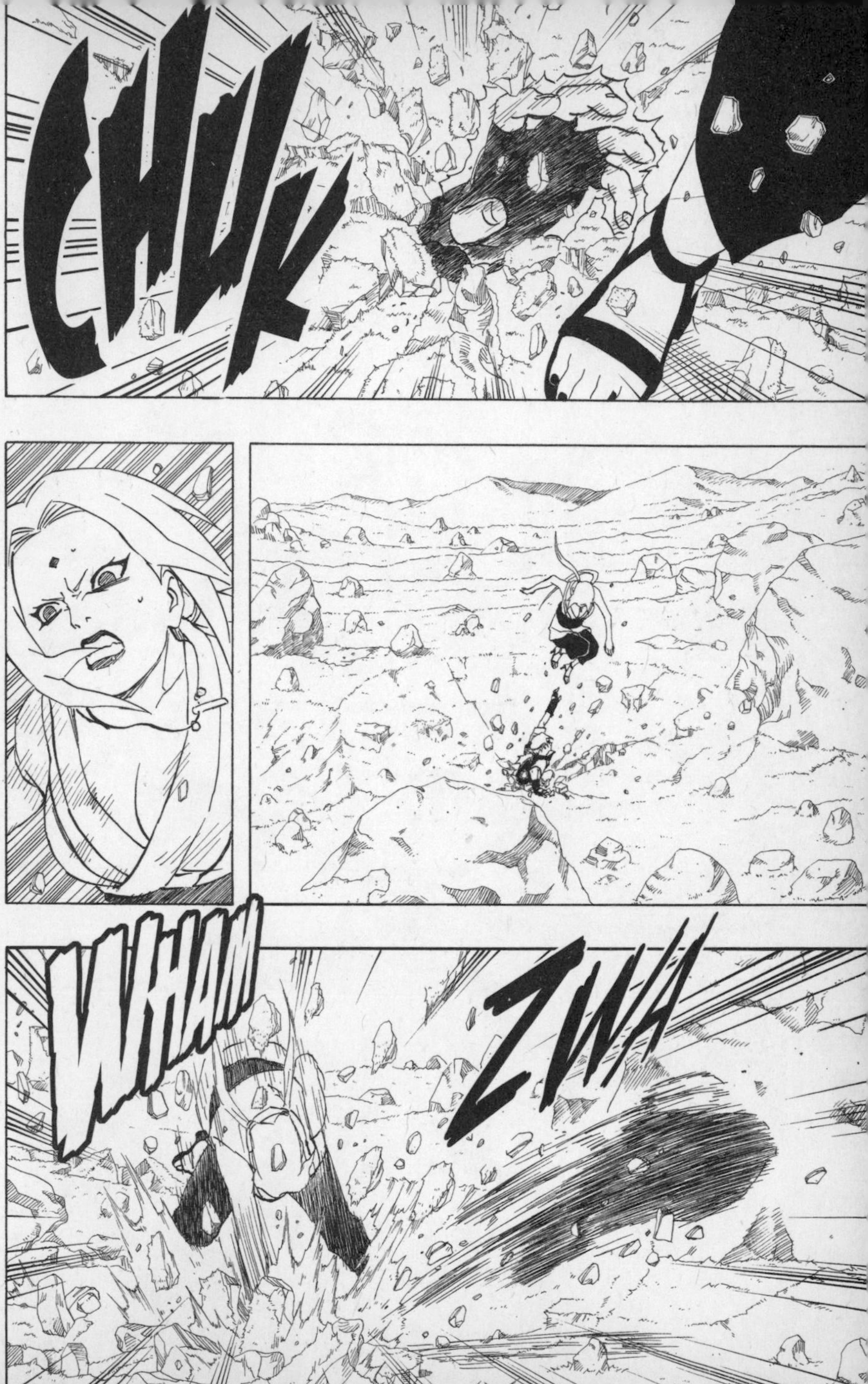
CHUK
ZWA
WHAM

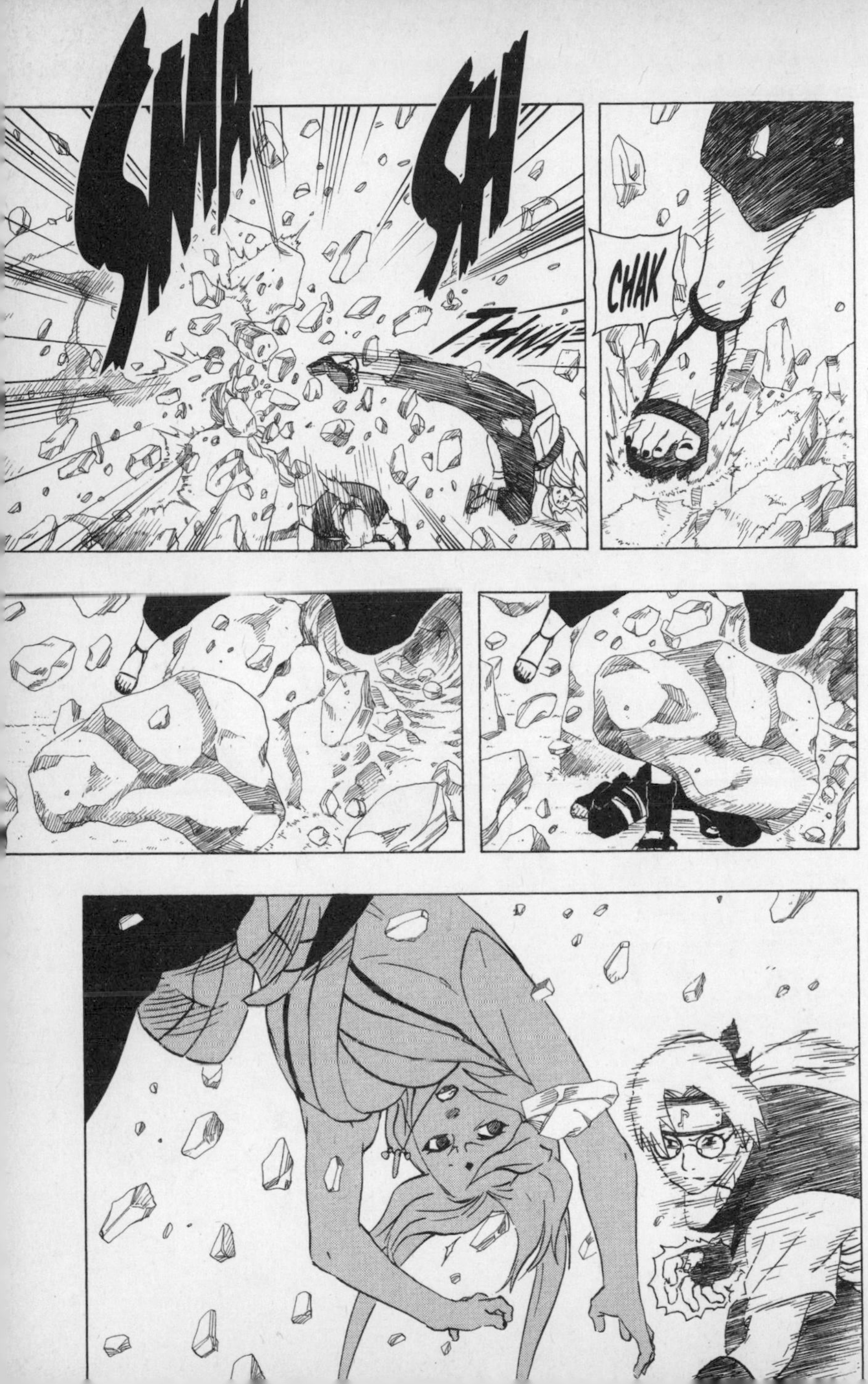
CHAK
SHWA
SH
THWA

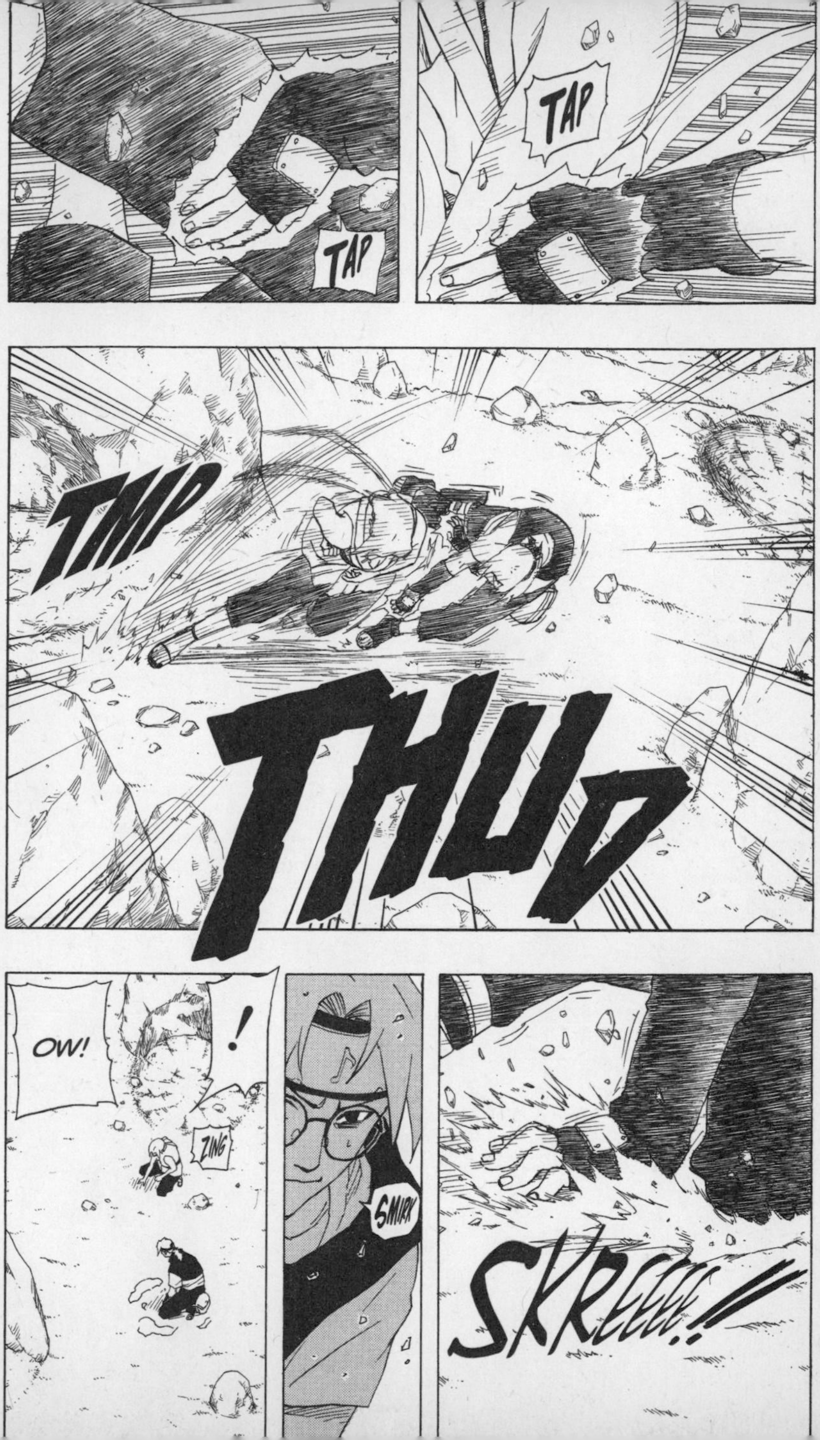
TAP
TAP
TMP
THUD
SKREEEE!!
SMIRK
!
OW!
ZING

READ THIS WAY

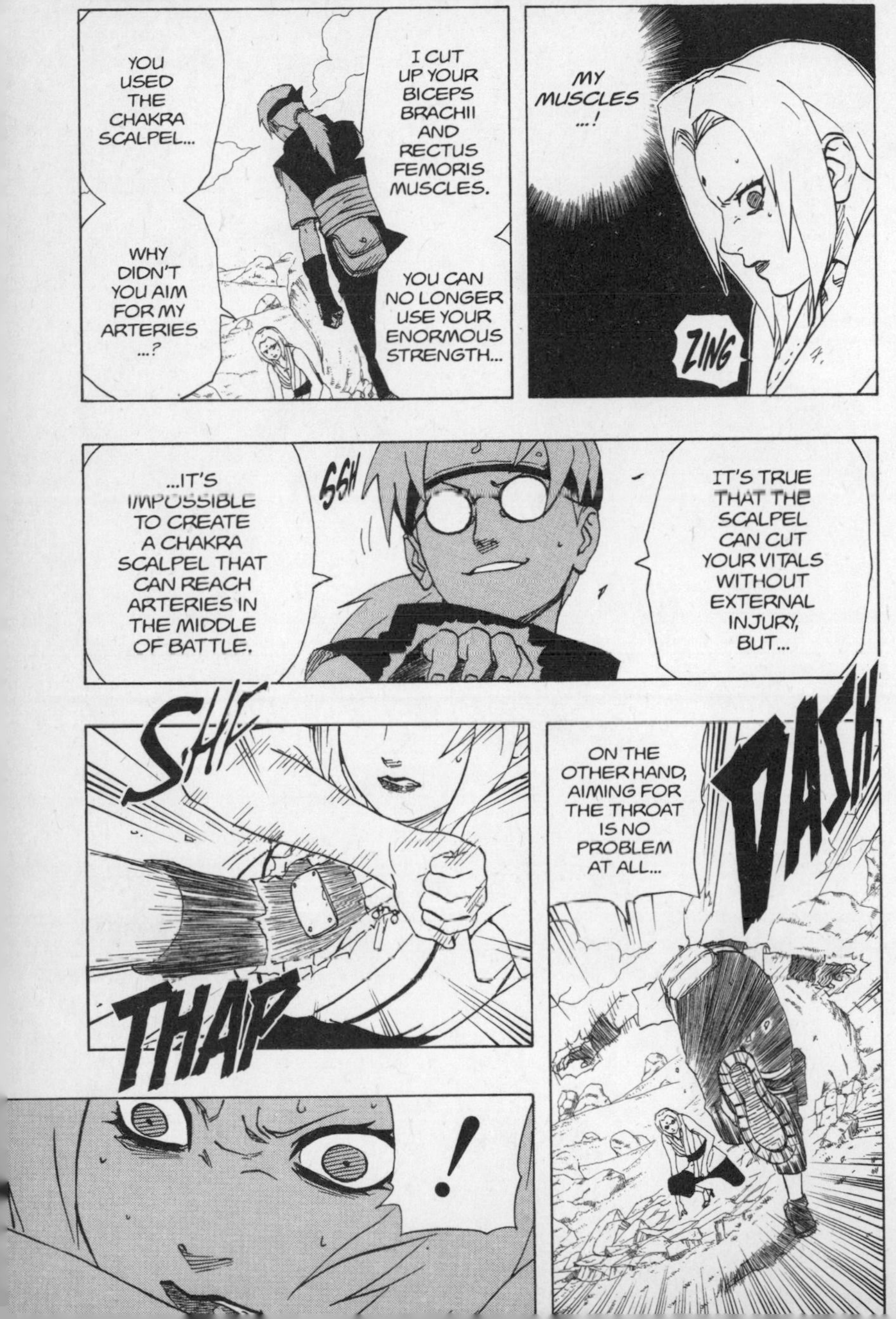
MY MUSCLES ...!
ZING
I CUT UP YOUR BICEPS BRACHII AND RECTUS FEMORIS MUSCLES.
YOU CAN NO LONGER USE YOUR ENORMOUS STRENGTH...
YOU USED THE CHAKRA SCALPEL...
WHY DIDN'T YOU AIM FOR MY ARTERIES ...?
IT'S TRUE THAT THE SCALPEL CAN CUT YOUR VITALS WITHOUT EXTERNAL INJURY, BUT...
SSH
...IT'S IMPOSSIBLE TO CREATE A CHAKRA SCALPEL THAT CAN REACH ARTERIES IN THE MIDDLE OF BATTLE.
DASH
ON THE OTHER HAND, AIMING FOR THE THROAT IS NO PROBLEM AT ALL...
SHF
THAP
!

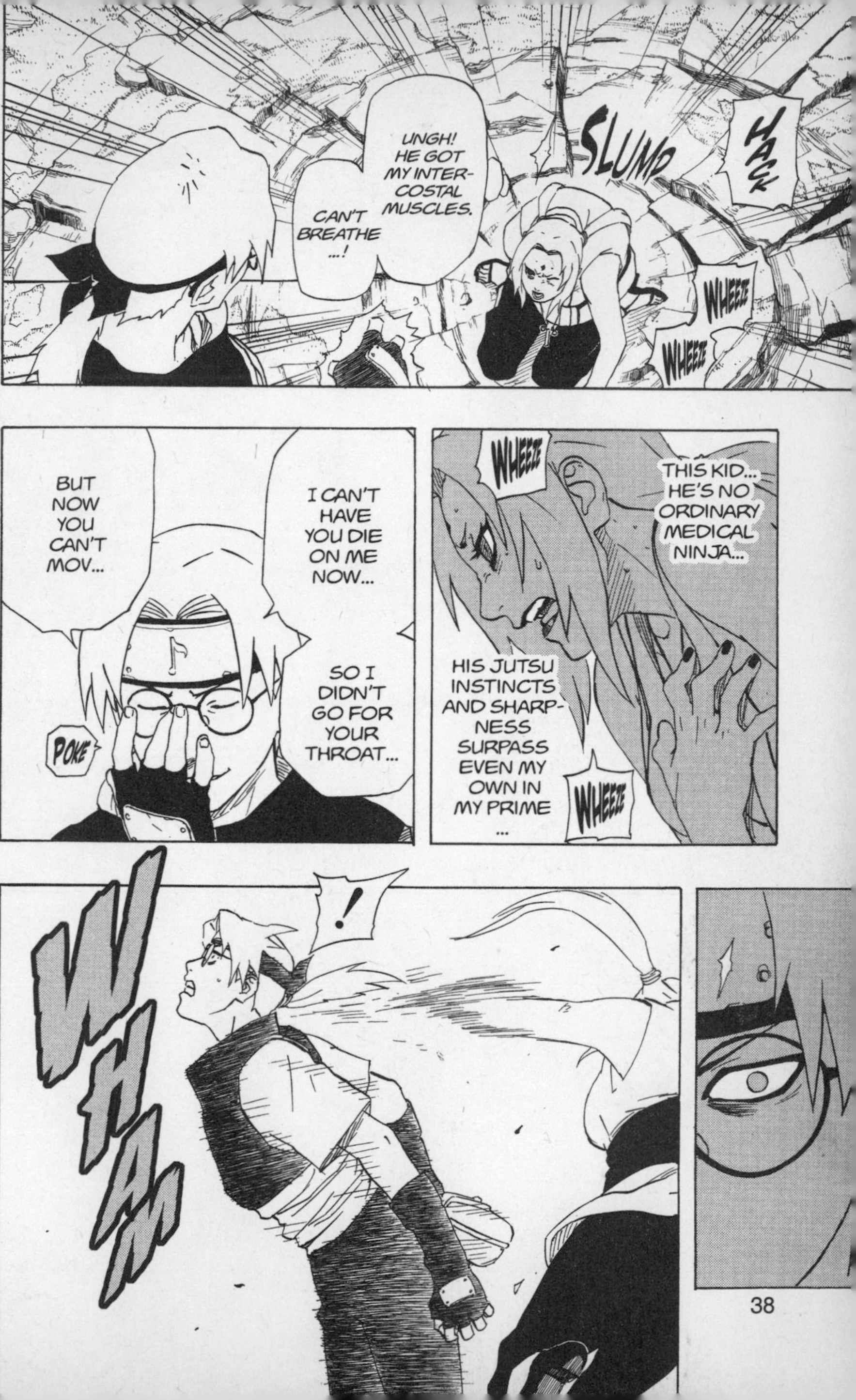
HACK
SLUMP
WHEEZE
WHEEZE
UNGH! HE GOT MY INTER-COSTAL MUSCLES.
CAN'T BREATHE ...!
WHEEZE
THIS KID... HE'S NO ORDINARY MEDICAL NINJA...
HIS JUTSU INSTINCTS AND SHARP-NESS SURPASS EVEN MY OWN IN MY PRIME ...
WHEEZE
I CAN'T HAVE YOU DIE ON ME NOW...
BUT NOW YOU CAN'T MOV...
SO I DIDN'T GO FOR YOUR THROAT...
POKE
!
WHAM

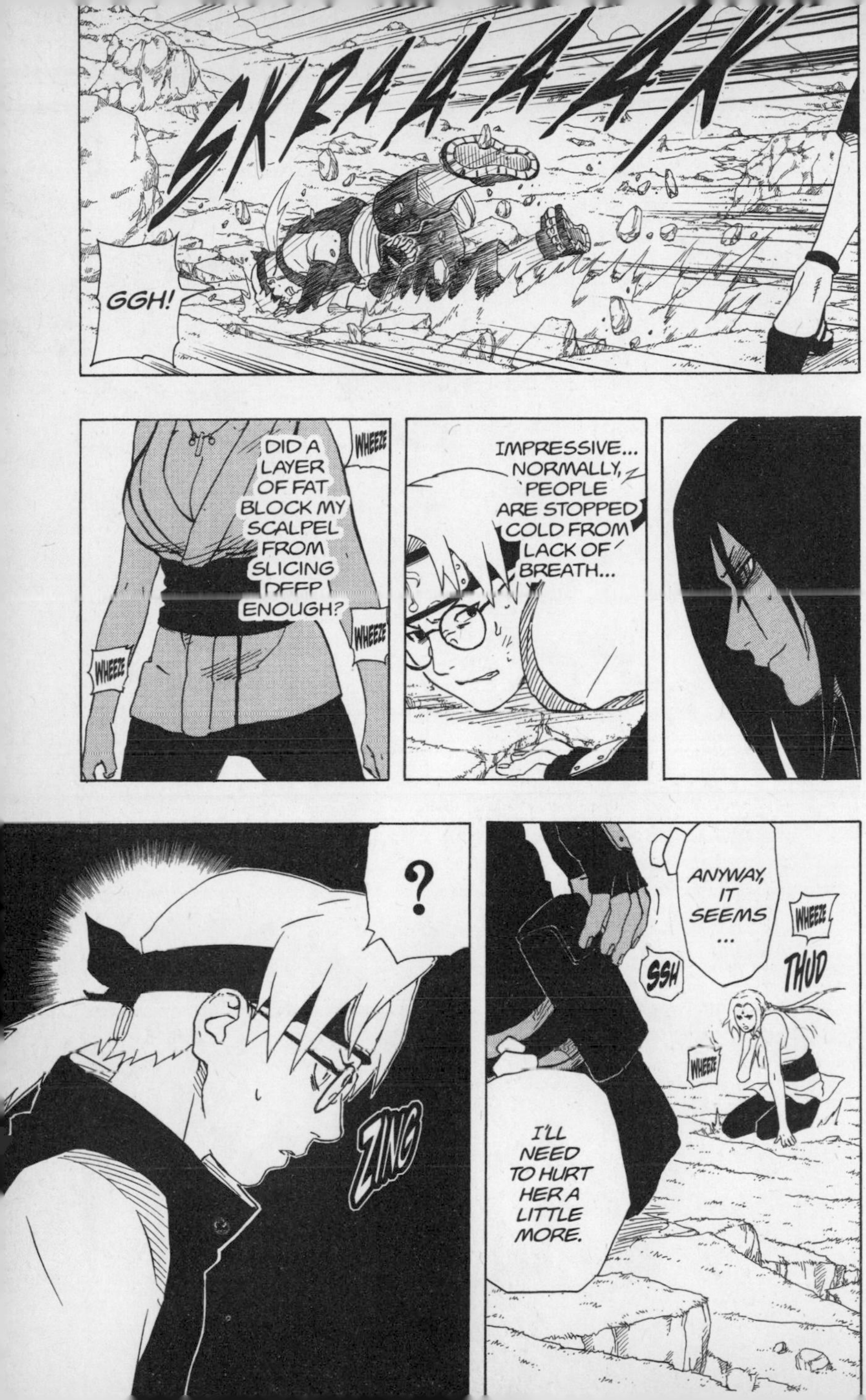
SKRAAAAK
GGH!
IMPRESSIVE... NORMALLY, PEOPLE ARE STOPPED COLD FROM LACK OF BREATH...
DID A LAYER OF FAT BLOCK MY SCALPEL FROM SLICING DEEP ENOUGH?
WHEEZE
WHEEZE
WHEEZE
ANYWAY, IT SEEMS ...
WHEEZE
THUD
SSH
WHEEZE
I'LL NEED TO HURT HER A LITTLE MORE.
?
ZING

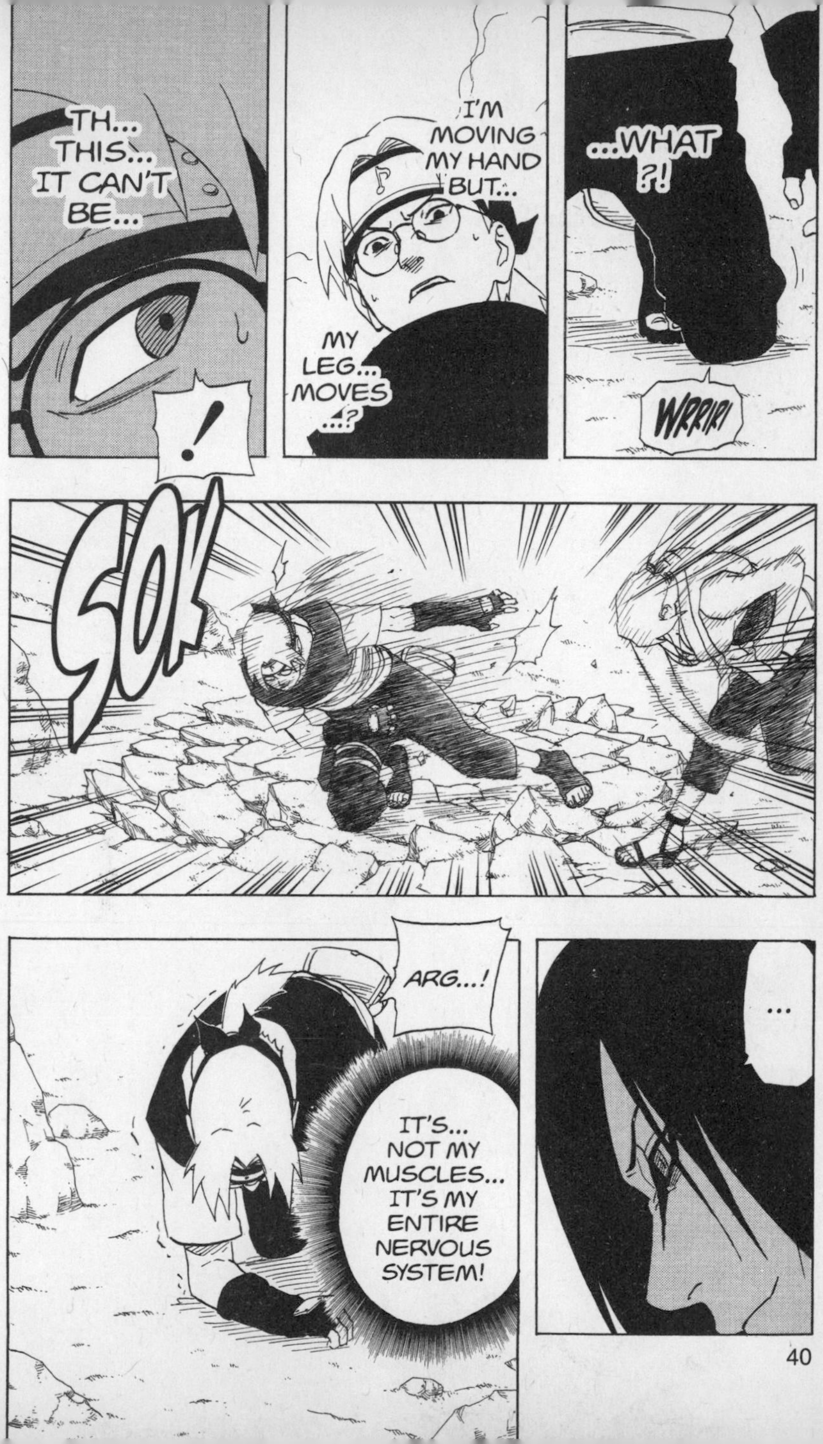
...WHAT ?!
WRRIR!
I'M MOVING MY HAND BUT...
MY LEG... MOVES ...?
TH... THIS... IT CAN'T BE...
!
SOK!
...
ARG...!
IT'S... NOT MY MUSCLES... IT'S MY ENTIRE NERVOUS SYSTEM!

READ THIS WAY

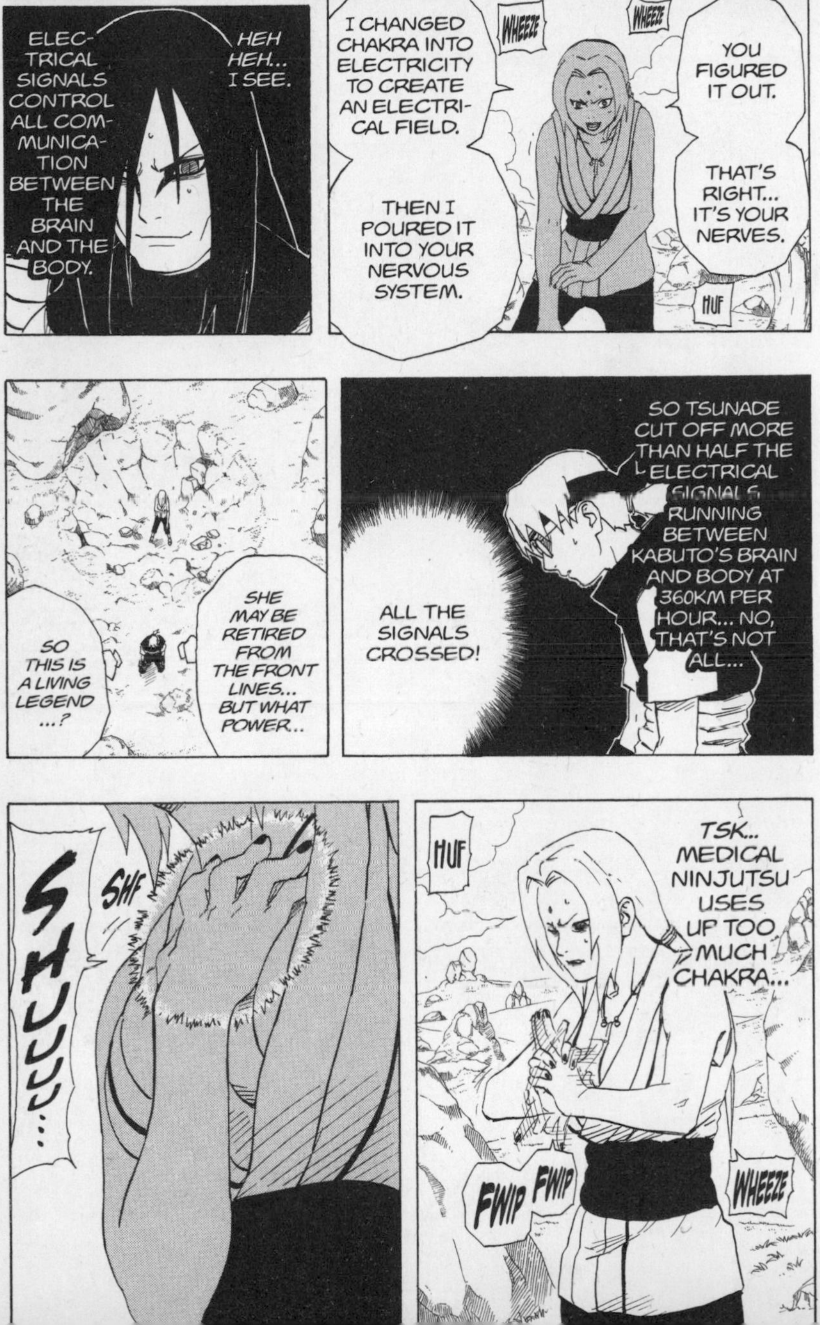
WHEEZE
YOU FIGURED IT OUT.
THAT'S RIGHT... IT'S YOUR NERVES.
WHEEZE
I CHANGED CHAKRA INTO ELECTRICITY TO CREATE AN ELECTRICAL FIELD.
THEN I POURED IT INTO YOUR NERVOUS SYSTEM.
HUF
HEH HEH... I SEE.
ELECTRICAL SIGNALS CONTROL ALL COMMUNICATION BETWEEN THE BRAIN AND THE BODY.
SO TSUNADE CUT OFF MORE THAN HALF THE ELECTRICAL SIGNALS RUNNING BETWEEN KABUTO'S BRAIN AND BODY AT 360KM PER HOUR... NO, THAT'S NOT ALL...
ALL THE SIGNALS CROSSED!
SHE MAY BE RETIRED FROM THE FRONT LINES... BUT WHAT POWER...
SO THIS IS A LIVING LEGEND...?
HUF
TSK... MEDICAL NINJUTSU USES UP TOO MUCH CHAKRA...
WHEEZE
FWIP
FWIP
SHF
SHUUUUU...

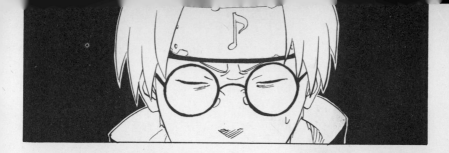

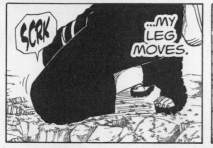

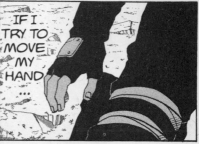

IF I TRY TO MOVE MY HAND ...
SCRK
...MY LEG MOVES.
WHEN I TRY TO MOVE MY LEFT ANKLE...
KRIK
MY RIGHT SHOULDER MOVES ...

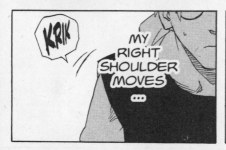

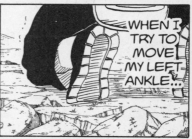

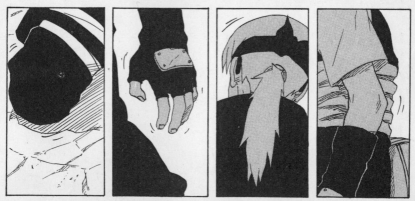

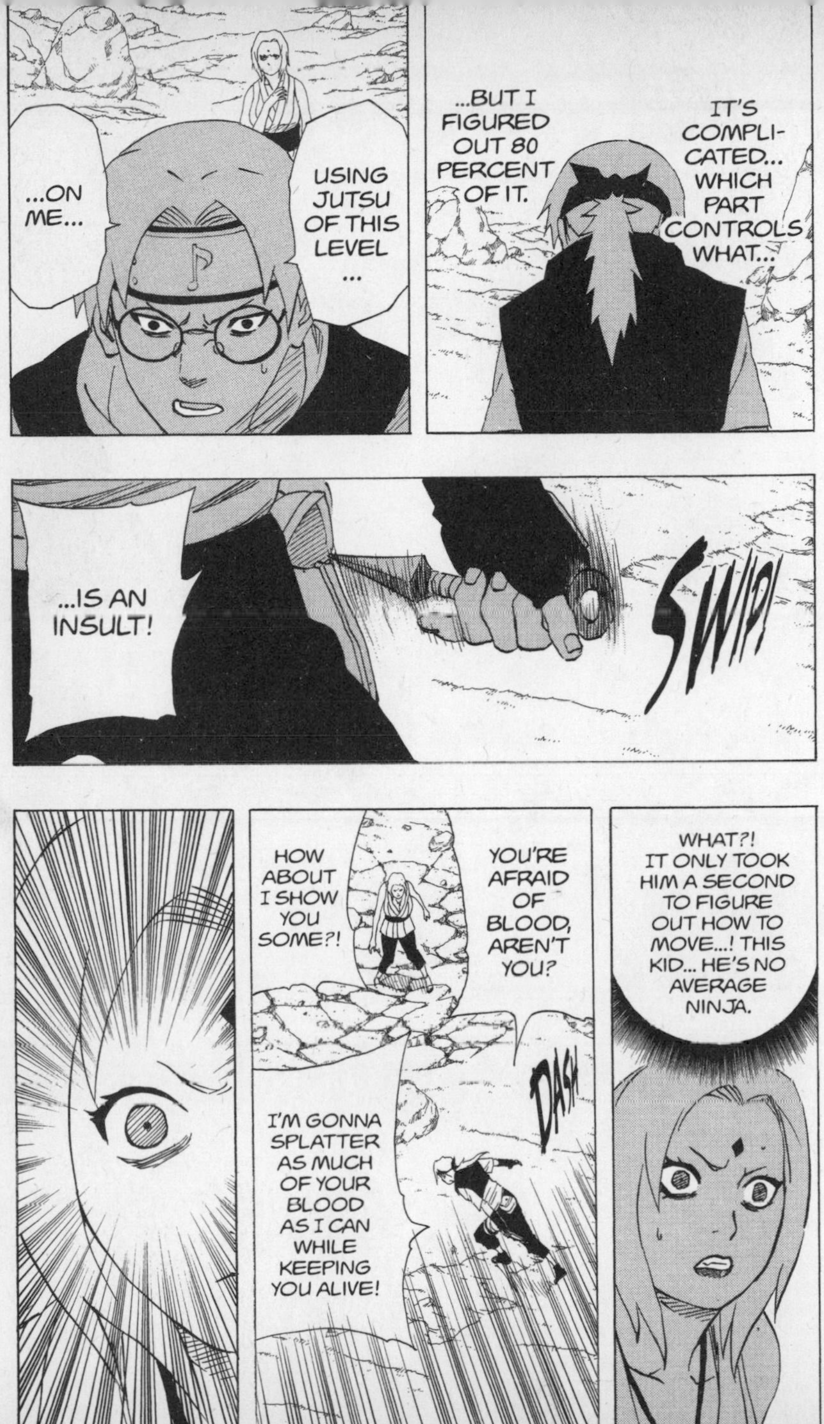
IT'S COMPLICATED... WHICH PART CONTROLS WHAT...
...BUT I FIGURED OUT 80 PERCENT OF IT.
USING JUTSU OF THIS LEVEL ...
...ON ME...
...IS AN INSULT!
SWIP!
WHAT?! IT ONLY TOOK HIM A SECOND TO FIGURE OUT HOW TO MOVE...! THIS KID... HE'S NO AVERAGE NINJA.
YOU'RE AFRAID OF BLOOD, AREN'T YOU?
HOW ABOUT I SHOW YOU SOME?!
DASH
I'M GONNA SPLATTER AS MUCH OF YOUR BLOOD AS I CAN WHILE KEEPING YOU ALIVE!

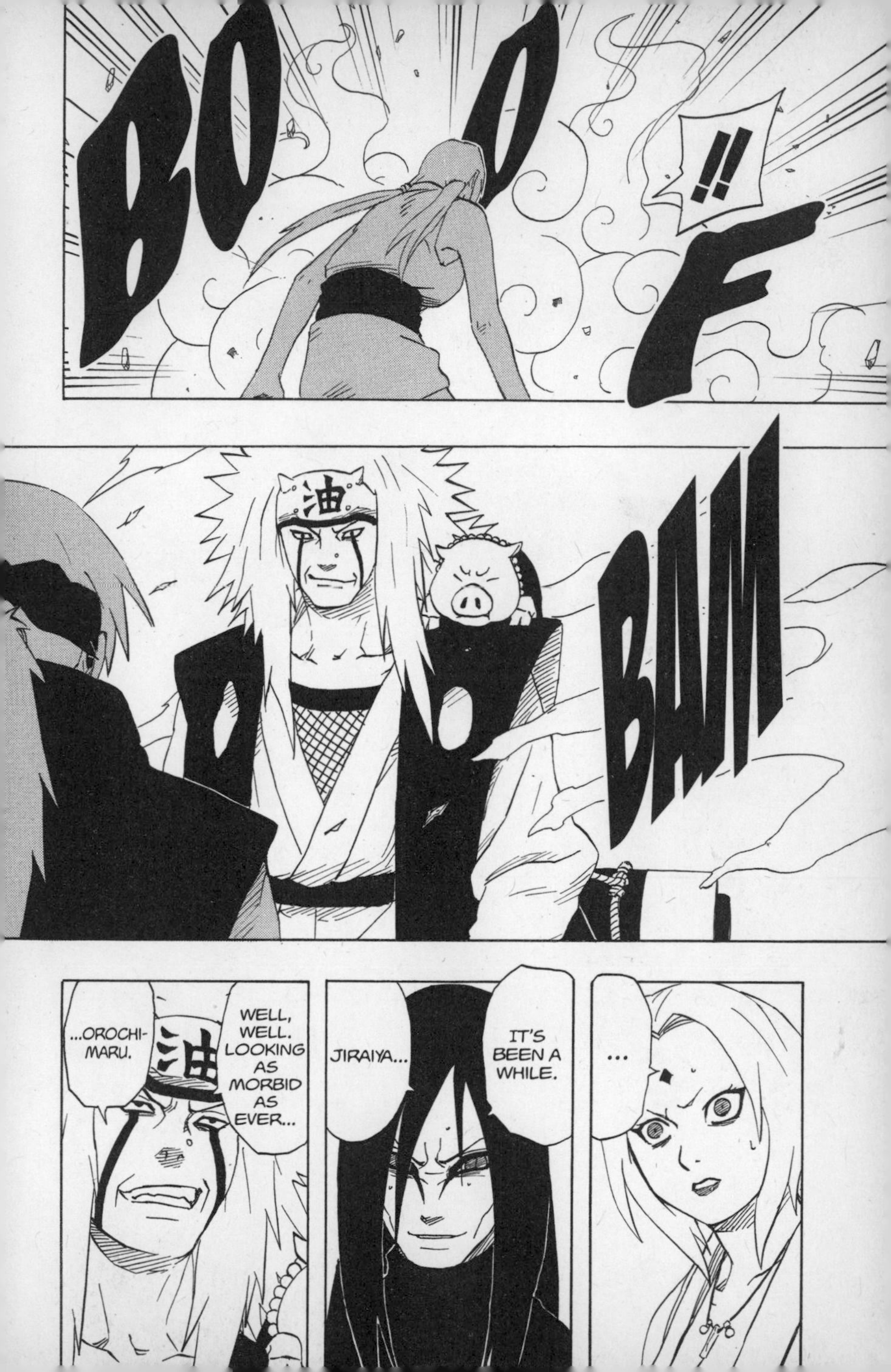
BOOF
!!
BAM
...
IT'S BEEN A WHILE.
JIRAIYA...
WELL, WELL. LOOKING AS MORBID AS EVER...
...OROCHIMARU.

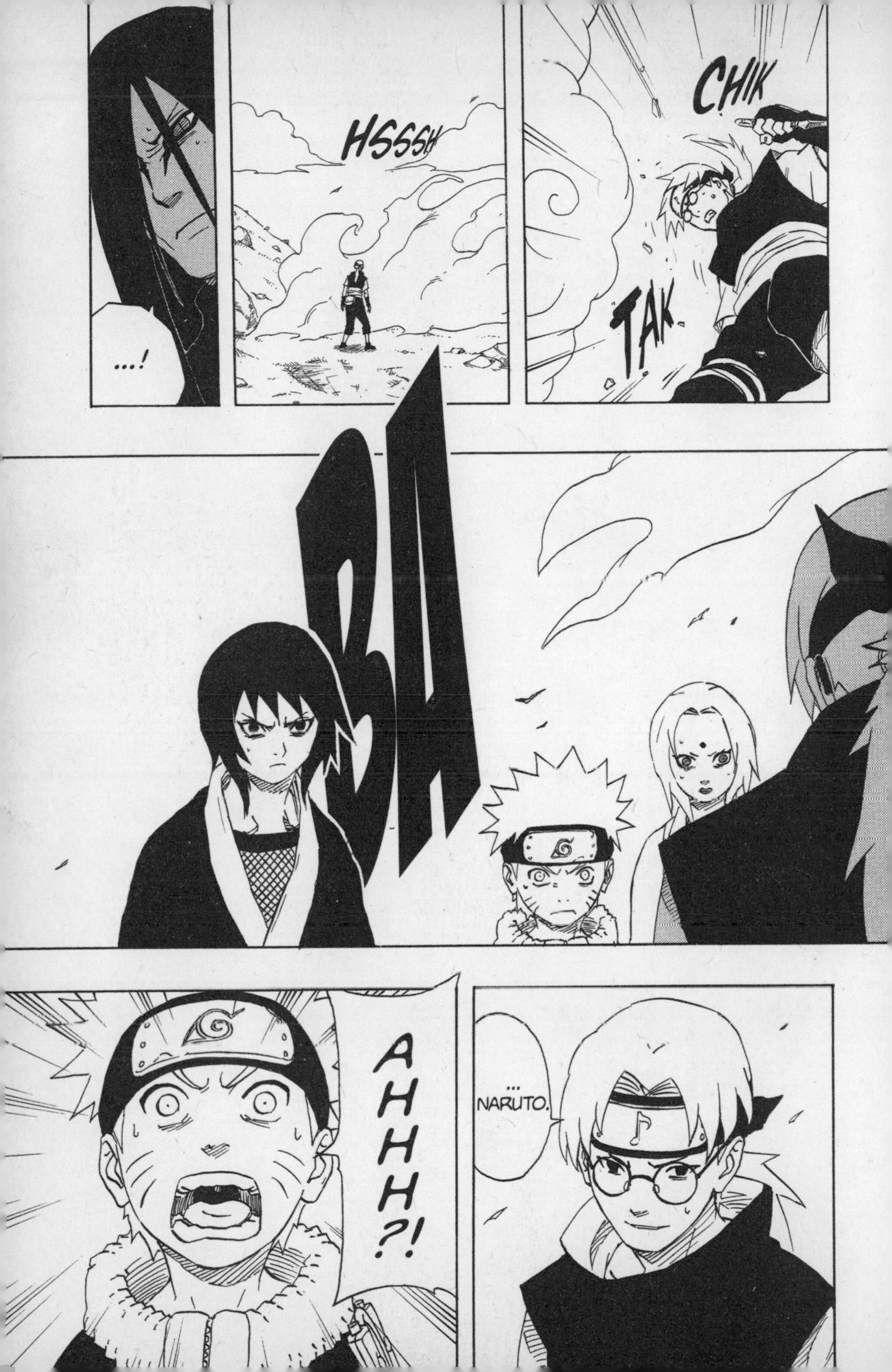
CHIK
TAK
HSSSH
...!
BA
... NARUTO.
AHHH?!

THE WORLD OF KISHIMOTO MASASHI
MY PERSONAL HISTORY, PART 30: NO. I

THIS TIME MY STORY IS ABOUT MY DARK AND DEPRESSING
YOUNGER DAYS... I WAS A FOURTH YEAR COLLEGE STUDENT
AND GRADUATION WAS RIGHT AROUND THE CORNER.
STILL, I HAD MADE NO PROGRESS AT ALL TOWARD
BECOMING A MANGA ARTIST. I FELT DOWN ALL THE TIME...
I HAD BEEN DRAWING THINGS LIKE BOYS' ACTION AND STUFF,
BUT NO MATTER WHAT I DREW IT ALWAYS CAME OUT LOOKING
DULL AND TYPICAL. EVERYTHING WAS TOTALLY, UNIFORMLY
REJECTED. LOOKING BACK ON THOSE DAYS NOW, I'D SAY
THAT THEY WERE PROBABLY THE MOST DIFFICULT OF MY LIFE.
CHANGING YOURSELF EVEN A LITTLE REQUIRES MUCH MORE
EFFORT THAN YOU THINK... TRANSFORMING MYSELF FROM
A YOUNG MAN WHO JUST ADORED MANGA INTO A
PROFESSIONAL MANGA ARTIST... THAT WAS A MASSIVE
CHANGE FOR ME AND IT REQUIRED AN ENORMOUS
AMOUNT OF ENERGY.

HAVING DREAMT ABOUT BECOMING A MANGA ARTIST, I FELT
A LITTLE TRIUMPHANT AFTER RECEIVING A MANGA AWARD.
I FELT AS THOUGH I HAD COME CLOSER TO BECOMING A PRO.
I HAD NO INTENTION OF SHOWING OFF MY AWARD, AND I
DON'T THINK THAT I DID. HOWEVER, DEEP DOWN I WAS
THINKING, "WELL, I CAN RELAX A BIT NOW. AFTER ALL, I'VE
WON AN AWARD."

BUT EVEN NOW I SOMETIMES THINK THAT WAS THE BIGGEST
MISTAKE OF MY LIFE. LIKE I SAID, CHANGING ONESELF TAKES
A LOT OF ENERGY. BUT MY RECEIVING THAT AWARD DIDN'T
MEAN THAT I HAD CHANGED THROUGH MY OWN EFFORTS;
IT WAS JUST AN ILLUSION THAT MADE IT LOOK THAT WAY.
AT OUR FIRST MEETING, MY EDITOR MR. YAHAGI GAVE ME A
WORD OF ADVICE: "IT'S AFTER YOU WIN AN AWARD THAT THE
HARD PART COMES...." OVER TIME I CAME TO UNDERSTAND
WHAT HE MEANT.

I THINK NOW THAT WINNING AWARDS OR NOT DOESN'T
REALLY MATTER VERY MUCH. WINNING AN AWARD DOESN'T
MAKE YOU A PRO. YOU'RE ONLY A STEP UP FROM BEING JUST
A MANGA LOVER. A TRUE PRO IS A TOTALLY DIFFERENT THING.
I KNOW THAT NOW. BUT THAT IS A TRAP THAT PEOPLE WHO
HAVE JUST BEGUN THEIR CAREERS AS MANGA ARTISTS
TEND TO GET CAUGHT IN. I'M NO EXCEPTION, AND IT TOOK
ME A TREMENDOUS AMOUNT OF TIME AND EFFORT TO GET
OUT OF THAT TRAP... BUT THAT'S A STORY I'LL CONTINUE
ANOTHER TIME... BOY...THAT'S A DISMAL STORY...

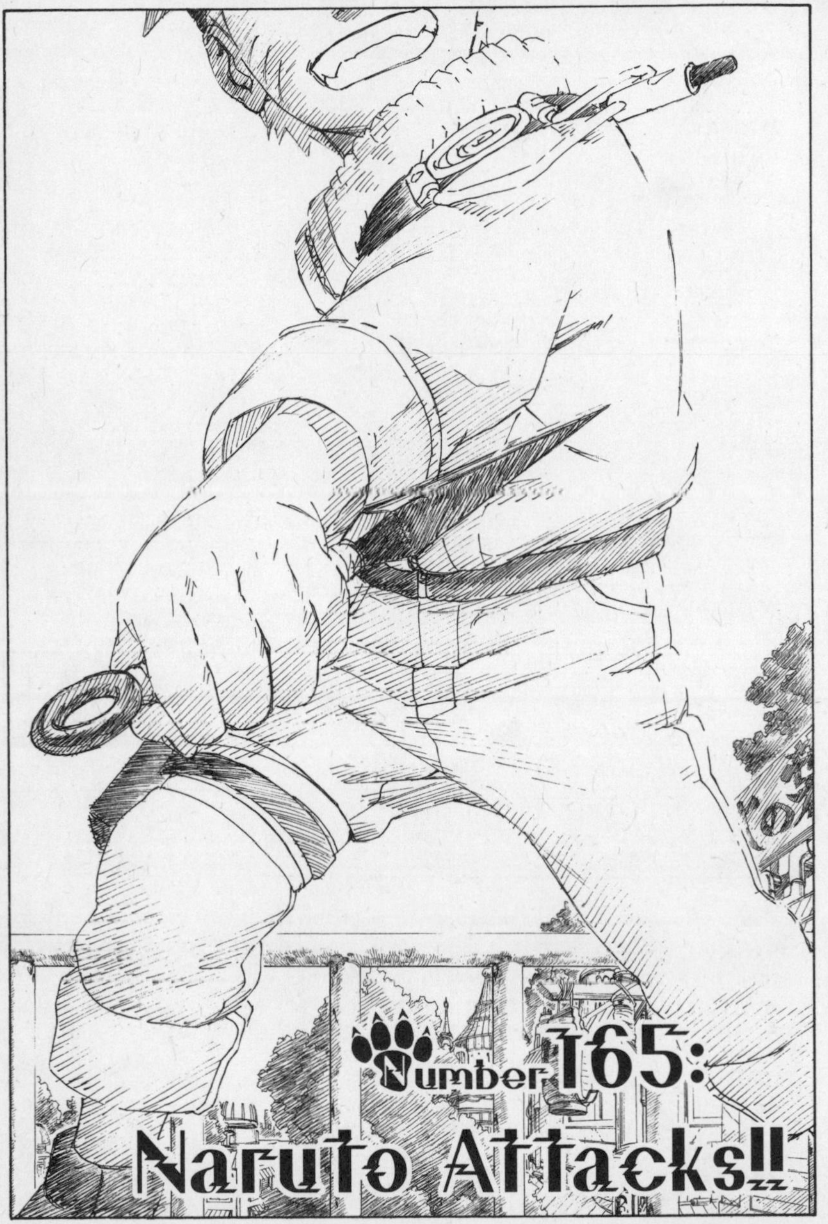
Number 165:
Naruto Attacks!!

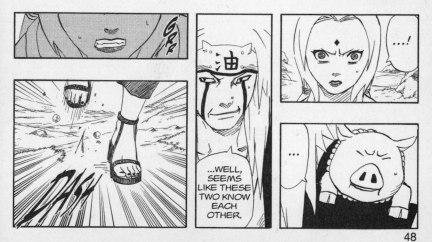

KA...
KABUTO
...?

....?

...

....!

...

...WELL,
SEEMS
LIKE THESE
TWO KNOW
EACH
OTHER.

READ THIS WAY

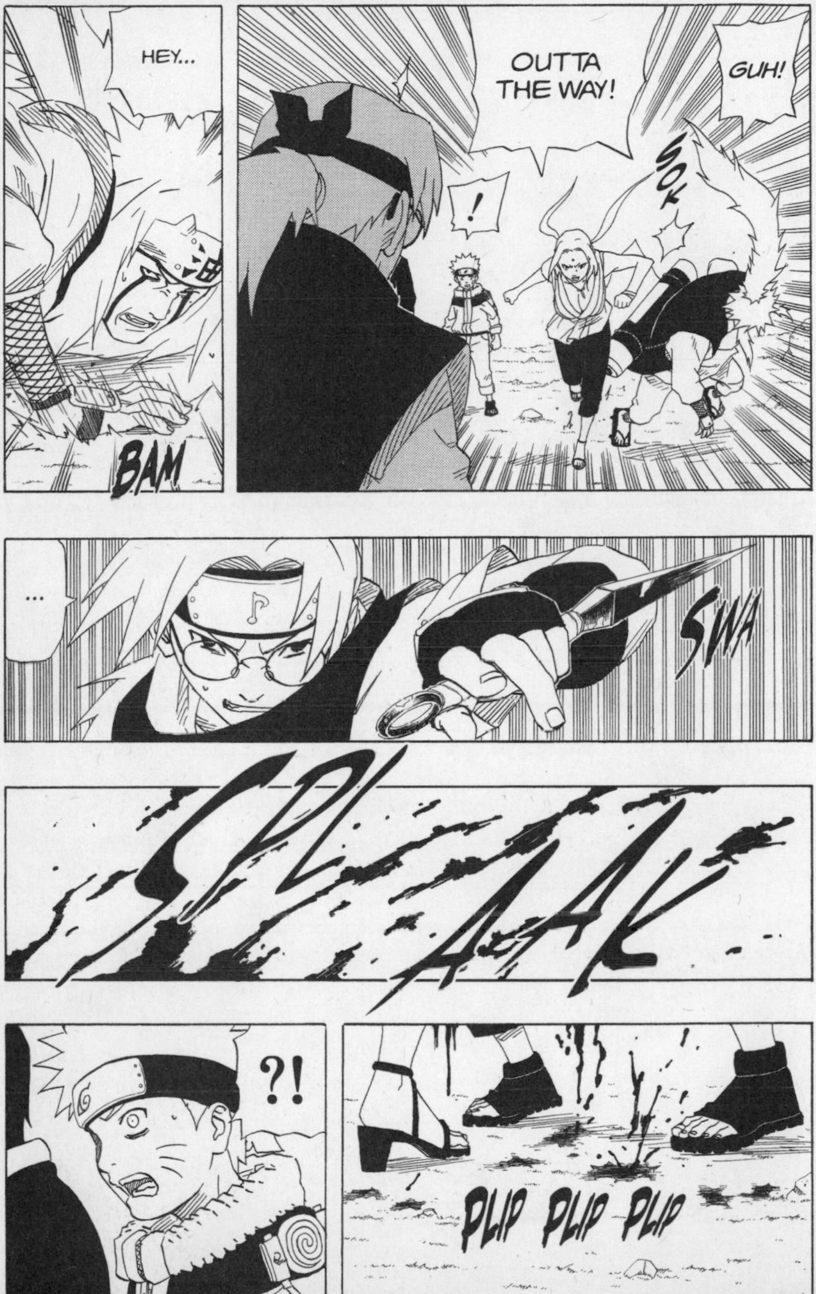
GUH!
OUTTA THE WAY!
SOK
!
HEY...
BAM
SWA
...
SPLAAK
PLIP PLIP PLIP
?!

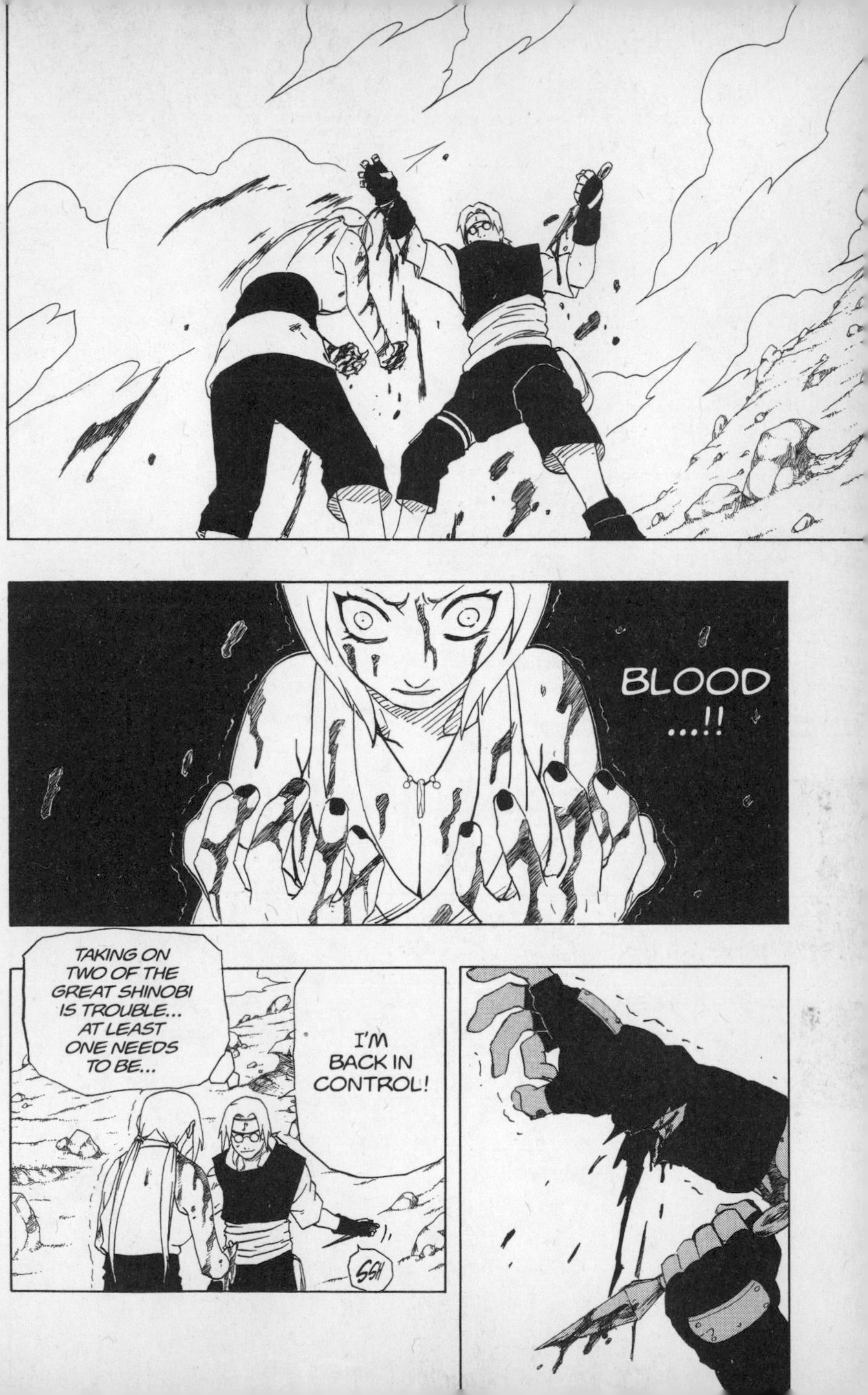
BLOOD ...!!
TAKING ON TWO OF THE GREAT SHINOBI IS TROUBLE... AT LEAST ONE NEEDS TO BE...
I'M BACK IN CONTROL!
SSH

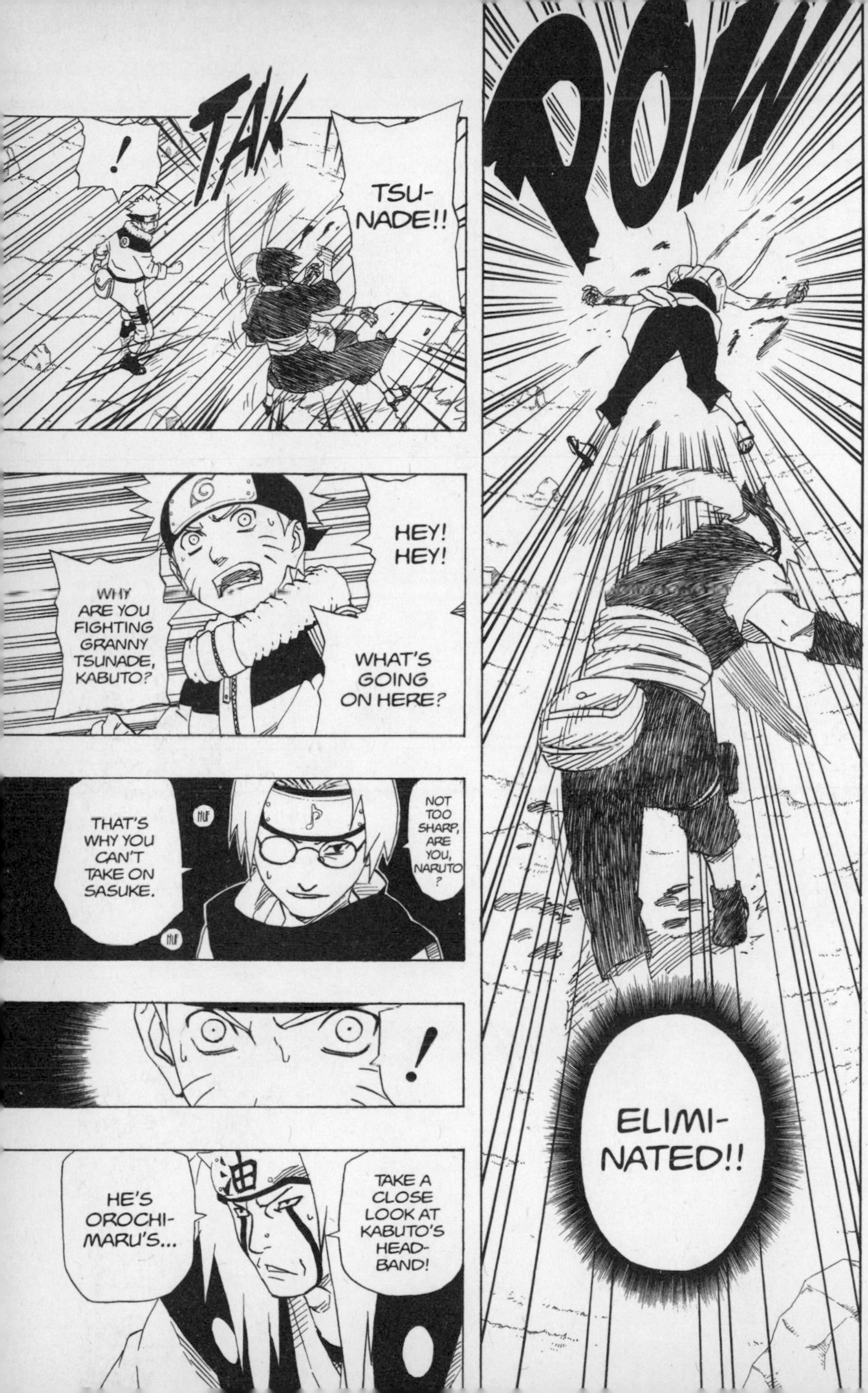
POW
ELIMI-NATED!!
TAK
TSU-NADE!!
!
HEY! HEY!
WHAT'S GOING ON HERE?
WHY ARE YOU FIGHTING GRANNY TSUNADE, KABUTO?
NOT TOO SHARP, ARE YOU, NARUTO?
HUF
THAT'S WHY YOU CAN'T TAKE ON SASUKE.
HUF
!
TAKE A CLOSE LOOK AT KABUTO'S HEAD-BAND!
HE'S OROCHI-MARU'S...

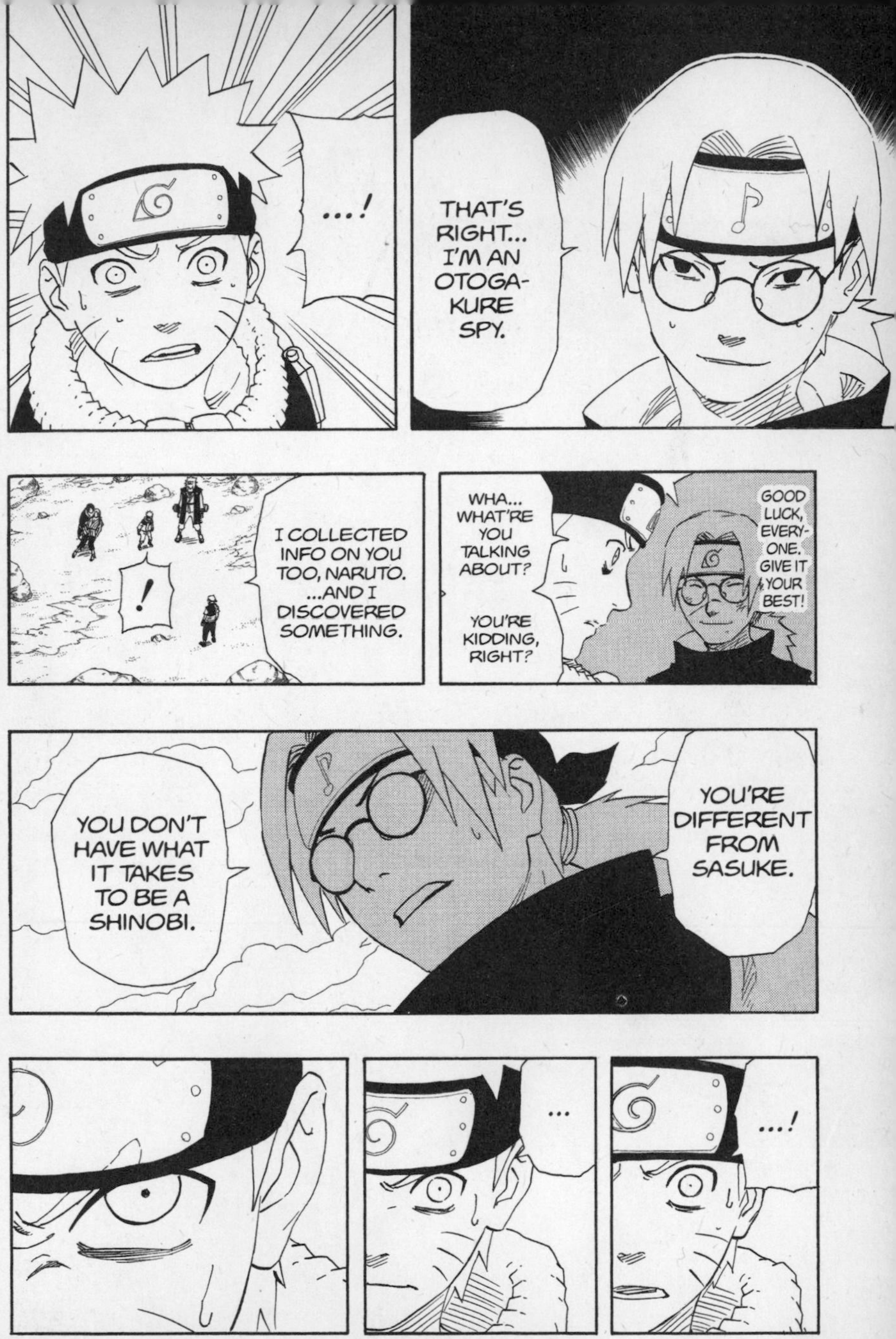
THAT'S RIGHT... I'M AN OTOGA-KURE SPY.
...!
GOOD LUCK, EVERY-ONE. GIVE IT YOUR BEST!
WHA... WHAT'RE YOU TALKING ABOUT?
YOU'RE KIDDING, RIGHT?
I COLLECTED INFO ON YOU TOO, NARUTO. ...AND I DISCOVERED SOMETHING.
!
YOU'RE DIFFERENT FROM SASUKE.
YOU DON'T HAVE WHAT IT TAKES TO BE A SHINOBI.
...!
...

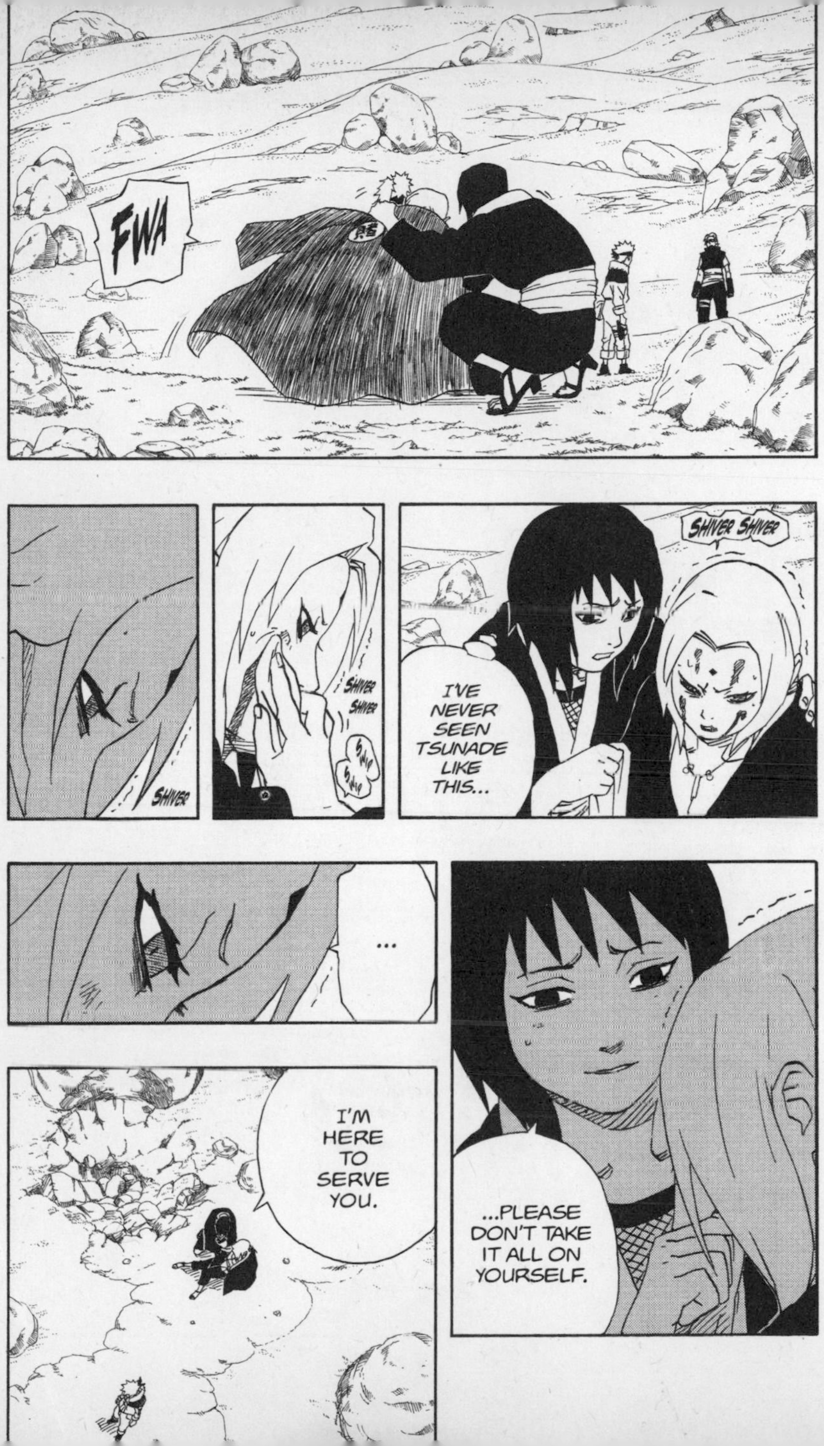
FWA
SHIVER SHIVER
I'VE NEVER SEEN TSUNADE LIKE THIS...
SHIVER SHIVER
SHIVER
...PLEASE DON'T TAKE IT ALL ON YOURSELF.
...
I'M HERE TO SERVE YOU.

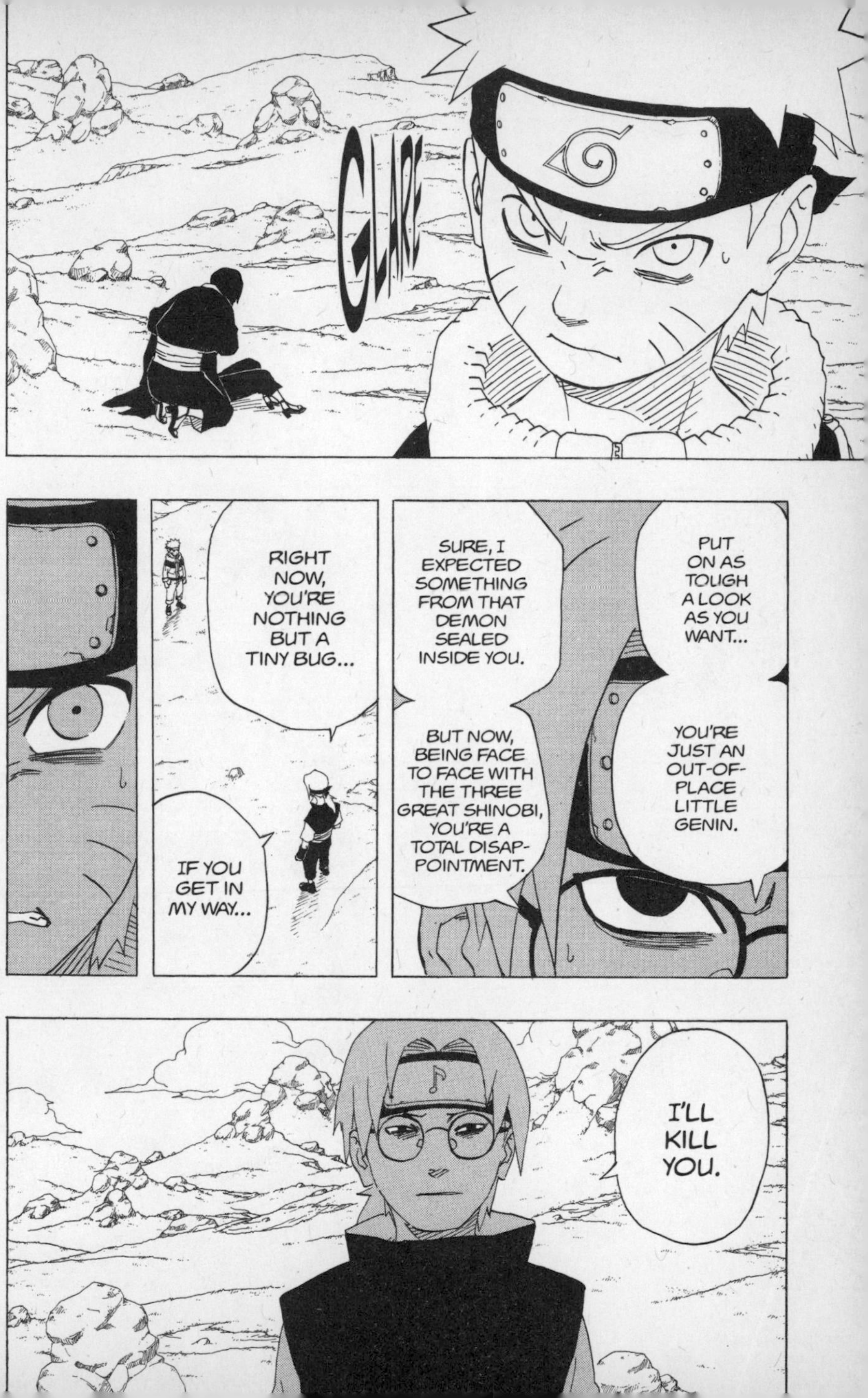
GLARE
PUT ON AS TOUGH A LOOK AS YOU WANT...
YOU'RE JUST AN OUT-OF-PLACE LITTLE GENIN.
SURE, I EXPECTED SOMETHING FROM THAT DEMON SEALED INSIDE YOU.
BUT NOW, BEING FACE TO FACE WITH THE THREE GREAT SHINOBI, YOU'RE A TOTAL DISAP-POINTMENT.
RIGHT NOW, YOU'RE NOTHING BUT A TINY BUG...
IF YOU GET IN MY WAY...
I'LL KILL YOU.

READ THIS WAY

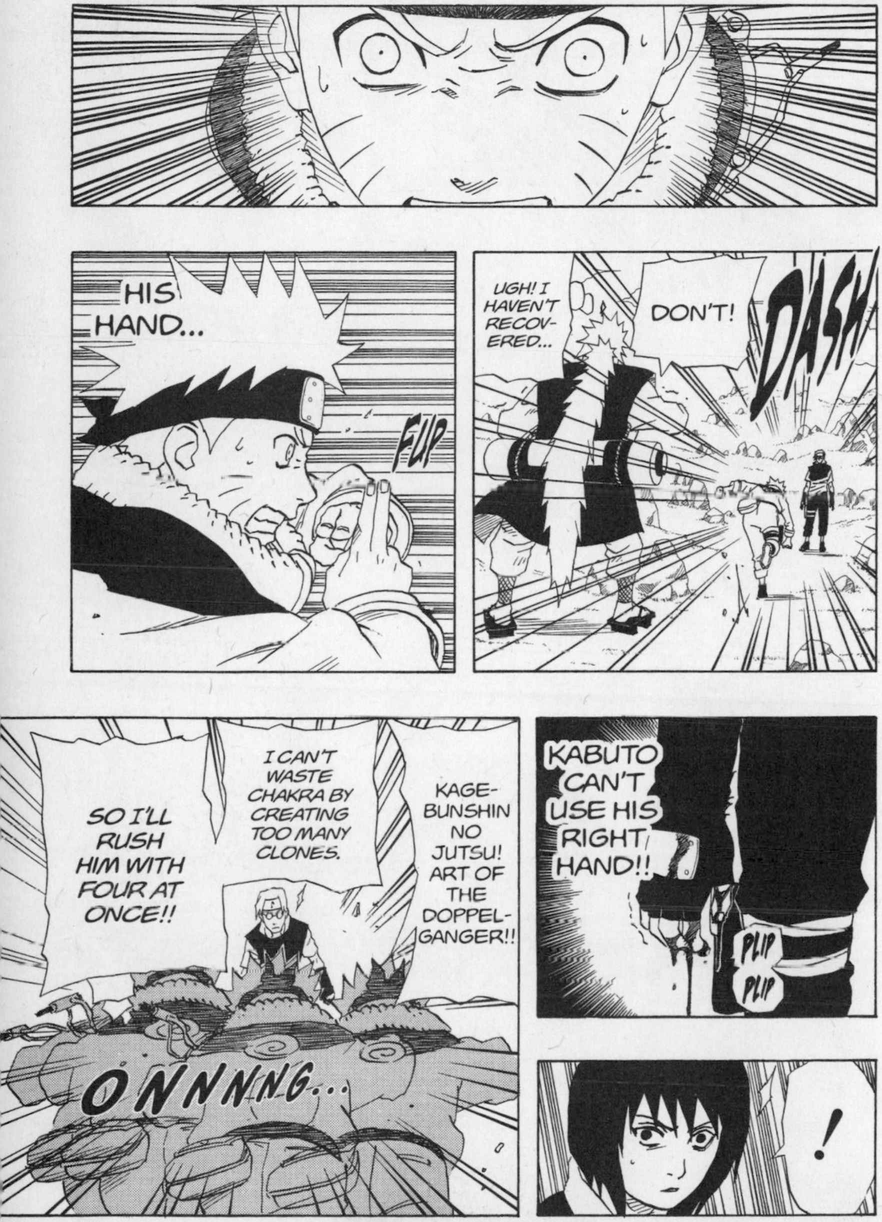

DASH
DON'T!
UGH! I HAVEN'T RECOVERED...
HIS HAND...
FUP
KABUTO CAN'T USE HIS RIGHT HAND!!
PLIP PLIP
!
KAGE-BUNSHIN NO JUTSU! ART OF THE DOPPELGANGER!!
I CAN'T WASTE CHAKRA BY CREATING TOO MANY CLONES.
SO I'LL RUSH HIM WITH FOUR AT ONCE!!
ONNNNG...

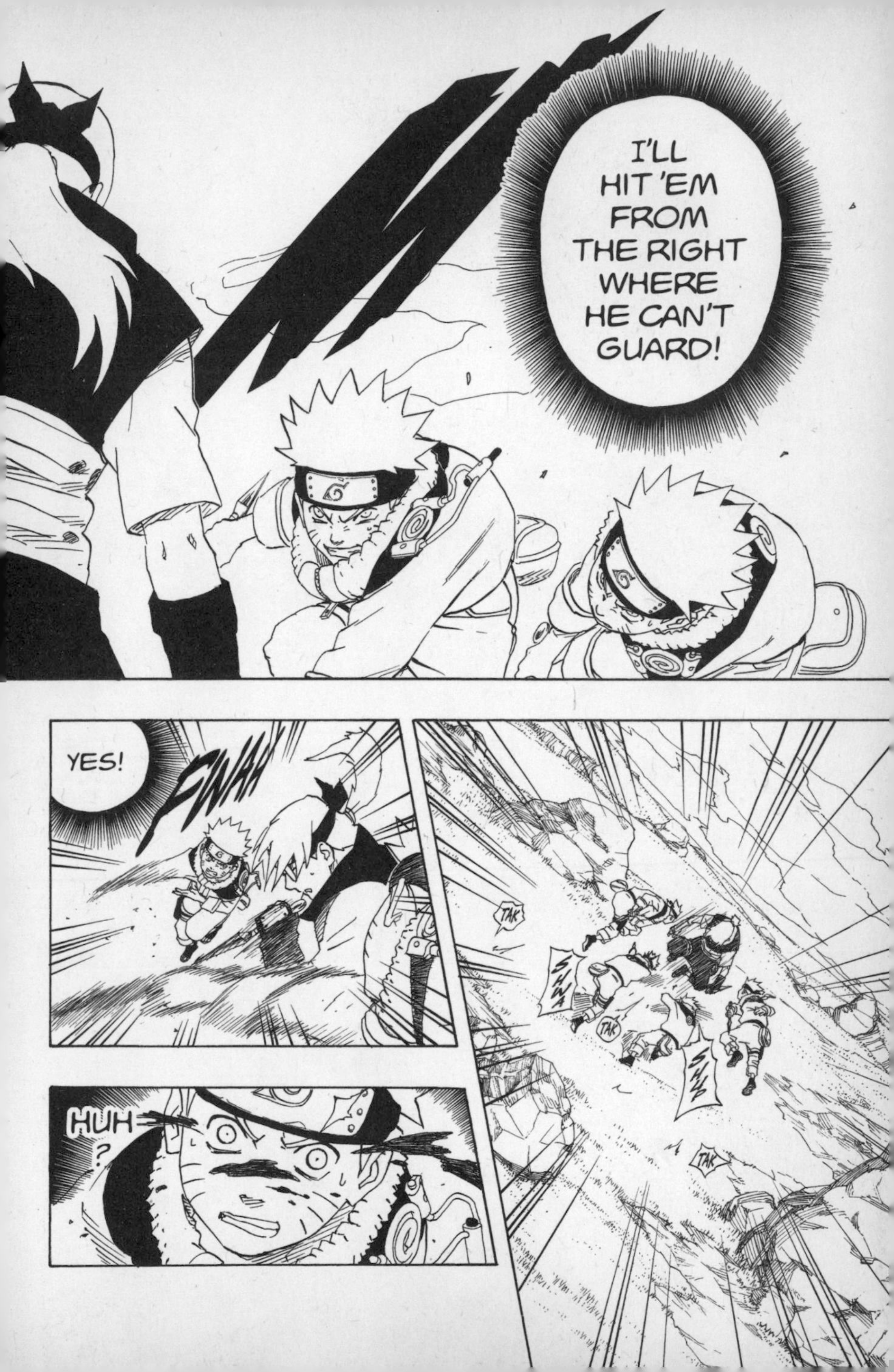
I'LL HIT 'EM FROM THE RIGHT WHERE HE CAN'T GUARD!
TAK
SHWA
TAK
SHHP
TAK
YES!
FWAH
HUH-?

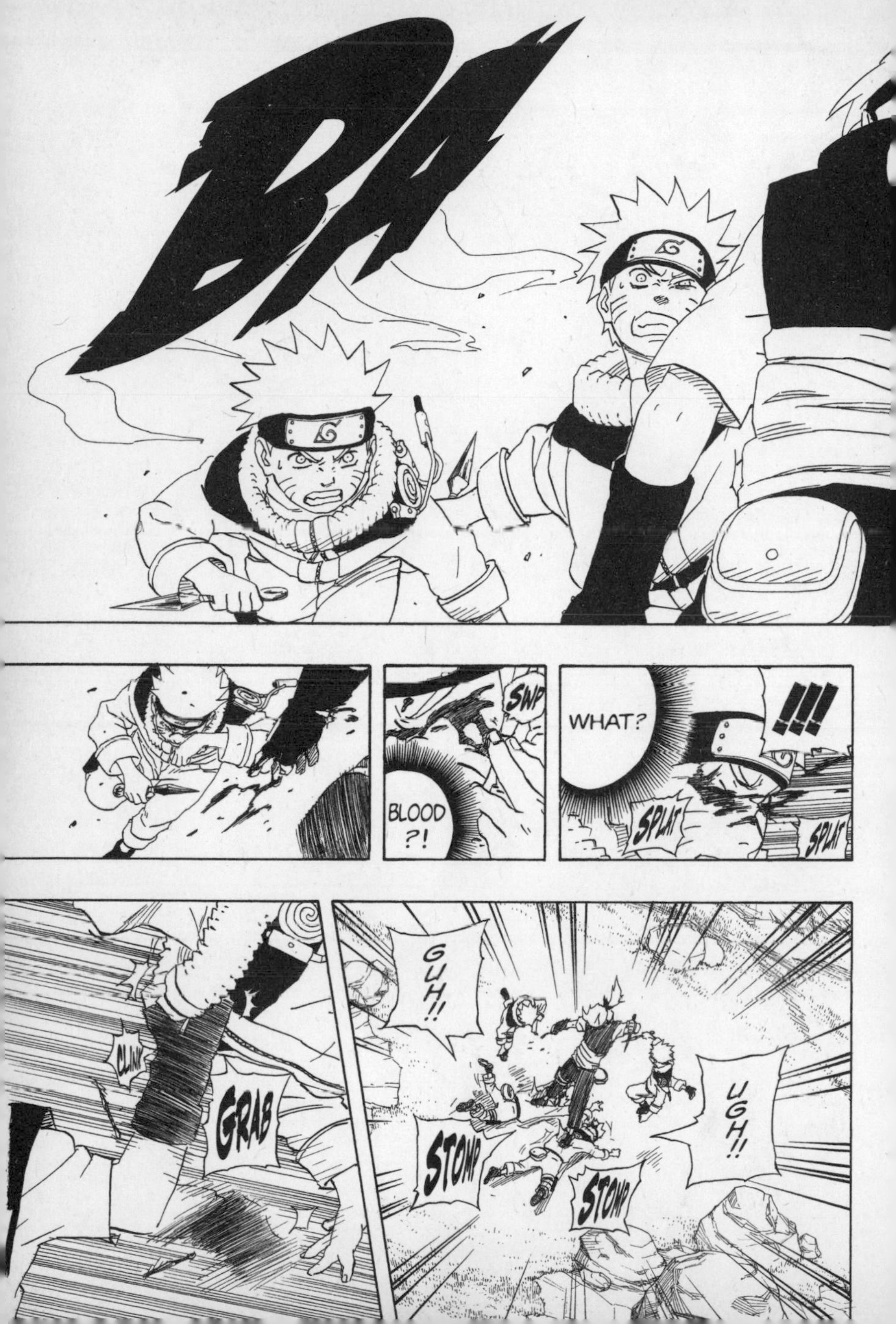
BA
!!!
WHAT?
SPLAT
SPLAT
SWP
BLOOD ?!
GUH!!
UGH!!
STOMP
STOMP
CLINK
GRAB

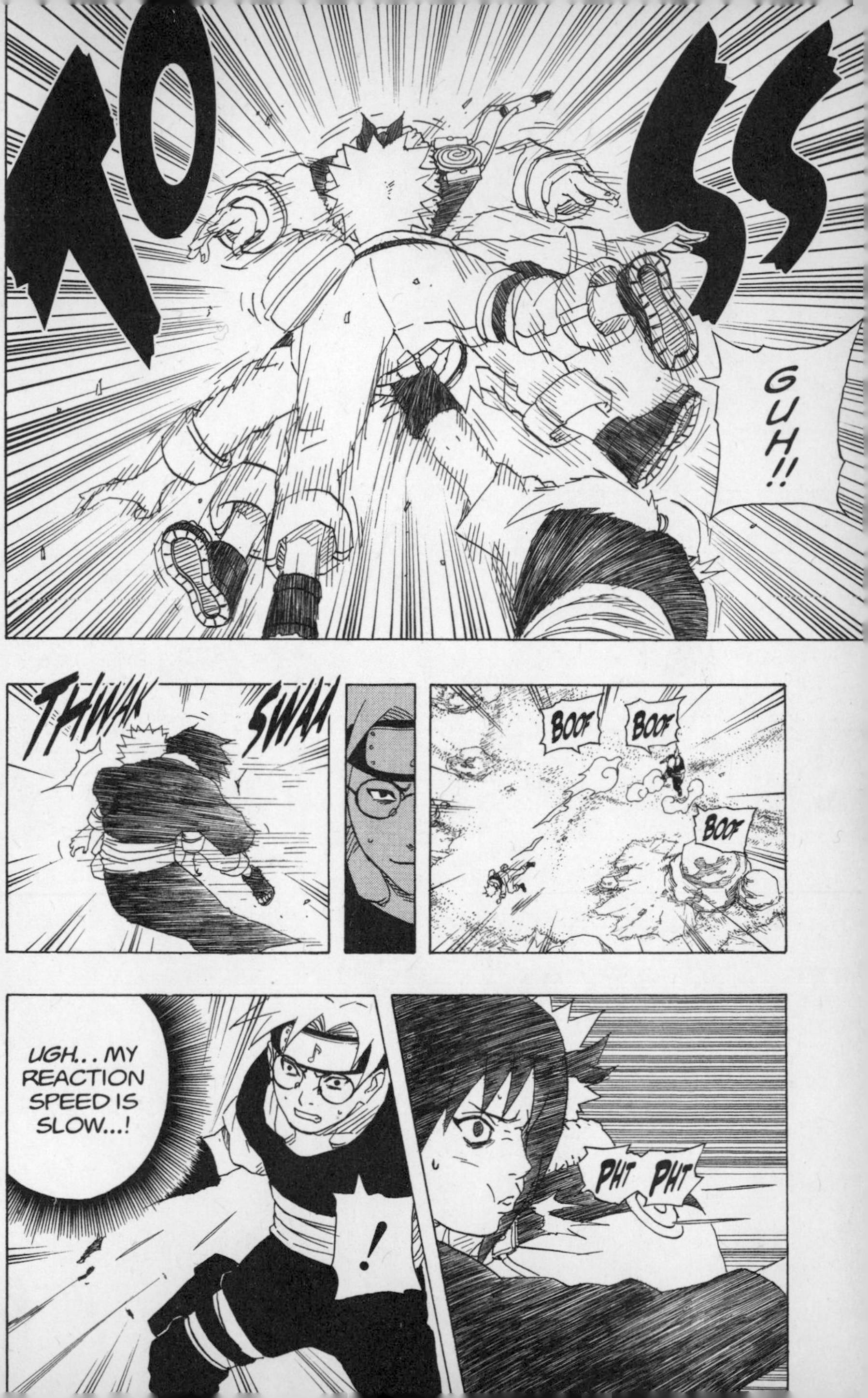
TOSS
GUH!!
BOOF
BOOF
BOOF
SWAA
THWAK
PHT PHT
!
UGH... MY REACTION SPEED IS SLOW...!

READ THIS WAY

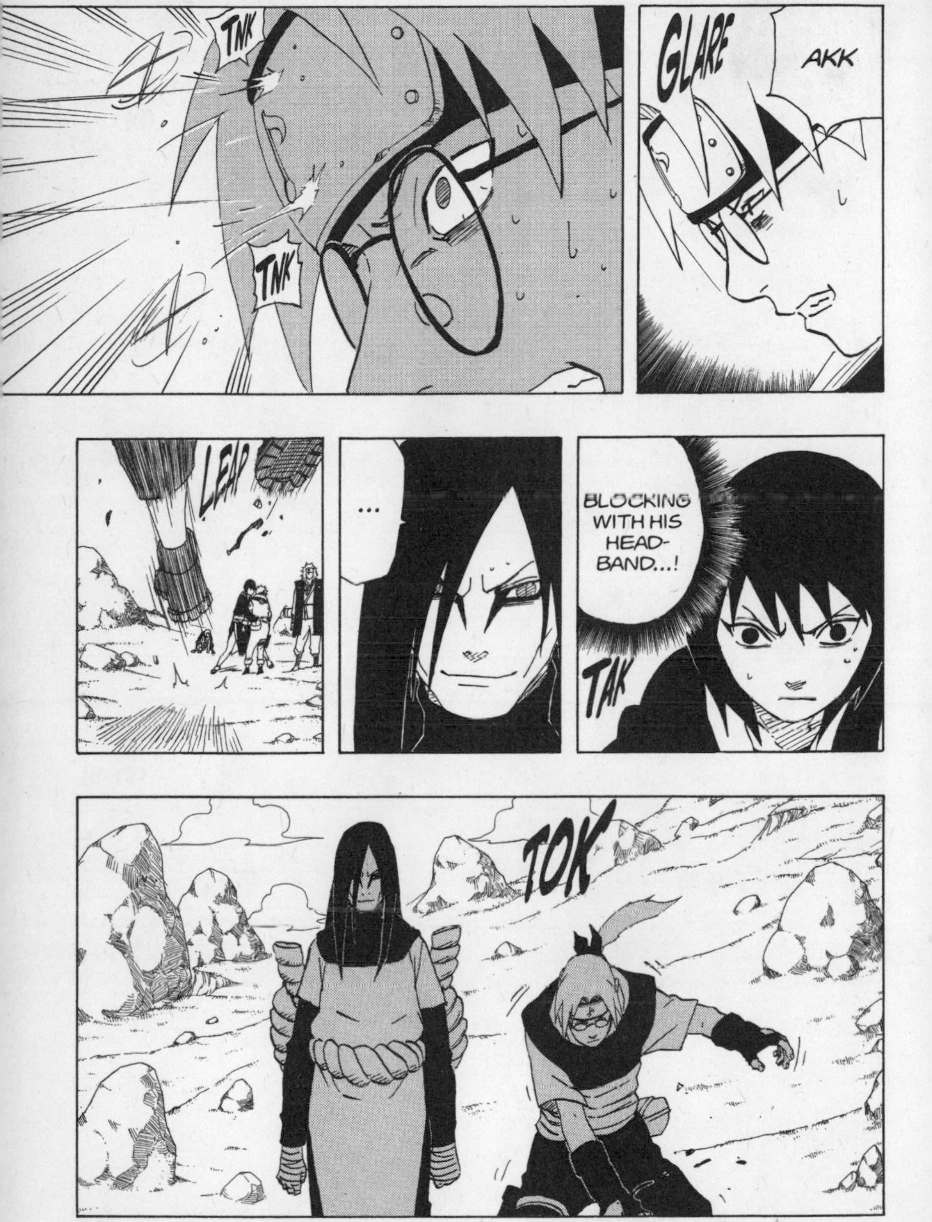
GLARE
AKK
TNK
TNK
BLOCKING WITH HIS HEAD-BAND...!
TAK
...
LEAP
TOK

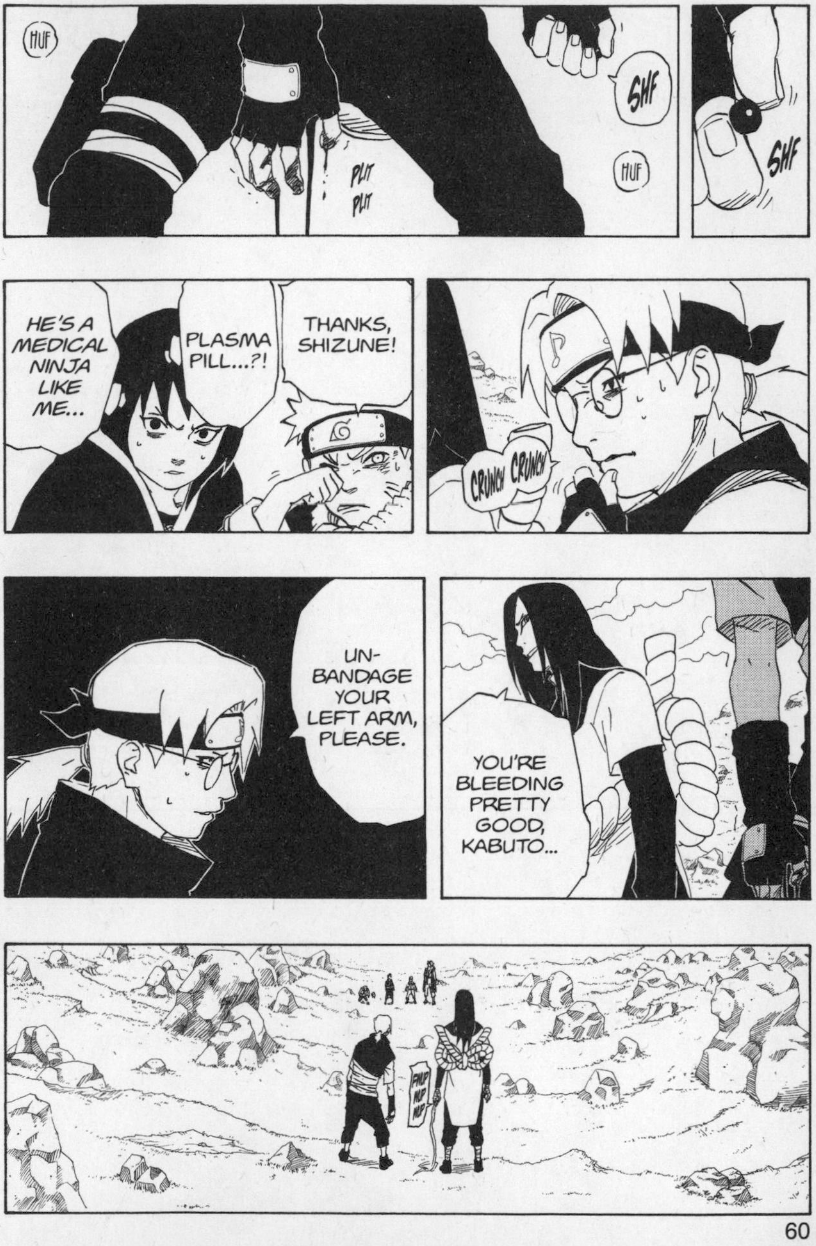
SHF
SHF
HUF
PLIT
PLIT
HUF
CRUNCH CRUNCH
THANKS, SHIZUNE!
PLASMA PILL...?!
HE'S A MEDICAL NINJA LIKE ME...
YOU'RE BLEEDING PRETTY GOOD, KABUTO...
UN-BANDAGE YOUR LEFT ARM, PLEASE.

READ THIS WAY

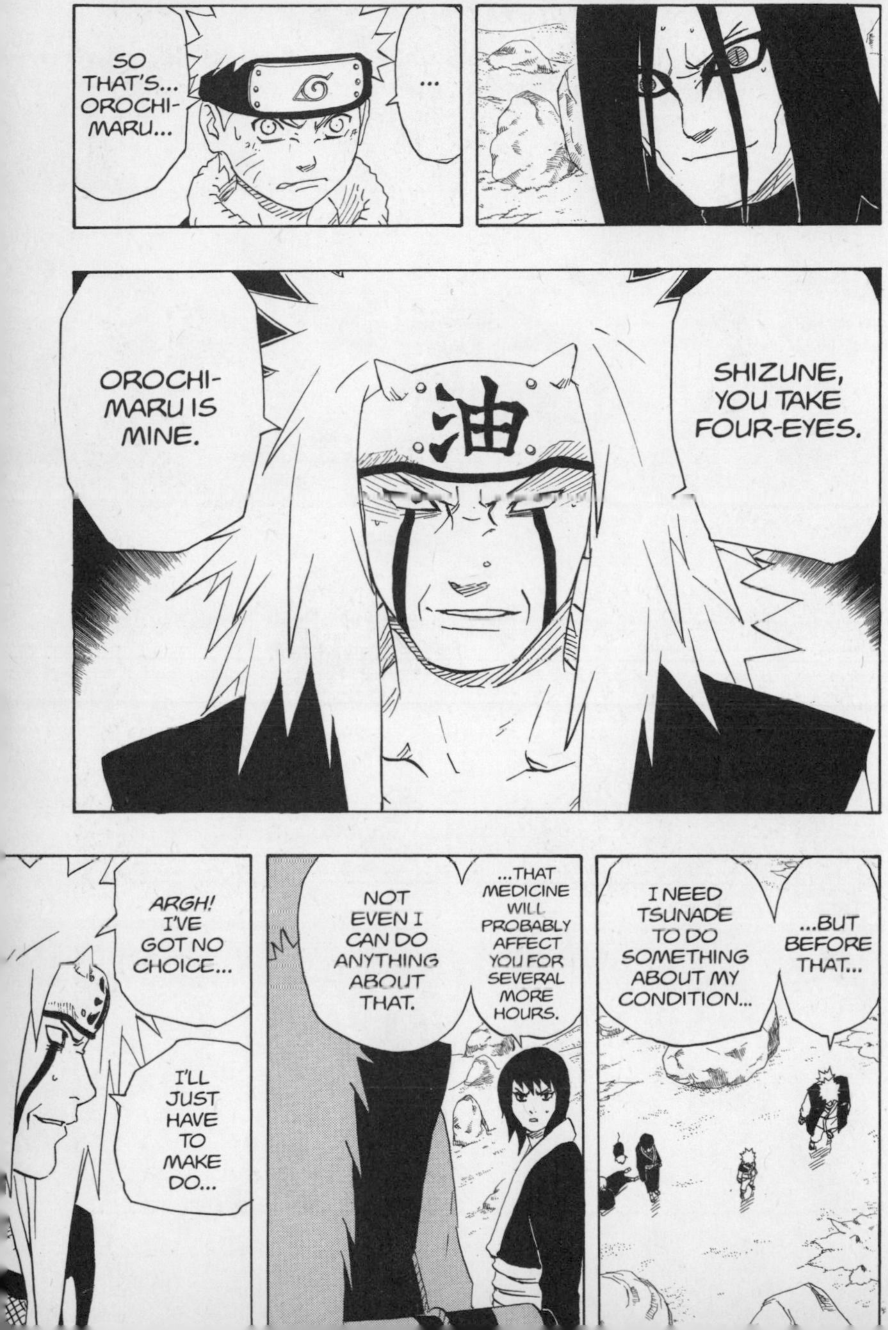
...
SO THAT'S... OROCHI-MARU...
SHIZUNE, YOU TAKE FOUR-EYES.
OROCHI-MARU IS MINE.
...BUT BEFORE THAT...
I NEED TSUNADE TO DO SOMETHING ABOUT MY CONDITION...
...THAT MEDICINE WILL PROBABLY AFFECT YOU FOR SEVERAL MORE HOURS.
NOT EVEN I CAN DO ANYTHING ABOUT THAT.
ARGH! I'VE GOT NO CHOICE...
I'LL JUST HAVE TO MAKE DO...

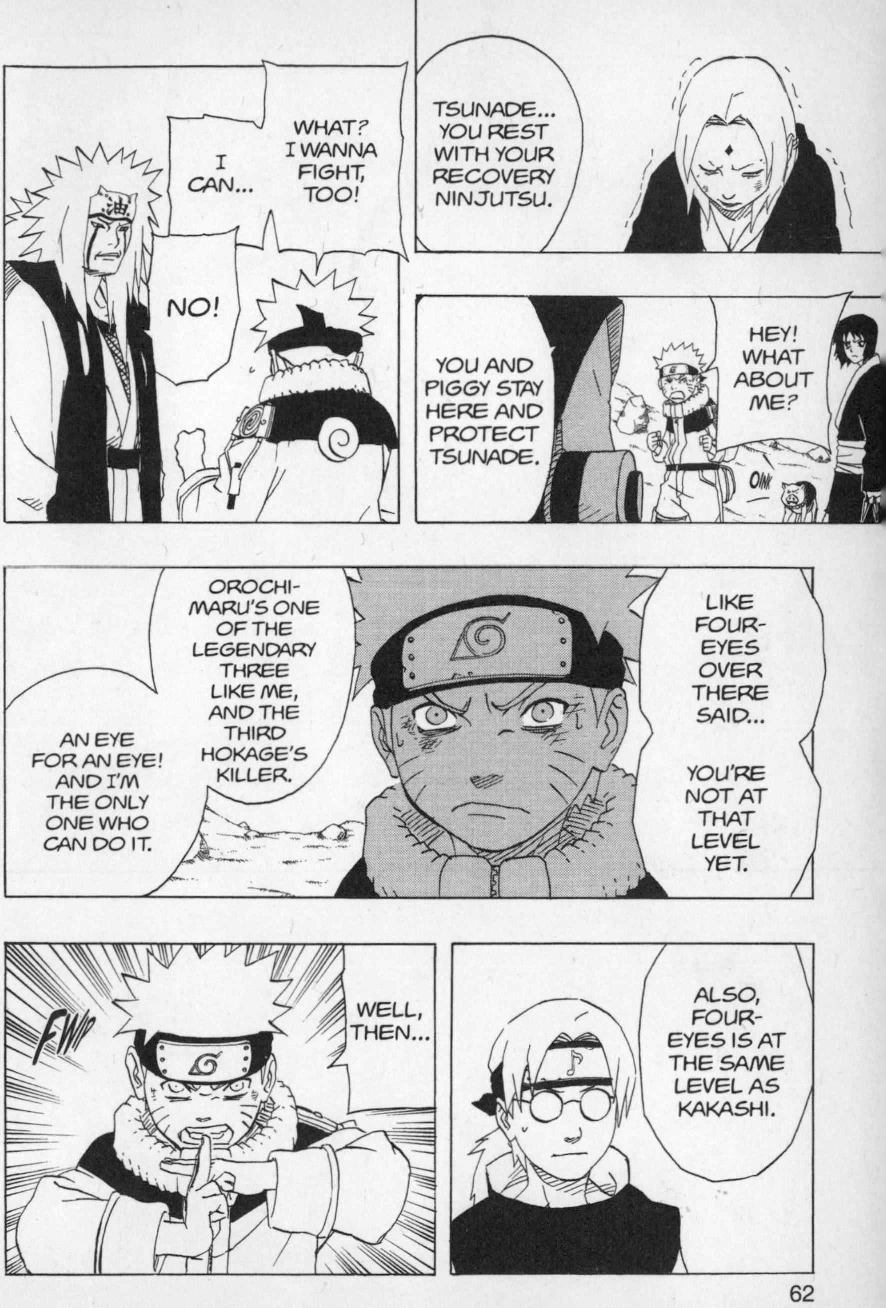
TSUNADE... YOU REST WITH YOUR RECOVERY NINJUTSU.
YOU AND PIGGY STAY HERE AND PROTECT TSUNADE.
HEY! WHAT ABOUT ME?
OINK
WHAT? I WANNA FIGHT, TOO!
I CAN...
NO!
LIKE FOUR-EYES OVER THERE SAID...
YOU'RE NOT AT THAT LEVEL YET.
OROCHI-MARU'S ONE OF THE LEGENDARY THREE LIKE ME, AND THE THIRD HOKAGE'S KILLER.
AN EYE FOR AN EYE! AND I'M THE ONLY ONE WHO CAN DO IT.
ALSO, FOUR-EYES IS AT THE SAME LEVEL AS KAKASHI.
WELL, THEN...
FWIP

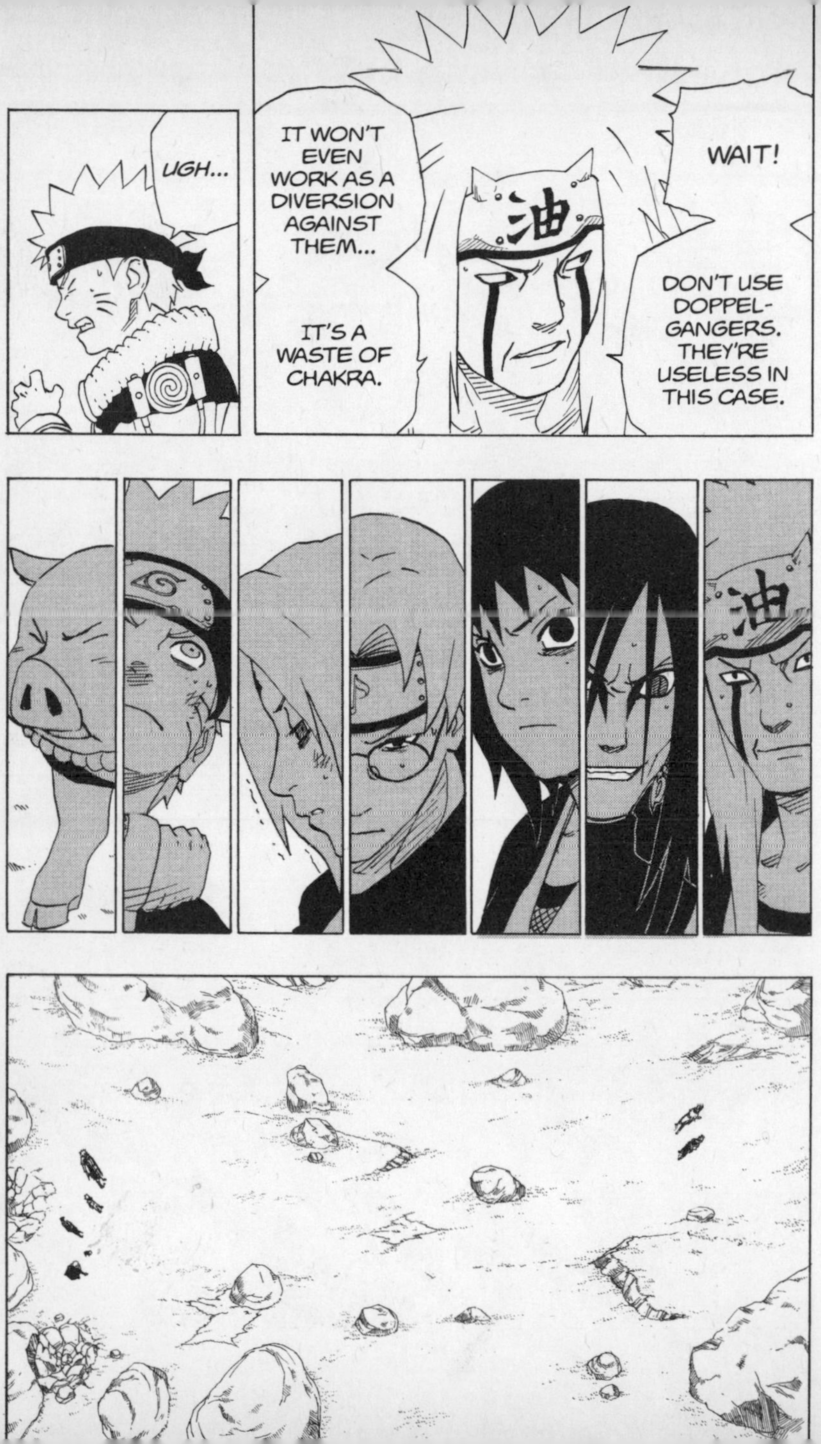
WAIT!
DON'T USE DOPPEL-GANGERS. THEY'RE USELESS IN THIS CASE.
IT WON'T EVEN WORK AS A DIVERSION AGAINST THEM...
IT'S A WASTE OF CHAKRA.
UGH...

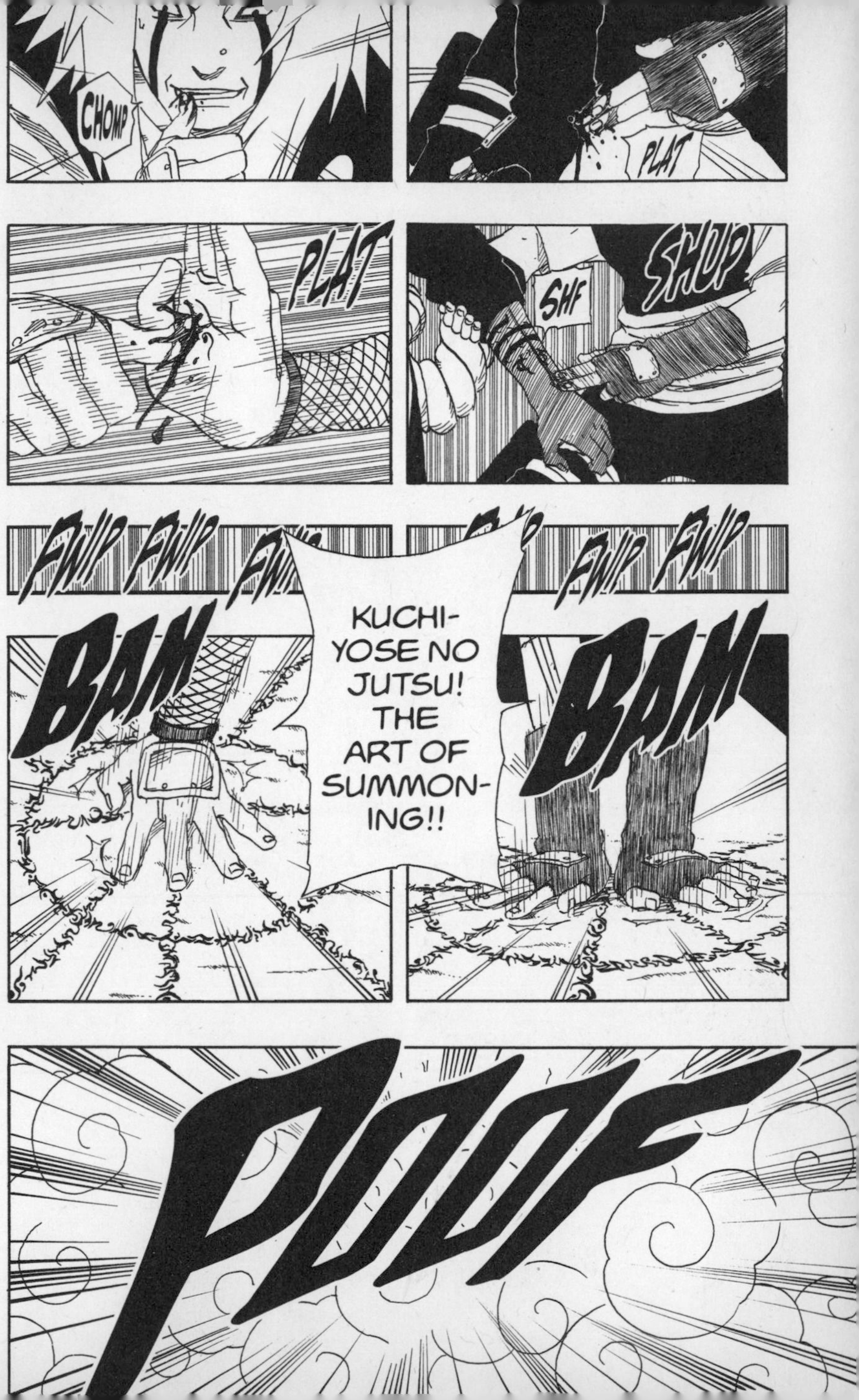
PLAT
CHOMP
SHUP
SHF
PLAT
FWIP FWIP
BAM
KUCHI-YOSE NO JUTSU! THE ART OF SUMMONING!!
FWIP FWIP FWIP
BAM
POOF

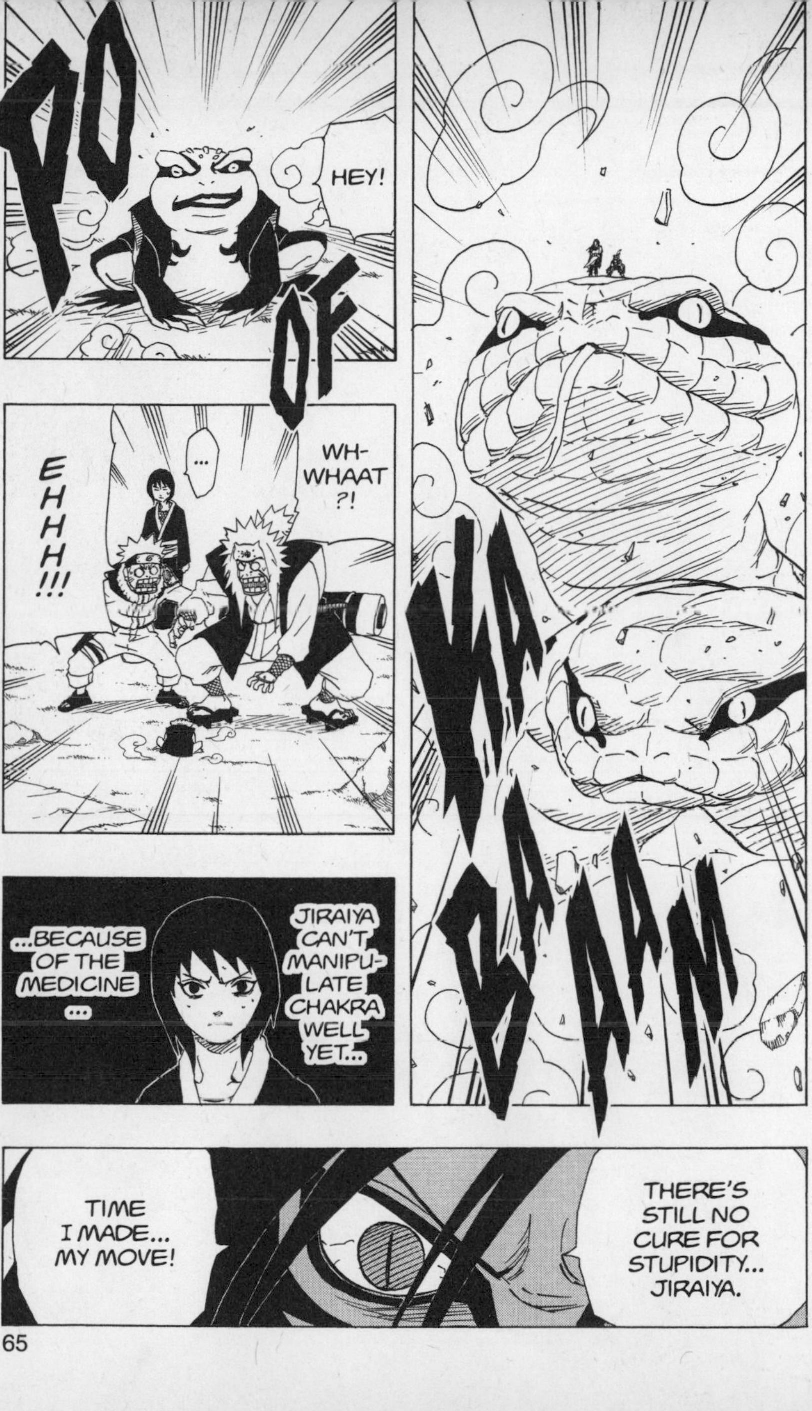
POOF
HEY!
WH-WHAAT?!
...
EHHH!!!
JIRAIYA CAN'T MANIPULATE CHAKRA WELL YET...
...BECAUSE OF THE MEDICINE...
THERE'S STILL NO CURE FOR STUPIDITY... JIRAIYA.
TIME I MADE... MY MOVE!

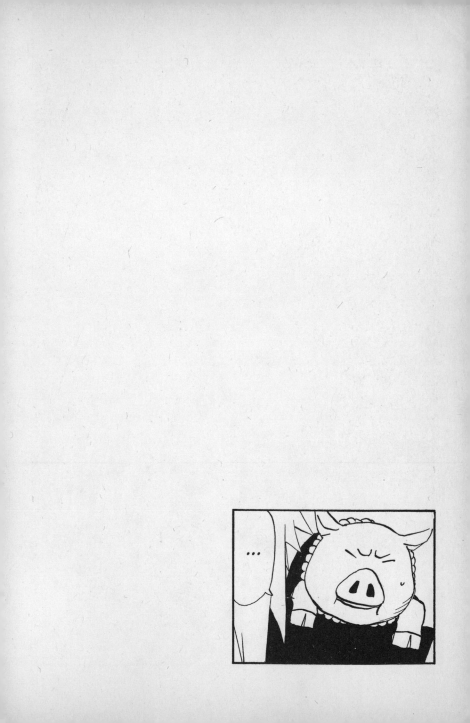

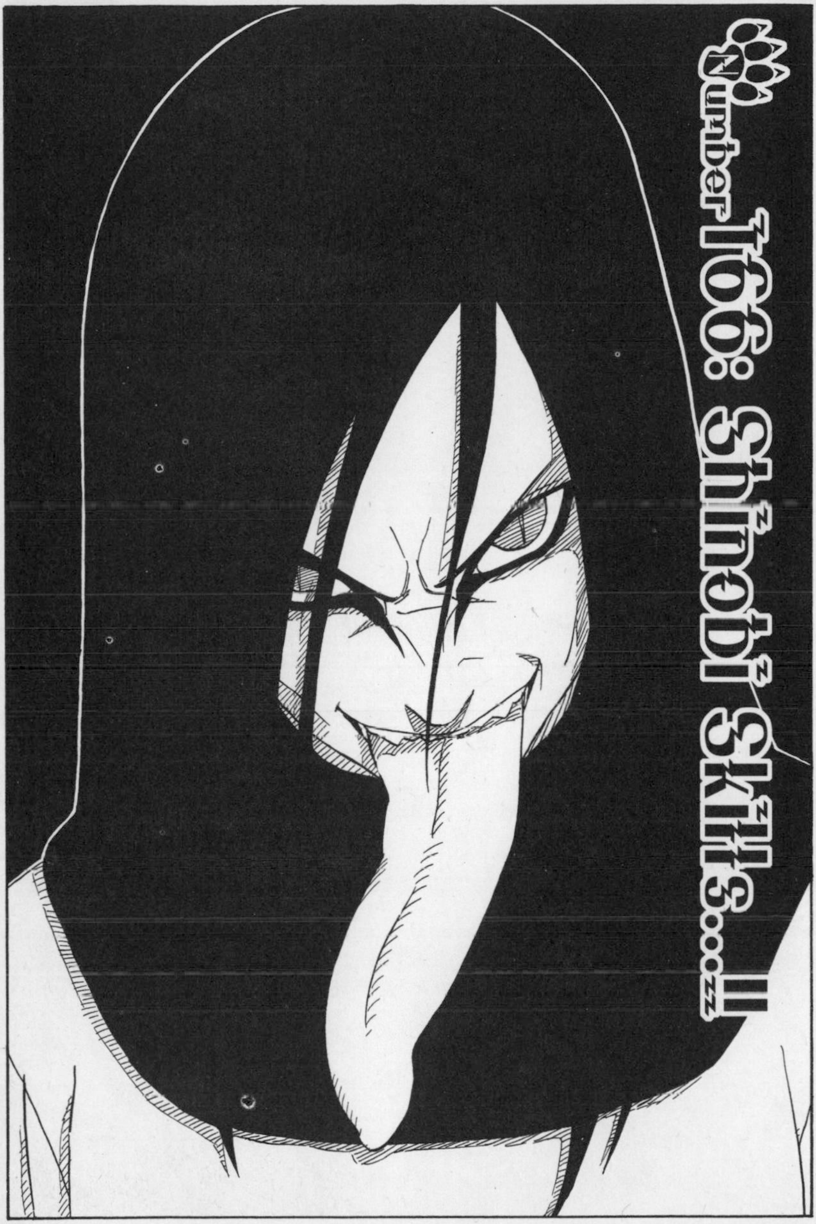
Number 166: Shinobi Skills...!!

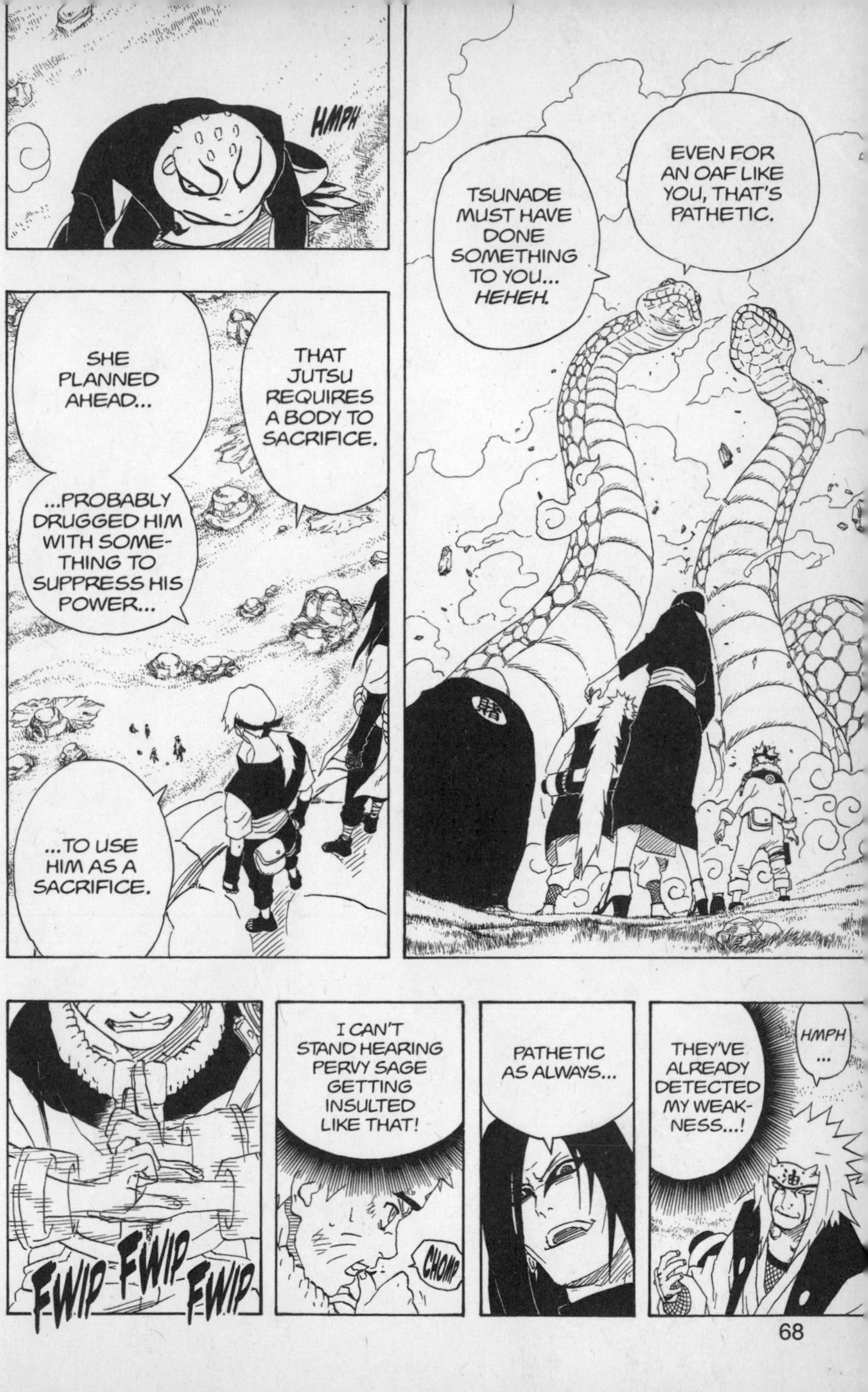
EVEN FOR AN OAF LIKE YOU, THAT'S PATHETIC.
TSUNADE MUST HAVE DONE SOMETHING TO YOU... HEHEH.
HMPH
THAT JUTSU REQUIRES A BODY TO SACRIFICE.
SHE PLANNED AHEAD...
...PROBABLY DRUGGED HIM WITH SOMETHING TO SUPPRESS HIS POWER...
...TO USE HIM AS A SACRIFICE.
HMPH...
THEY'VE ALREADY DETECTED MY WEAKNESS...!
PATHETIC AS ALWAYS...
I CAN'T STAND HEARING PERVY SAGE GETTING INSULTED LIKE THAT!
CHOMP
FWIP FWIP FWIP

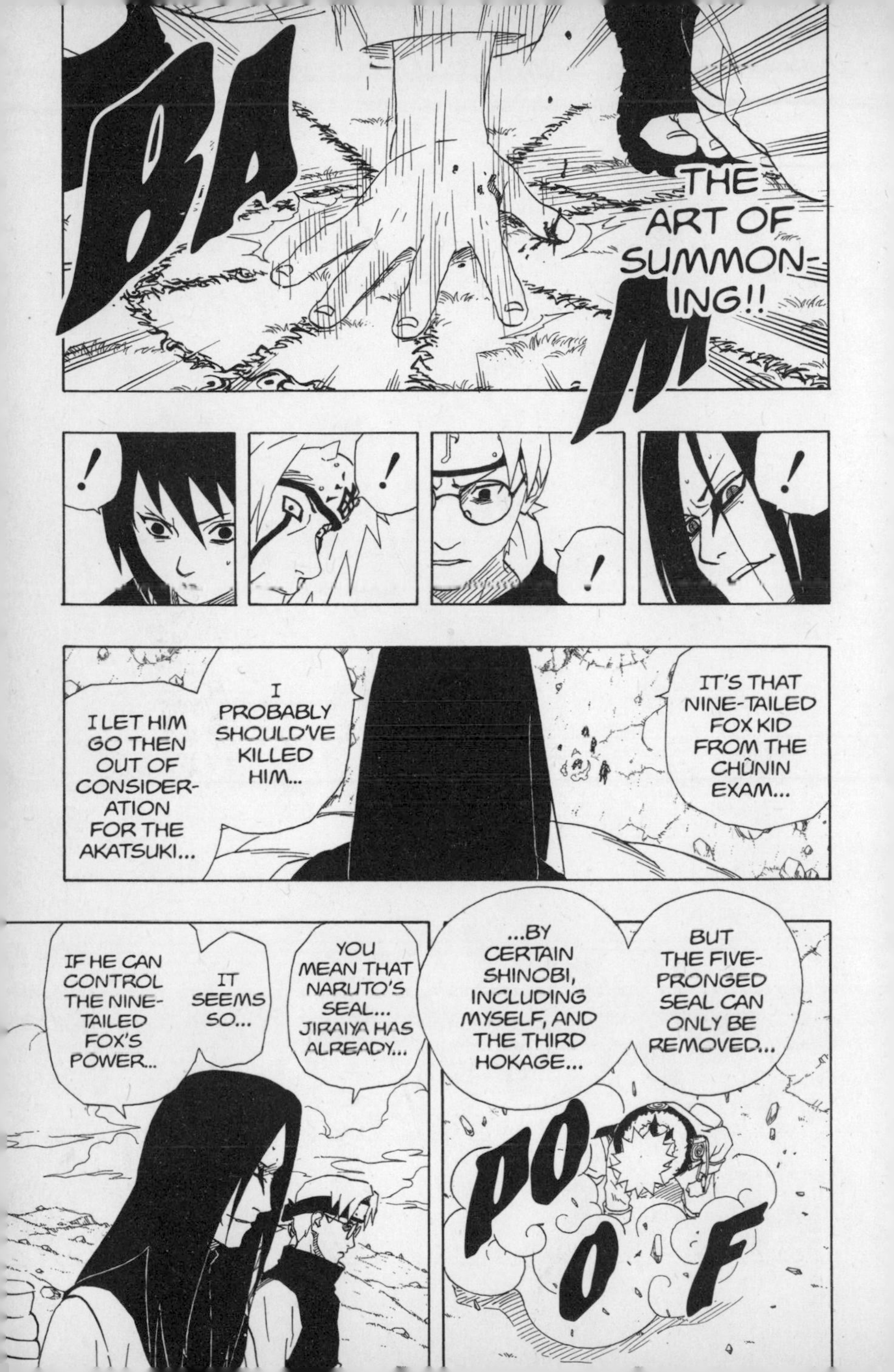
THE ART OF SUMMONING!!
BAM
!
!
!
!
IT'S THAT NINE-TAILED FOX KID FROM THE CHŪNIN EXAM...
I PROBABLY SHOULD'VE KILLED HIM...
I LET HIM GO THEN OUT OF CONSIDERATION FOR THE AKATSUKI...
BUT THE FIVE-PRONGED SEAL CAN ONLY BE REMOVED...
...BY CERTAIN SHINOBI, INCLUDING MYSELF, AND THE THIRD HOKAGE...
POOF
YOU MEAN THAT NARUTO'S SEAL... JIRAIYA HAS ALREADY...
IT SEEMS SO...
IF HE CAN CONTROL THE NINE-TAILED FOX'S POWER...

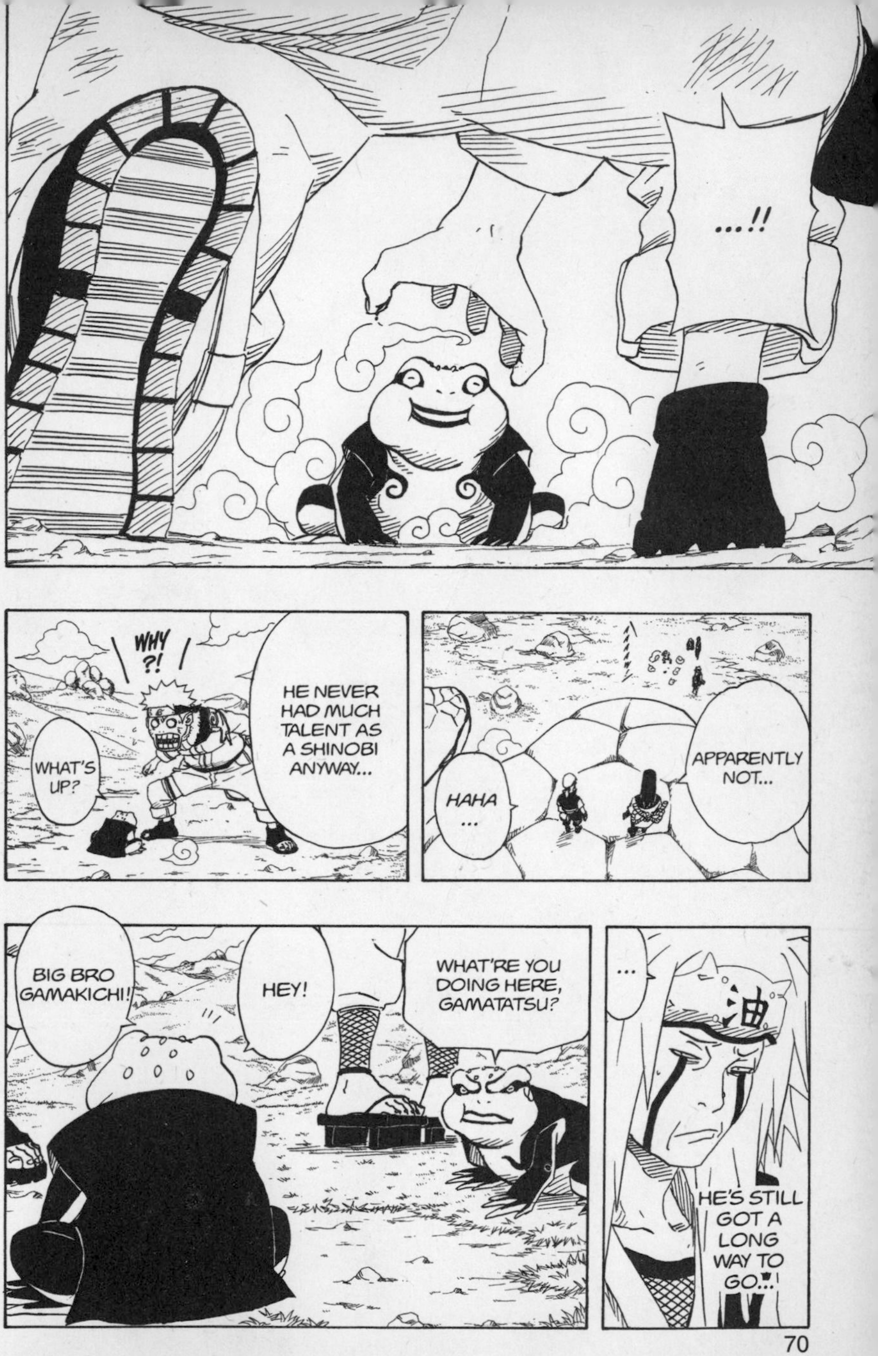
...!!
APPARENTLY NOT...
HAHA ...
HE NEVER HAD MUCH TALENT AS A SHINOBI ANYWAY...
WHY ?!
WHAT'S UP?
...
HE'S STILL GOT A LONG WAY TO GO...
WHAT'RE YOU DOING HERE, GAMATATSU?
HEY!
BIG BRO GAMAKICHI!

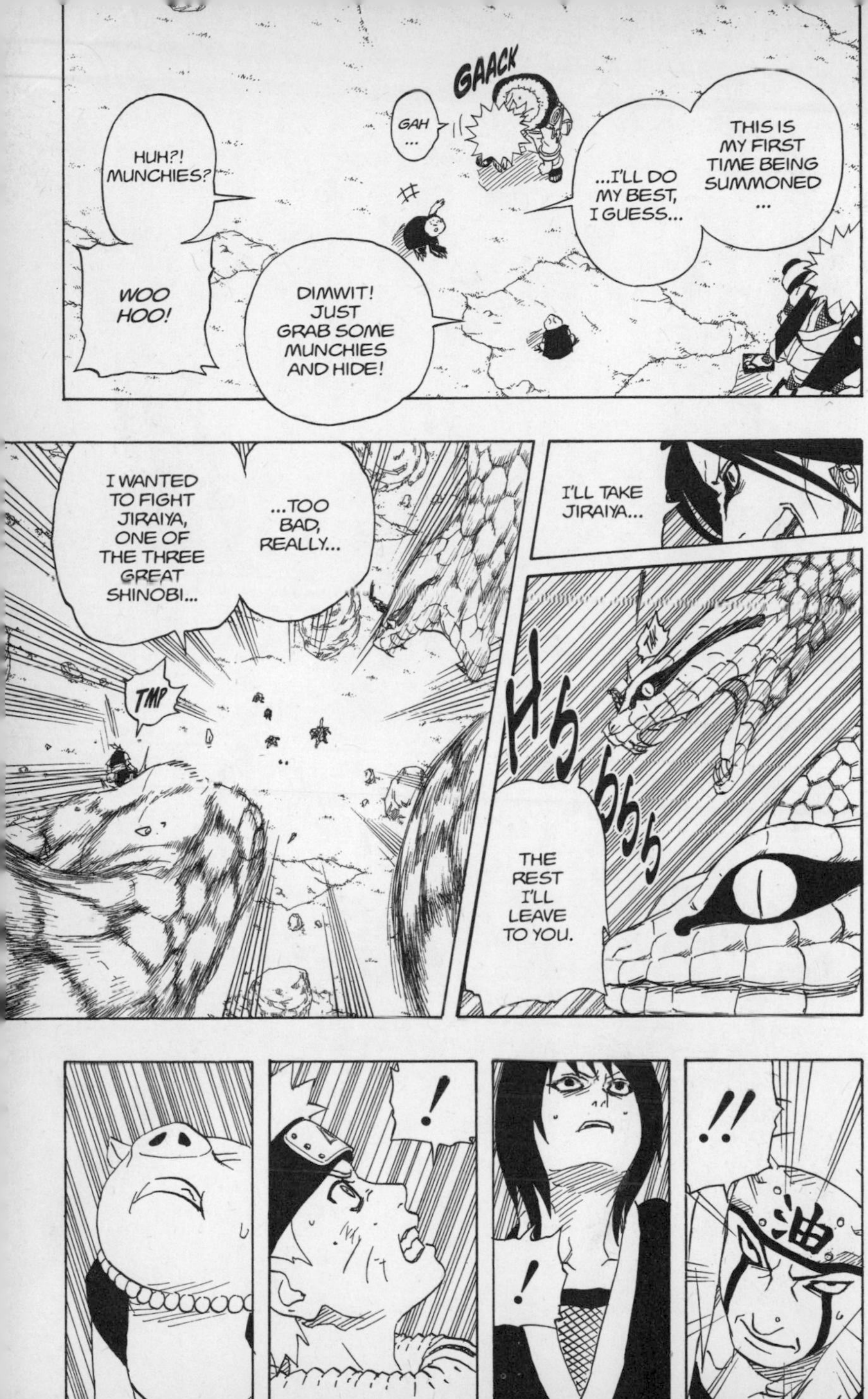

THIS IS MY FIRST TIME BEING SUMMONED...
...I'LL DO MY BEST, I GUESS...
GAACK
GAH...
HUH?! MUNCHIES?
DIMWIT! JUST GRAB SOME MUNCHIES AND HIDE!
WOO HOO!
I'LL TAKE JIRAIYA...
HSSSS
THE REST I'LL LEAVE TO YOU.
...TOO BAD, REALLY...
I WANTED TO FIGHT JIRAIYA, ONE OF THE THREE GREAT SHINOBI...
TMP
!!
!
!

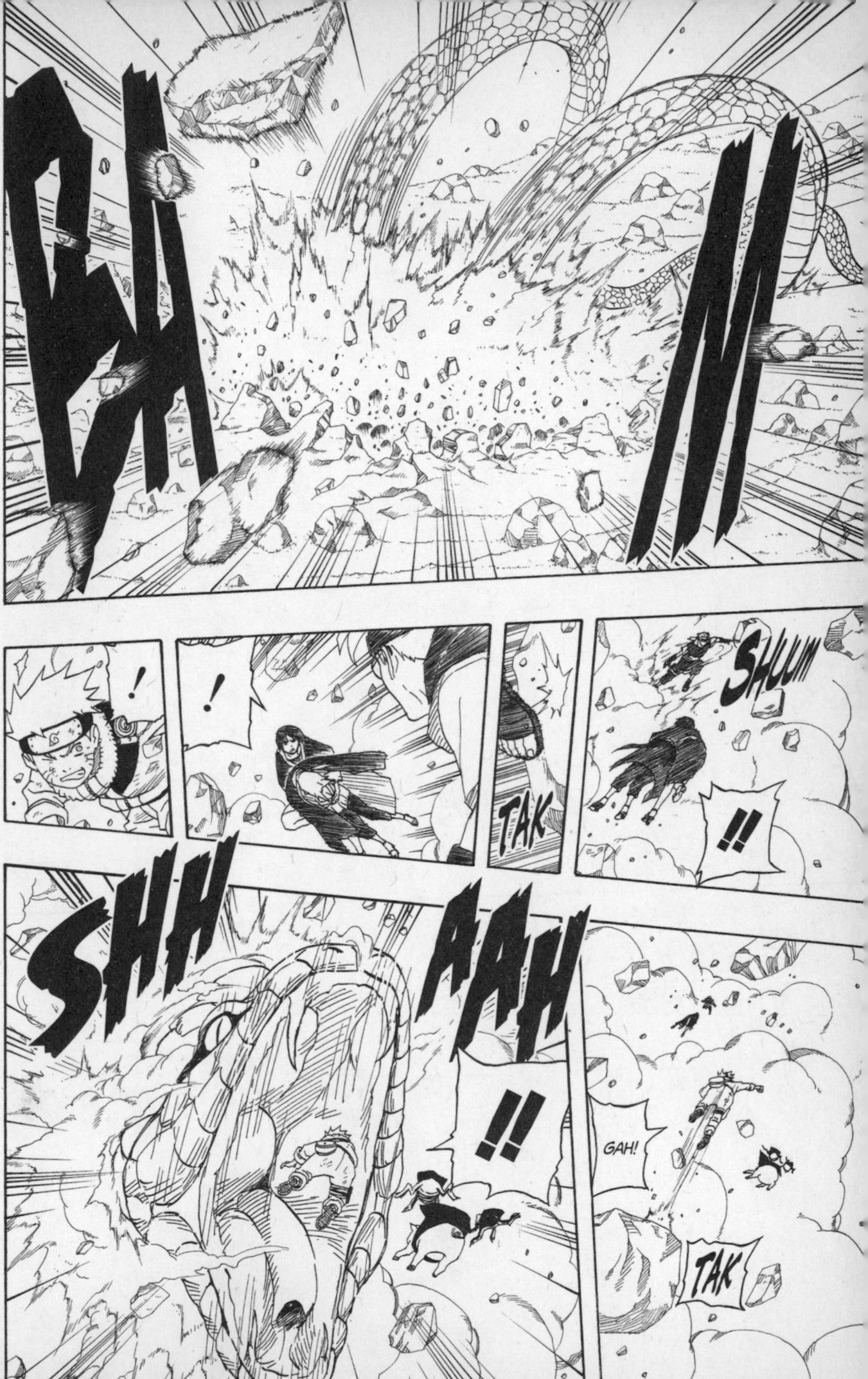
SHUUN
!!
TAK
!
!
GAH!
TAK
SHH
AAH
!!

« READ THIS WAY «

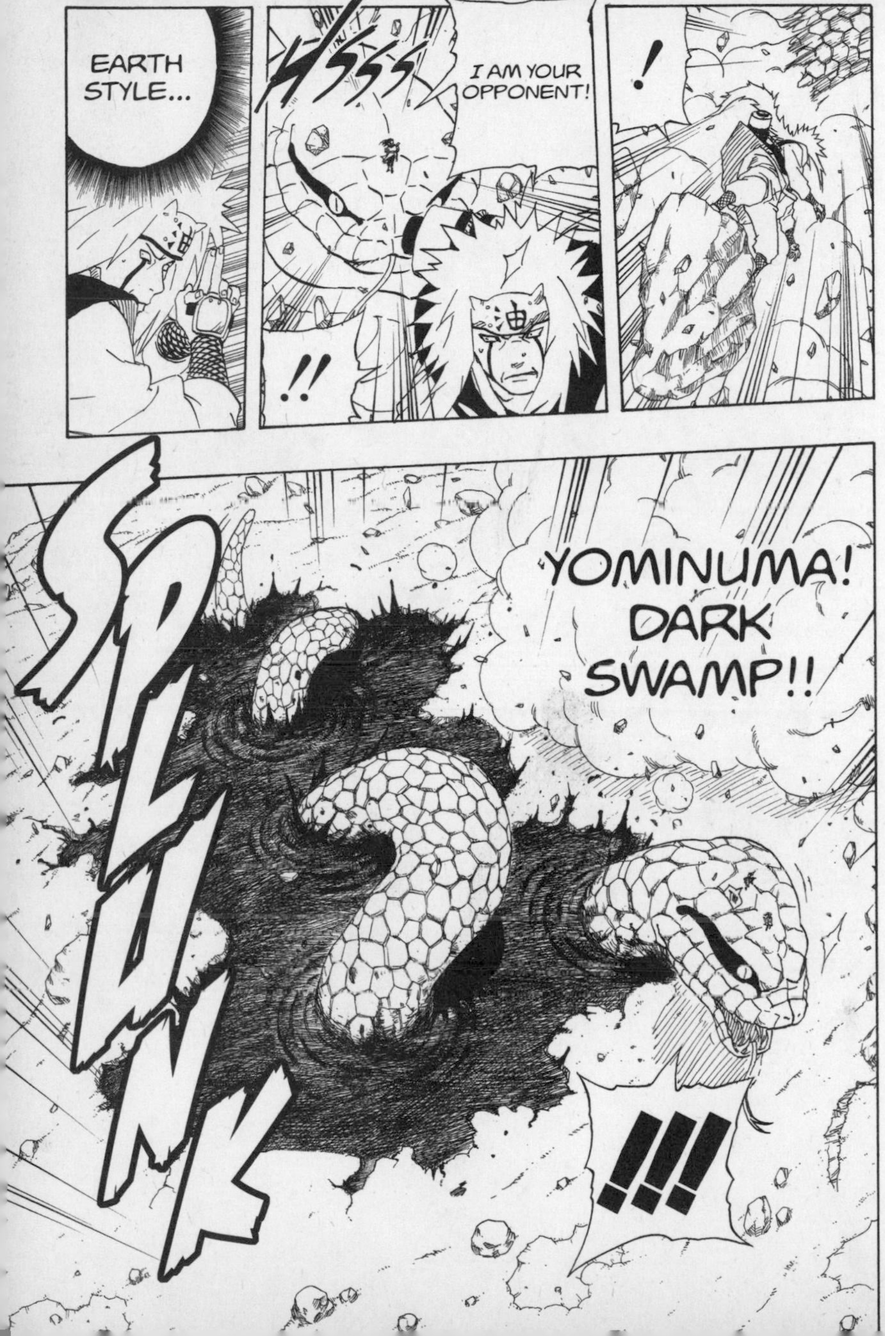
!
I AM YOUR OPPONENT!
!!
EARTH STYLE...
YOMINUMA! DARK SWAMP!!
!!!

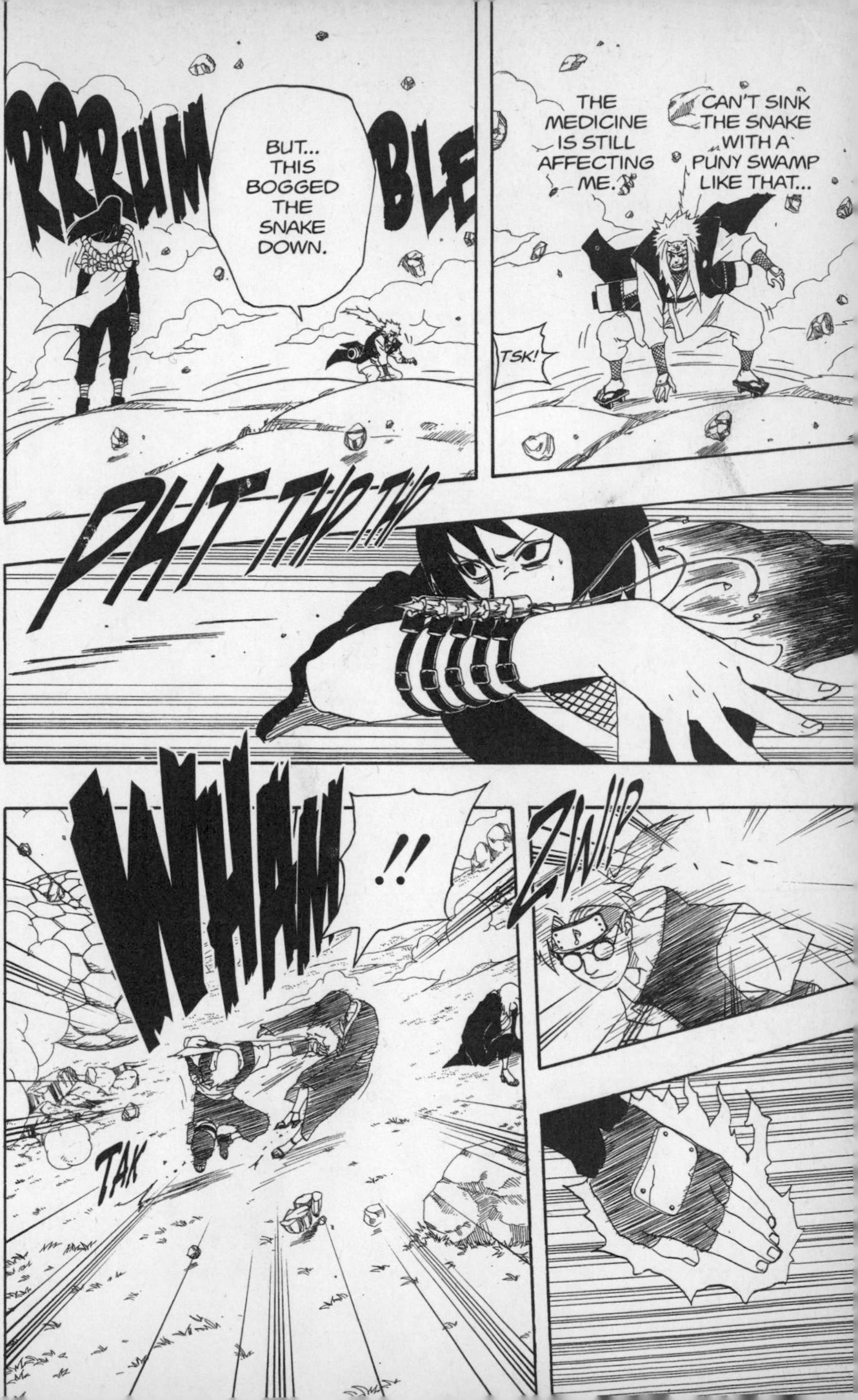

CAN'T SINK THE SNAKE WITH A PUNY SWAMP LIKE THAT...
THE MEDICINE IS STILL AFFECTING ME.
TSK!
RRRUMBLE
BUT... THIS BOGGED THE SNAKE DOWN.
PHT THP THP
ZWIP
WHAM!!
TAK

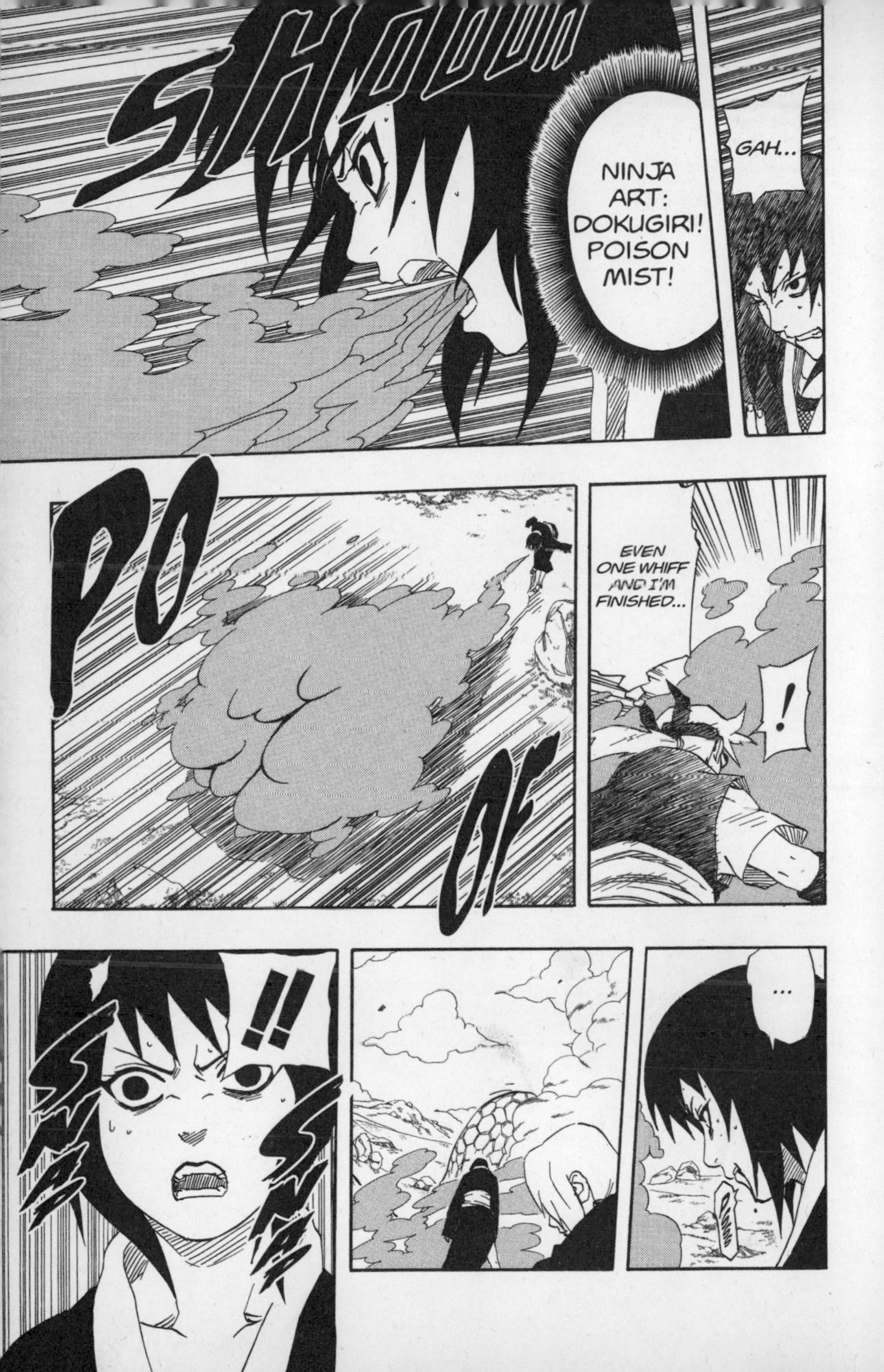
GAH...
SHOOOM
NINJA ART: DOKUGIRI! POISON MIST!
EVEN ONE WHIFF AND I'M FINISHED...
!
POOF
...
!!

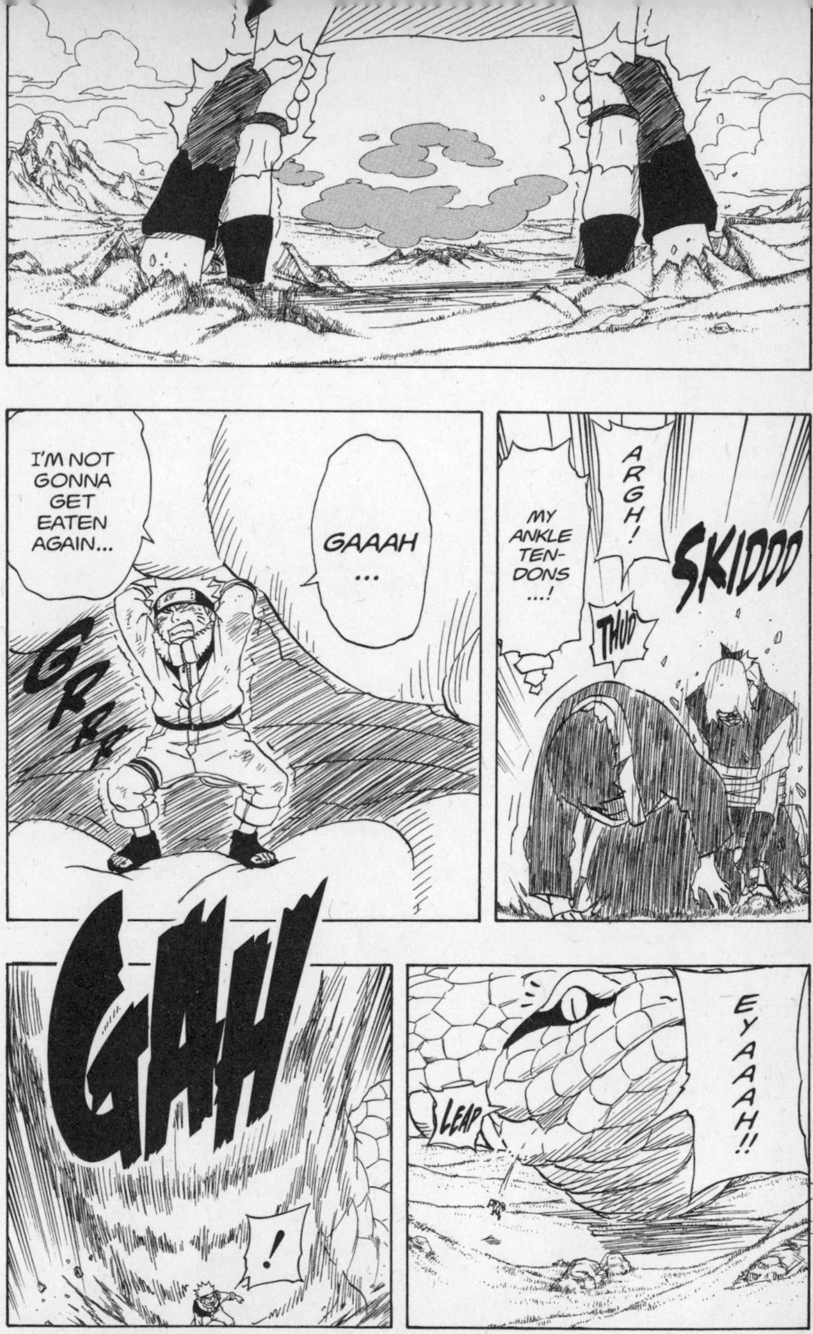

ARGH!
MY ANKLE TEN-DONS ...!
SKIDDD
THUD
I'M NOT GONNA GET EATEN AGAIN...
GAAAH ...
GRRR
EYAAAAH!!
LEAP
GAH
!

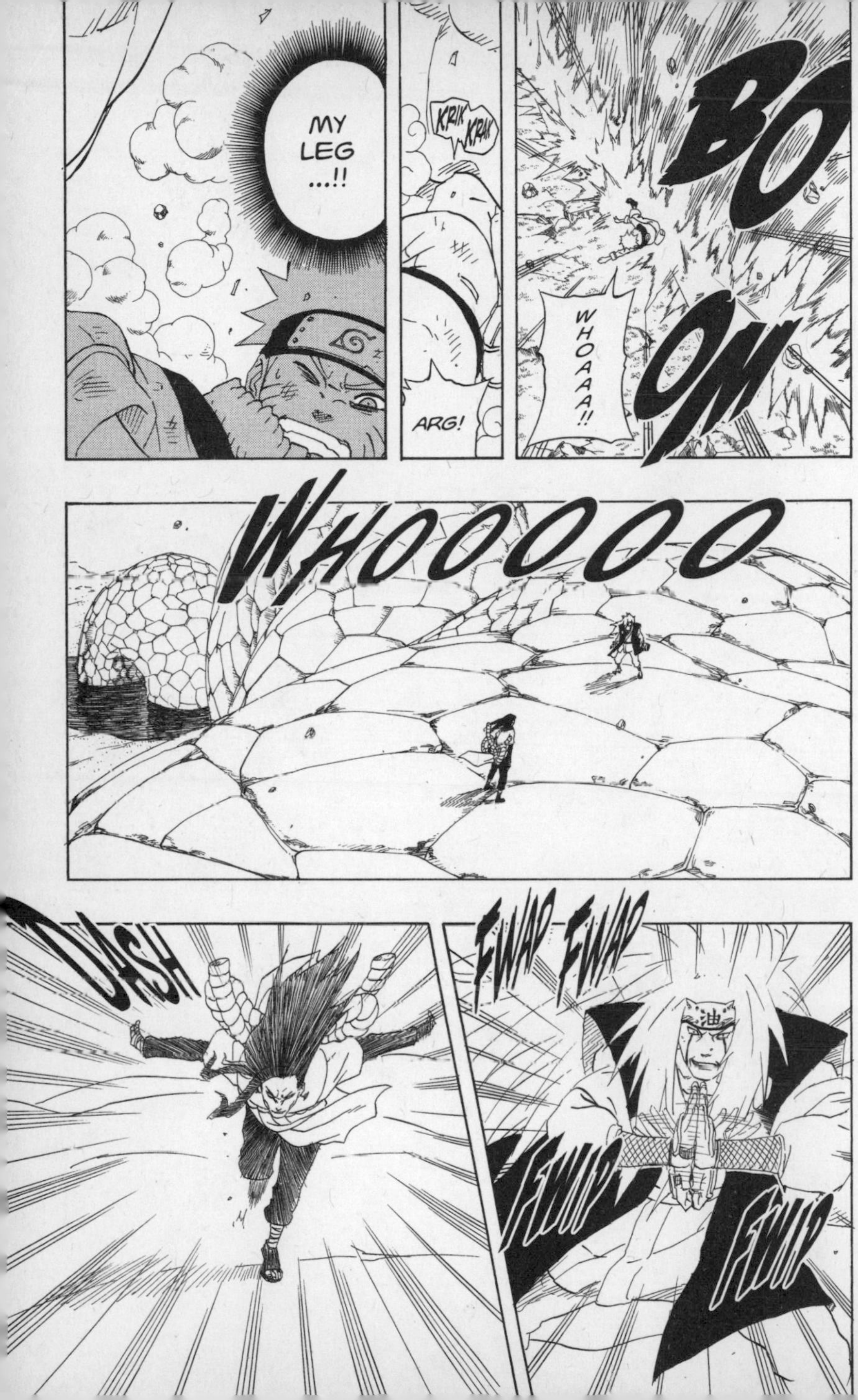
BOOM
WHOAAAA!!
KRIK KRAK
ARG!
MY LEG ...!!
WHOOOOO
FWAP FWAP
FWUP
FWUP
DASH

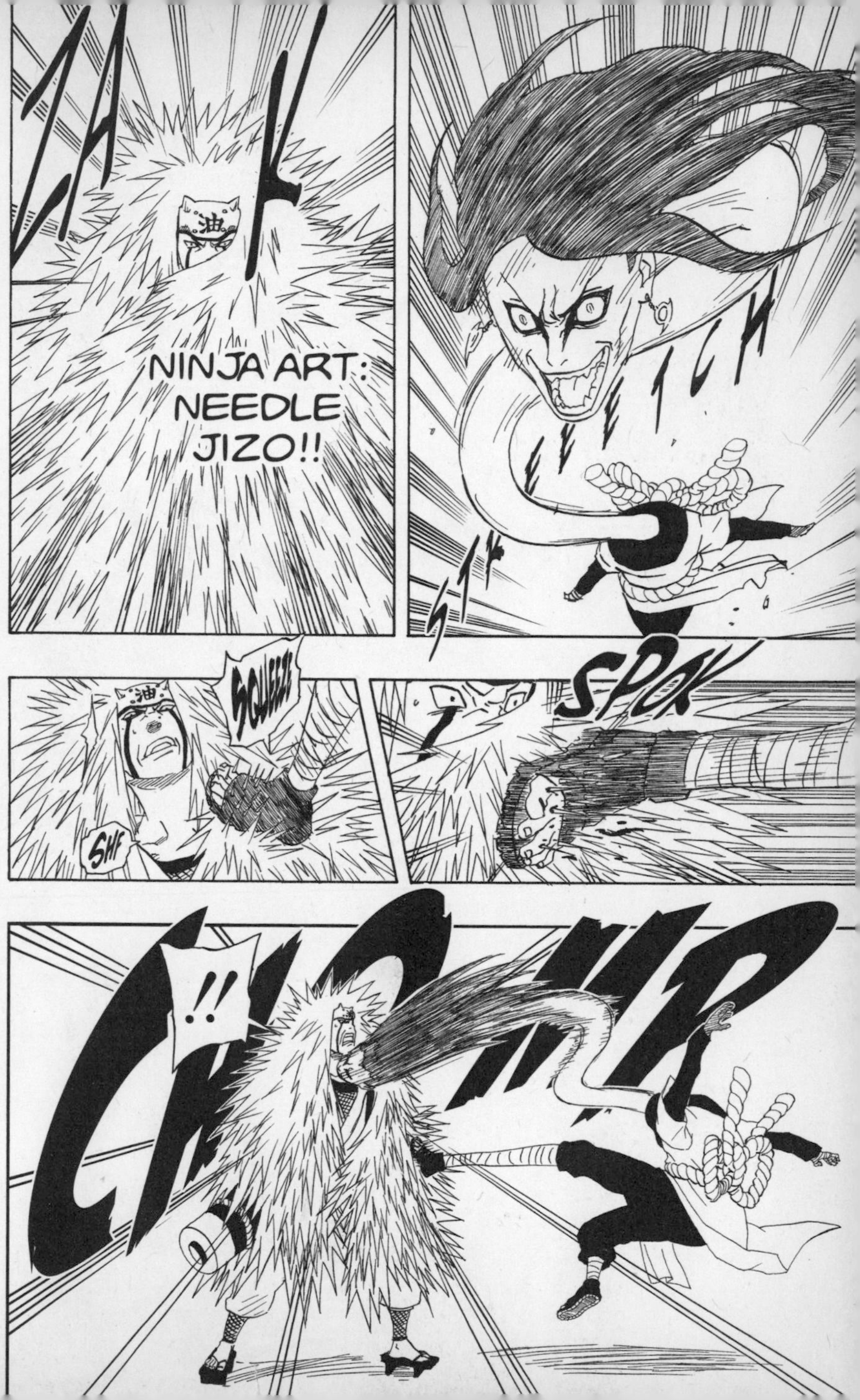
STRETCH
ZAK
NINJA ART: NEEDLE JIZO!!
SPOK
SQUEEZE
SHF
CHOMP
!!

READ THIS WAY

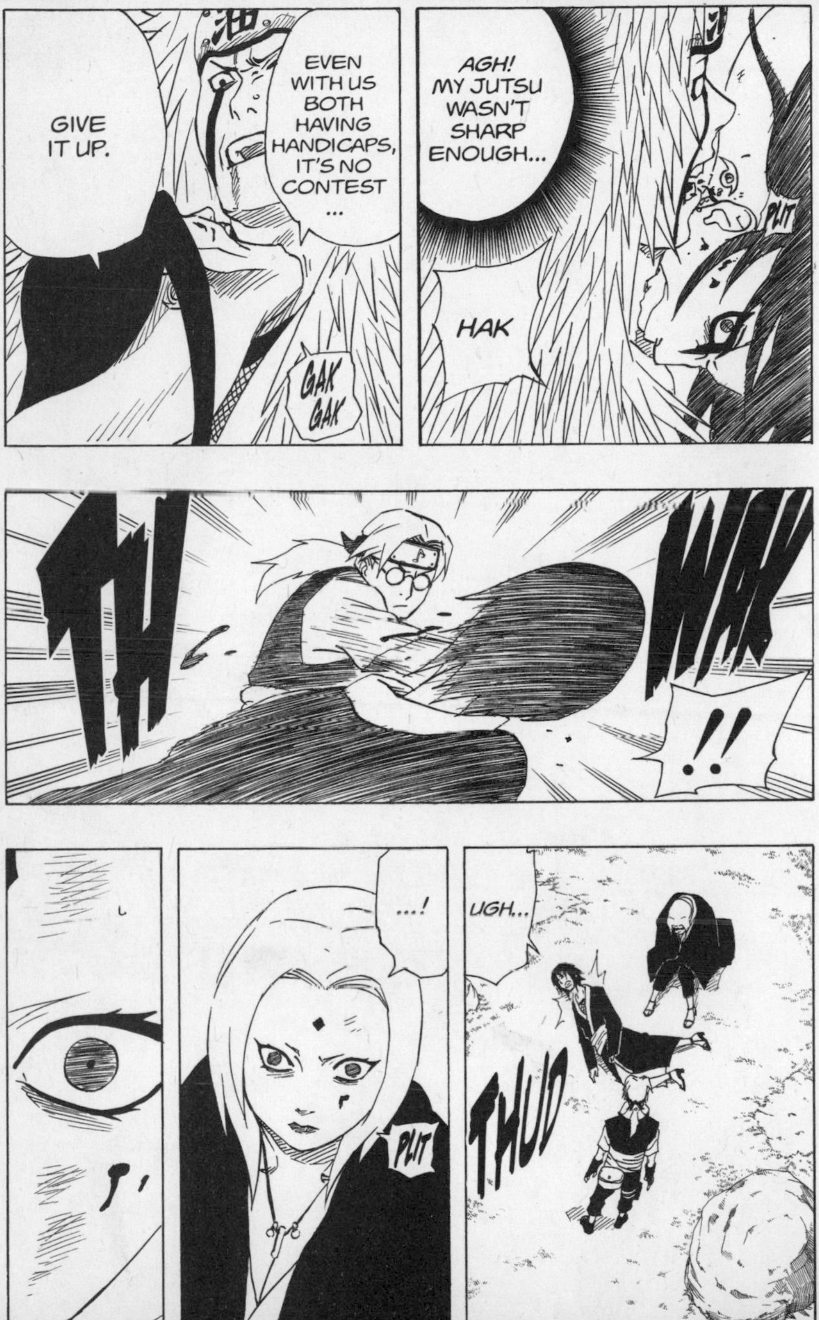
AGH! MY JUTSU WASN'T SHARP ENOUGH...
PLIT
HAK
EVEN WITH US BOTH HAVING HANDICAPS, IT'S NO CONTEST ...
GIVE IT UP.
GAK GAK
WAK
!!
TH
UGH...
THUD
...!
PLIT

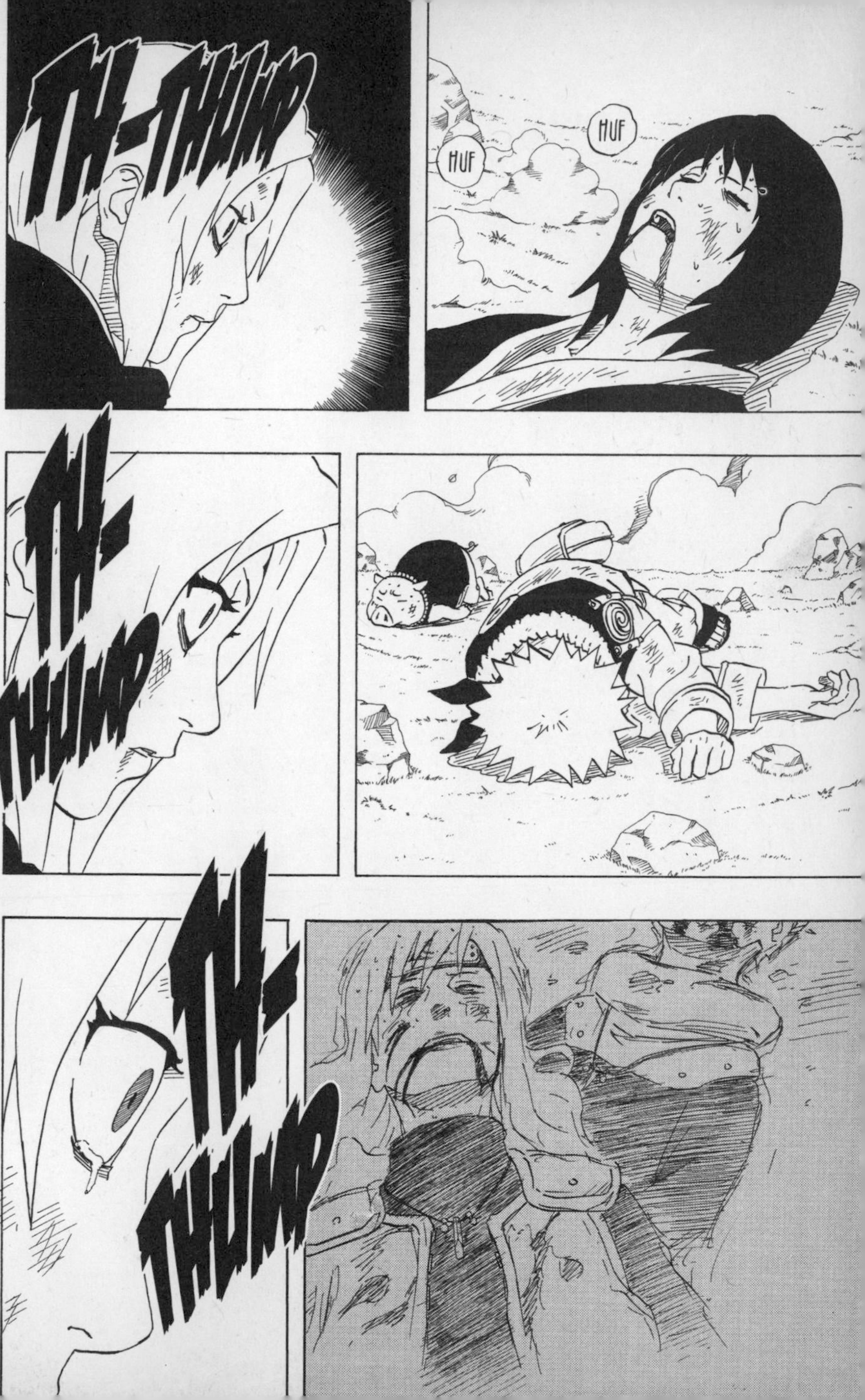
HUF
HUF
TH-THUMP
TH-THUMP
TH-THUMP

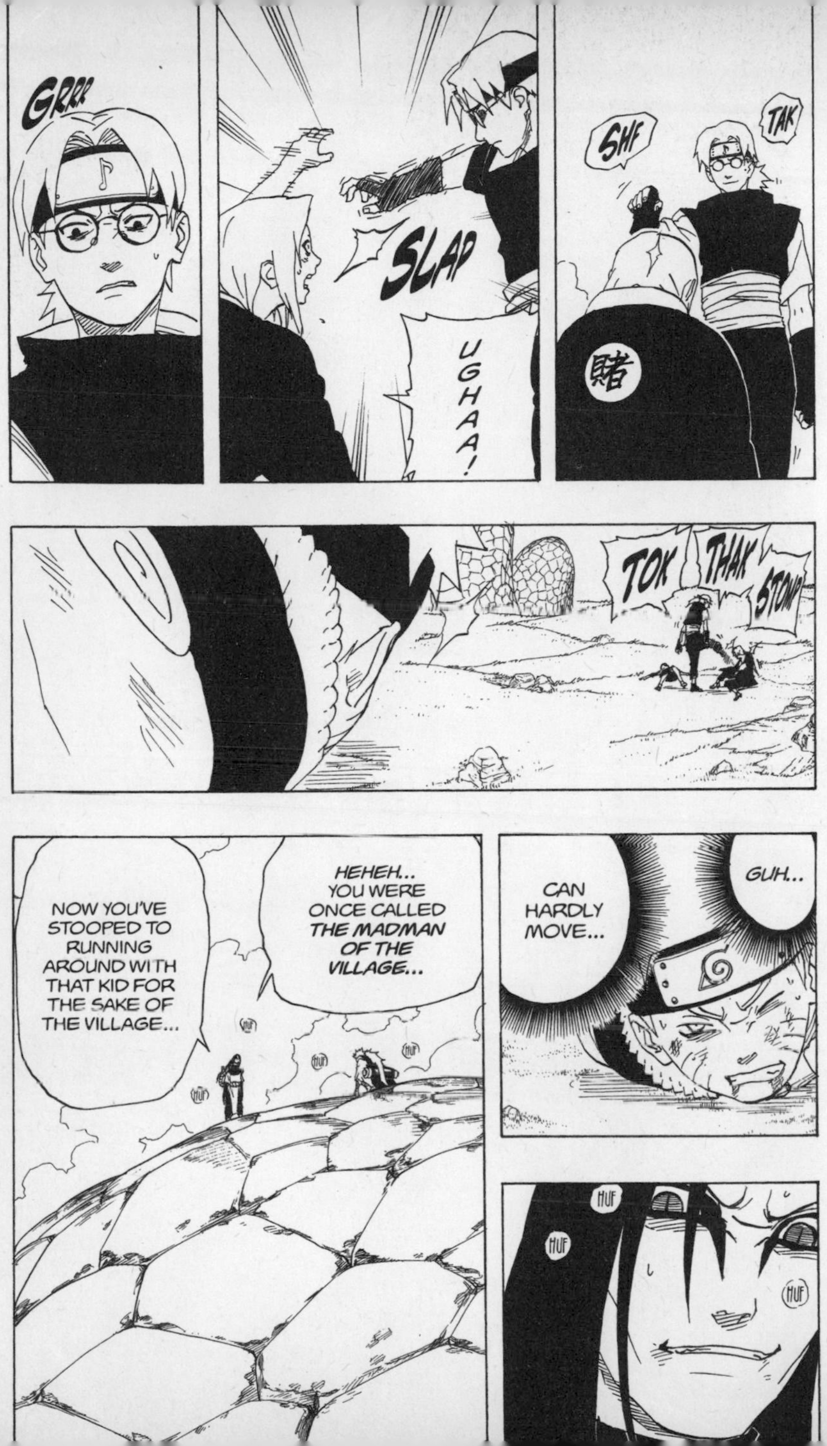
SHF
TAK
SLAP
UGHAA!
GRRR
THAK
TOK
STOMP
GUH...
CAN HARDLY MOVE...
HUF
HUF
HUF
HEHEH... YOU WERE ONCE CALLED THE MADMAN OF THE VILLAGE...
NOW YOU'VE STOOPED TO RUNNING AROUND WITH THAT KID FOR THE SAKE OF THE VILLAGE...
HUF
HUF
HUF

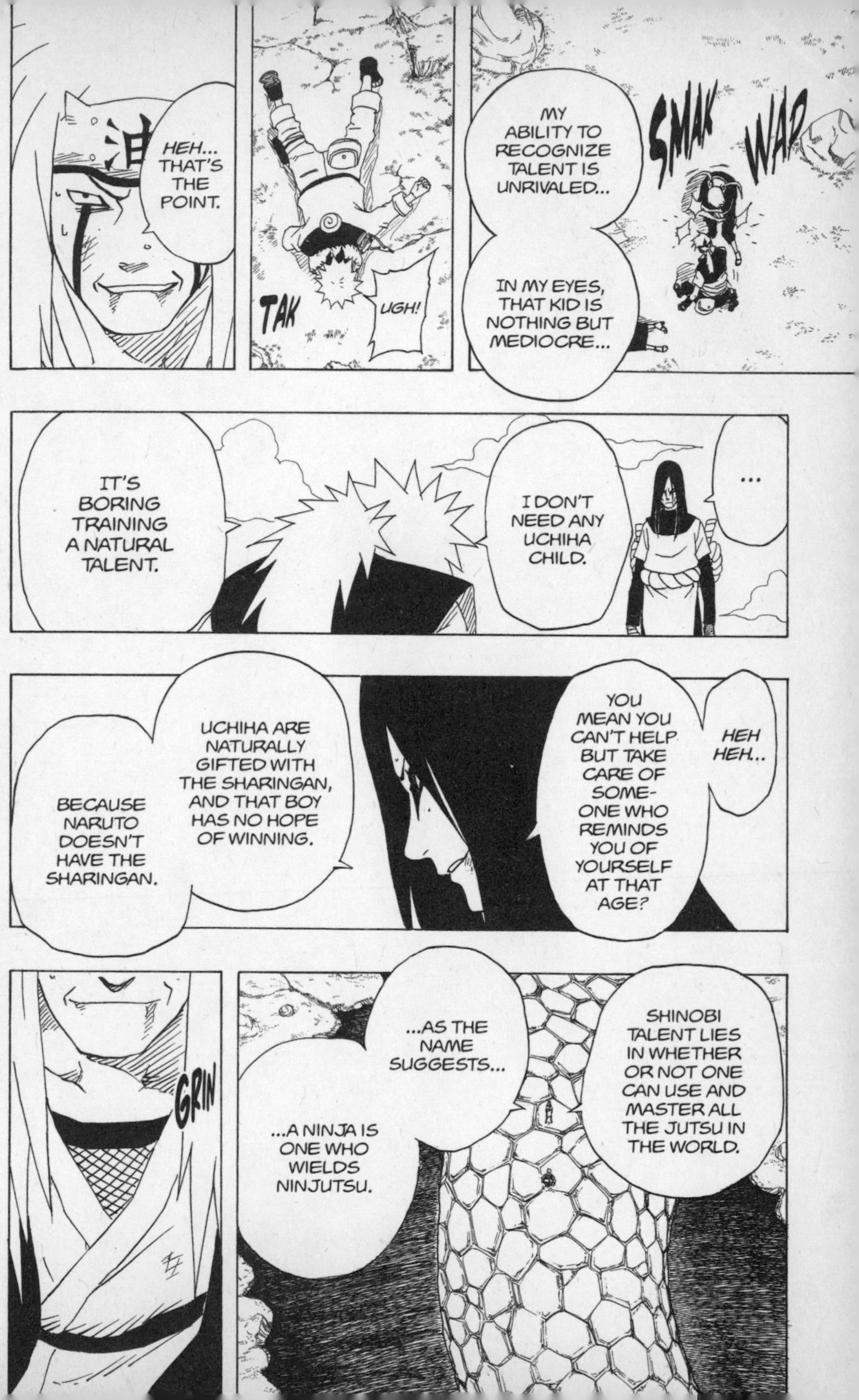

MY ABILITY TO RECOGNIZE TALENT IS UNRIVALED...
SMAK
WAP
IN MY EYES, THAT KID IS NOTHING BUT MEDIOCRE...
UGH!
TAK
HEH... THAT'S THE POINT.
...
I DON'T NEED ANY UCHIHA CHILD.
IT'S BORING TRAINING A NATURAL TALENT.
HEH HEH...
YOU MEAN YOU CAN'T HELP BUT TAKE CARE OF SOME-ONE WHO REMINDS YOU OF YOURSELF AT THAT AGE?
UCHIHA ARE NATURALLY GIFTED WITH THE SHARINGAN, AND THAT BOY HAS NO HOPE OF WINNING.
BECAUSE NARUTO DOESN'T HAVE THE SHARINGAN.
SHINOBI TALENT LIES IN WHETHER OR NOT ONE CAN USE AND MASTER ALL THE JUTSU IN THE WORLD.
...AS THE NAME SUGGESTS...
...A NINJA IS ONE WHO WIELDS NINJUTSU.
GRIN

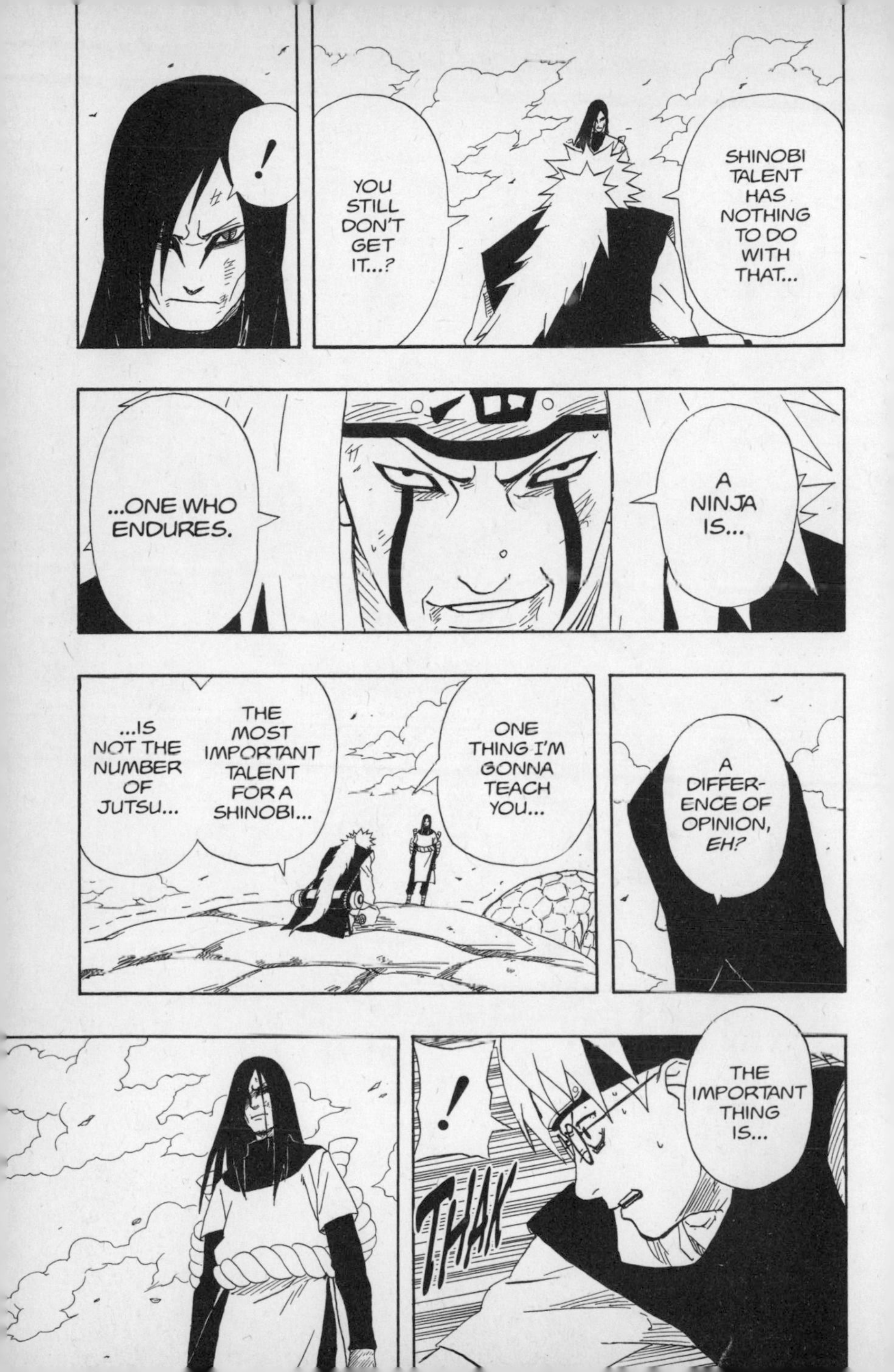
SHINOBI TALENT HAS NOTHING TO DO WITH THAT...
YOU STILL DON'T GET IT...?
!
A NINJA IS...
...ONE WHO ENDURES.
A DIFFERENCE OF OPINION, EH?
ONE THING I'M GONNA TEACH YOU...
THE MOST IMPORTANT TALENT FOR A SHINOBI...
...IS NOT THE NUMBER OF JUTSU...
THE IMPORTANT THING IS...
!
THAK

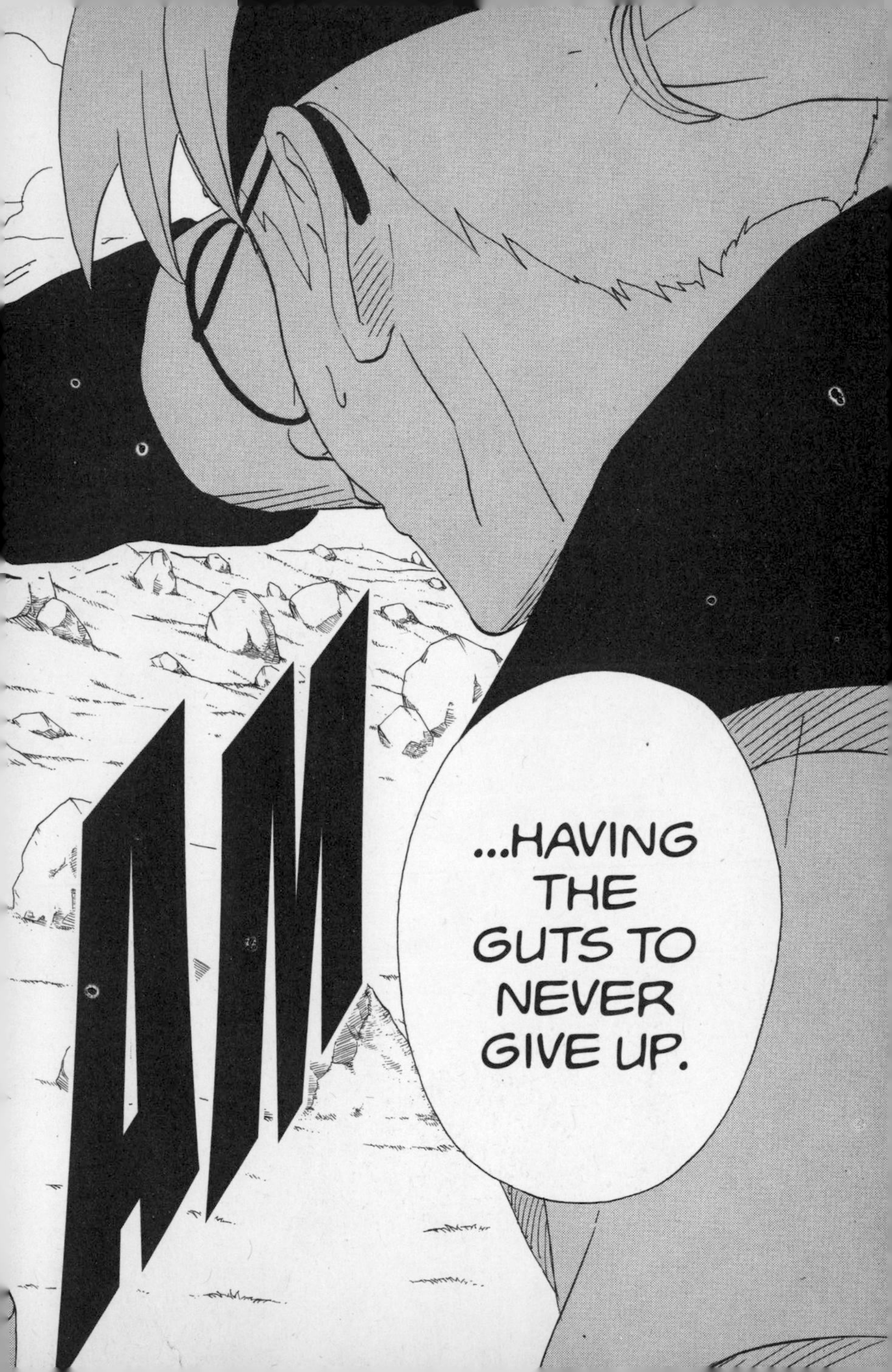
...HAVING THE GUTS TO NEVER GIVE UP.

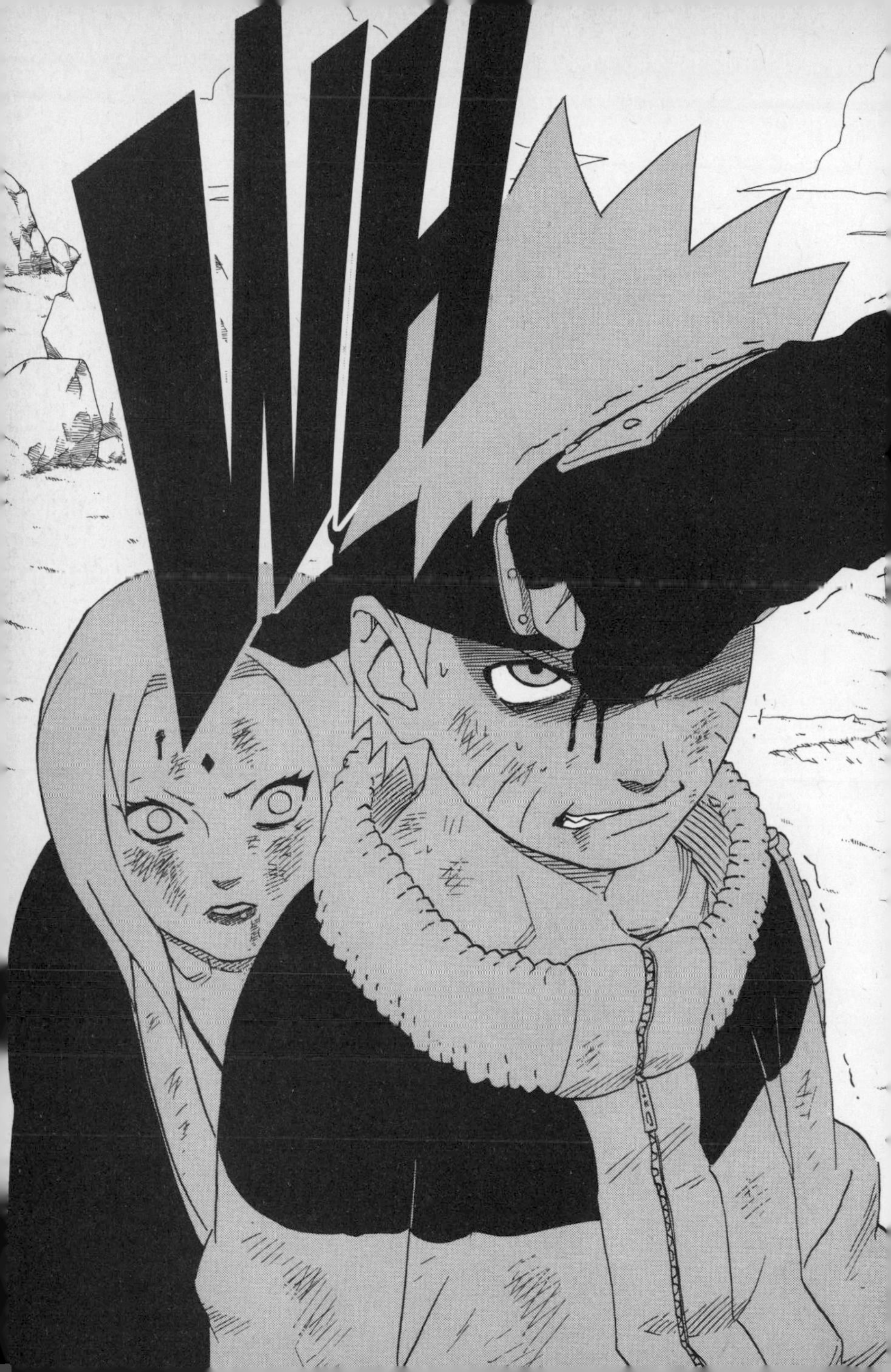
WH

THE WORLD OF KISHIMOTO MASASHI
MY PERSONAL HISTORY, PART 30: NO. 2

IN THE PREVIOUS STORY, I SAID THAT I WAS CAUGHT IN A TRAP. THIS TRAP WAS A STRONG ONE AND SO ONCE TRAPPED, I COULDN'T ESCAPE FROM IT EASILY.

AFTER WINNING AN AWARD, MY THOUGHTS WERE: "BECOMING A PROFESSIONAL WON'T BE FAR OFF NOW THAT I'VE WON AN AWARD WITH MY WORK. I'LL JUST REARRANGE MY AWARD-WINNING MANGA 'KARAKURI' AND CREATE ANOTHER STORY." IN THIS LIGHTHEARTED STATE OF MIND, I CONTINUED WRITING ANOTHER MANGA. BUT, AS I SHOULD HAVE EXPECTED, MY WORK WAS CONSISTENTLY TURNED DOWN. I SPENT A YEAR MUCKING AROUND WITH THE STORY, SETTING AND CHARACTERS IN VAIN. AROUND THIS TIME, I BEGAN TO DOUBT MY TALENT AND ABILITY AND BEGAN TO THINK THAT I MIGHT NOT BE ABLE TO BECOME A MANGA ARTIST AFTER ALL.

MEANWHILE, MOST OF MY FRIENDS STARTED JOB-HUNTING AND GETTING JOBS. I, ON THE OTHER HAND, WAS DETERMINED TO BECOME A MANGA ARTIST AFTER GRADUATING, AND DIDN'T DO ANYTHING ABOUT GETTING OTHER JOBS AT ALL. SURE ENOUGH, I WAS A LITTLE SCARED... AFTER ALL, THIS WAS A PERIOD WHEN I DOUBTED WHETHER I COULD EVEN BECOME A MANGA ARTIST. BUT CREATING AN ESCAPE ROUTE WOULD HAVE MEANT ACKNOWLEDGING TO MYSELF THAT I COULD NEVER DO IT.

I WAS IMPATIENT AND WENT ROUND AND ROUND IN CIRCLES AND GOT NOWHERE. I CREATED DRAFTS DESPERATELY WANTING TO FEEL LIKE A PRO. ALL REJECTS.

IN THE END, I WOUND UP GRADUATING FROM COLLEGE HAVING ACCOMPLISHED NOTHING.

MY PARENTS HAD SPENT A LOT OF MONEY SENDING ME TO COLLEGE AND I OWED THEM A LOT, AND NOT JUST FOR THAT. YET I DID NOTHING TO GET ANY OTHER JOB AND JUST KEPT TELLING MY PARENTS THAT I WOULD BECOME A MANGA ARTIST AS THOUGH I WERE IN A DREAM... MY PARENTS WERE STRICT IN RAISING ME AND SO I WAS PREPARED FOR A SCOLDING. ON THE CONTRARY, HOWEVER, THEY SUPPORTED MY UNREALISTIC DREAMS. ONE DAY MY PARENTS AND MY YOUNGER BROTHER WERE TALKING ABOUT HOW TO MAKE MONEY FOR HIS COLLEGE TUITION. MY BROTHER SAID TO ME "WE COULD HAVE BOUGHT A FERRARI WITH THE MONEY SPENT ON YOUR EDUCATION!" THEN I REALIZED HOW MUCH MONEY IT HAD COST THEM SENDING ME TO COLLEGE... WHEN I RECALLED MY COLLEGE DAYS ALWAYS PLAYING MAHJONG WITH MY FRIENDS, I REALIZED HOW STUPID I HAD BEEN AND FELT ANGRY WITH MYSELF. AROUND THIS TIME, MY FATHER STOPPED BY TO TALK OVER HIS IDEAS OF A NEW MANGA STORY AND CHARACTERS. WHILE LISTENING TO HIS MOSTLY UNINTERESTING IDEAS, I REALIZED THAT I HAD TO BECOME A MANGA ARTIST SOON AND PUT MY PARENTS AT EASE. THINGS COULDN'T STAY THE WAY THEY WERE.
TO BE CONTINUED... IT'S SOOOO DEPRESSING...

Number 167: As Promised...!!

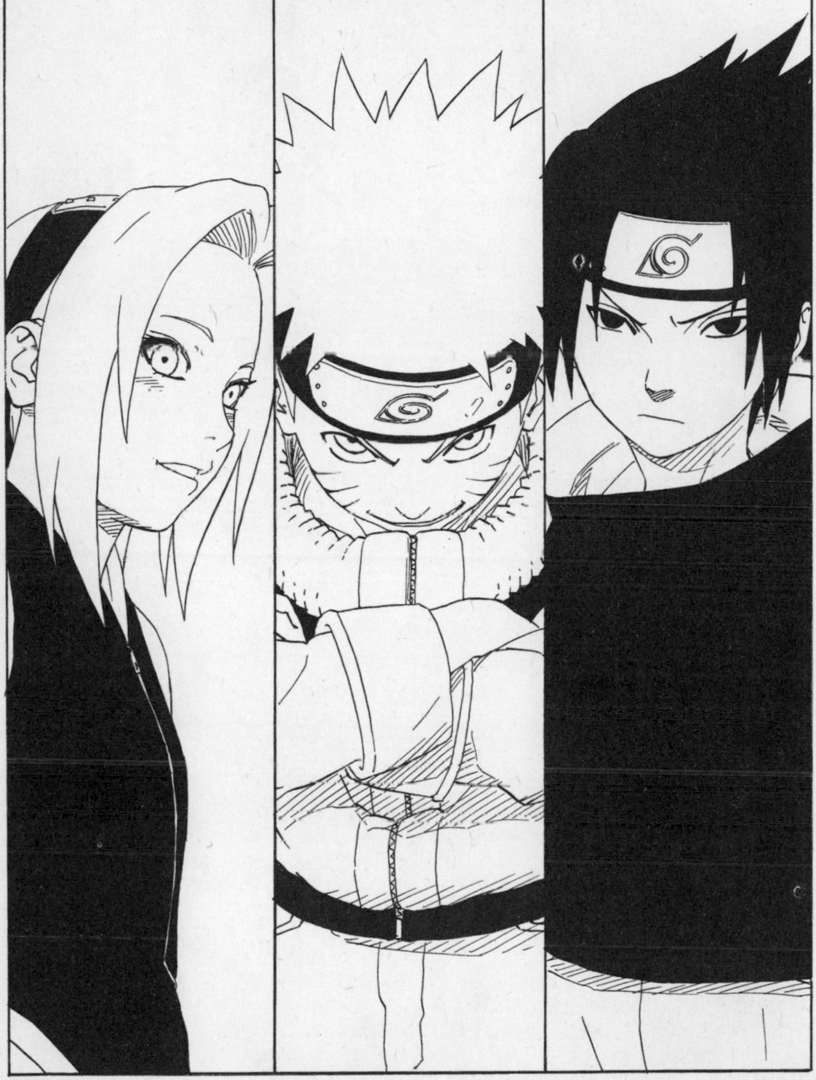

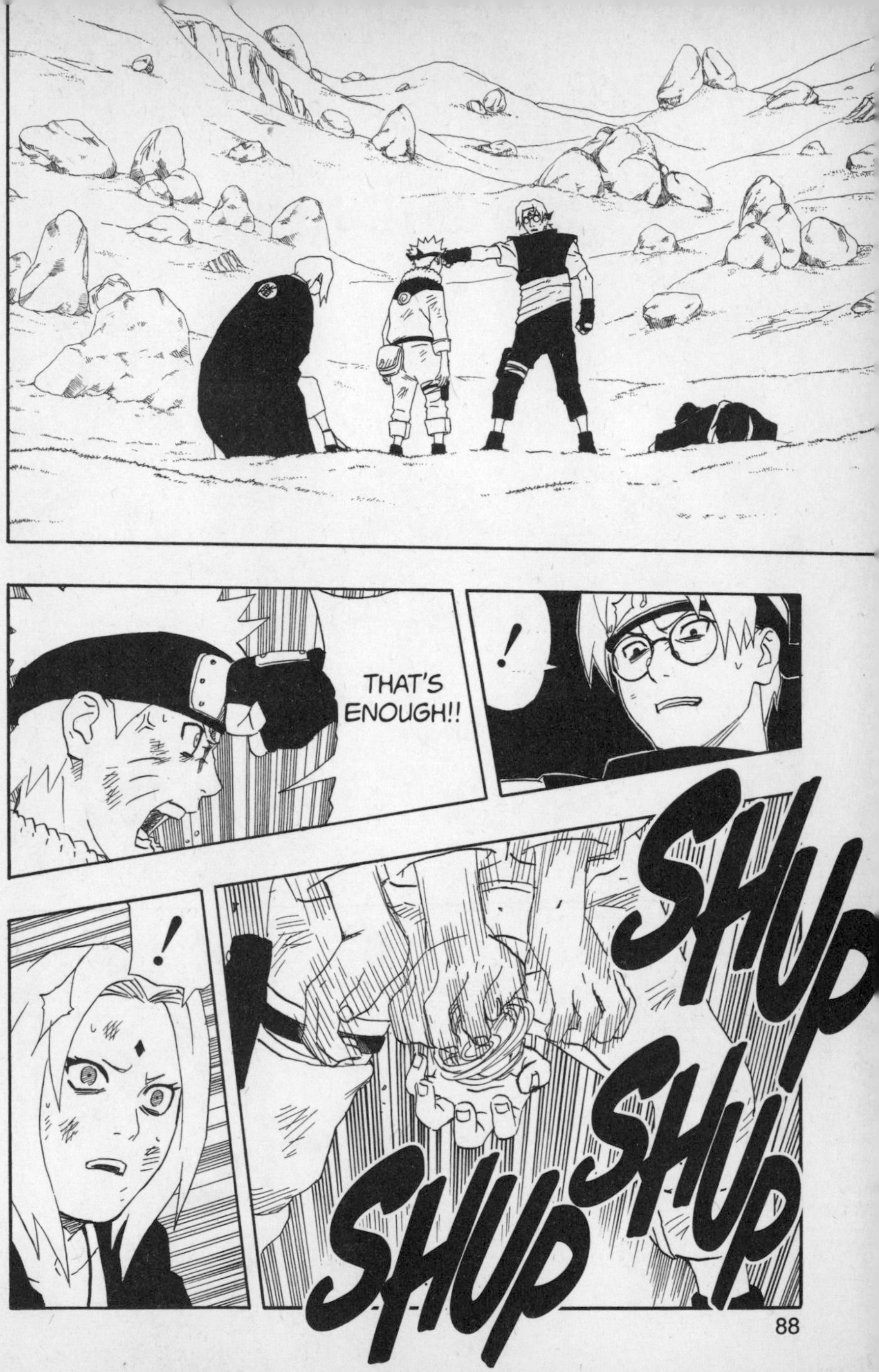
!
THAT'S ENOUGH!!
SHUP
SHUP
SHUP
!

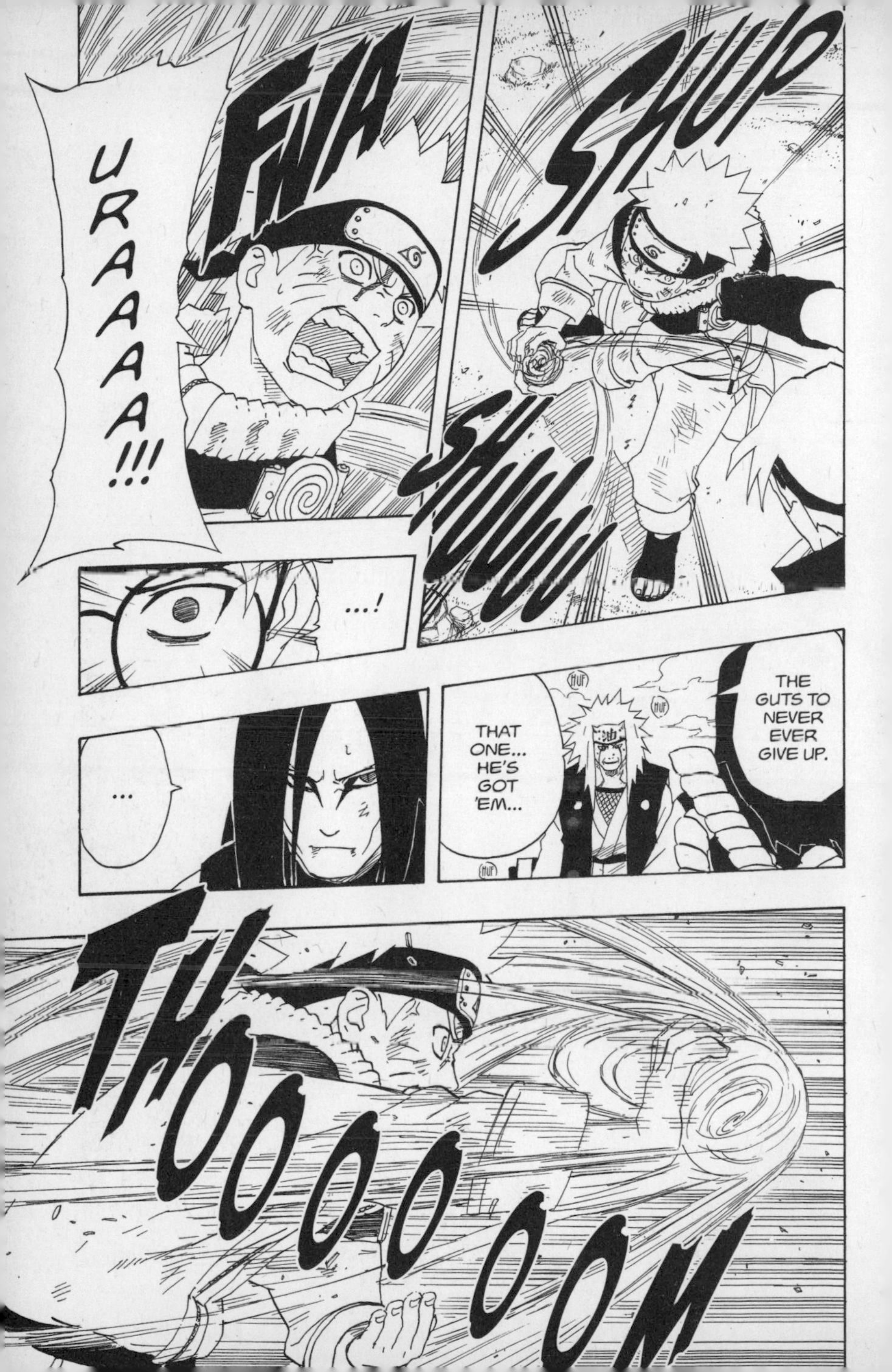
SHUP
SHUUUU
FWA
URAAAAA!!!
...!
HUF
HUF
THAT ONE... HE'S GOT 'EM...
THE GUTS TO NEVER EVER GIVE UP.
HUF
...
THOOOOOOOM

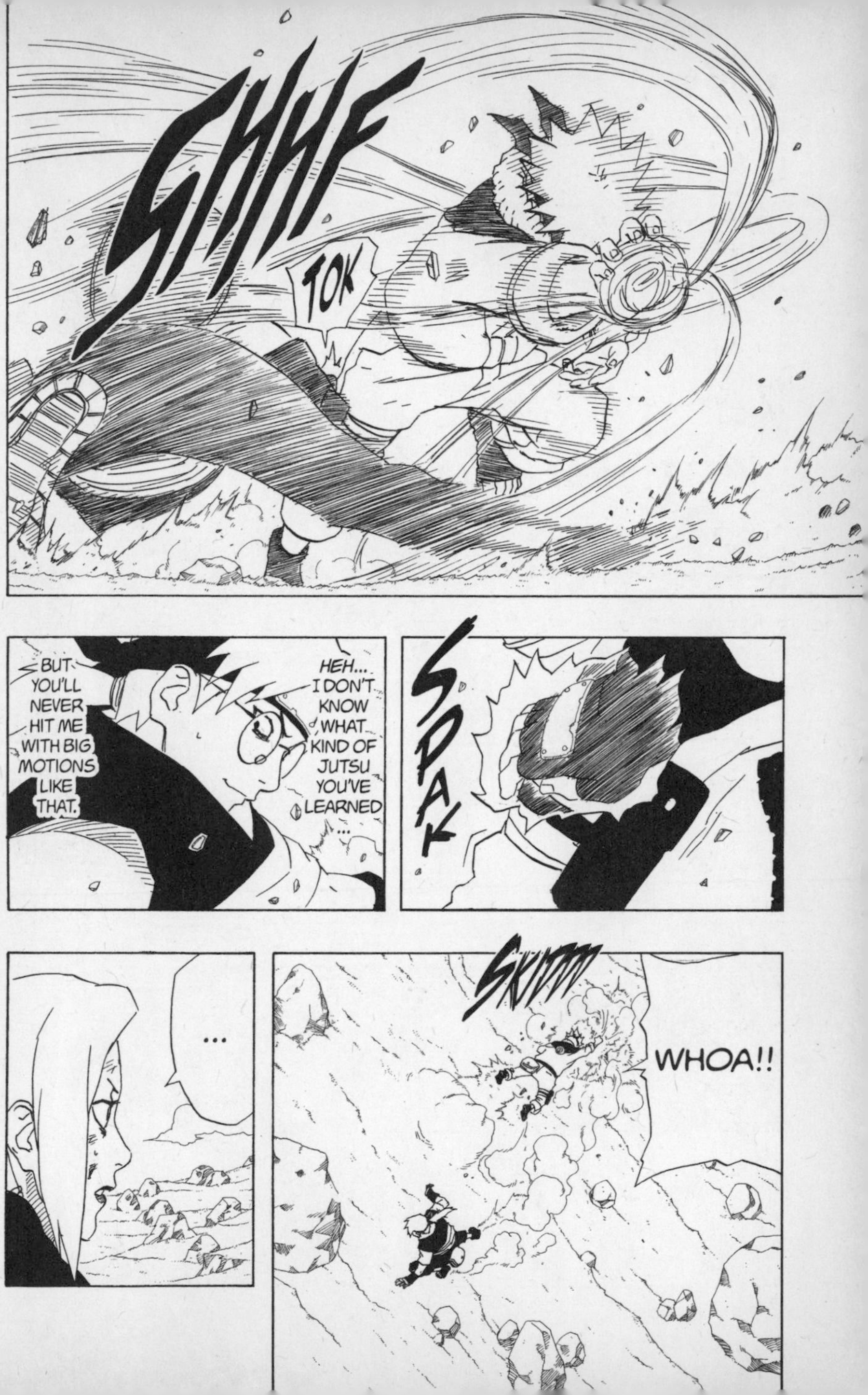
SHHF
TOK
SPAK
HEH... I DON'T KNOW WHAT KIND OF JUTSU YOU'VE LEARNED...
BUT YOU'LL NEVER HIT ME WITH BIG MOTIONS LIKE THAT.
SKIDDD
WHOA!!
...

READ THIS WAY

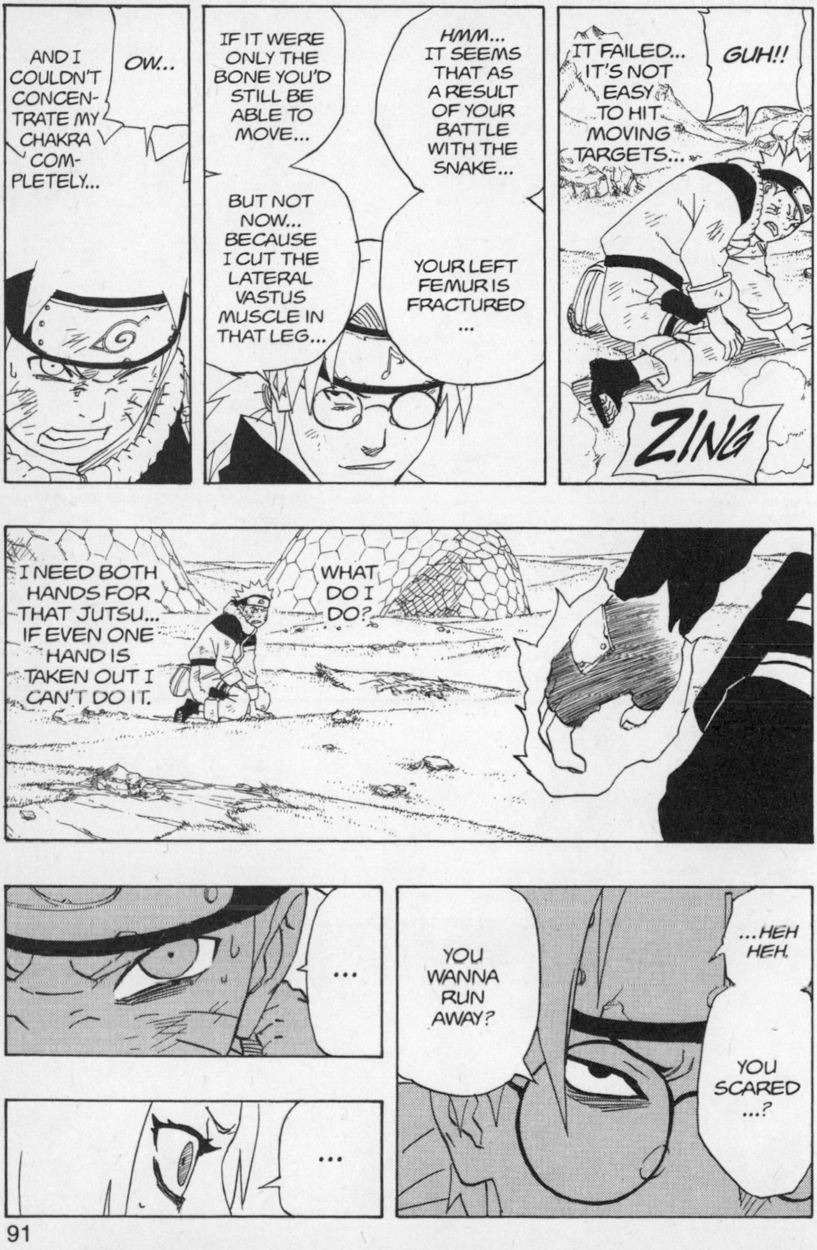

GUH!!
IT FAILED... IT'S NOT EASY TO HIT MOVING TARGETS...
ZING
HMM... IT SEEMS THAT AS A RESULT OF YOUR BATTLE WITH THE SNAKE...
YOUR LEFT FEMUR IS FRACTURED ...
IF IT WERE ONLY THE BONE YOU'D STILL BE ABLE TO MOVE...
BUT NOT NOW... BECAUSE I CUT THE LATERAL VASTUS MUSCLE IN THAT LEG...
OW...
AND I COULDN'T CONCENTRATE MY CHAKRA COMPLETELY...
WHAT DO I DO?
I NEED BOTH HANDS FOR THAT JUTSU... IF EVEN ONE HAND IS TAKEN OUT I CAN'T DO IT.
...HEH HEH.
YOU WANNA RUN AWAY?
YOU SCARED ...?
...
...

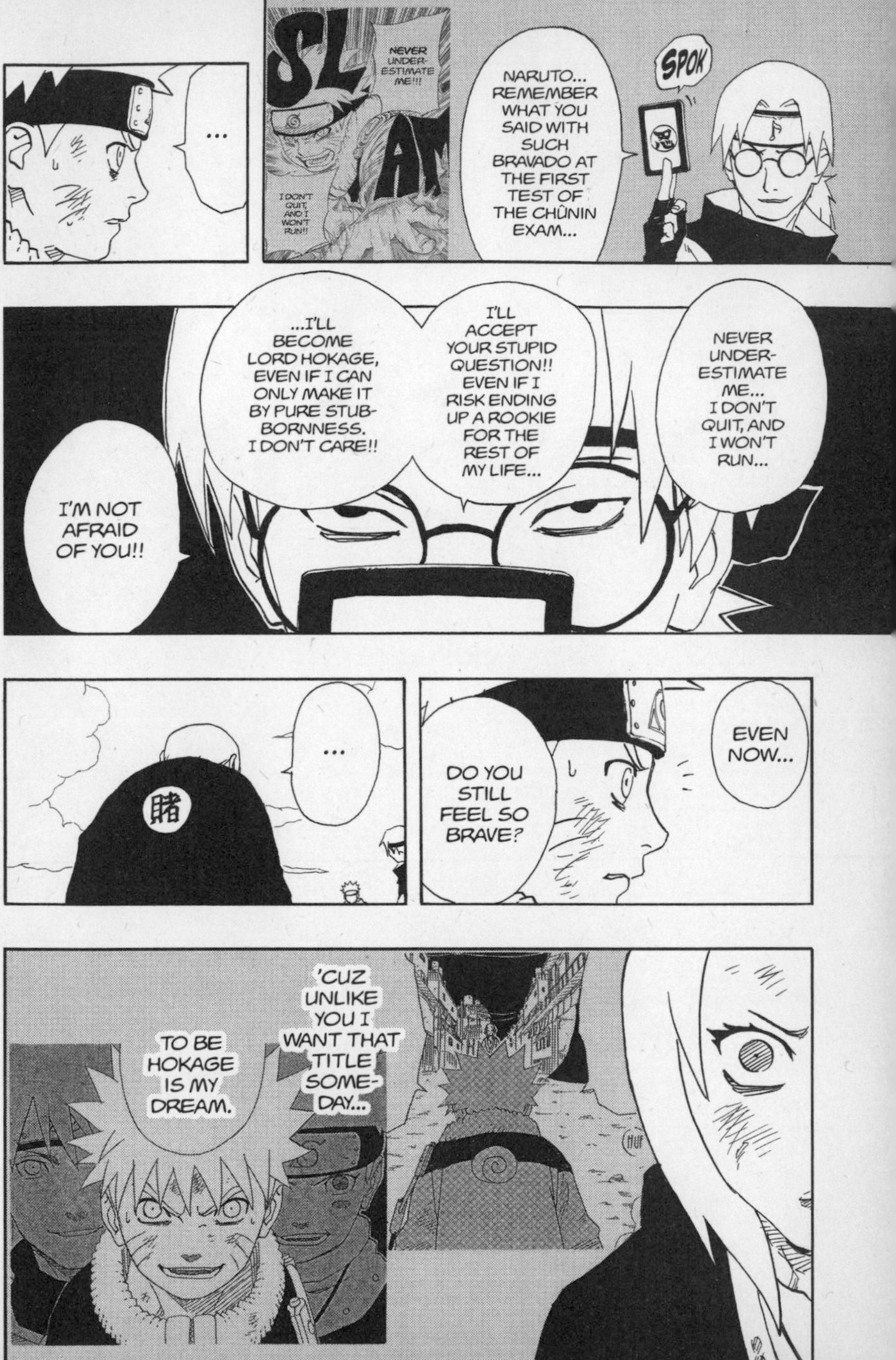
SPOK
NARUTO... REMEMBER WHAT YOU SAID WITH SUCH BRAVADO AT THE FIRST TEST OF THE CHÛNIN EXAM...
NEVER UNDER-ESTIMATE ME!!!
SLAM
I DON'T QUIT, AND I WON'T RUN!!
...
NEVER UNDER-ESTIMATE ME... I DON'T QUIT, AND I WON'T RUN...
I'LL ACCEPT YOUR STUPID QUESTION!! EVEN IF I RISK ENDING UP A ROOKIE FOR THE REST OF MY LIFE...
...I'LL BECOME LORD HOKAGE, EVEN IF I CAN ONLY MAKE IT BY PURE STUB-BORNNESS. I DON'T CARE!!
I'M NOT AFRAID OF YOU!!
EVEN NOW...
DO YOU STILL FEEL SO BRAVE?
...
HUF
'CUZ UNLIKE YOU I WANT THAT TITLE SOME-DAY...
TO BE HOKAGE IS MY DREAM.

READ THIS WAY

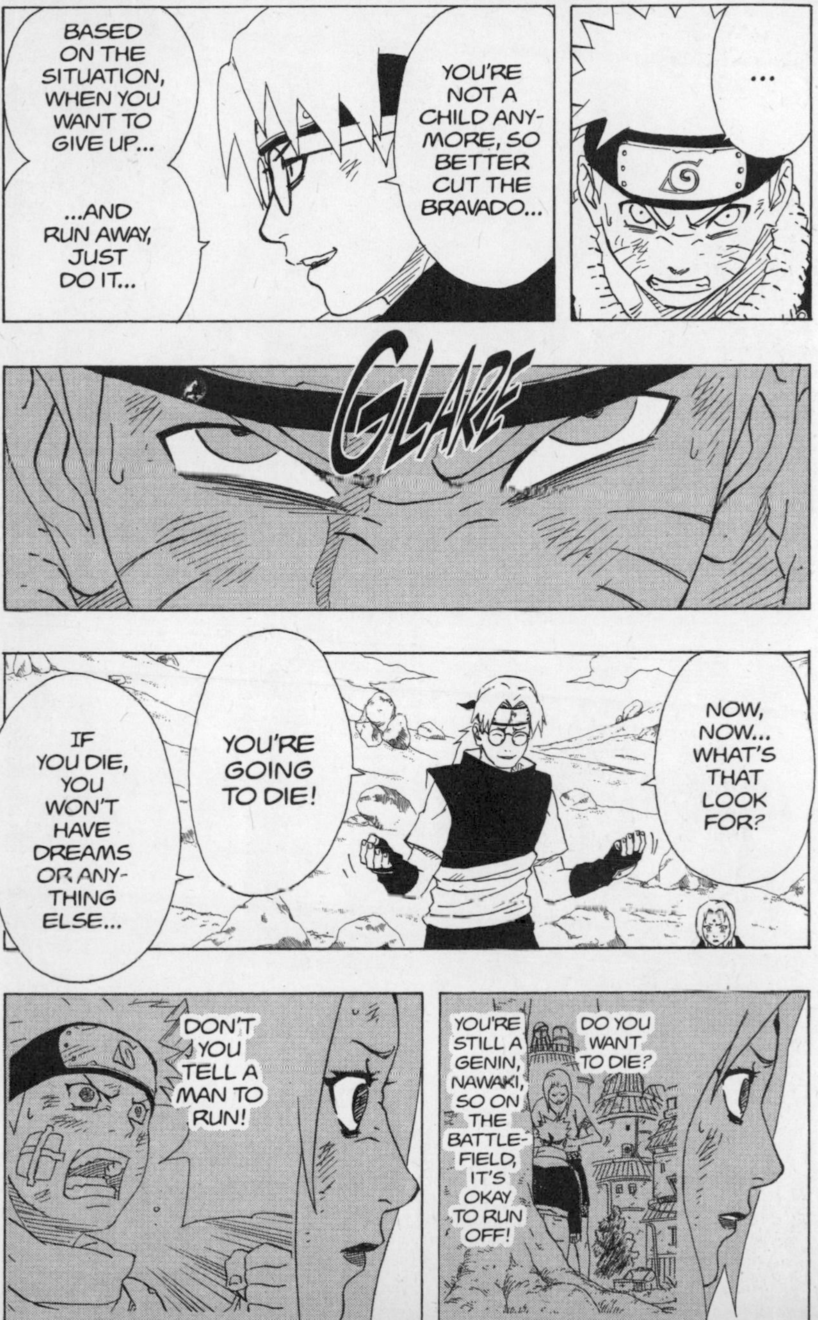
...
YOU'RE NOT A CHILD ANYMORE, SO BETTER CUT THE BRAVADO...
BASED ON THE SITUATION, WHEN YOU WANT TO GIVE UP...
...AND RUN AWAY, JUST DO IT...
GLARE
NOW, NOW... WHAT'S THAT LOOK FOR?
YOU'RE GOING TO DIE!
IF YOU DIE, YOU WON'T HAVE DREAMS OR ANYTHING ELSE...
DO YOU WANT TO DIE?
YOU'RE STILL A GENIN, NAWAKI, SO ON THE BATTLEFIELD, IT'S OKAY TO RUN OFF!
DON'T YOU TELL A MAN TO RUN!

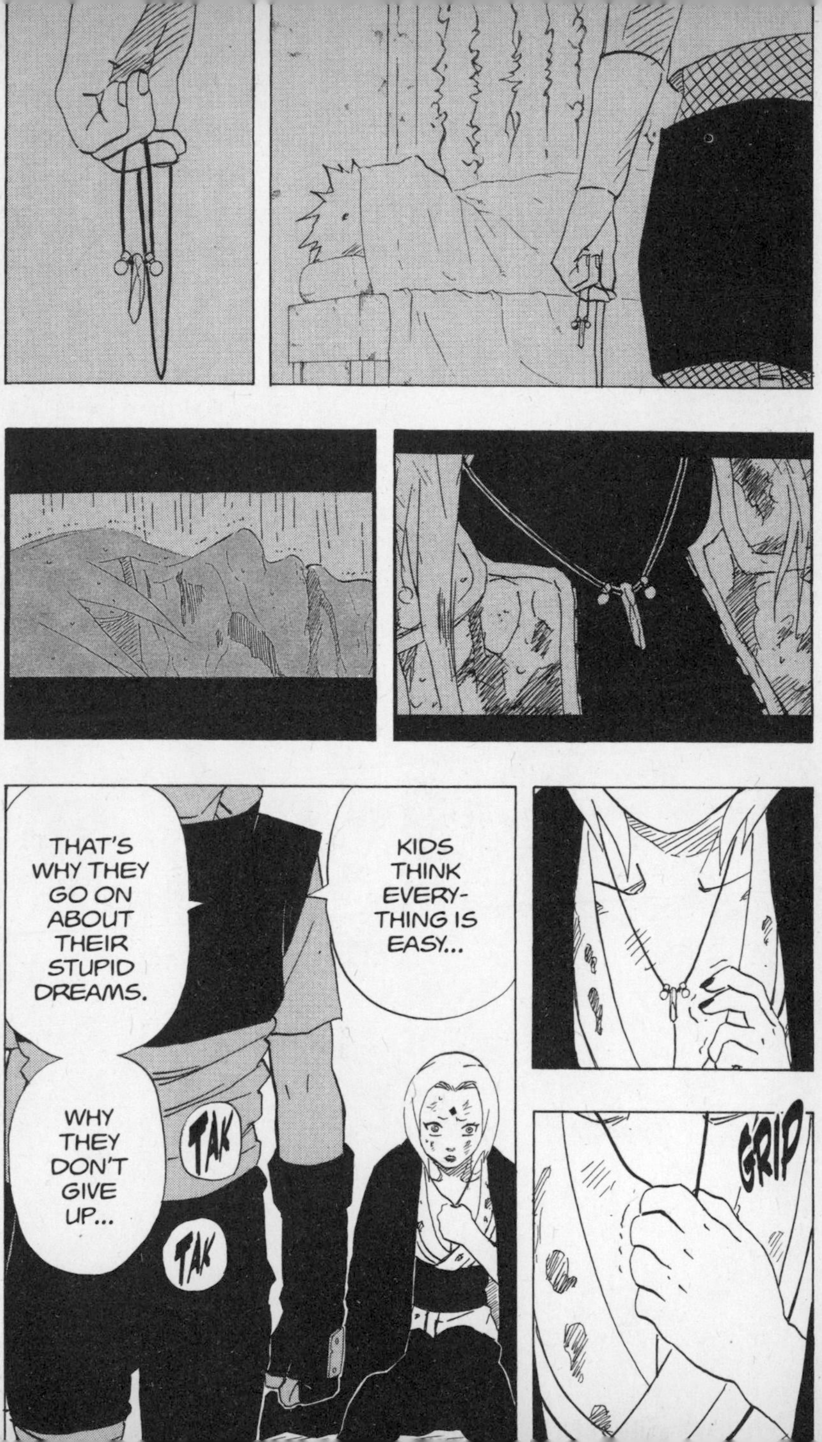
GRIP
KIDS THINK EVERYTHING IS EASY...
THAT'S WHY THEY GO ON ABOUT THEIR STUPID DREAMS.
TAK
WHY THEY DON'T GIVE UP...
TAK

READ THIS WAY

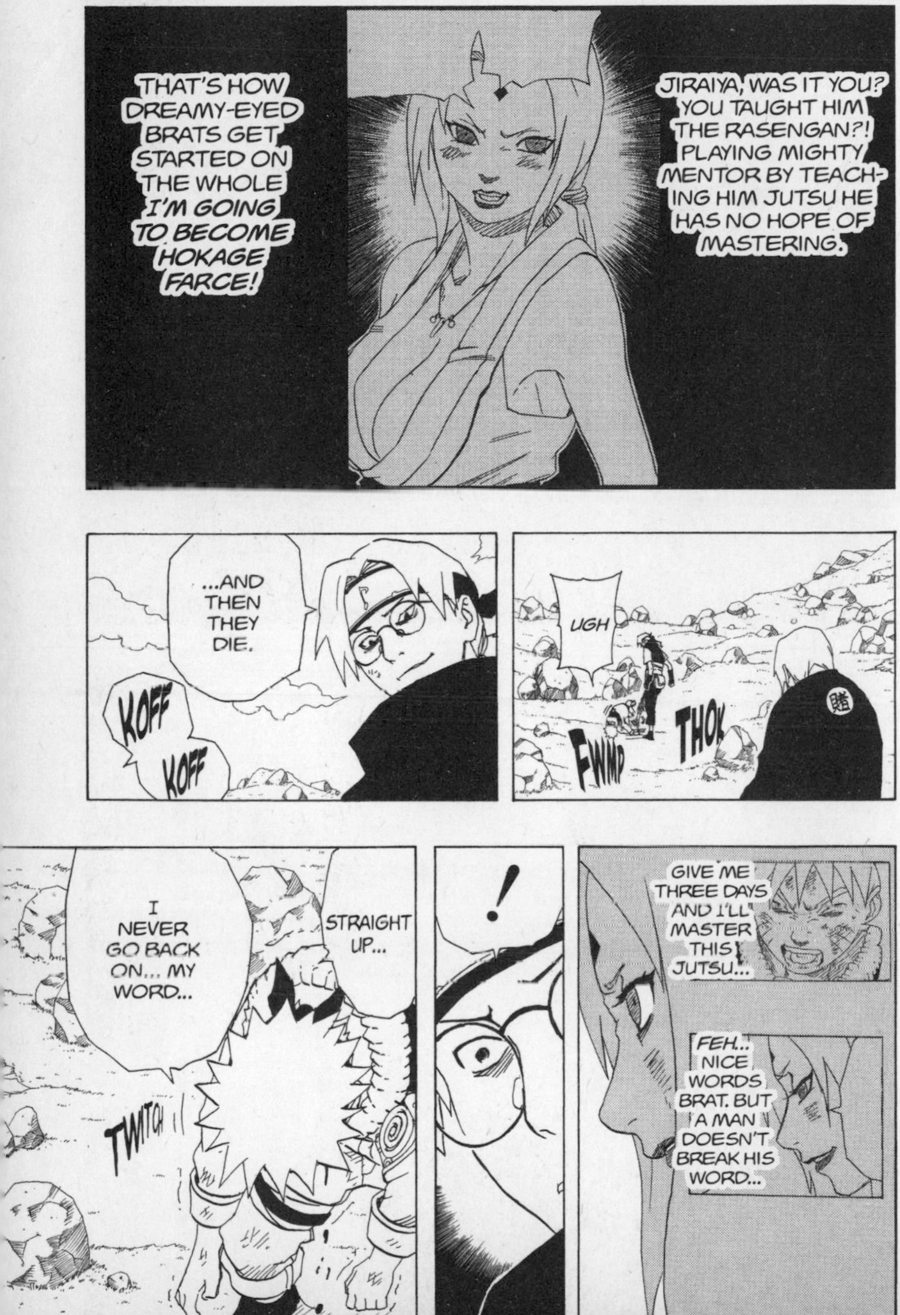
JIRAIYA, WAS IT YOU? YOU TAUGHT HIM THE RASENGAN?! PLAYING MIGHTY MENTOR BY TEACHING HIM JUTSU HE HAS NO HOPE OF MASTERING.
THAT'S HOW DREAMY-EYED BRATS GET STARTED ON THE WHOLE *I'M GOING TO BECOME HOKAGE* FARCE!
UGH
THOK
FWMP
...AND THEN THEY DIE.
KOFF
KOFF
GIVE ME THREE DAYS AND I'LL MASTER THIS JUTSU...
FEH... NICE WORDS BRAT. BUT A MAN DOESN'T BREAK HIS WORD...
!
STRAIGHT UP...
I NEVER GO BACK ON... MY WORD...
TWITCH

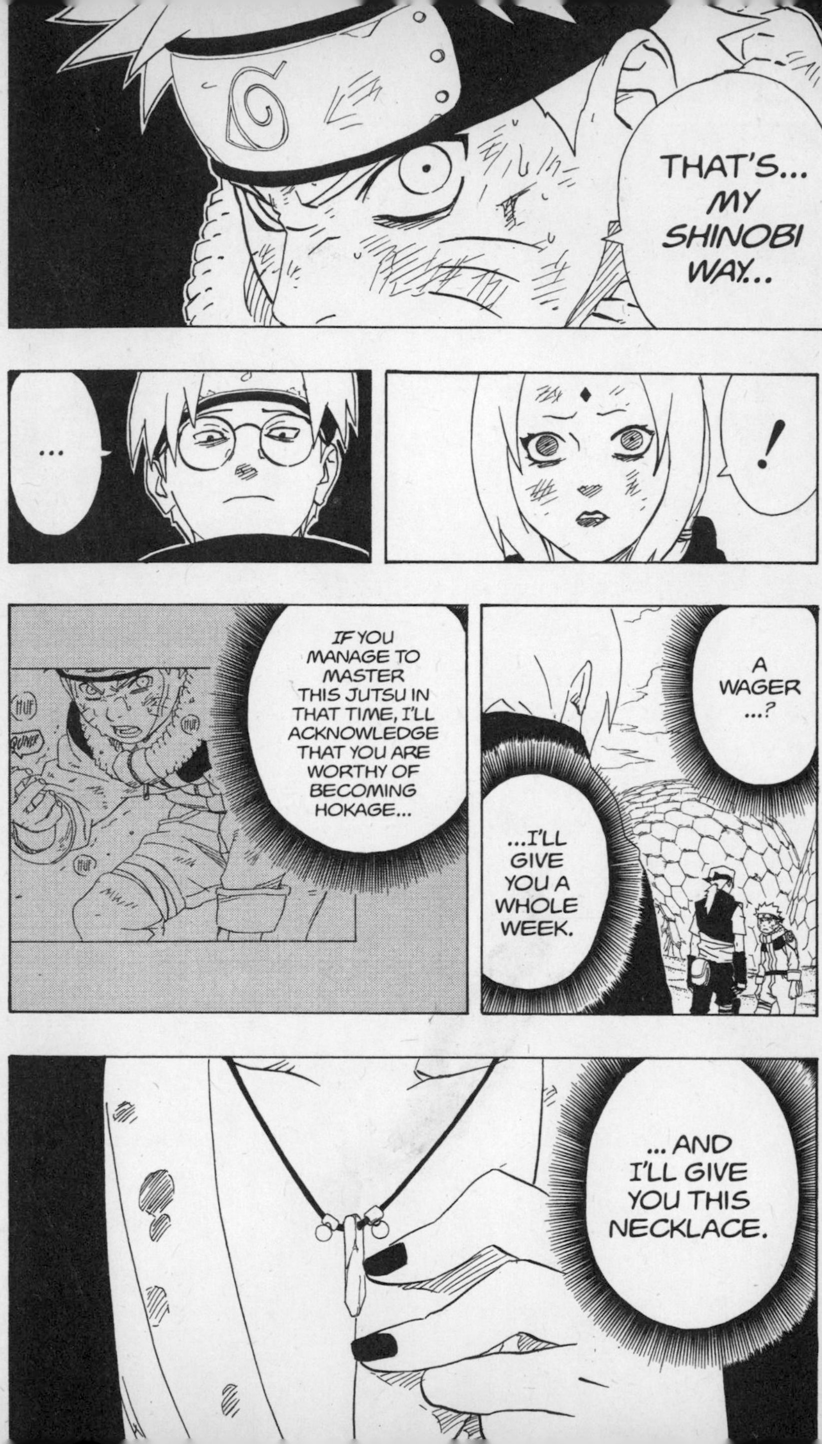
THAT'S... MY SHINOBI WAY...
!
...
A WAGER ...?
...I'LL GIVE YOU A WHOLE WEEK.
IF YOU MANAGE TO MASTER THIS JUTSU IN THAT TIME, I'LL ACKNOWLEDGE THAT YOU ARE WORTHY OF BECOMING HOKAGE...
... AND I'LL GIVE YOU THIS NECKLACE.

READ THIS WAY

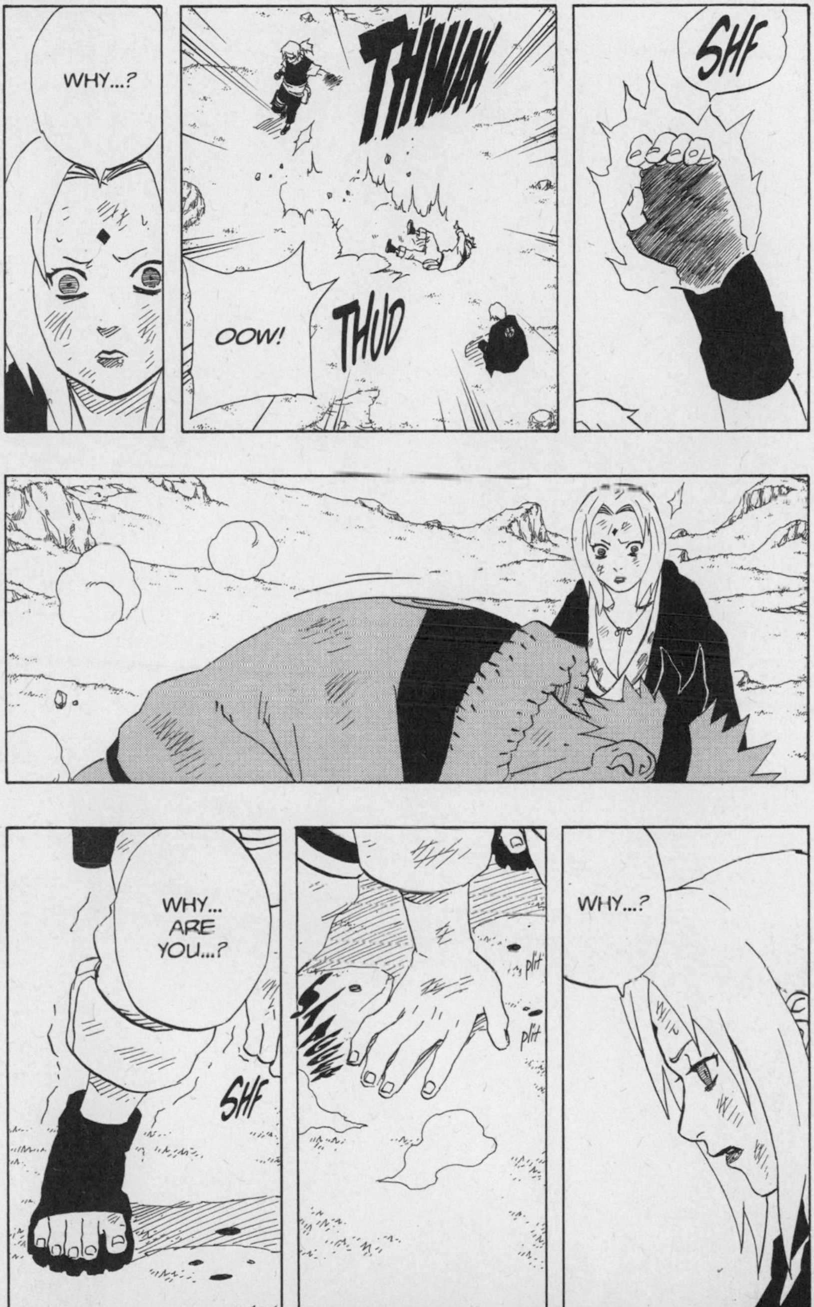
SHF
THWAK
OOW!
THUD
WHY...?
WHY...?
plit
plit
WHY... ARE YOU...?
SHF

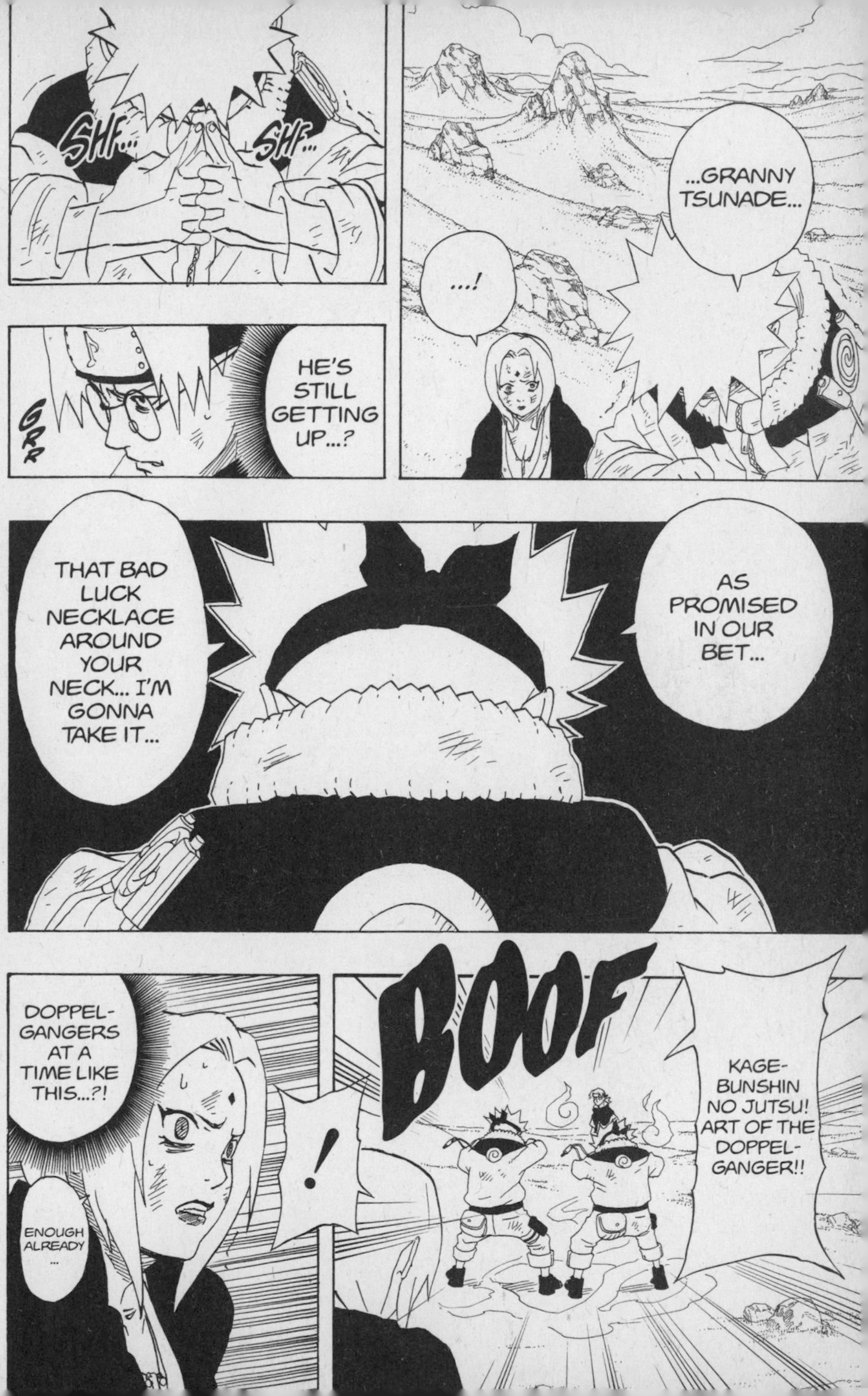
...GRANNY TSUNADE...
...!
SHF...
SHF...
HE'S STILL GETTING UP...?
GRR
AS PROMISED IN OUR BET...
THAT BAD LUCK NECKLACE AROUND YOUR NECK... I'M GONNA TAKE IT...
KAGE-BUNSHIN NO JUTSU! ART OF THE DOPPEL-GANGER!!
BOOF
!
DOPPEL-GANGERS AT A TIME LIKE THIS...?!
ENOUGH ALREADY ...

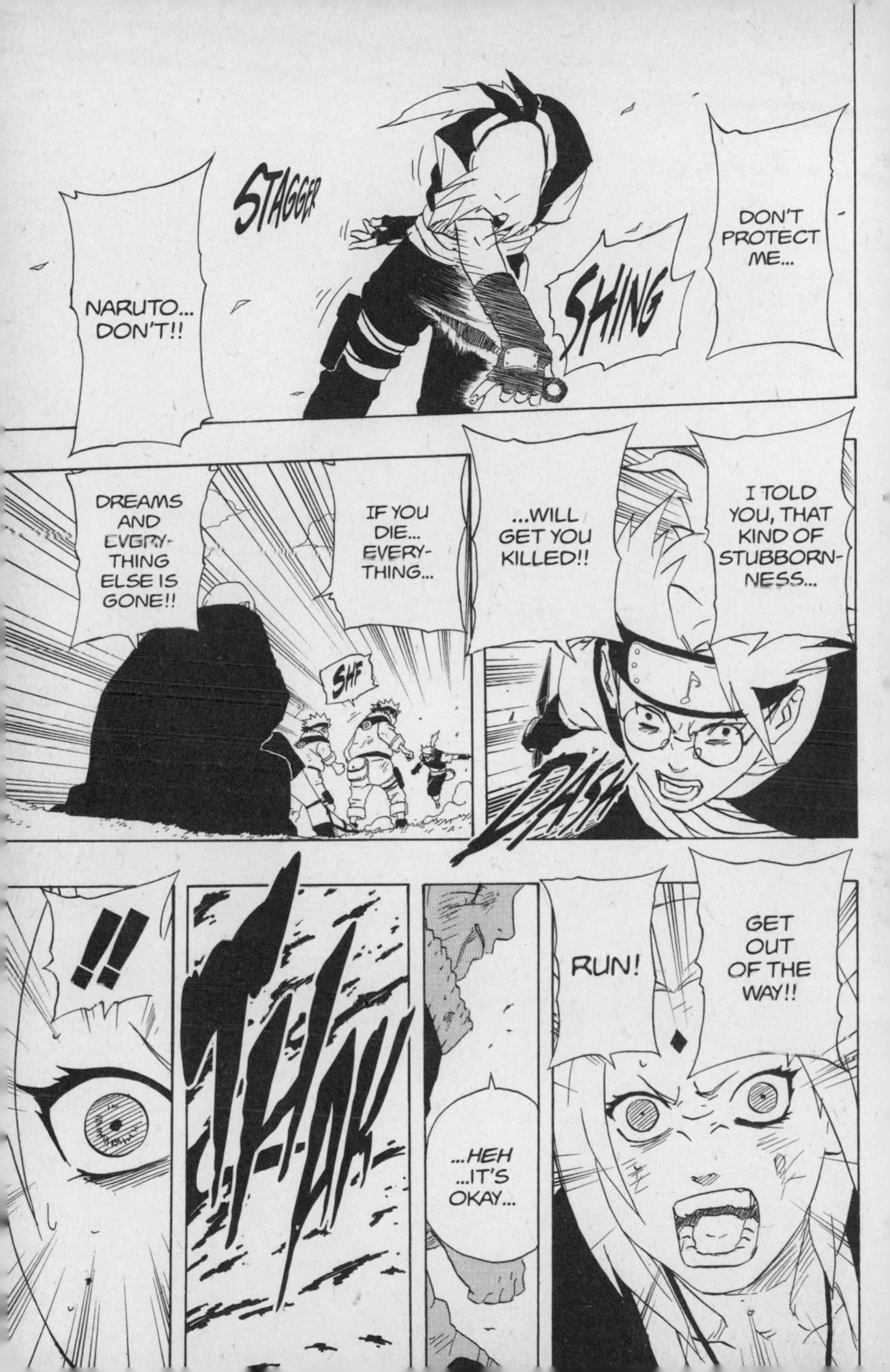
DON'T PROTECT ME...
SHING
STAGGER
NARUTO... DON'T!!
I TOLD YOU, THAT KIND OF STUBBORN-NESS...
...WILL GET YOU KILLED!!
DASH
IF YOU DIE... EVERY-THING...
DREAMS AND EVERY-THING ELSE IS GONE!!
SHF
GET OUT OF THE WAY!!
RUN!
...HEH ...IT'S OKAY...
!!

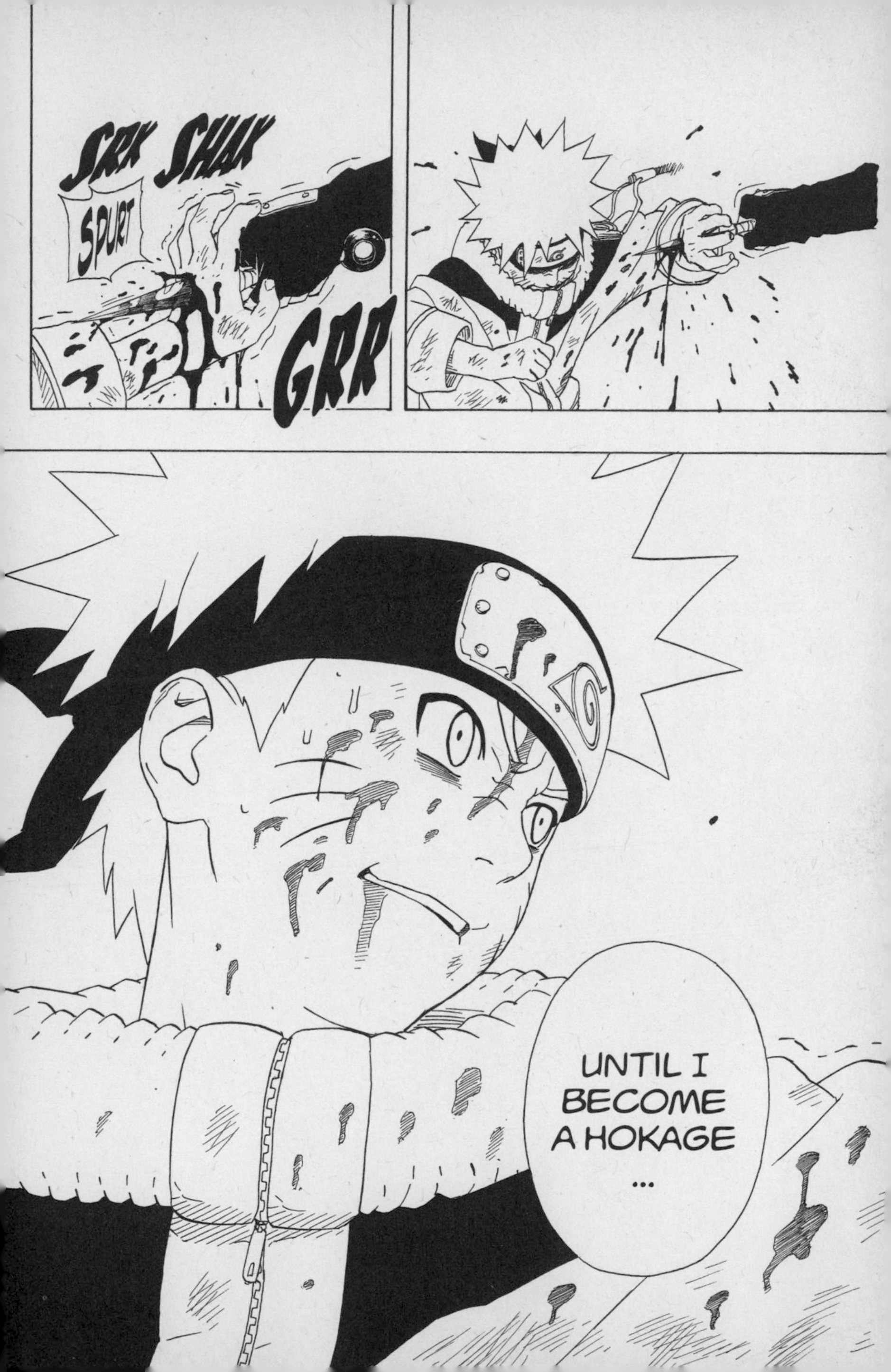
SRK SHAK
SPURT
GRR
UNTIL I BECOME A HOKAGE ...

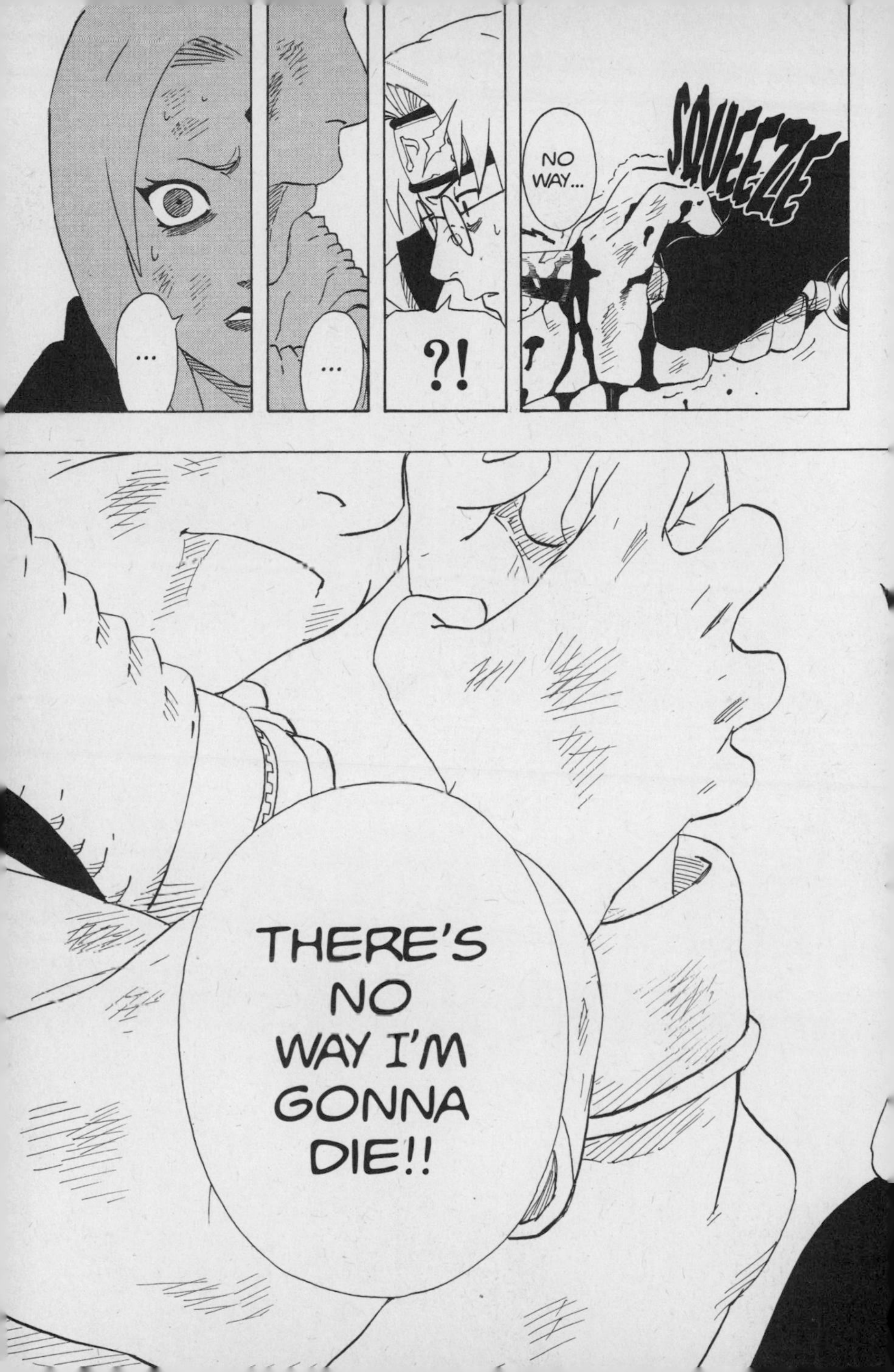
SQUEEZE
NO WAY...
?!
...
...
THERE'S NO WAY I'M GONNA DIE!!

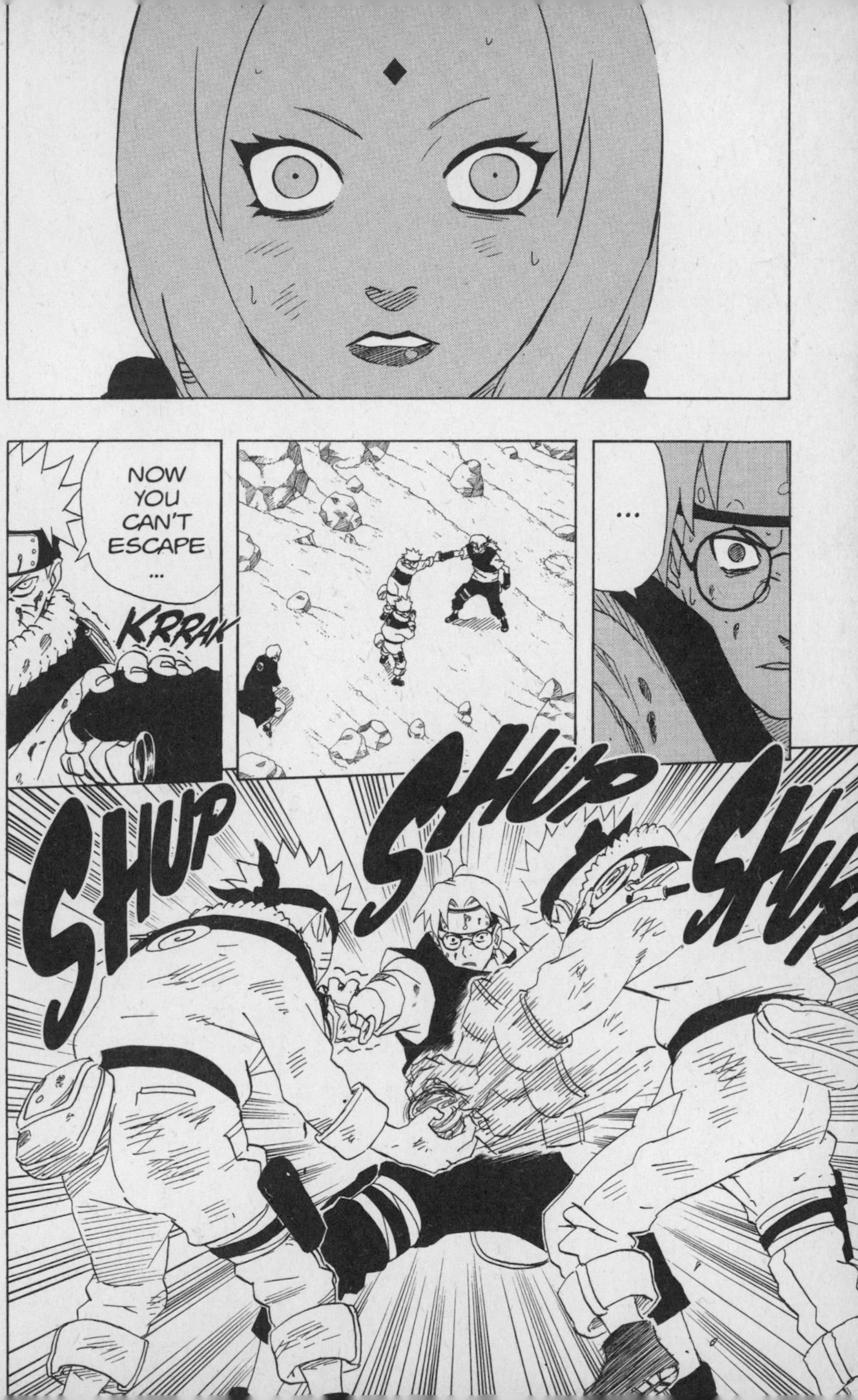
...
NOW YOU CAN'T ESCAPE ...
KRRAK
SHUP
SHUP
SHUP

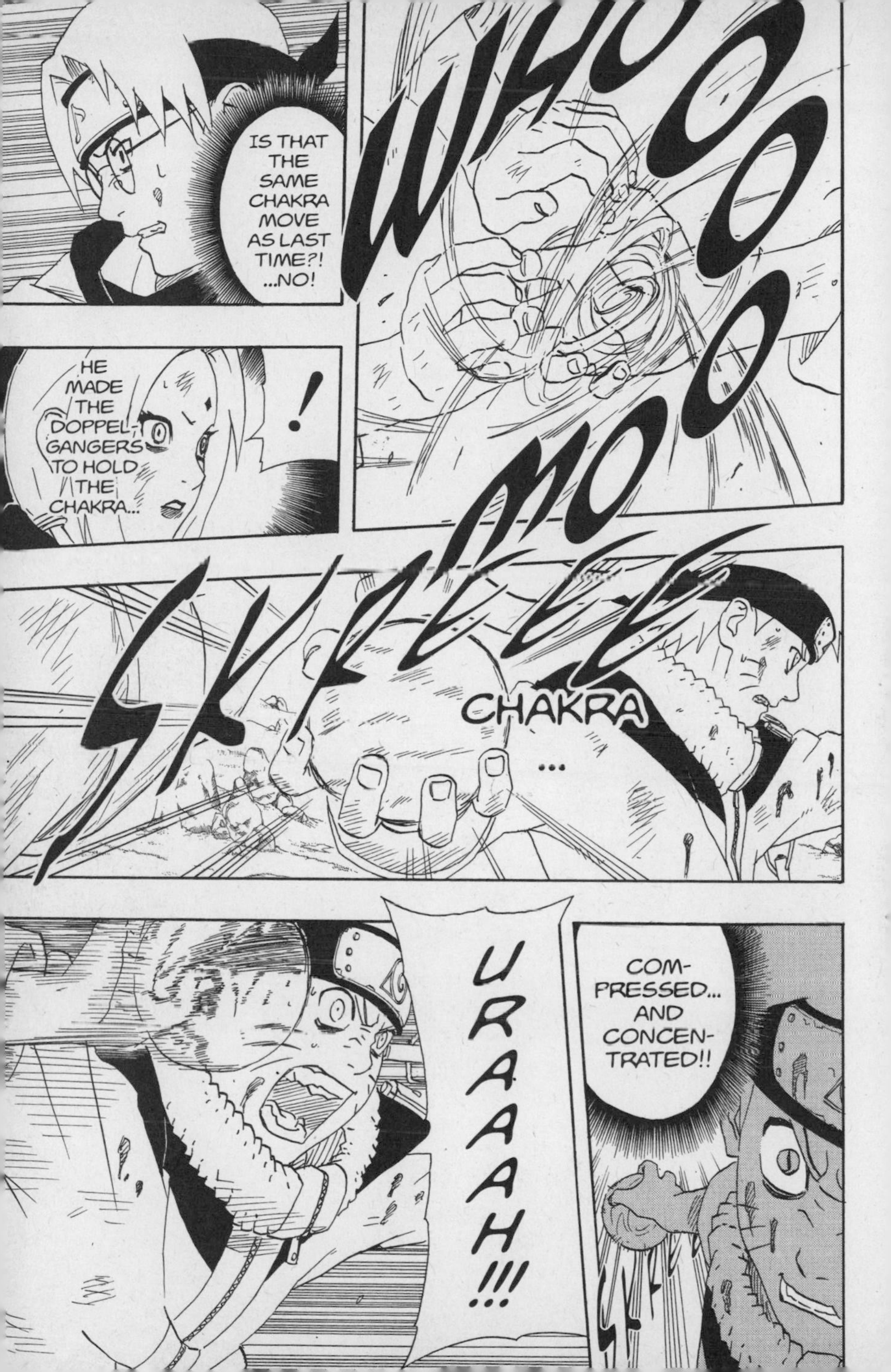
WHOOOOOOMO
IS THAT THE SAME CHAKRA MOVE AS LAST TIME?! ...NO!
!
HE MADE THE DOPPELGANGERS TO HOLD THE CHAKRA...
SKREEEE
CHAKRA ...
COMPRESSED... AND CONCENTRATED!!
URAAAAH!!!

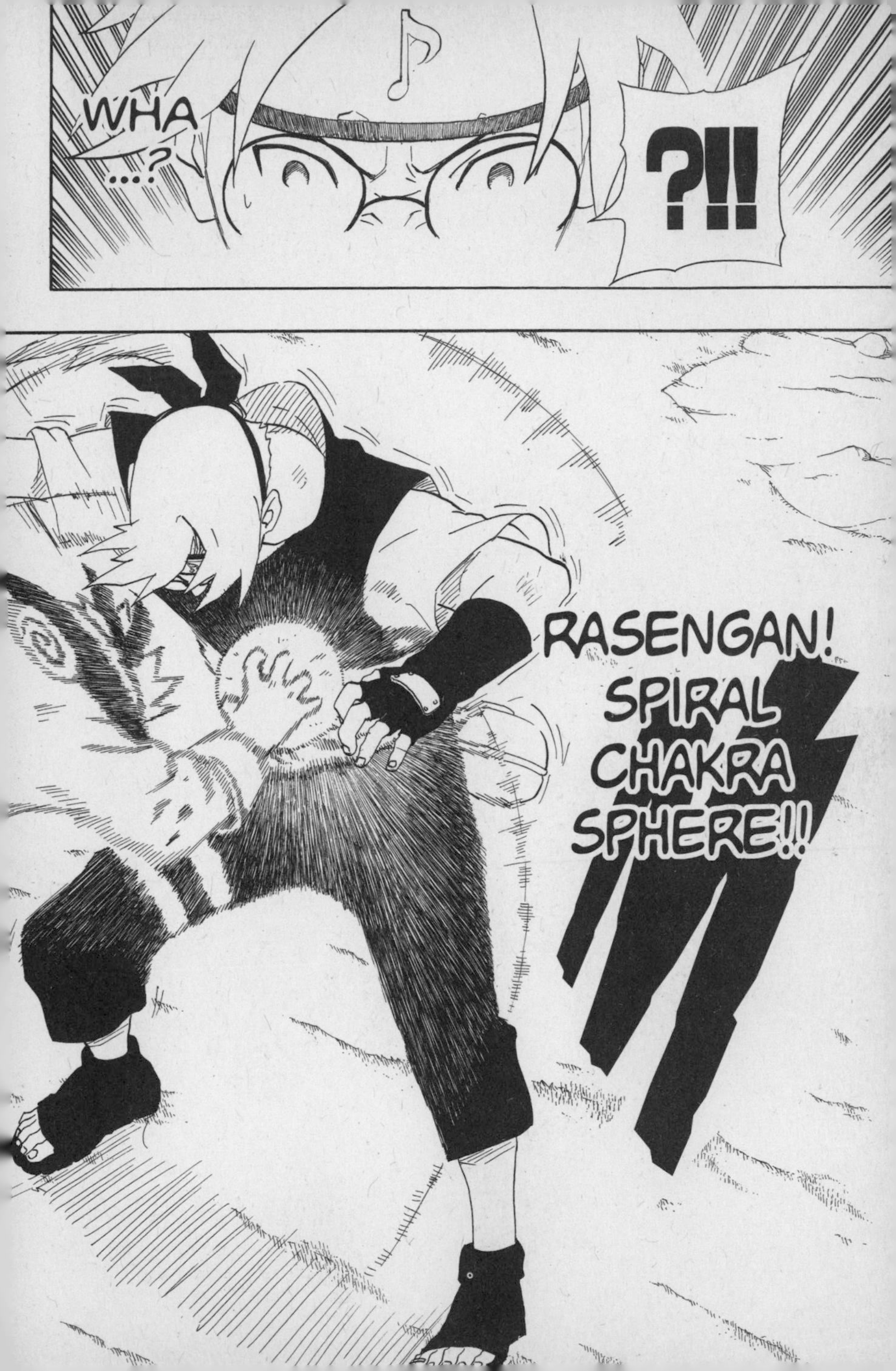
?!!
WHA ...?
RASENGAN! SPIRAL CHAKRA SPHERE!!

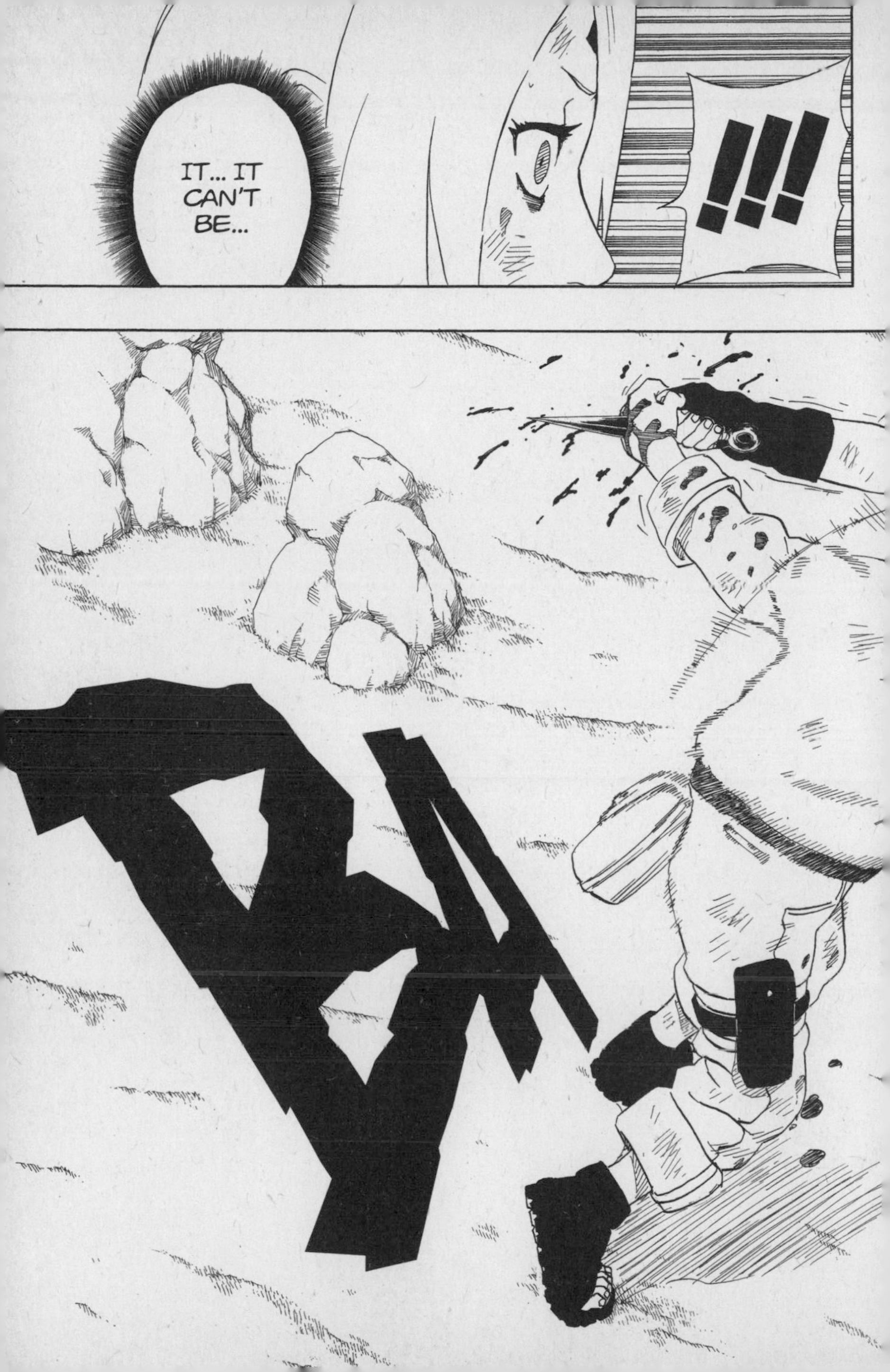
!!!
IT... IT CAN'T BE...

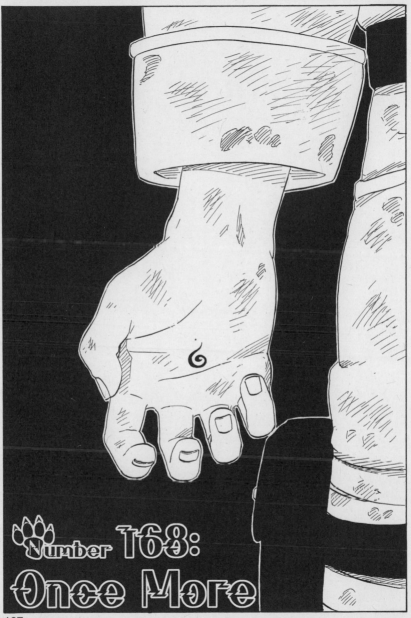

Number 168:
Once More

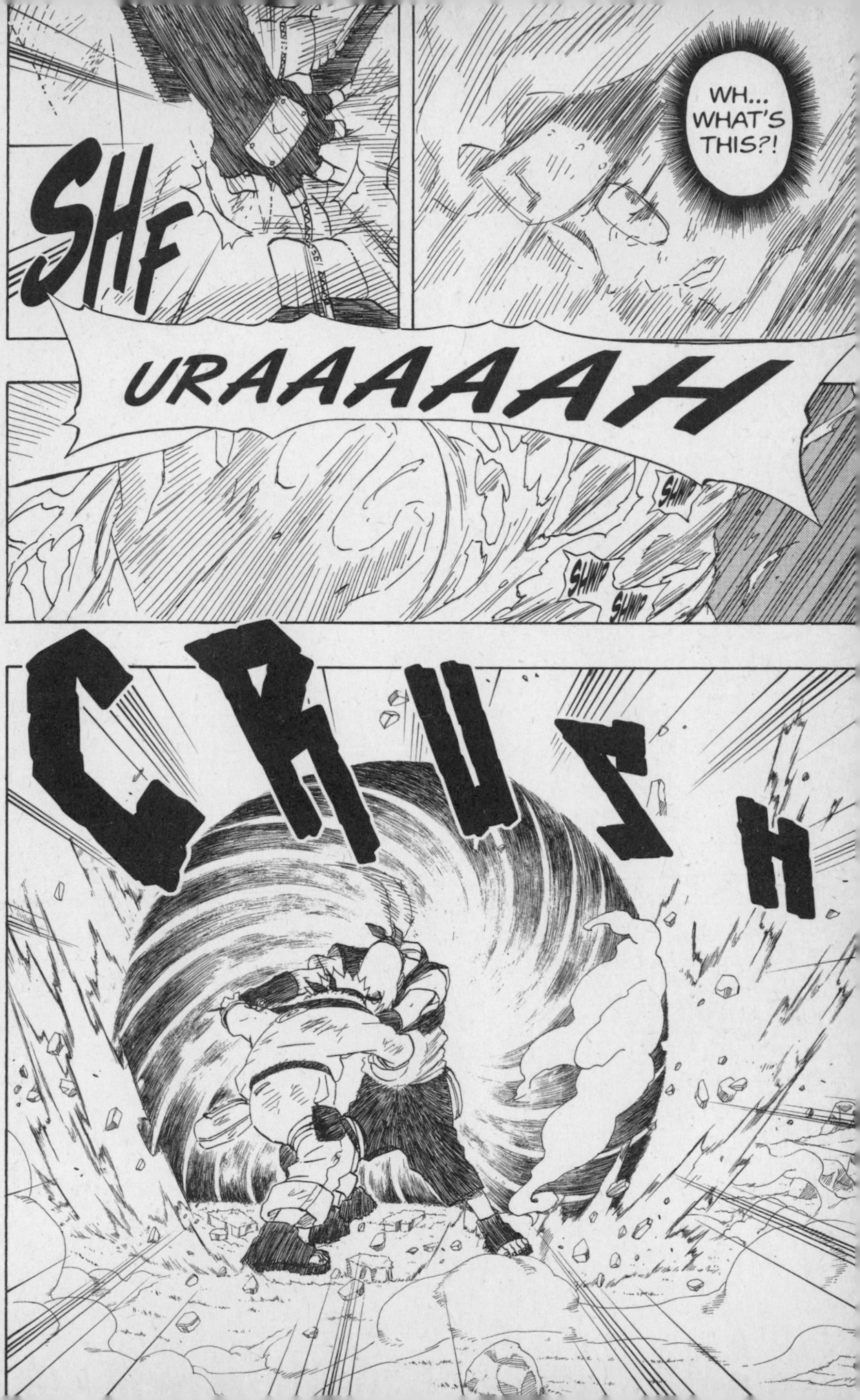
WH... WHAT'S THIS?!
SHF
URAAAAAH
SHNP
SHNP
SHNP
CRUSH

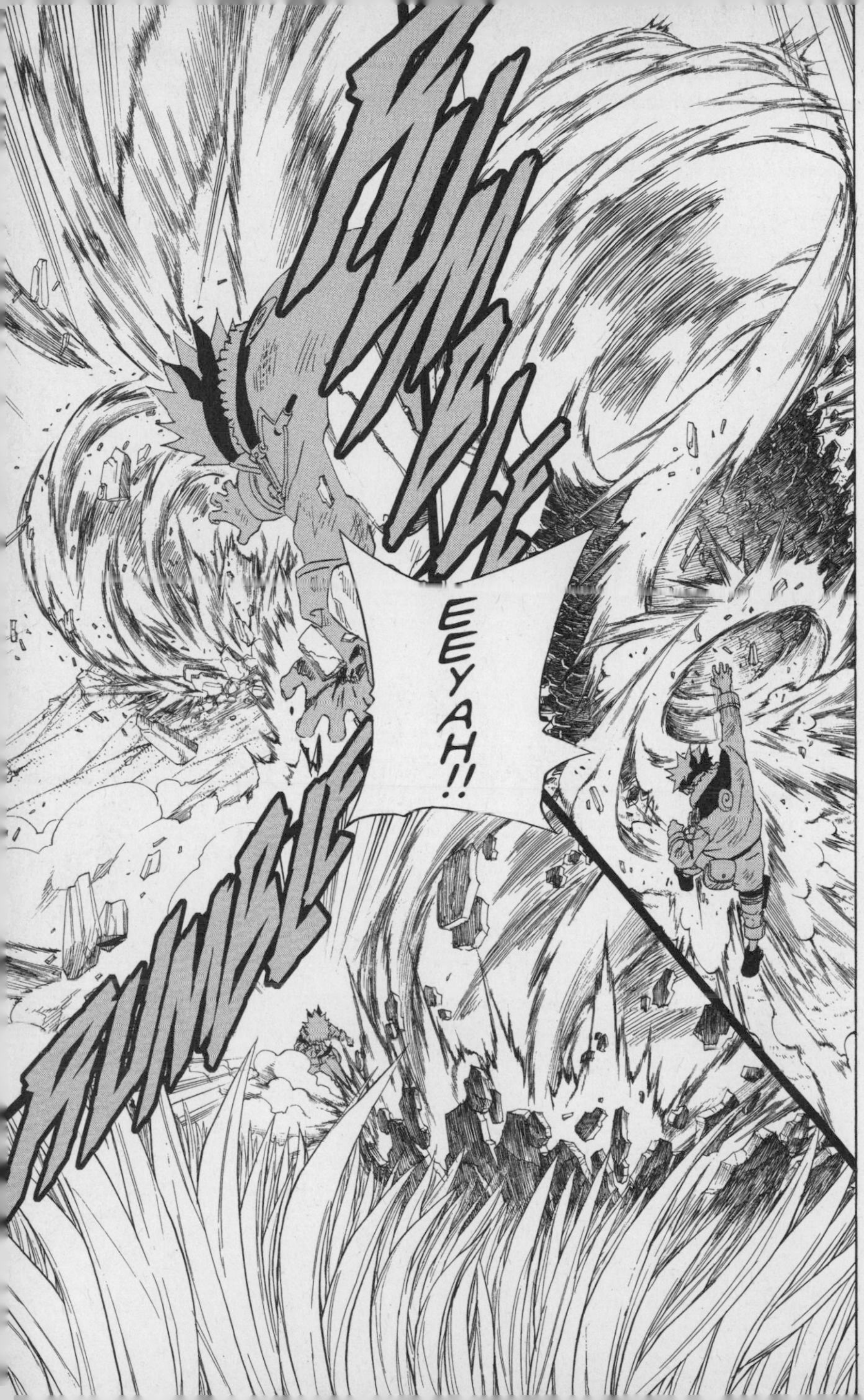
EEYAH!!

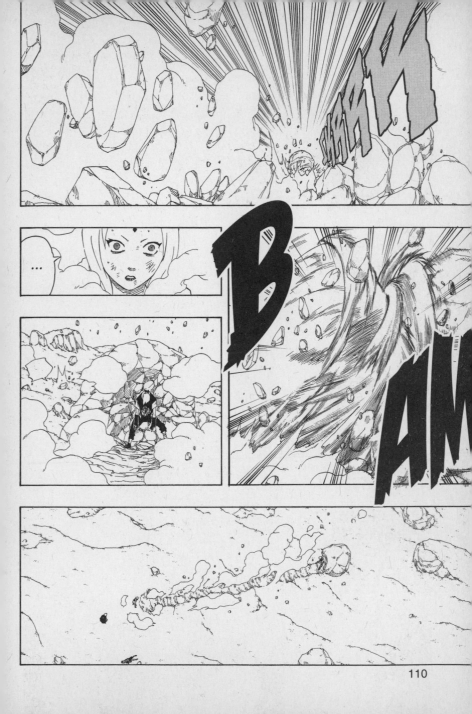

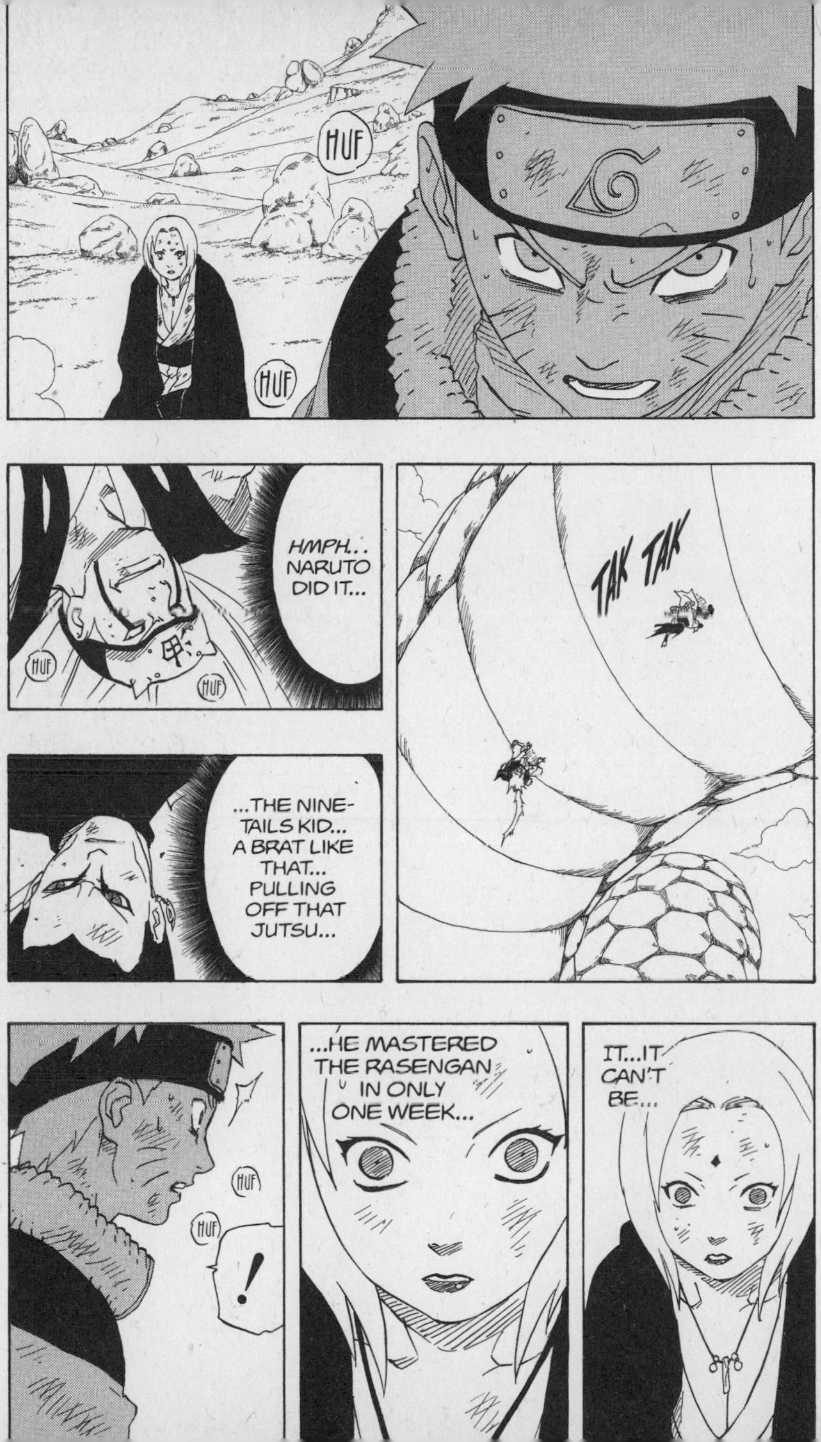
HUF
HUF
TAK TAK
HMPH... NARUTO DID IT...
HUF
HUF
...THE NINE-TAILS KID... A BRAT LIKE THAT... PULLING OFF THAT JUTSU...
IT...IT CAN'T BE...
...HE MASTERED THE RASENGAN IN ONLY ONE WEEK...
HUF
HUF
!

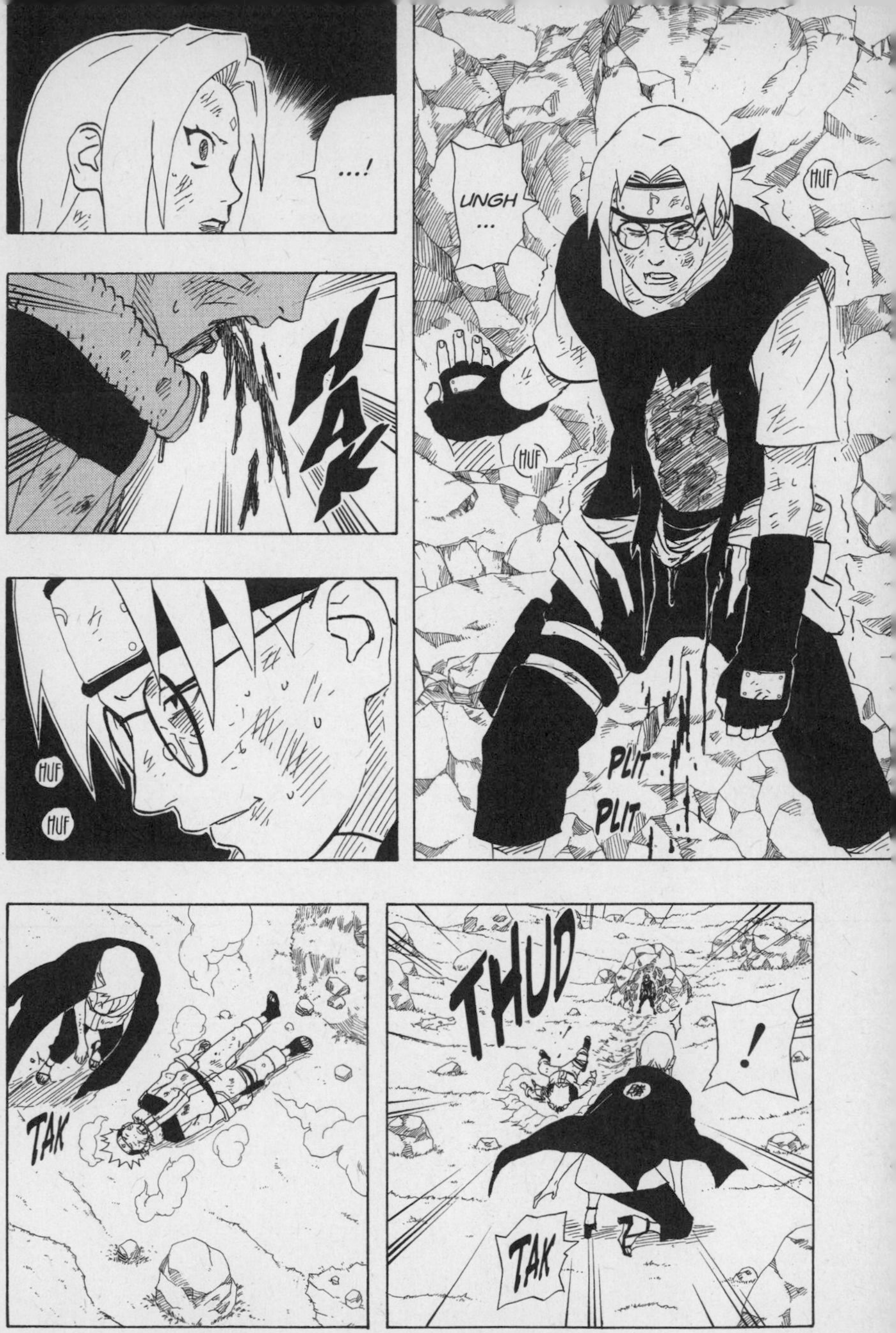
UNGH ...
HUF
HUF
PLIT
PLIT
...!
HAK
HUF
HUF
THUD
!
TAK
TAK

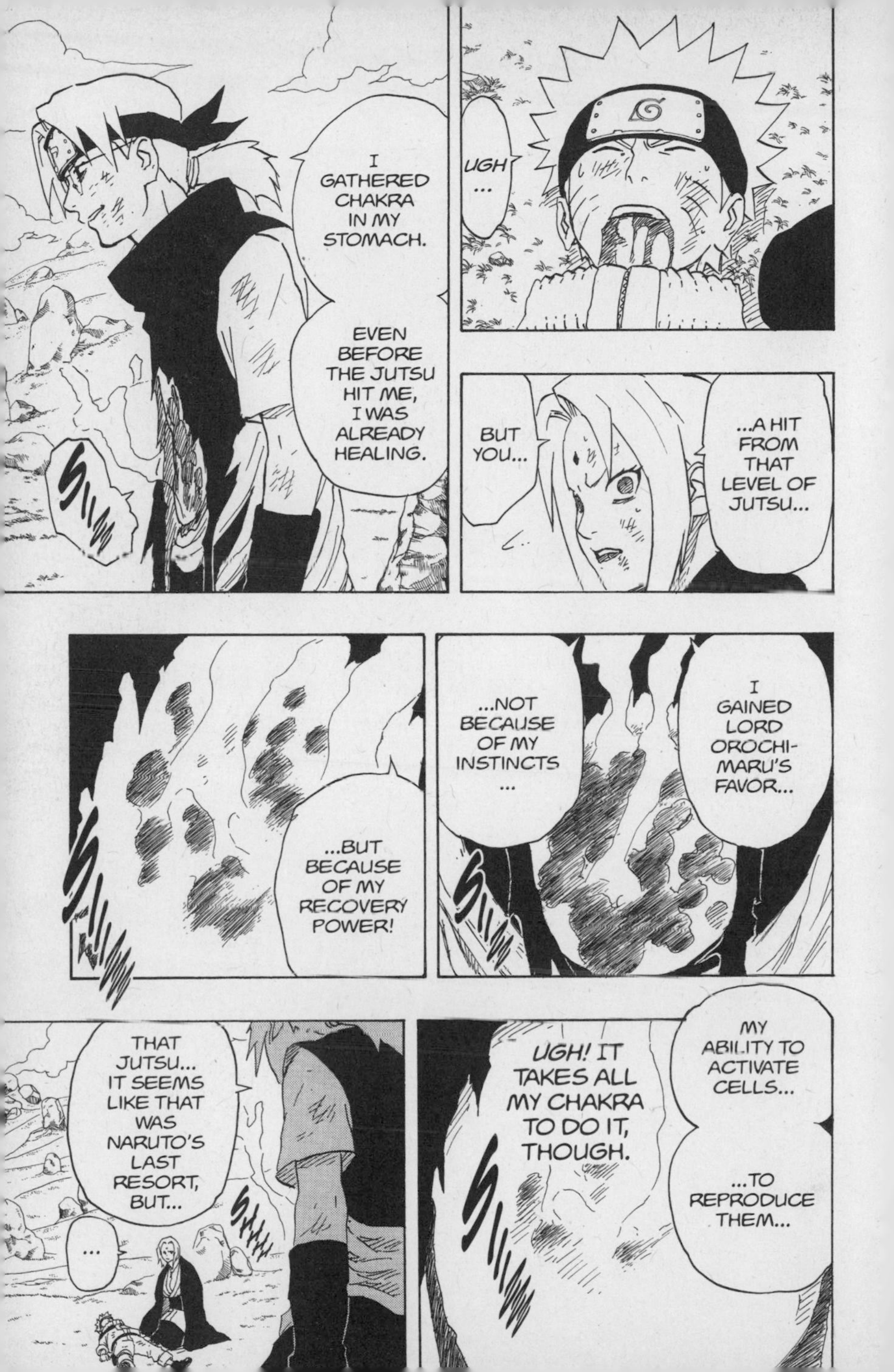
UGH ...
...A HIT FROM THAT LEVEL OF JUTSU...
BUT YOU...
I GATHERED CHAKRA IN MY STOMACH.
EVEN BEFORE THE JUTSU HIT ME, I WAS ALREADY HEALING.
I GAINED LORD OROCHI-MARU'S FAVOR...
...NOT BECAUSE OF MY INSTINCTS ...
...BUT BECAUSE OF MY RECOVERY POWER!
MY ABILITY TO ACTIVATE CELLS...
...TO REPRODUCE THEM...
UGH! IT TAKES ALL MY CHAKRA TO DO IT, THOUGH.
THAT JUTSU... IT SEEMS LIKE THAT WAS NARUTO'S LAST RESORT, BUT...
...

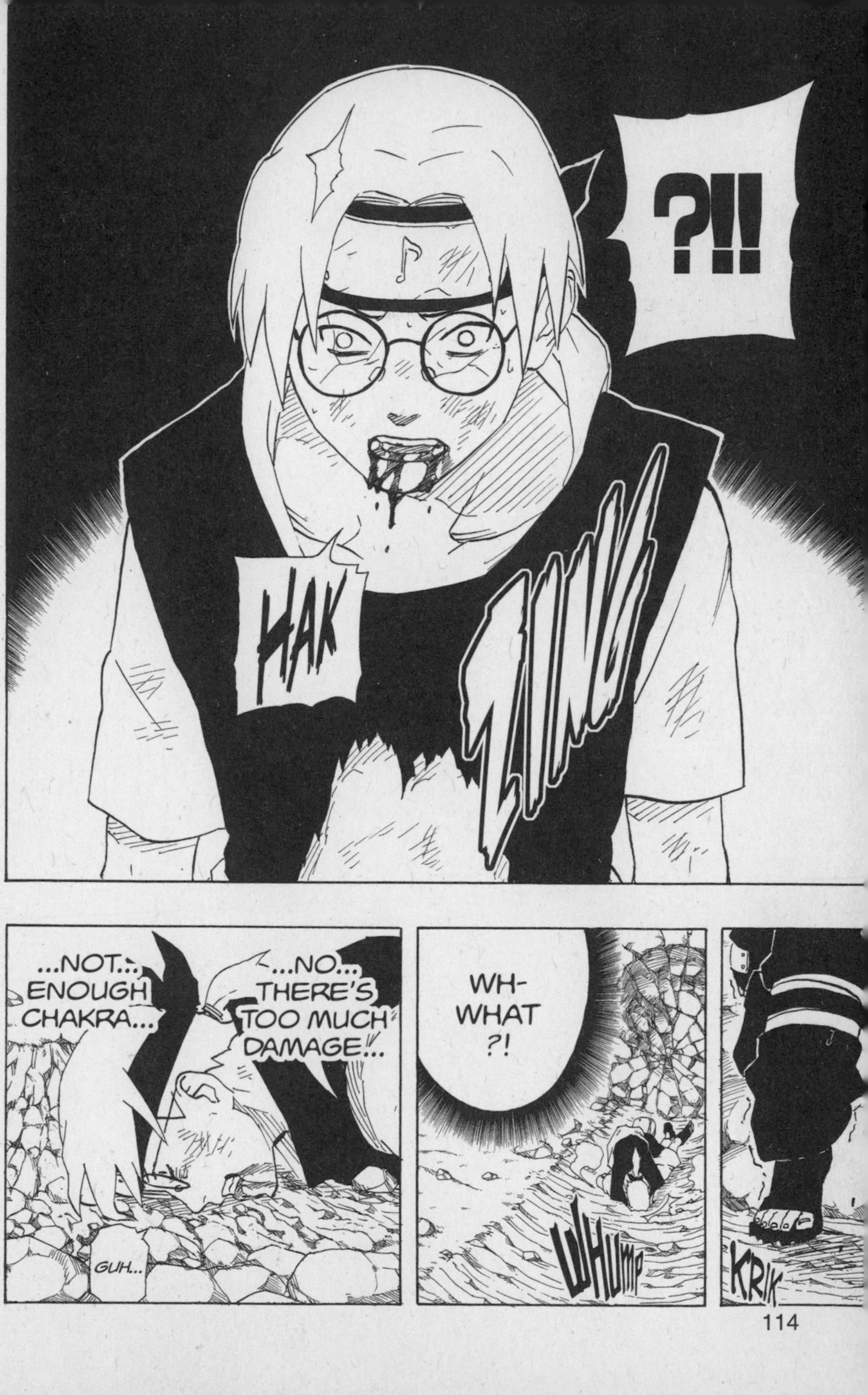
?!!
HAK
KRIK
WH- WHAT ?!
WHUMP
...NO... THERE'S TOO MUCH DAMAGE!!...
...NOT... ENOUGH CHAKRA...
GUH...

READ THIS WAY

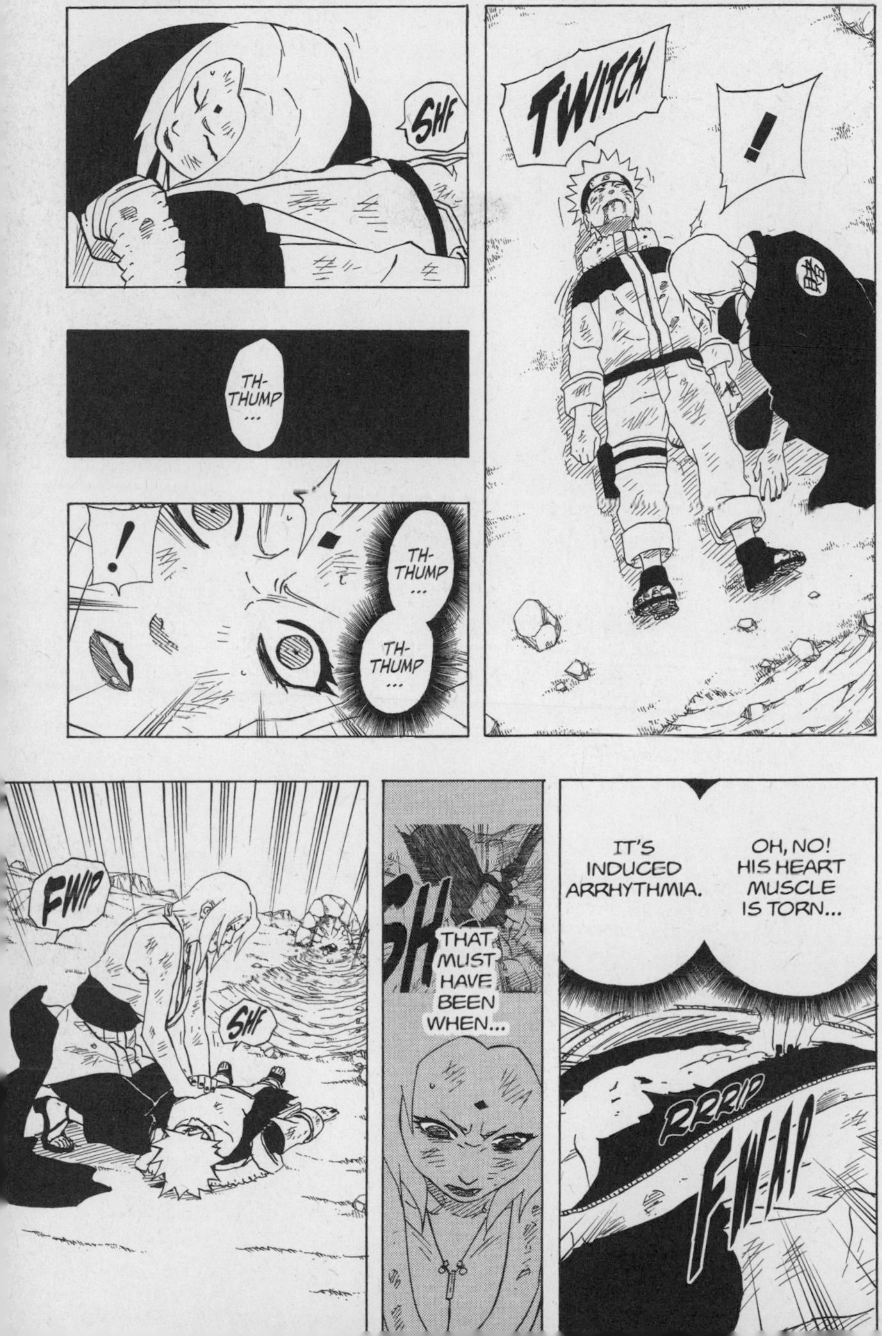
TWITCH
!
SHF
TH-THUMP...
!
TH-THUMP...
TH-THUMP...
OH, NO! HIS HEART MUSCLE IS TORN...
IT'S INDUCED ARRHYTHMIA.
RRRIP
FWAP
SH
THAT MUST HAVE BEEN WHEN...
FWIP
SHF

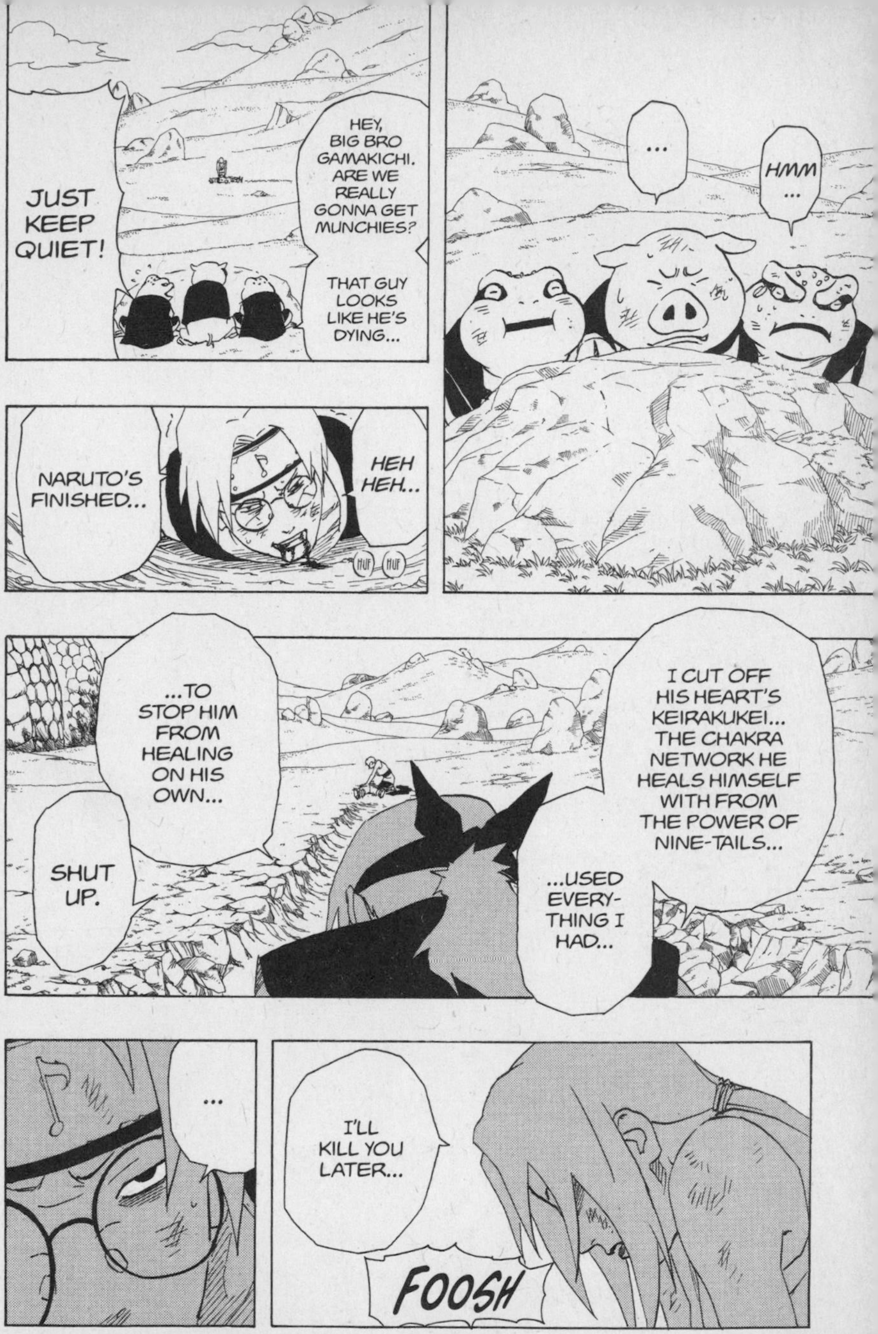
HMM ...
...
HEY, BIG BRO GAMAKICHI. ARE WE REALLY GONNA GET MUNCHIES?
THAT GUY LOOKS LIKE HE'S DYING...
JUST KEEP QUIET!
HEH HEH...
HUF HUF
NARUTO'S FINISHED...
I CUT OFF HIS HEART'S KEIRAKUKEI... THE CHAKRA NETWORK HE HEALS HIMSELF WITH FROM THE POWER OF NINE-TAILS...
...USED EVERY-THING I HAD...
...TO STOP HIM FROM HEALING ON HIS OWN...
SHUT UP.
I'LL KILL YOU LATER...
FOOSH
...

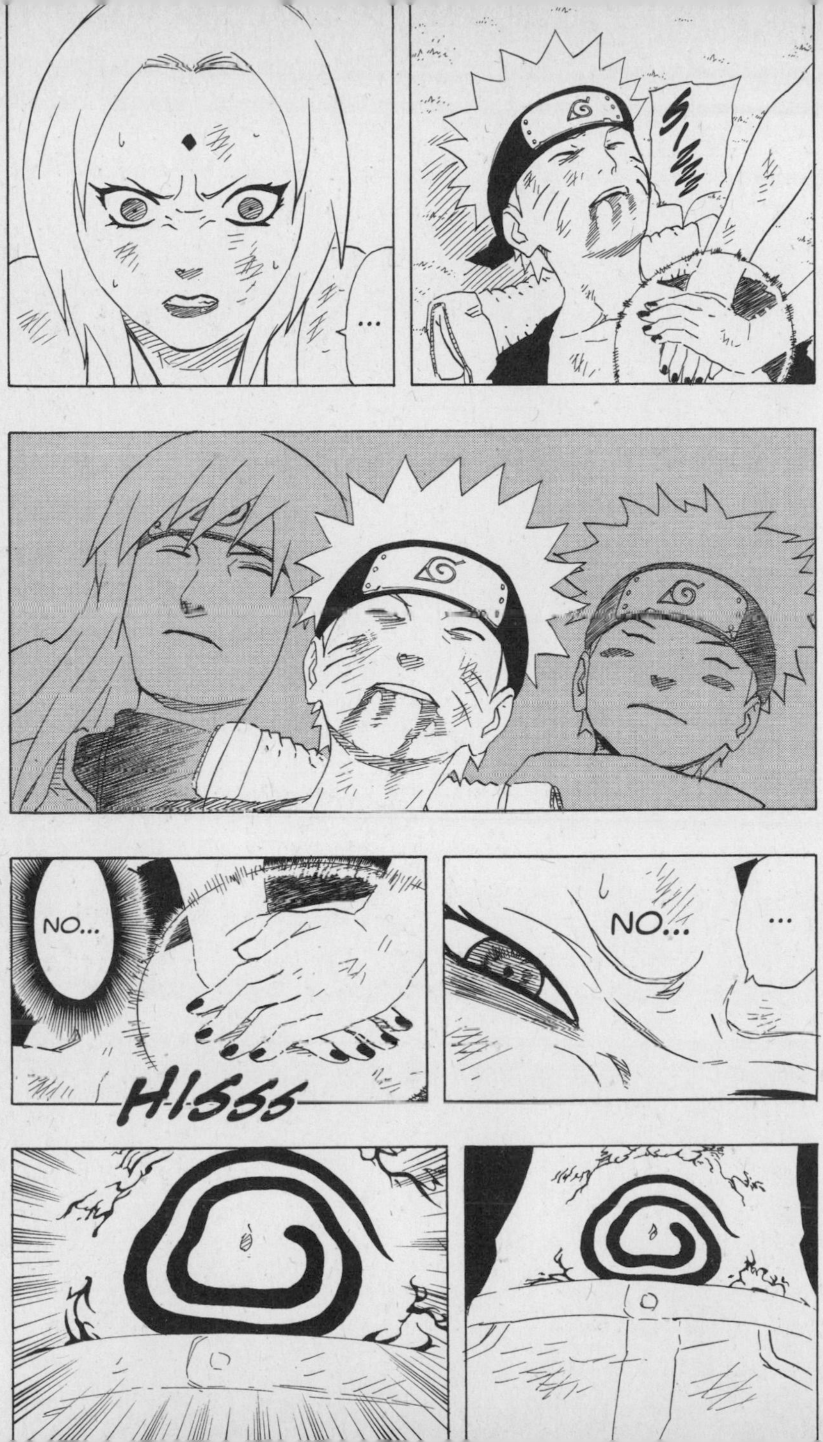
SIZZZ
...
NO...
...
NO...
HISSS

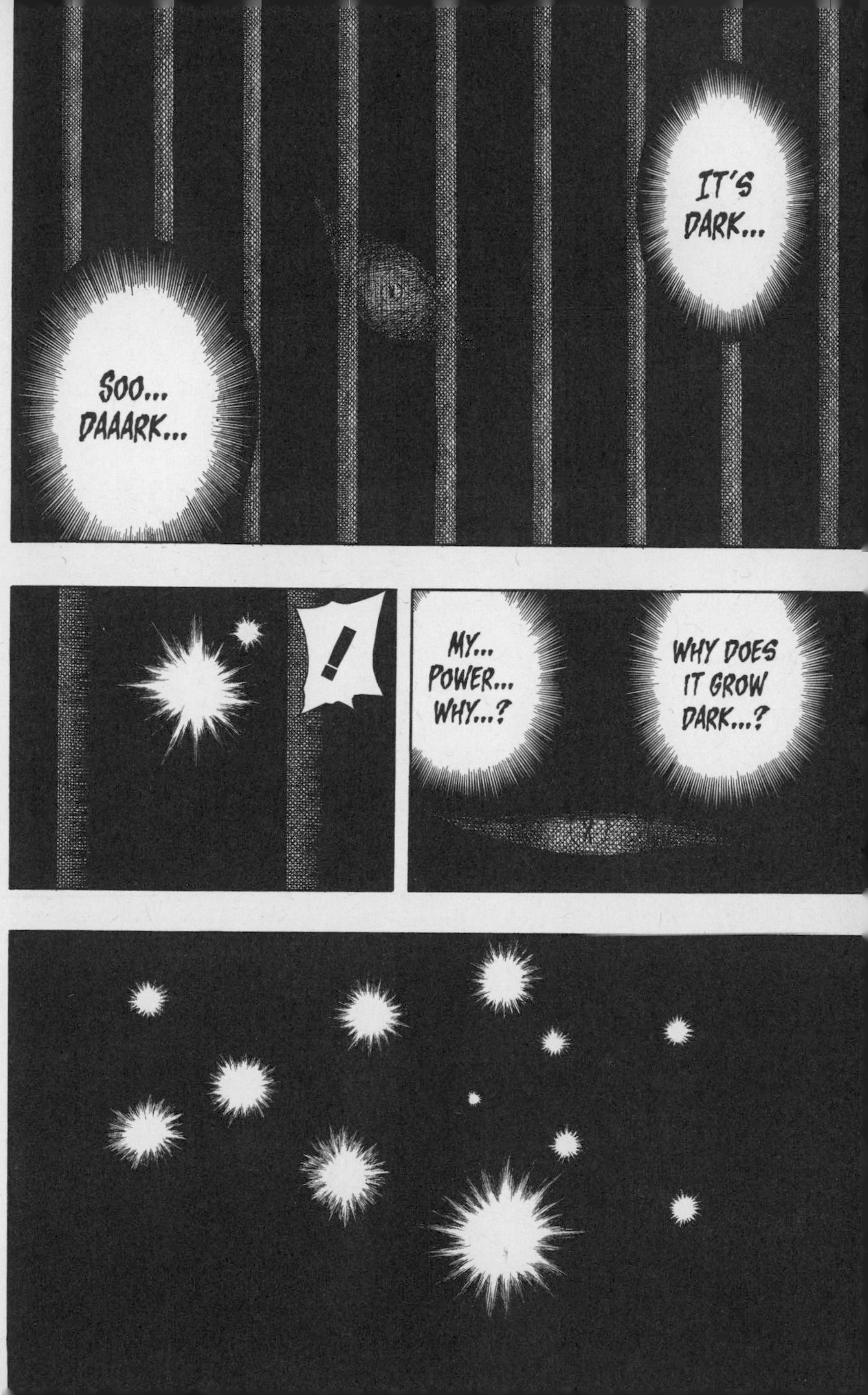
IT'S DARK...
SOO... DAAARK...
WHY DOES IT GROW DARK...?
MY... POWER... WHY...?
!

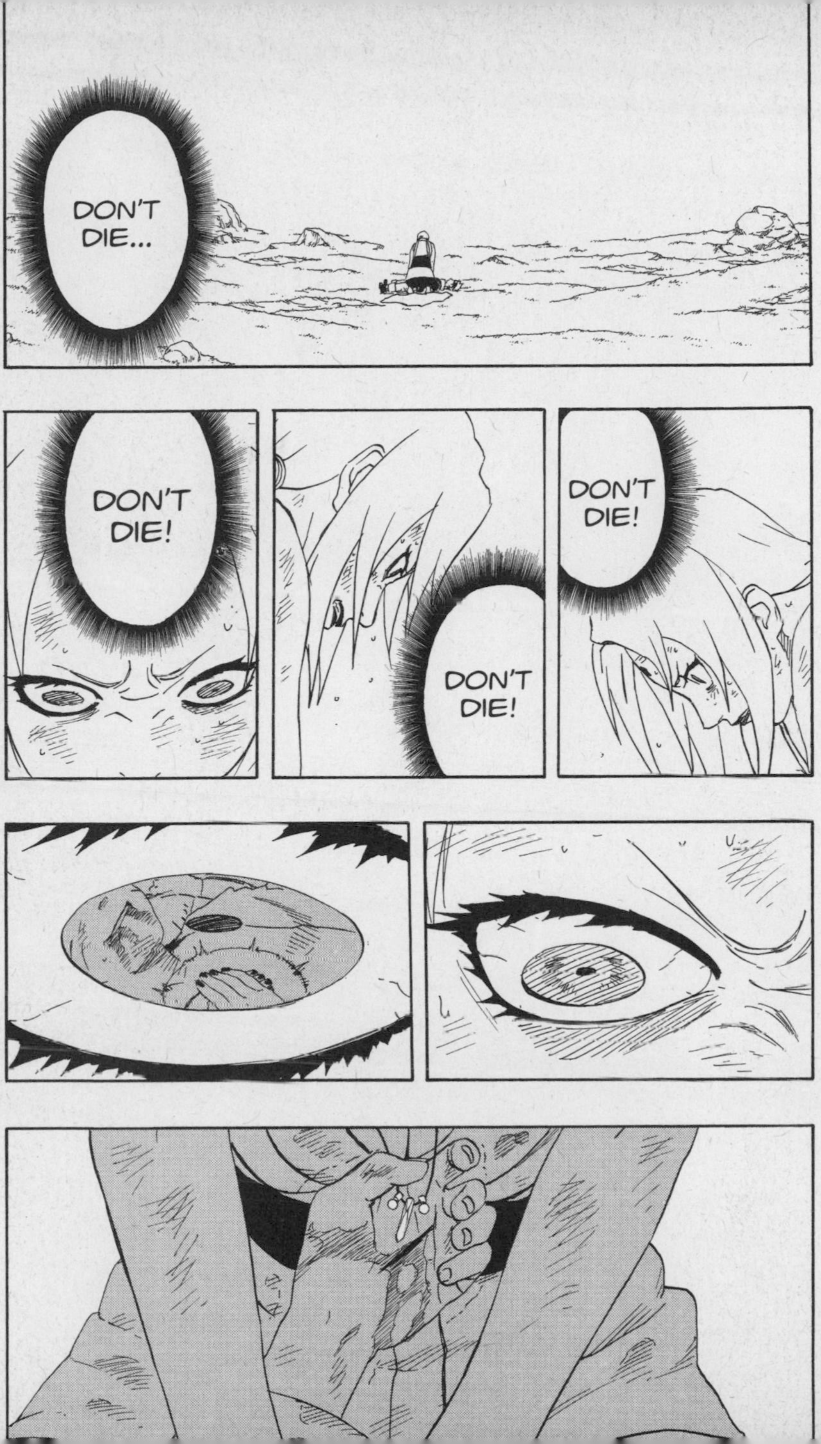
DON'T DIE...
DON'T DIE!
DON'T DIE!
DON'T DIE!

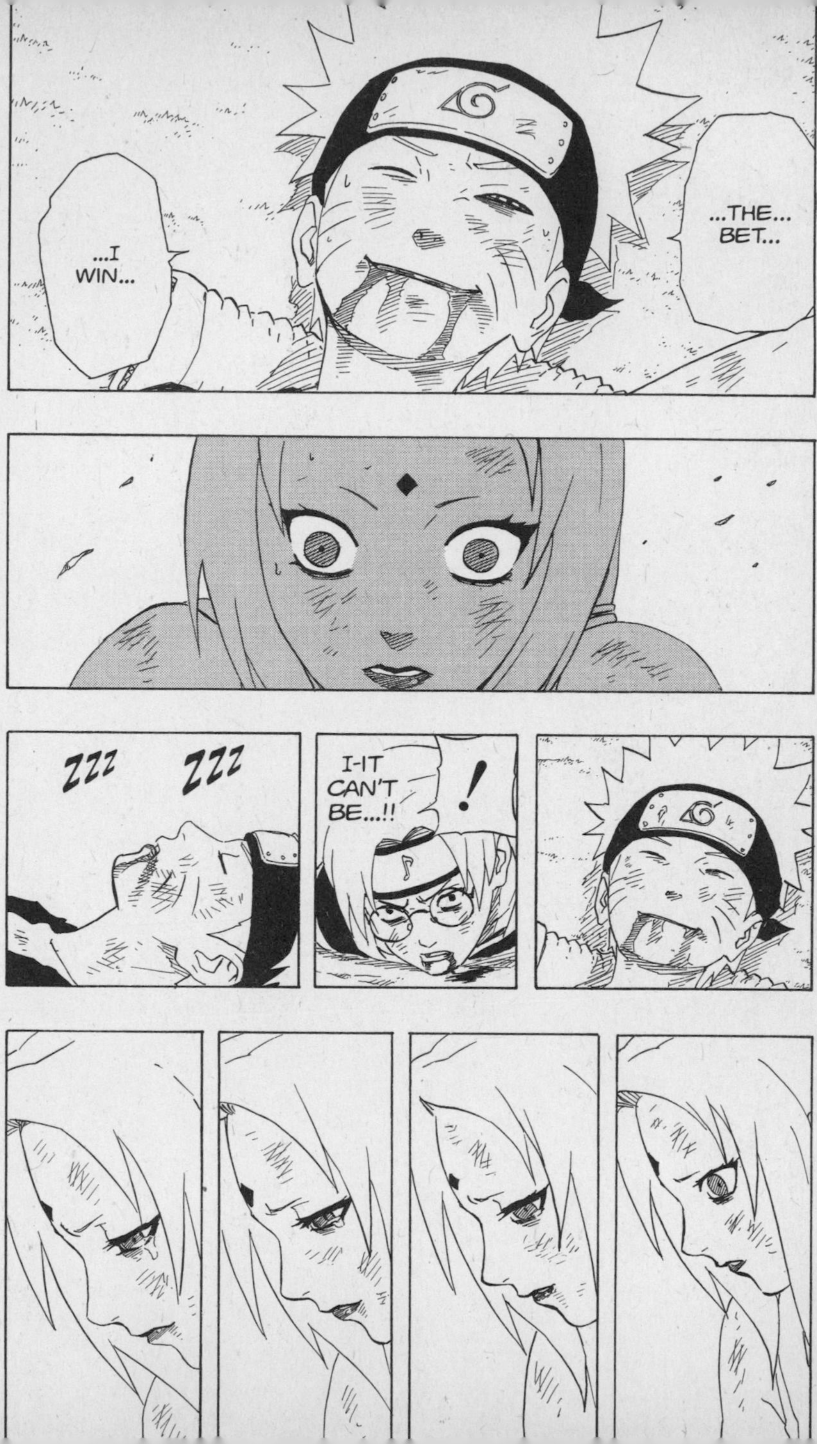
...THE... BET...
...I WIN...
!
I-IT CAN'T BE...!!
ZZZ
ZZZ

READ THIS WAY

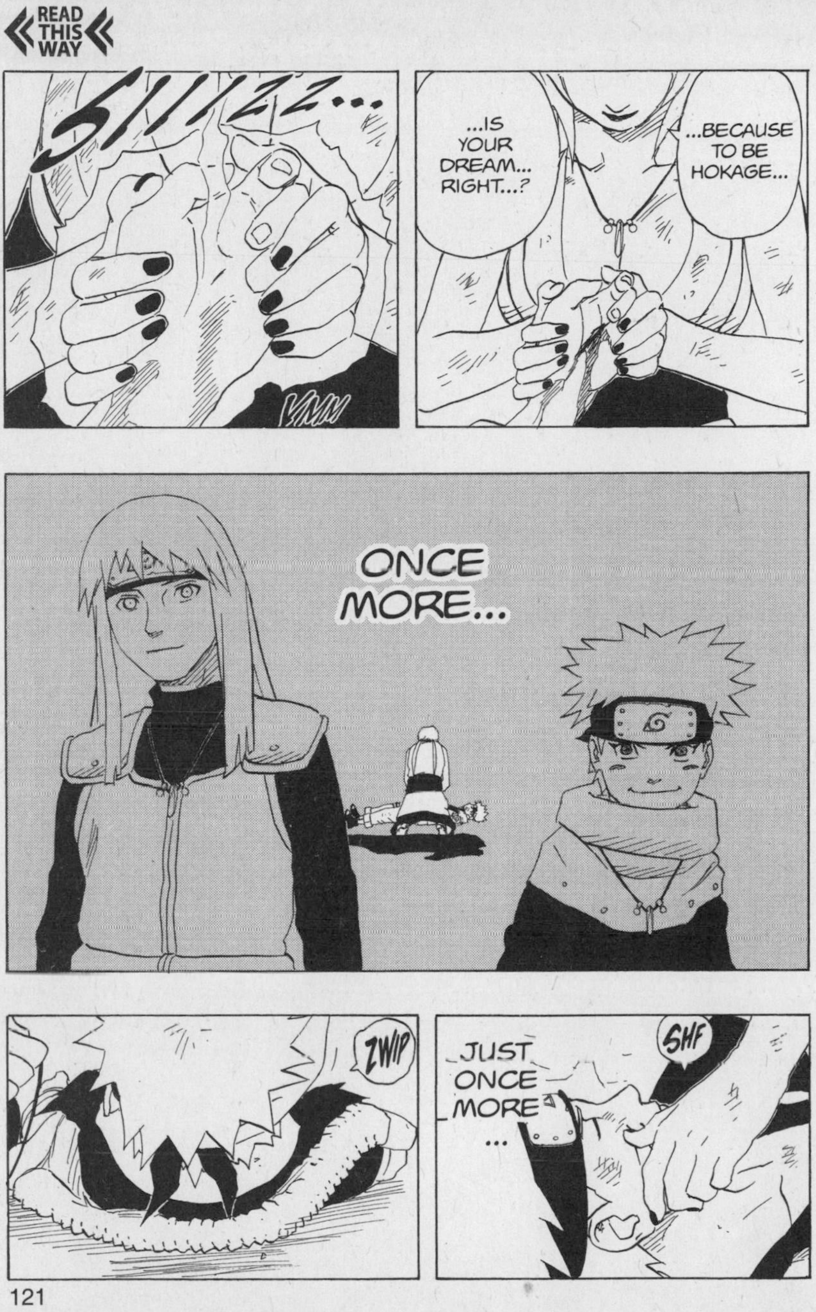
...BECAUSE TO BE HOKAGE...
...IS YOUR DREAM... RIGHT...?
SIIIZZ...
VMM
ONCE MORE...
SHF
JUST ONCE MORE ...
ZWIP

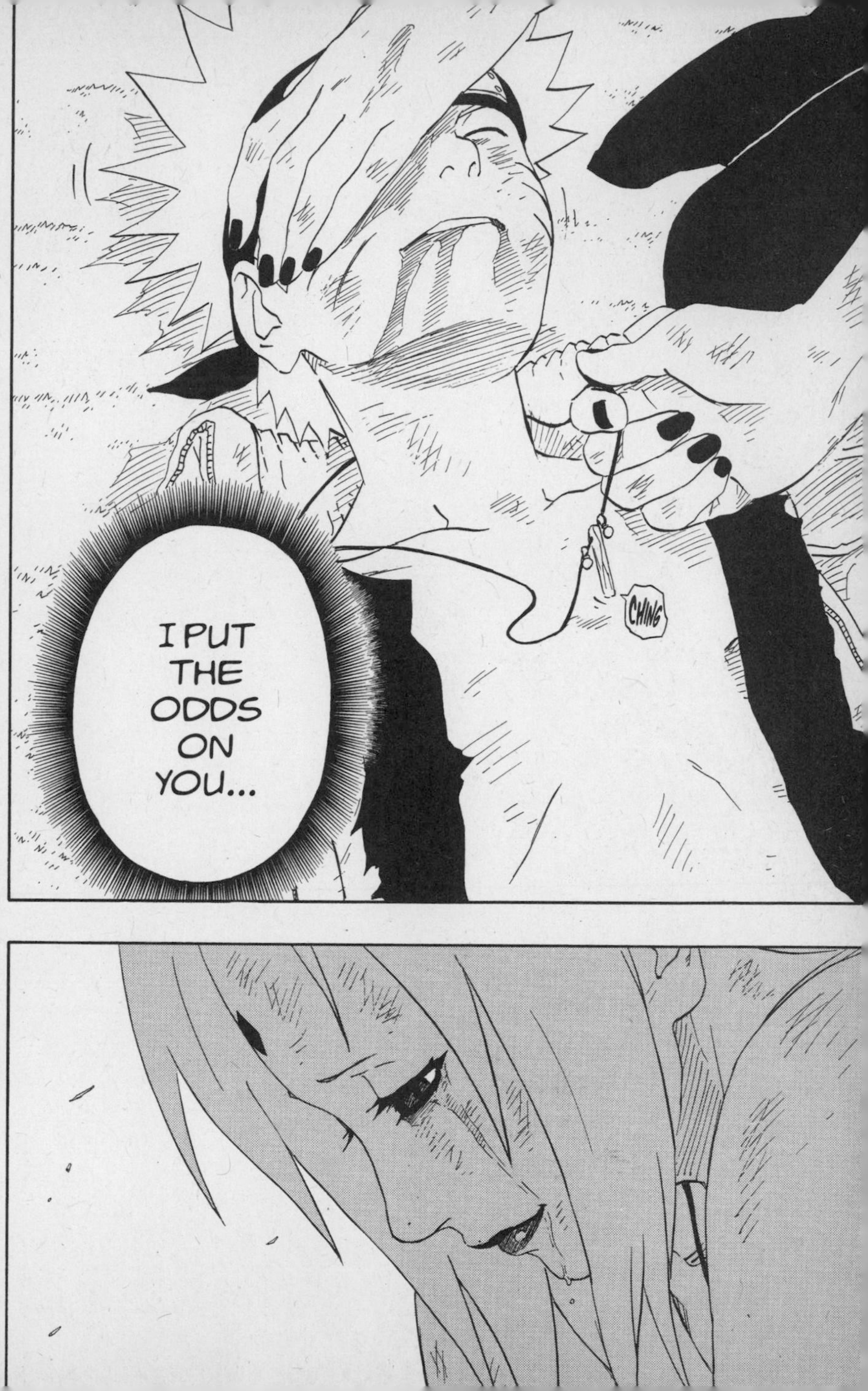
CHING
I PUT THE ODDS ON YOU...

READ THIS WAY

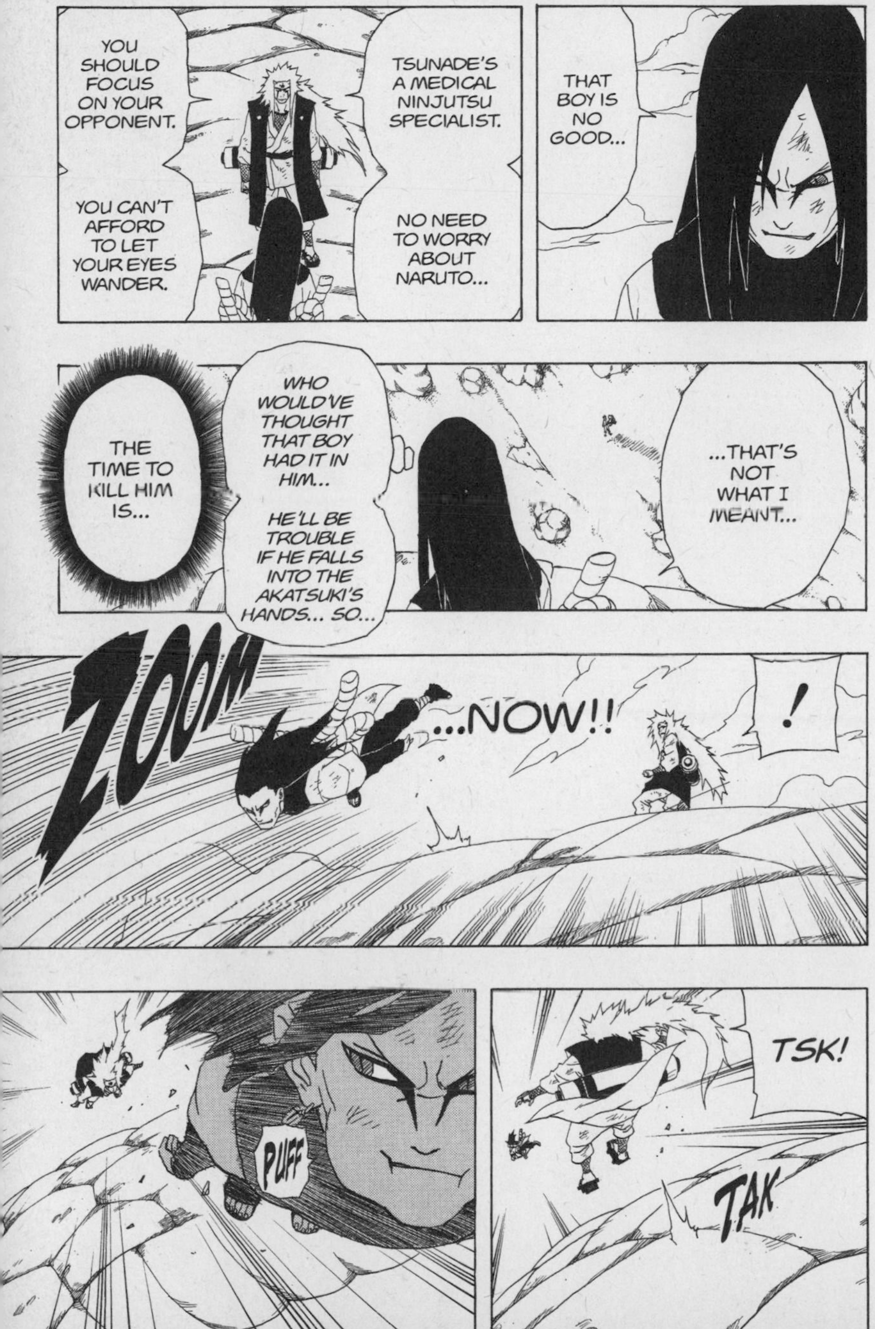
THAT BOY IS NO GOOD...
TSUNADE'S A MEDICAL NINJUTSU SPECIALIST.
NO NEED TO WORRY ABOUT NARUTO...
YOU SHOULD FOCUS ON YOUR OPPONENT.
YOU CAN'T AFFORD TO LET YOUR EYES WANDER.
...THAT'S NOT WHAT I MEANT...
WHO WOULD'VE THOUGHT THAT BOY HAD IT IN HIM...
HE'LL BE TROUBLE IF HE FALLS INTO THE AKATSUKI'S HANDS... SO...
THE TIME TO KILL HIM IS...
!
...NOW!!
ZOOM
TSK!
TAK
PUFF

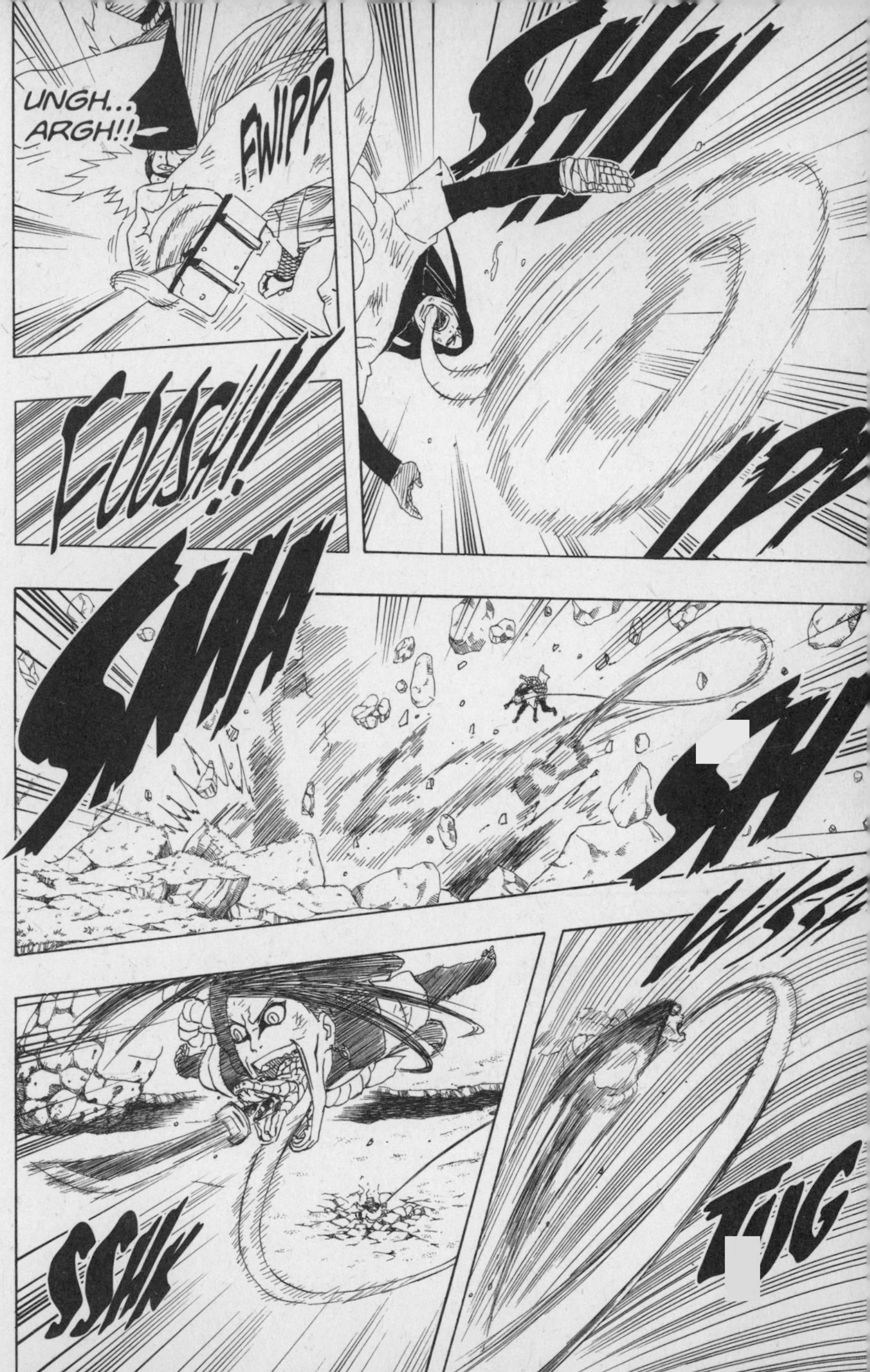
SHN
UNGH... ARGH!!
FWIPP
FOOSH!!
SWA
TIG
SSHK

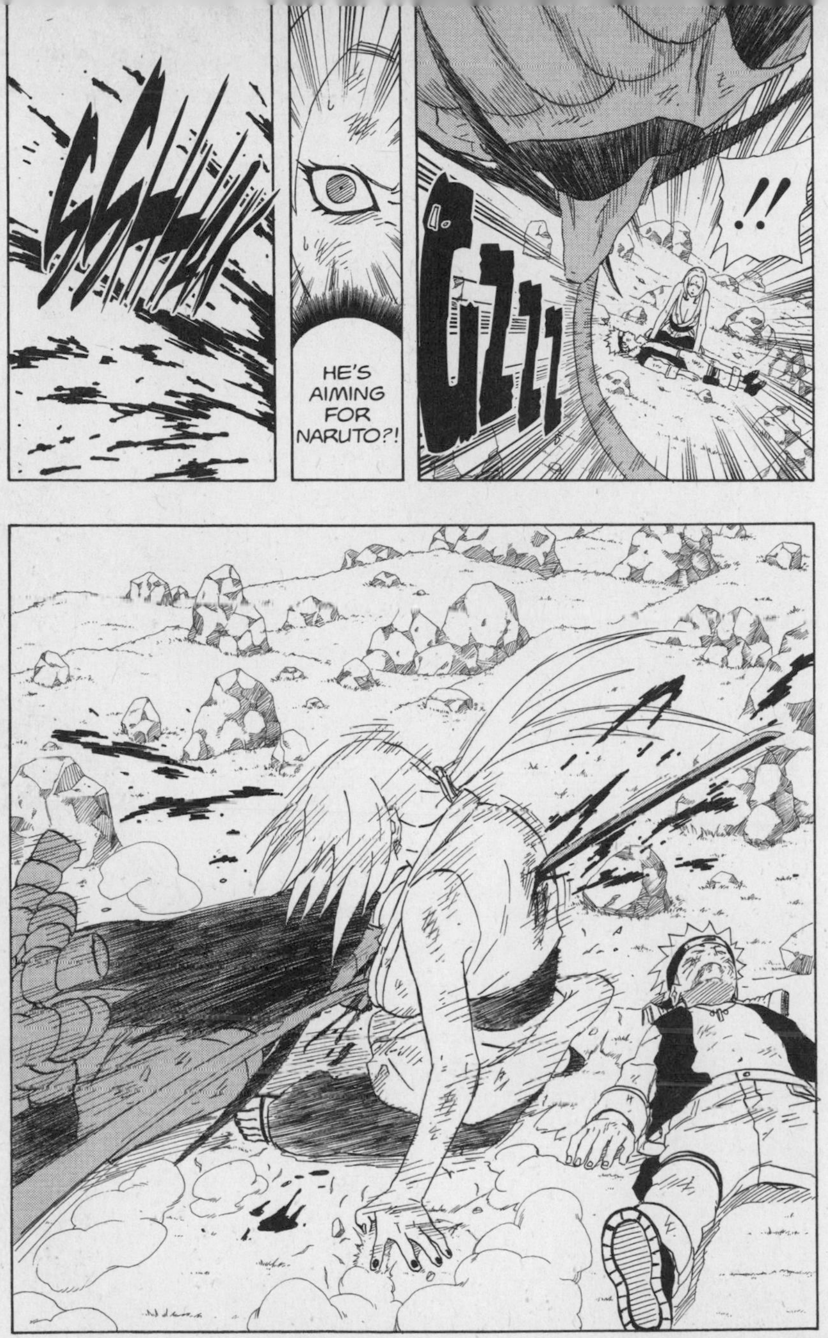
!!
HE'S AIMING FOR NARUTO?!

THE WORLD OF KISHIMOTO MASASHI
MY PERSONAL HISTORY, PART 30: NO.3

BECOMING A MANGA ARTIST IS NOT SOMETHING ONE DOES TO SATISFY THEIR PARENTS OR FOR MONEY. BUT AS LONG AS ONE AIMS TO BE A MANGA ARTIST, VARIOUS CIRCUMSTANCES ARE BOUND TO ARISE ALONG THE WAY. IN THE END, MAKING THESE THINGS GO SMOOTHLY WAS SOMETHING I DID FOR MYSELF... IN OTHER WORDS, IT WAS A PART OF MY BECOMING A MANGA ARTIST.

TO THAT END, I REALIZED THAT MY LIFE COULDN'T CONTINUE GOING THE WAY IT HAD BEEN.

I DECIDED TO GO BACK TO BASICS AND THOROUGHLY RESTUDY MANGA FROM THE BEGINNING.

FIRST, I BEGAN WITH THE FOLLOWING QUESTION: WHAT IS A STORY? THEN I LOOKED UP THE MEANINGS OF ALL MANGA-RELATED TERMS, ASKING MYSELF: WHAT DOES THEME REALLY MEAN? WHAT DO EPISODE, STRUCTURE, CHARACTERS AND DIRECTION MEAN? I STUDIED THEM AND TRIED TO UNDERSTAND WHAT THOSE WORDS MEANT AND HOW TO USE THEM.

WHAT I ACTUALLY DID WAS VISIT LIBRARIES AND STUDY THE THINGS NECESSARY TO CREATE A STORY, SUCH AS HOW TO WRITE A STORY, MAKING SCENARIO SYNOPSES, MISLEADING, HOOK TECHNIQUES, CATCH, THREE-ACT STRUCTURE, SET-UP ORDER, HOW TO CREATE AND DISPLAY CHARACTERS, THEIR ROLES, STORY PATTERNS, AND SO ON... THESE THINGS I LEARNED BY READING HOW-TO BOOKS ON SCRIPTWRITING AND BECOMING A WRITER.

I ACTUALLY WATCHED THE MOVIES USED AS EXAMPLES IN THOSE BOOKS TO LEARN DIRECTING TECHNIQUES, CHARACTER DEVELOPMENT AND STORY STRUCTURE. I ALSO READ SUSPENSE NOVELS TO STUDY METHODS OF LEADING AND HOLDING, TECHNIQUES OF DELIBERATELY NOT USING NOUNS, AND MISLEADING TECHNIQUES NECESSARY TO MAKE THE STORY ENTERTAINING. IN SHORT, I LEARNED HOW TO WRITE A STORY BY READING BOOKS.

...BUT I COULDN'T ACQUIRE THESE TECHNIQUES JUST BY READING. SO I WATCHED LOTS OF MOVIES TO FIND HOW, AND IN WHICH SCENES, THE TECHNIQUES INTRODUCED IN THOSE BOOKS WERE ACTUALLY USED AND I WROTE THEM DOWN IN NOTEBOOKS AND STOCKPILED THEM. THEN I SET ABOUT DEVELOPING THIS MATERIAL AND THUS MADE THE TECHNIQUES MY OWN.

I WROTE OUT EACH LINE OF PULP FICTION TO STUDY CHARACTERS AND STORY STRUCTURE. I READ NOVELS WRITTEN BY DAZAI OSAMU TO LEARN HOW TO TREAT THEME, AND DISCOVERED SOME PATTERNS. I SUNK MY TEETH INTO WHATEVER I THOUGHT OF AS ENTERTAINMENT AND SEARCHED FOR ANSWERS TO THE QUESTIONS, "WHAT'S INTERESTING?" AND "HOW IS IT INTERESTING?" I WOKE UP IN THE MORNING AND VISITED LIBRARIES, BOOKSTORES AND VIDEO STORES... I SPENT EVERY DAY LIKE THAT FOR TWO YEARS AFTER GRADUATING COLLEGE.

I DIDN'T MAKE MANY STORYBOARDS DURING THAT TIME. BUT IT APPEARED THAT MY FIRST VERSION OF *NARUTO*, A ONE-SHOT MANGA I WROTE SOON AFTER STARTING THIS RESEARCH, SOMEHOW GAINED POPULARITY IN *AKAMARU JUMP*, ROUGH WORK THOUGH IT WAS.

TO BE CONTINUED. SEE, THE STORY'S GETTING BRIGHTER, RIGHT?

Number 169: Risking Everything...!!

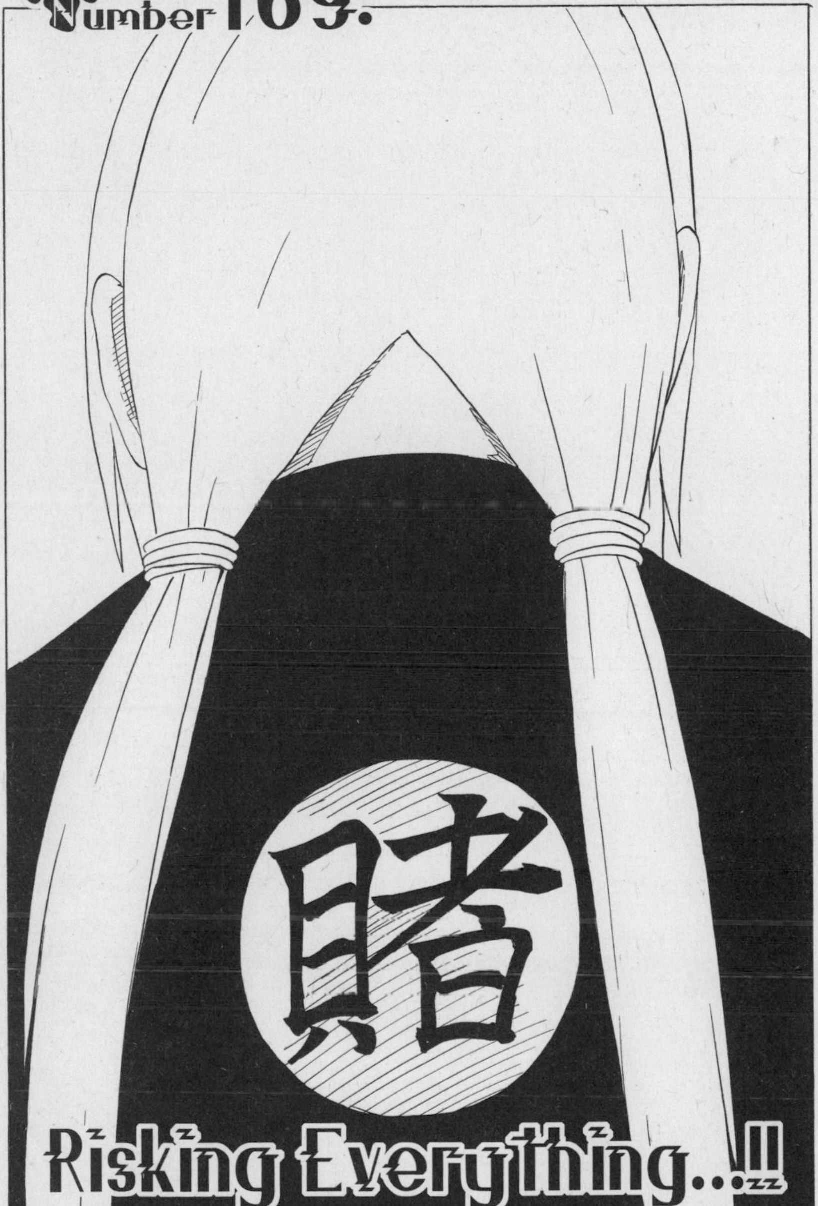
賭

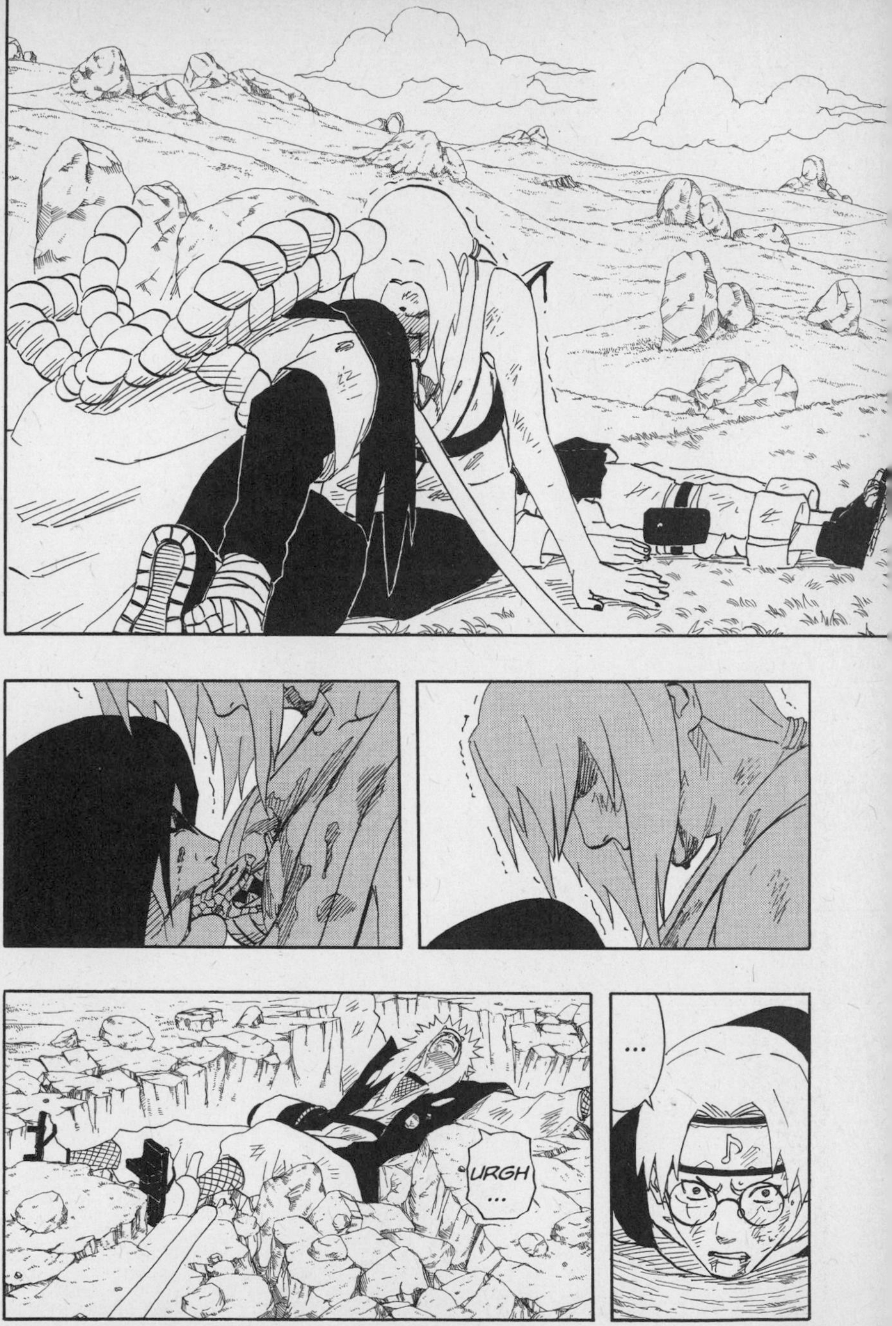
...
URGH ...

READ THIS WAY

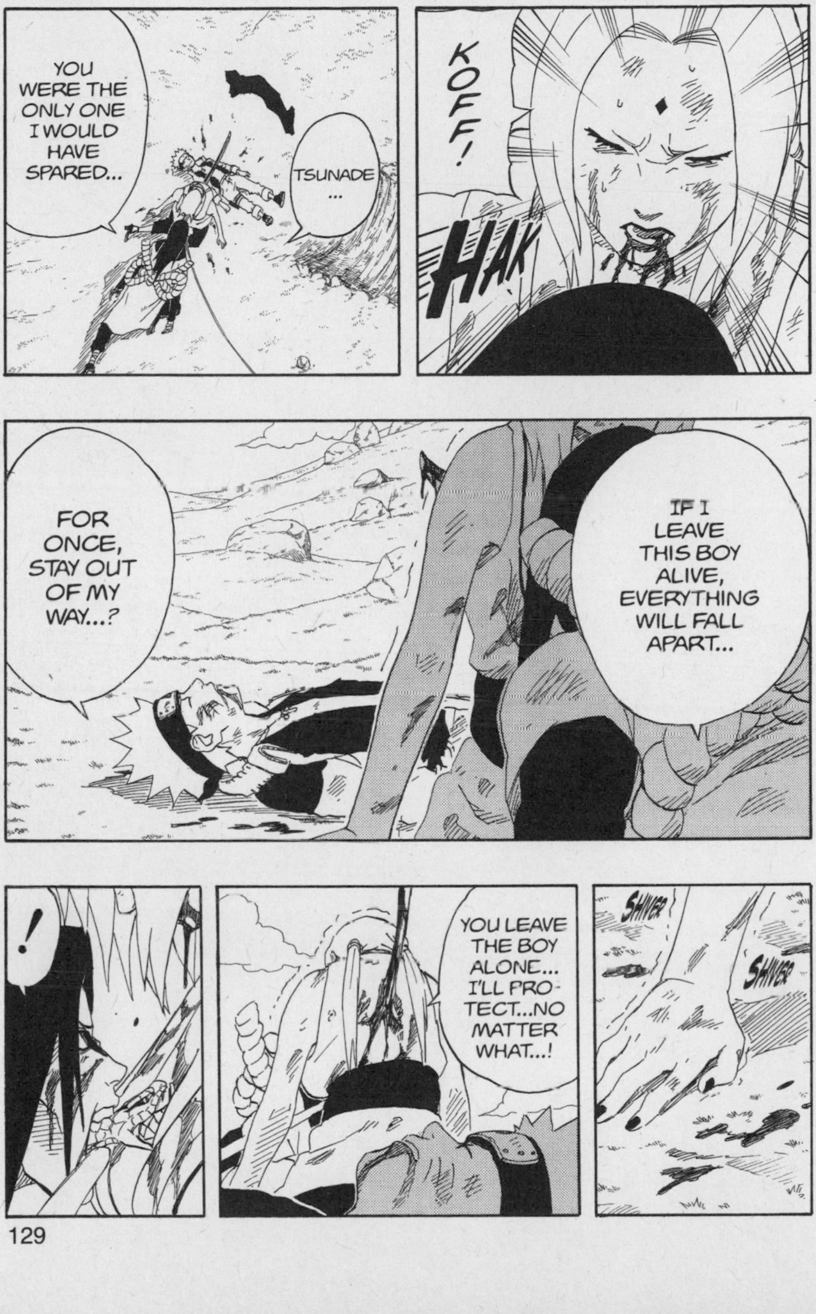
KOFF!
HAK
TSUNADE...
YOU WERE THE ONLY ONE I WOULD HAVE SPARED...
IF I LEAVE THIS BOY ALIVE, EVERYTHING WILL FALL APART...
FOR ONCE, STAY OUT OF MY WAY...?
SHIVER
SHIVER
YOU LEAVE THE BOY ALONE... I'LL PROTECT...NO MATTER WHAT...!
!

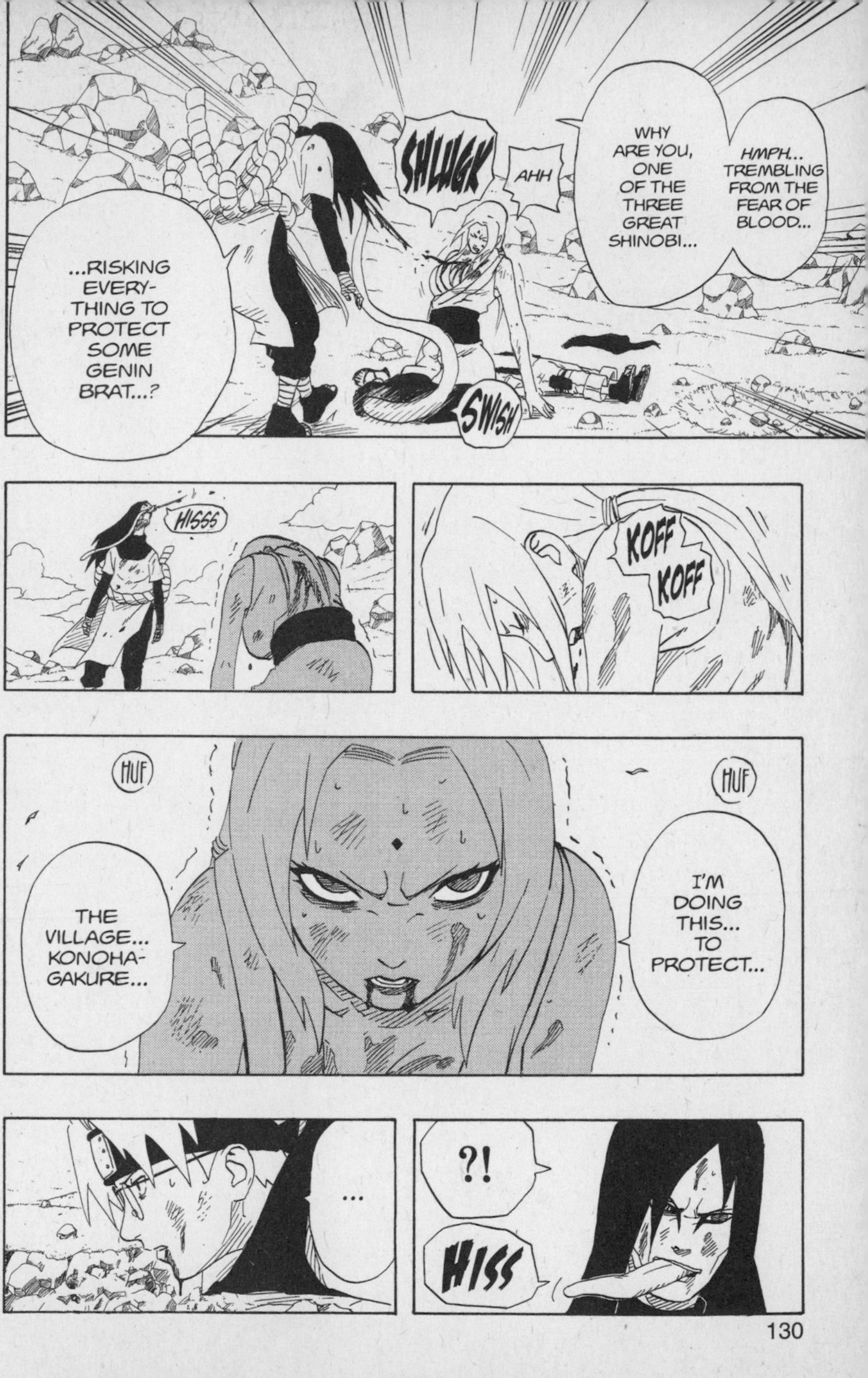

HMPH... TREMBLING FROM THE FEAR OF BLOOD...
WHY ARE YOU, ONE OF THE THREE GREAT SHINOBI...
AHH
SHLUGK
...RISKING EVERY-THING TO PROTECT SOME GENIN BRAT...?
SWISH
KOFF KOFF
HISSS
HUF
I'M DOING THIS... TO PROTECT...
HUF
THE VILLAGE... KONOHA-GAKURE...
?!
HISS
...

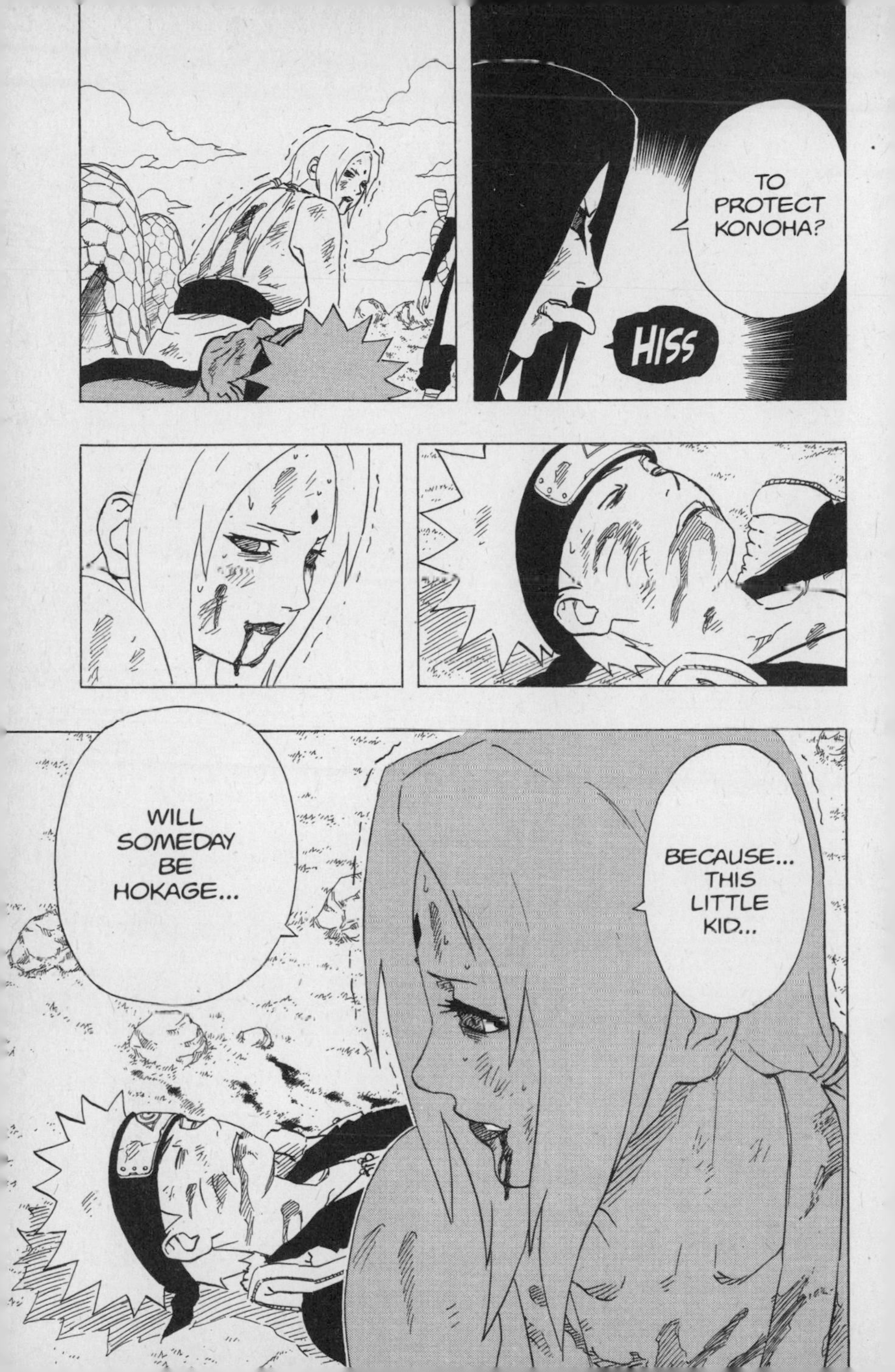
TO PROTECT KONOHA?
HISS
BECAUSE... THIS LITTLE KID...
WILL SOMEDAY BE HOKAGE...

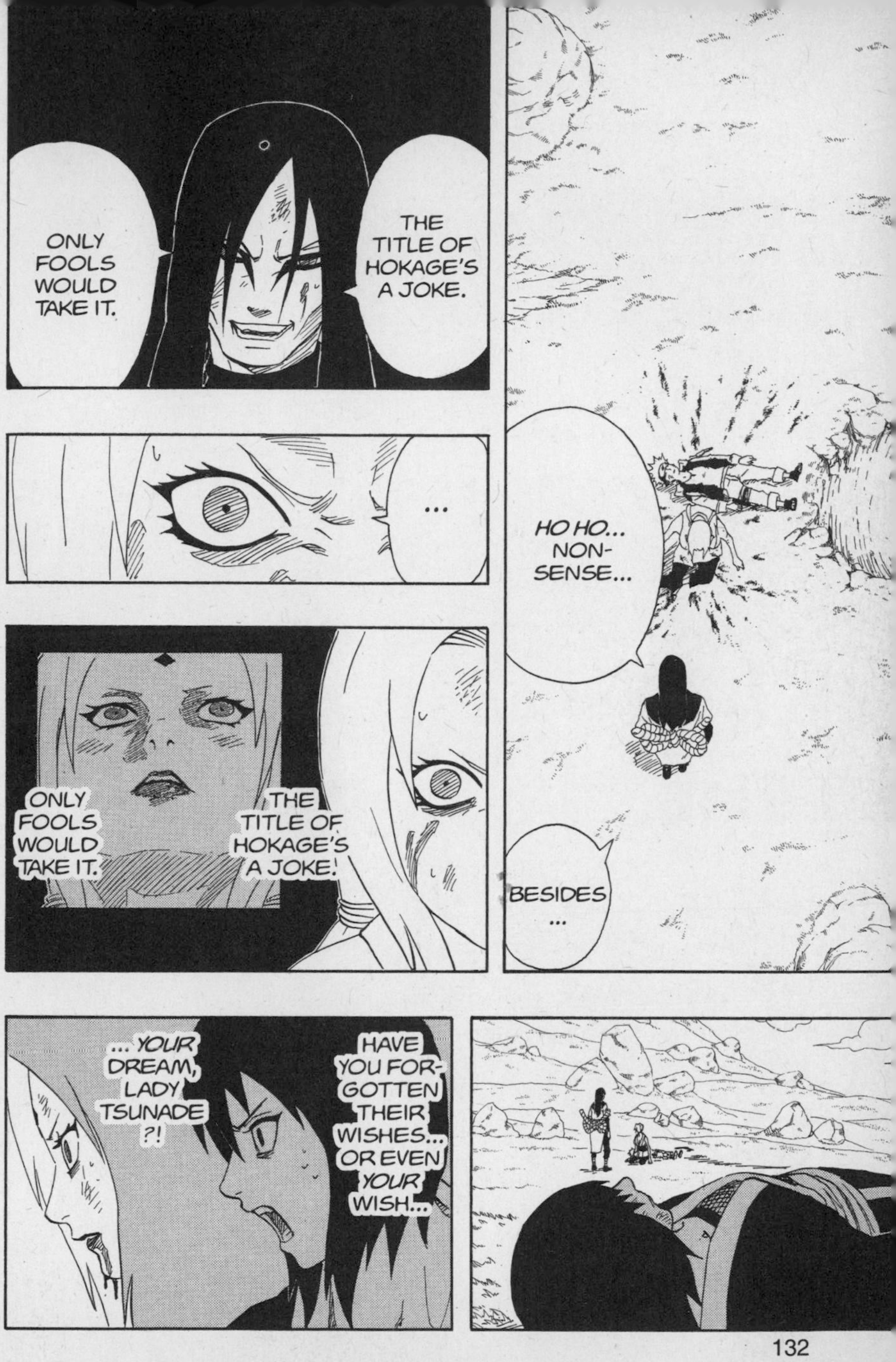
HO HO... NON-SENSE...
BESIDES ...
THE TITLE OF HOKAGE'S A JOKE.
ONLY FOOLS WOULD TAKE IT.
...
THE TITLE OF HOKAGE'S A JOKE!
ONLY FOOLS WOULD TAKE IT.
HAVE YOU FOR-GOTTEN THEIR WISHES... OR EVEN YOUR WISH...
... YOUR DREAM, LADY TSUNADE ?!

READ THIS WAY

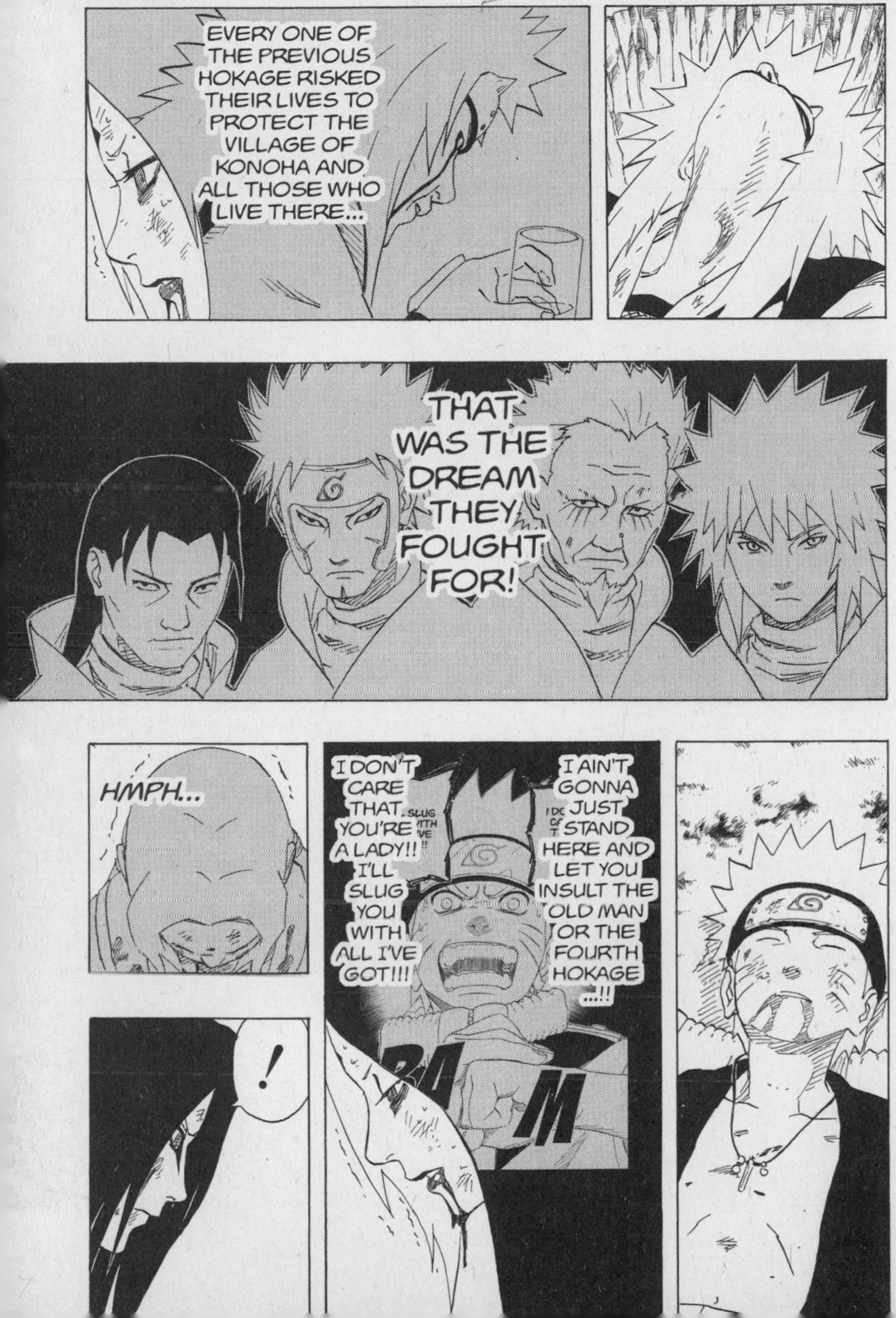
EVERY ONE OF THE PREVIOUS HOKAGE RISKED THEIR LIVES TO PROTECT THE VILLAGE OF KONOHA AND ALL THOSE WHO LIVE THERE...
THAT WAS THE DREAM THEY FOUGHT FOR!
I AIN'T GONNA JUST STAND HERE AND LET YOU INSULT THE OLD MAN OR THE FOURTH HOKAGE ...!!
I DON'T CARE THAT YOU'RE A LADY!! I'LL SLUG YOU WITH ALL I'VE GOT!!!
HMPH...
BAM
!

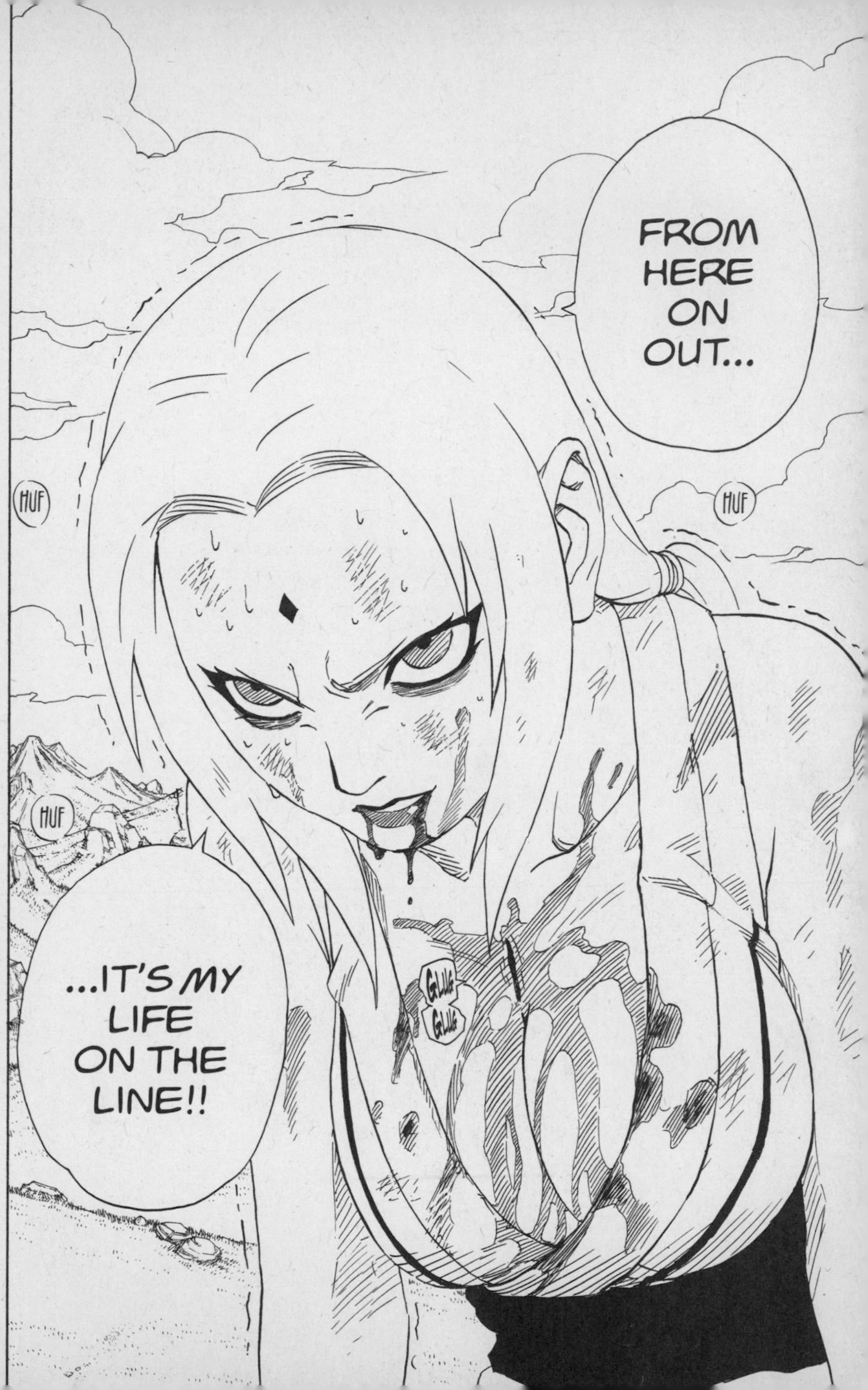
FROM HERE ON OUT...
HUF
HUF
HUF
GLUG
GLUG
...IT'S MY LIFE ON THE LINE!!

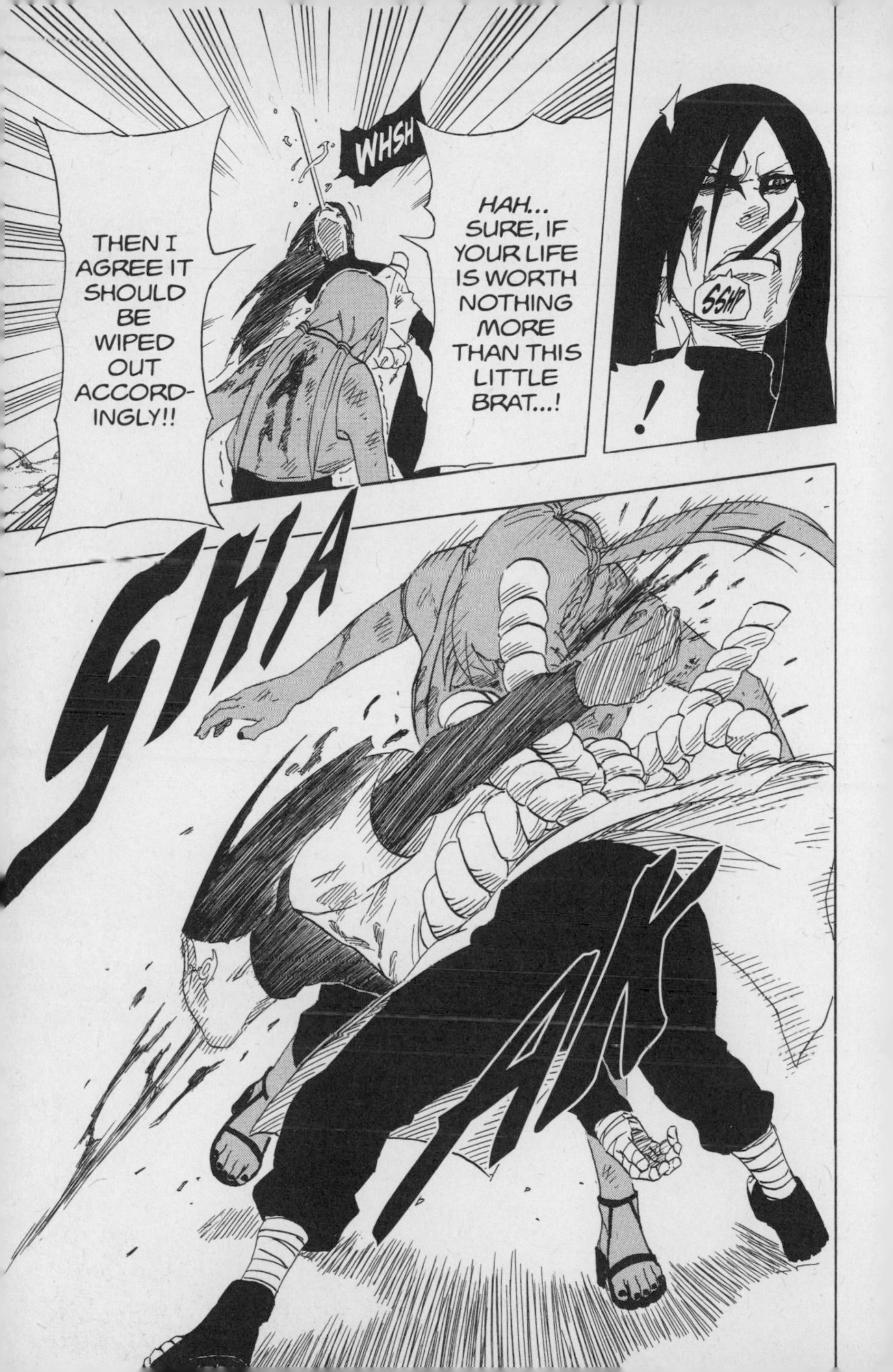
SSHP
!
HAH... SURE, IF YOUR LIFE IS WORTH NOTHING MORE THAN THIS LITTLE BRAT...!
WHSH
THEN I AGREE IT SHOULD BE WIPED OUT ACCORD-INGLY!!
SHA

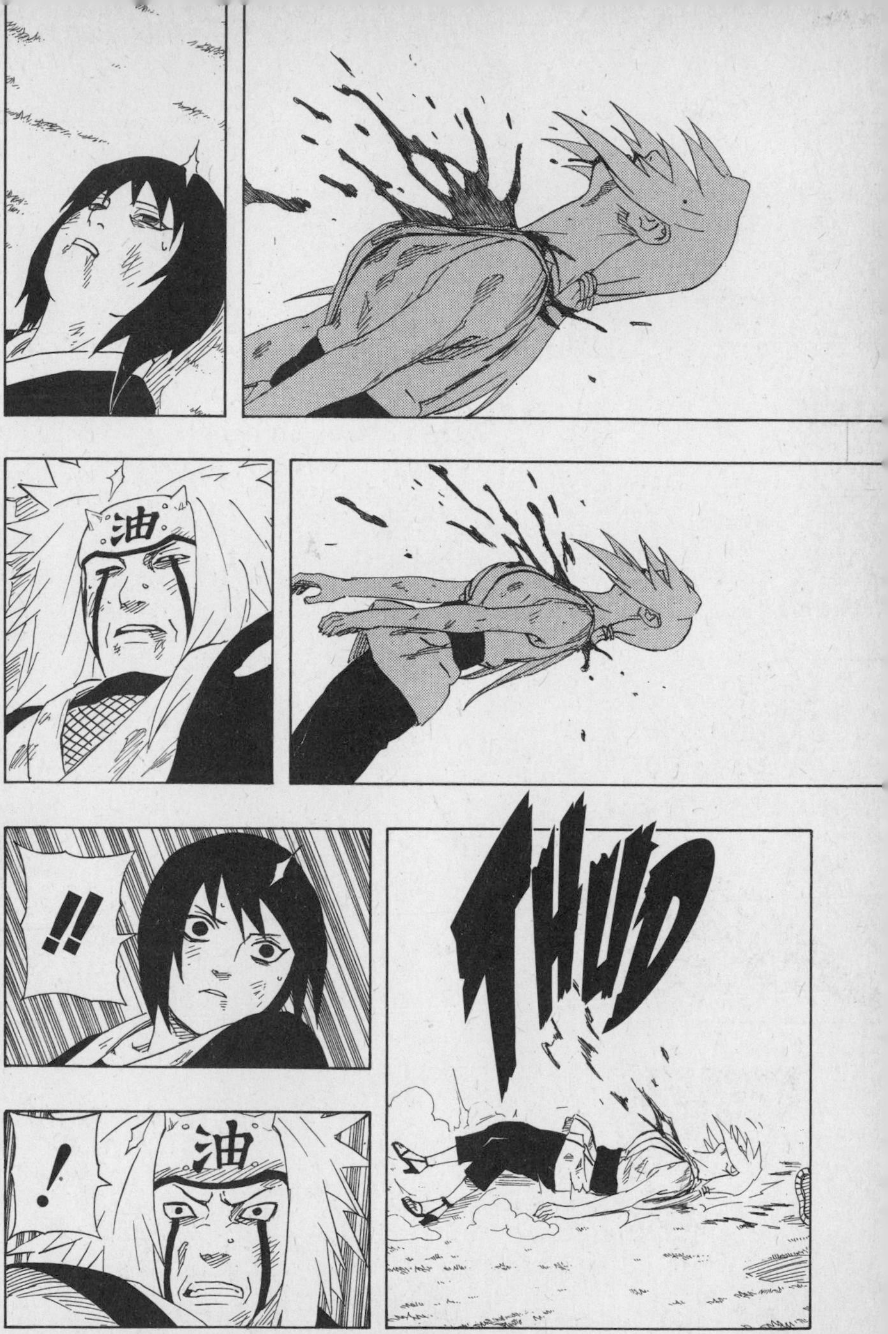
!!
!
THUD

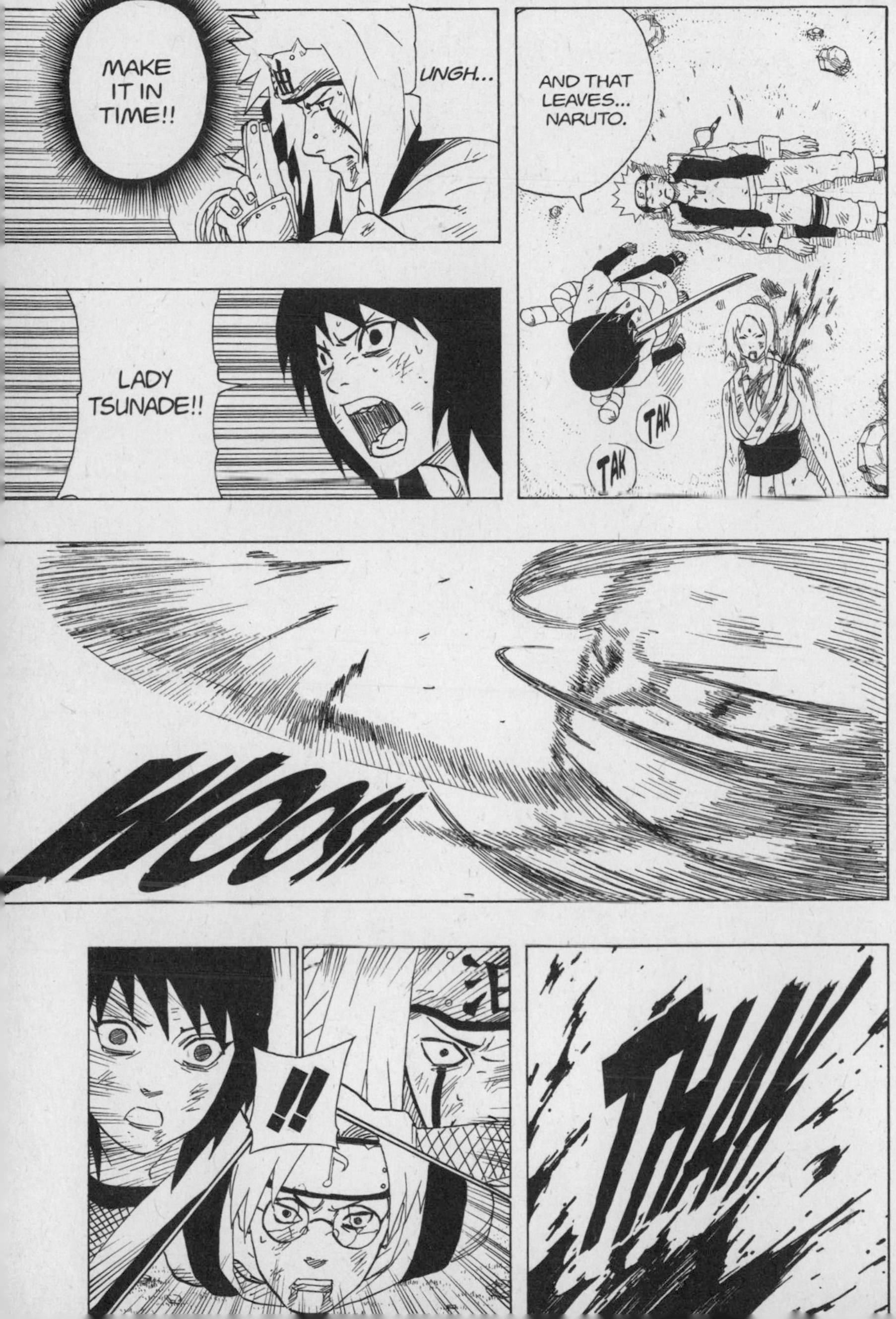
AND THAT LEAVES... NARUTO.
TAK
TAK
UNGH...
MAKE IT IN TIME!!
LADY TSUNADE!!
WOOSH
THAK
!!

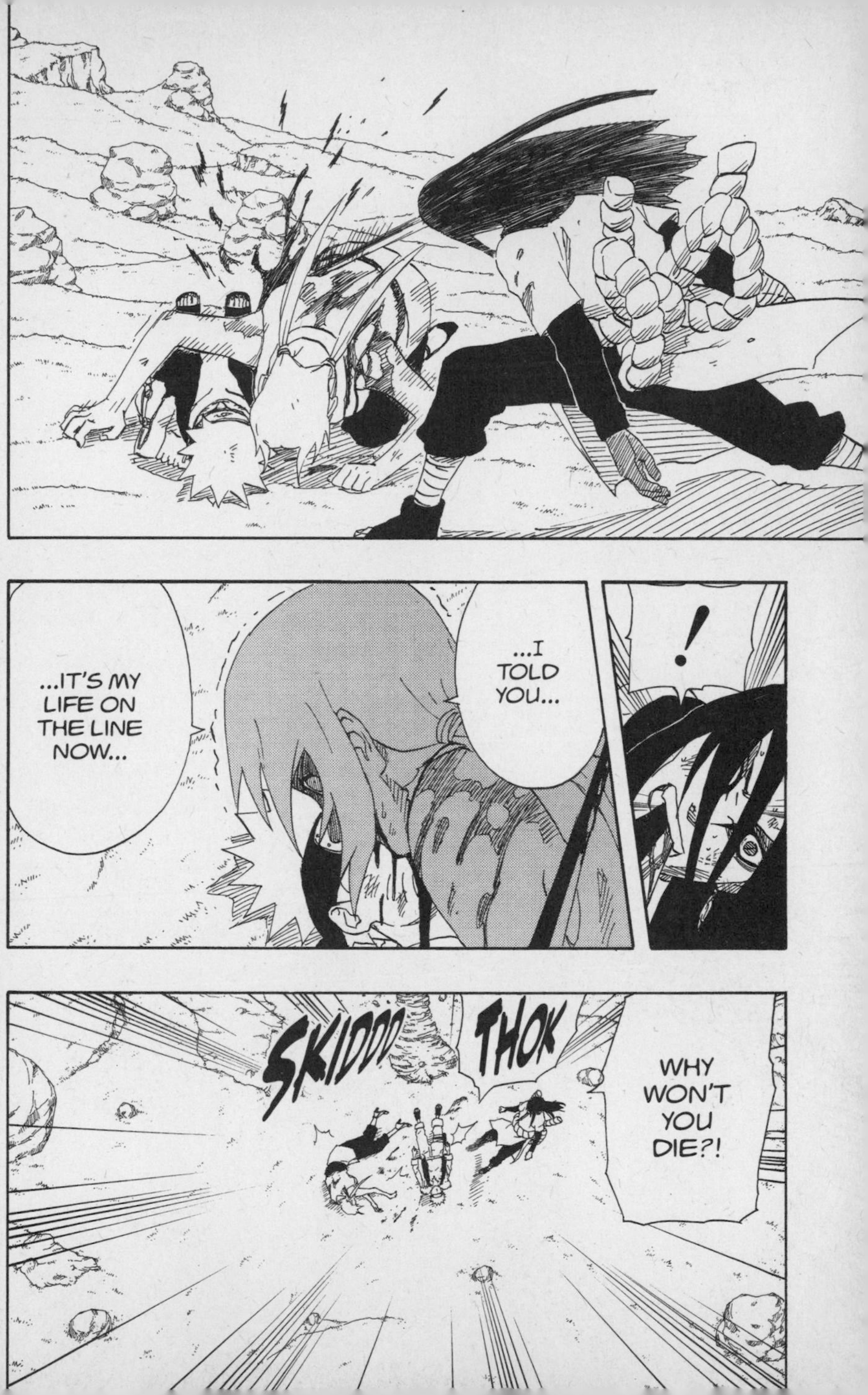
!
...I TOLD YOU...
...IT'S MY LIFE ON THE LINE NOW...
WHY WON'T YOU DIE?!
THOK
SKIDDD

READ THIS WAY

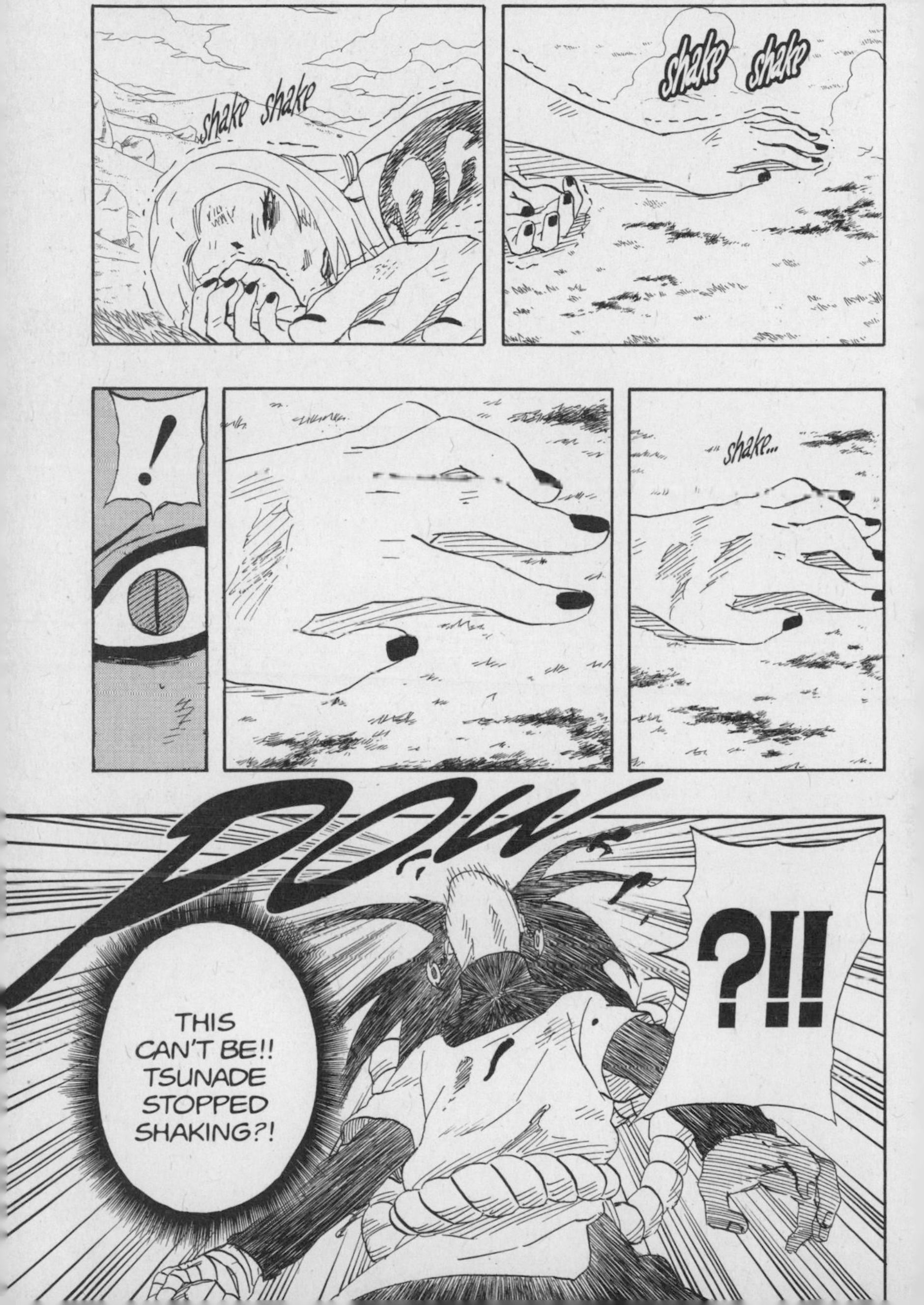

shake shake
shake shake
shake...
!
POW
?!!
THIS CAN'T BE!! TSUNADE STOPPED SHAKING?!

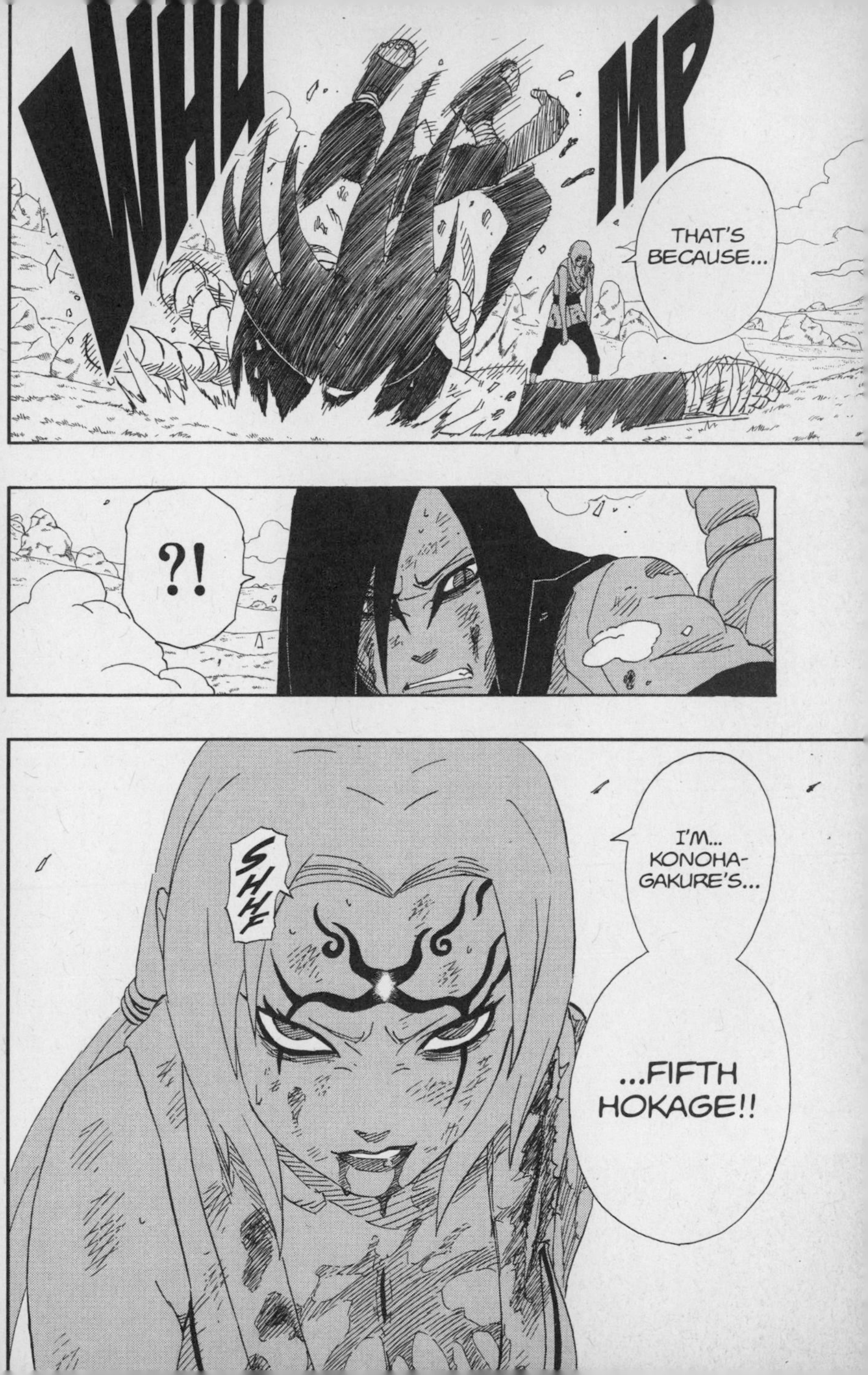
WHH
MP
THAT'S BECAUSE...
?!
SHHF
I'M... KONOHA-GAKURE'S...
...FIFTH HOKAGE!!

READ THIS WAY

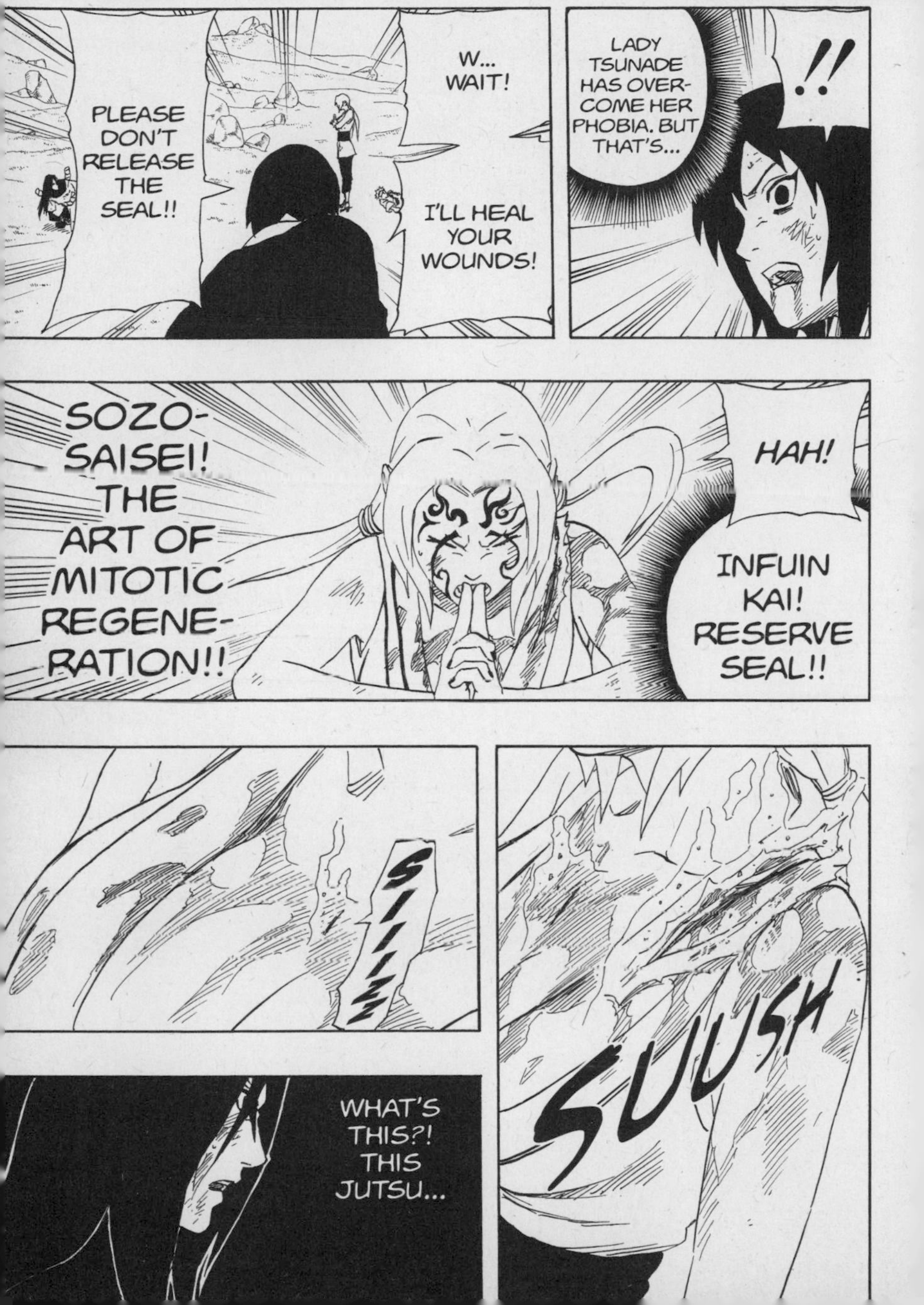

LADY TSUNADE HAS OVERCOME HER PHOBIA. BUT THAT'S...
!!
W... WAIT!
I'LL HEAL YOUR WOUNDS!
PLEASE DON'T RELEASE THE SEAL!!
HAH!
INFUIN KAI! RESERVE SEAL!!
SOZO-SAISEI! THE ART OF MITOTIC REGENERATION!!
SUUSH
SIIIZZ
WHAT'S THIS?! THIS JUTSU...

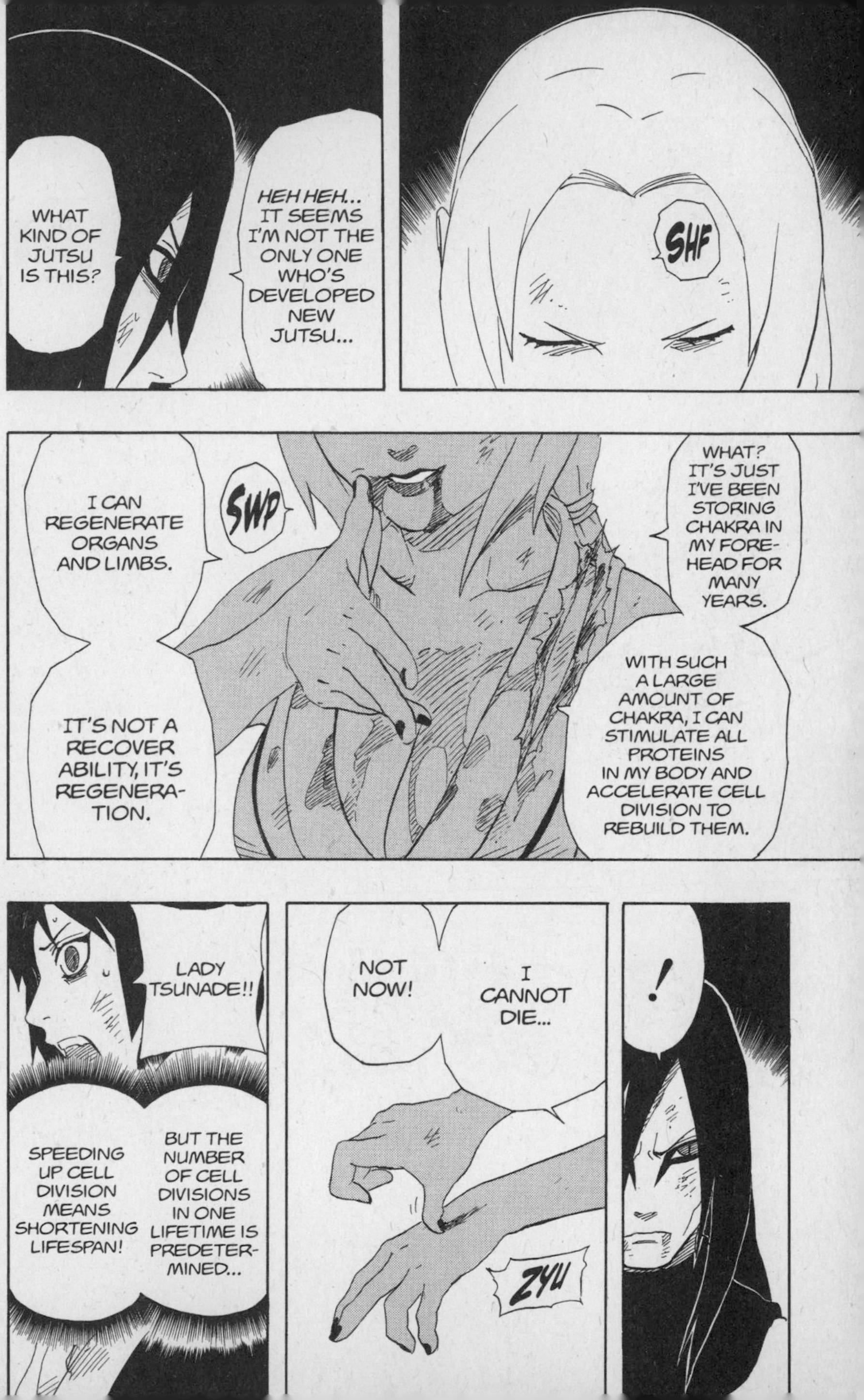
SHF
HEH HEH... IT SEEMS I'M NOT THE ONLY ONE WHO'S DEVELOPED NEW JUTSU...
WHAT KIND OF JUTSU IS THIS?
WHAT? IT'S JUST I'VE BEEN STORING CHAKRA IN MY FORE-HEAD FOR MANY YEARS.
WITH SUCH A LARGE AMOUNT OF CHAKRA, I CAN STIMULATE ALL PROTEINS IN MY BODY AND ACCELERATE CELL DIVISION TO REBUILD THEM.
SWP
I CAN REGENERATE ORGANS AND LIMBS.
IT'S NOT A RECOVER ABILITY, IT'S REGENERA-TION.
!
I CANNOT DIE...
NOT NOW!
ZYU
LADY TSUNADE!!
BUT THE NUMBER OF CELL DIVISIONS IN ONE LIFETIME IS PREDETER-MINED...
SPEEDING UP CELL DIVISION MEANS SHORTENING LIFESPAN!

READ THIS WAY

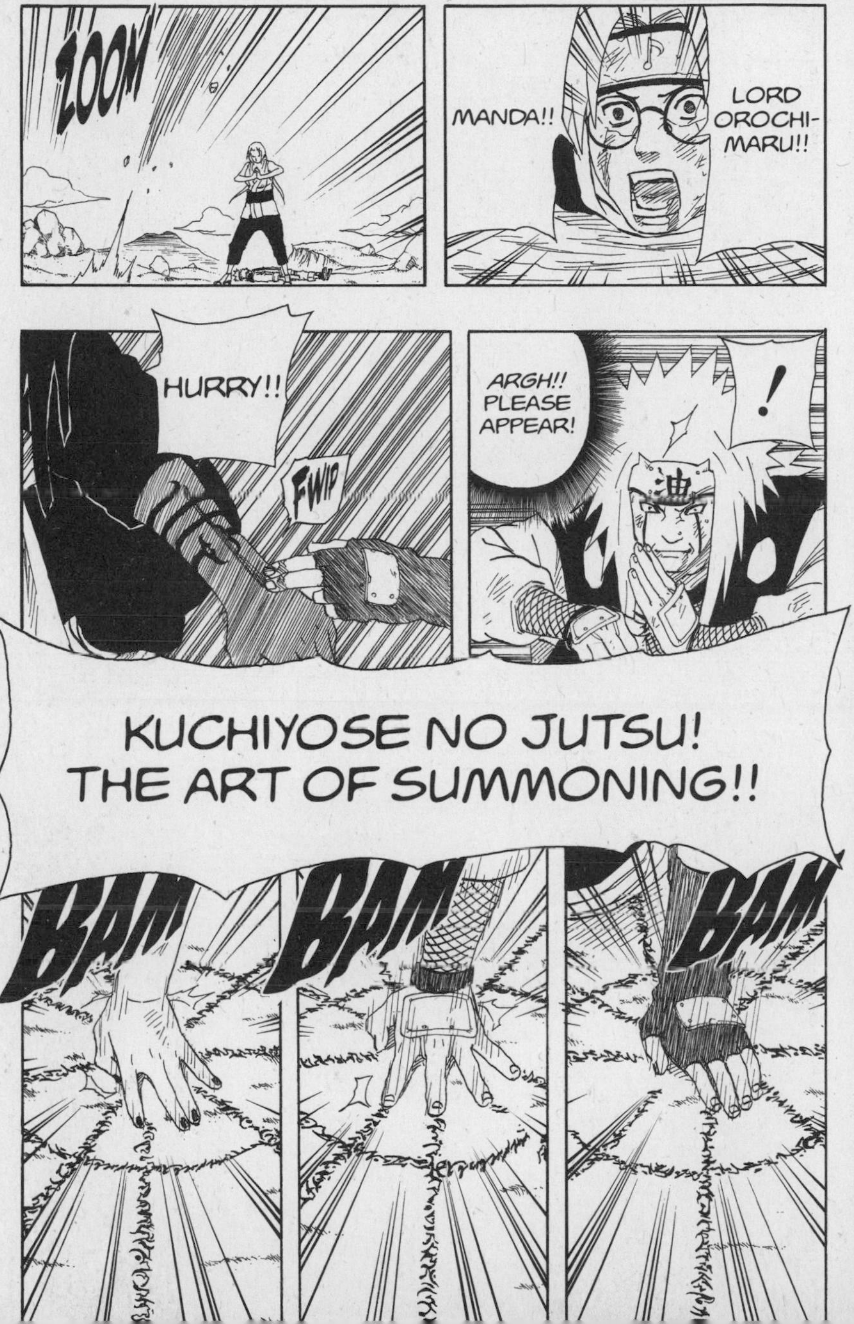
LORD OROCHI-MARU!!
MANDA!!
ZOOM
!
ARGH!! PLEASE APPEAR!
HURRY!!
FWIP
KUCHIYOSE NO JUTSU! THE ART OF SUMMONING!!
BAM
BAM
BAM

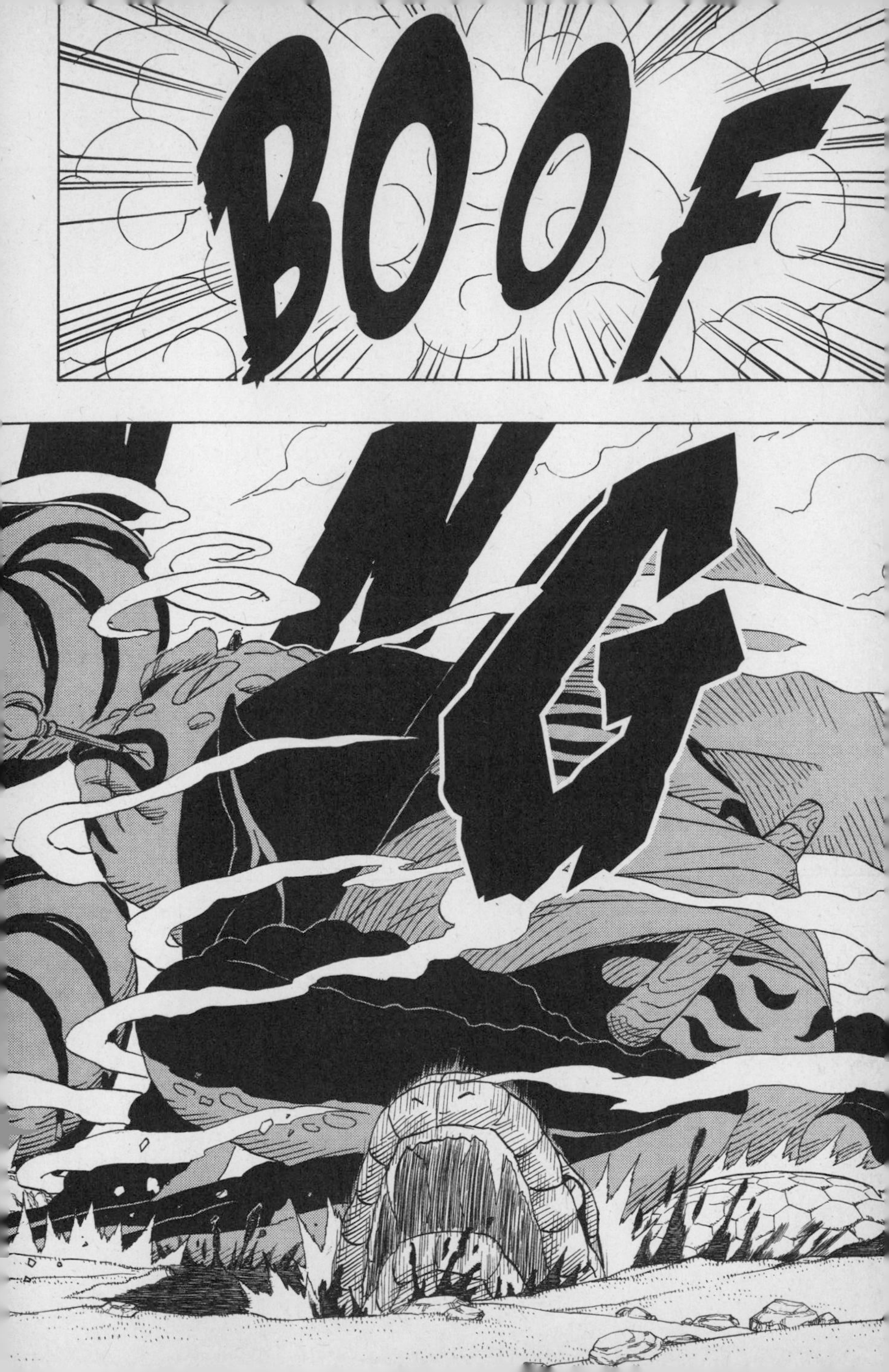
BOOF

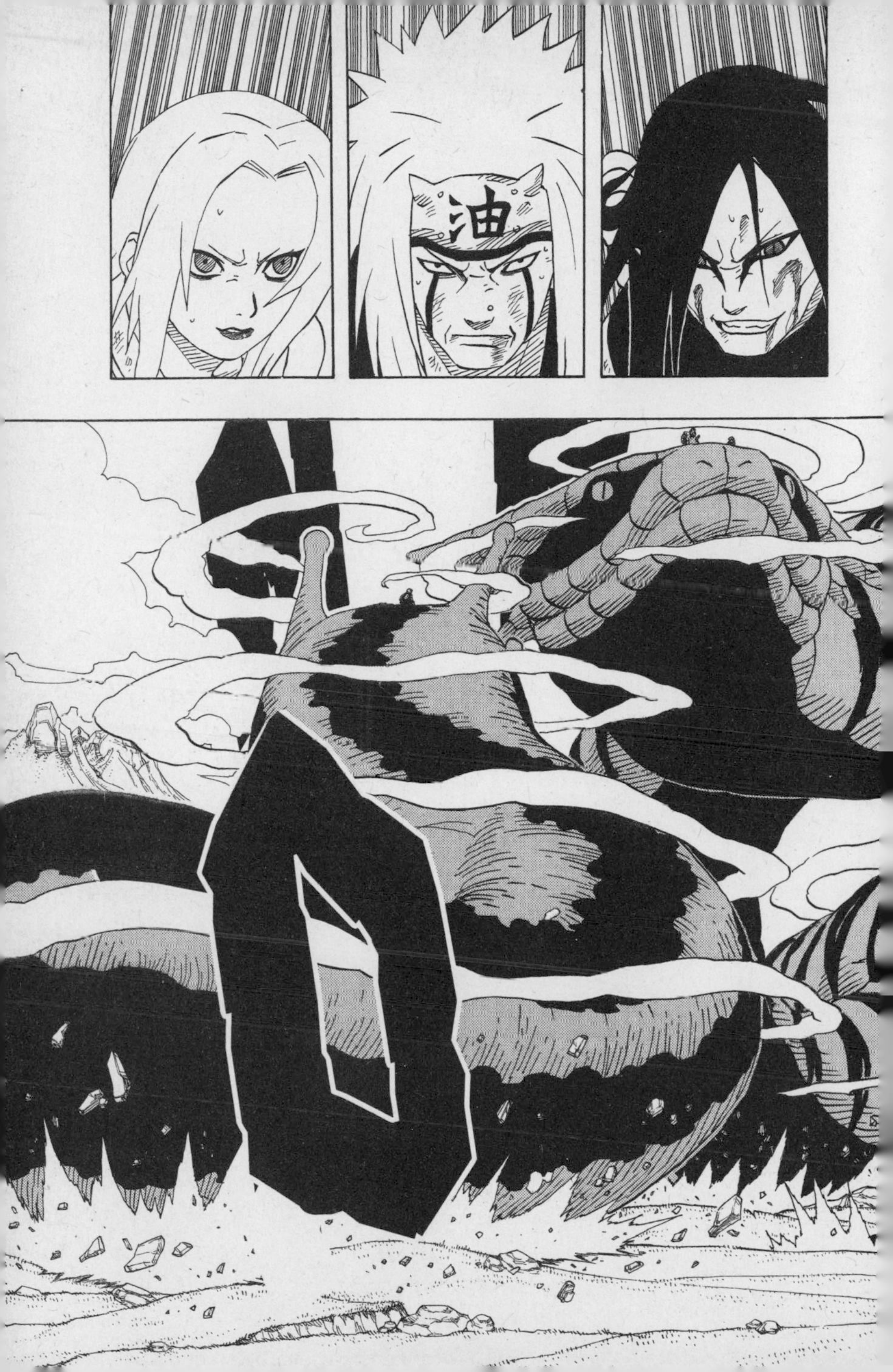
油

Number 170: Deadlock!!!

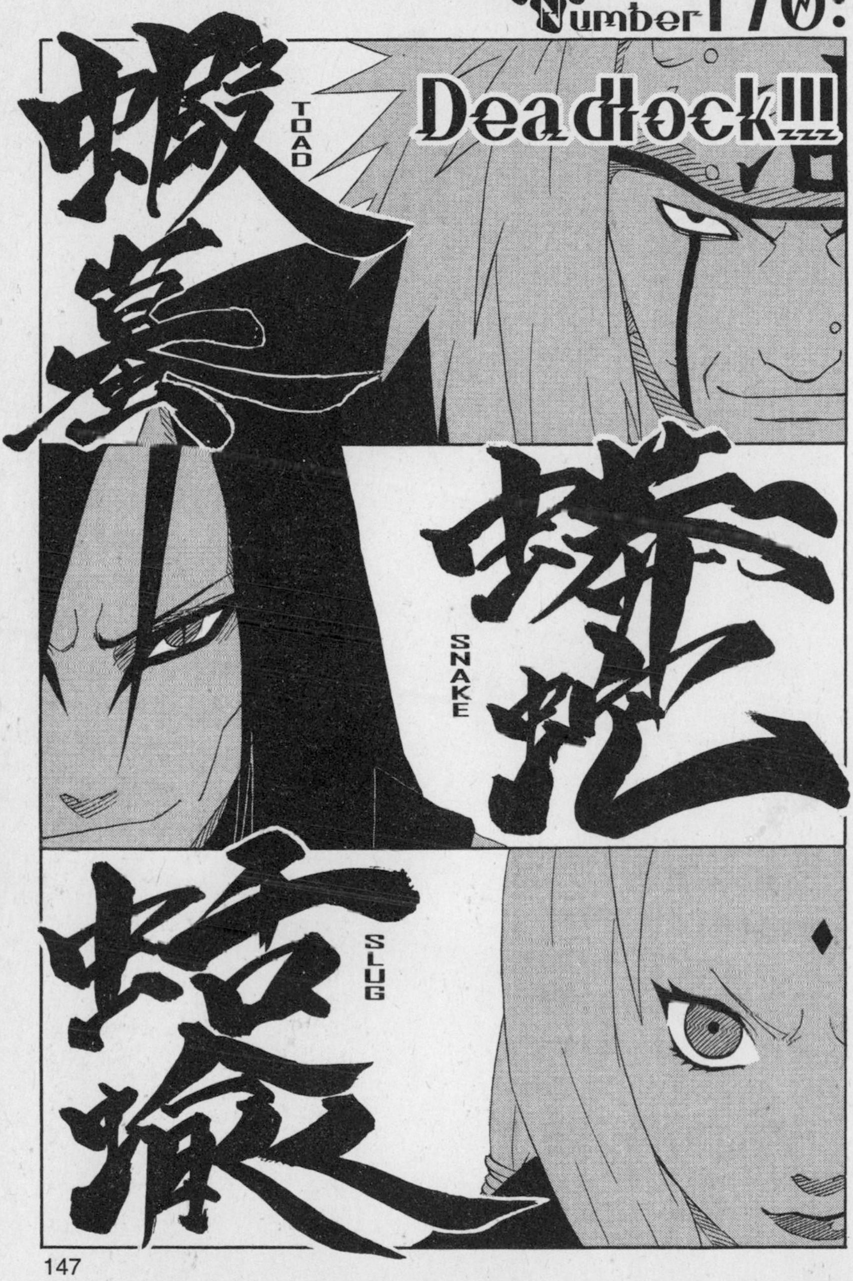
蝦蟇
TOAD
蟒蛇
SNAKE
蛞蝓
SLUG

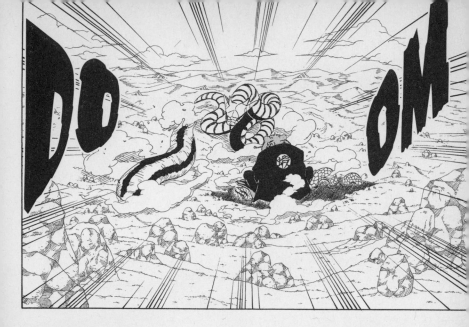

NO! GAMA-TATSU...

WE'RE GETTING OUTTA HERE!!

HEY! IT'S DAD!!

READ THIS WAY

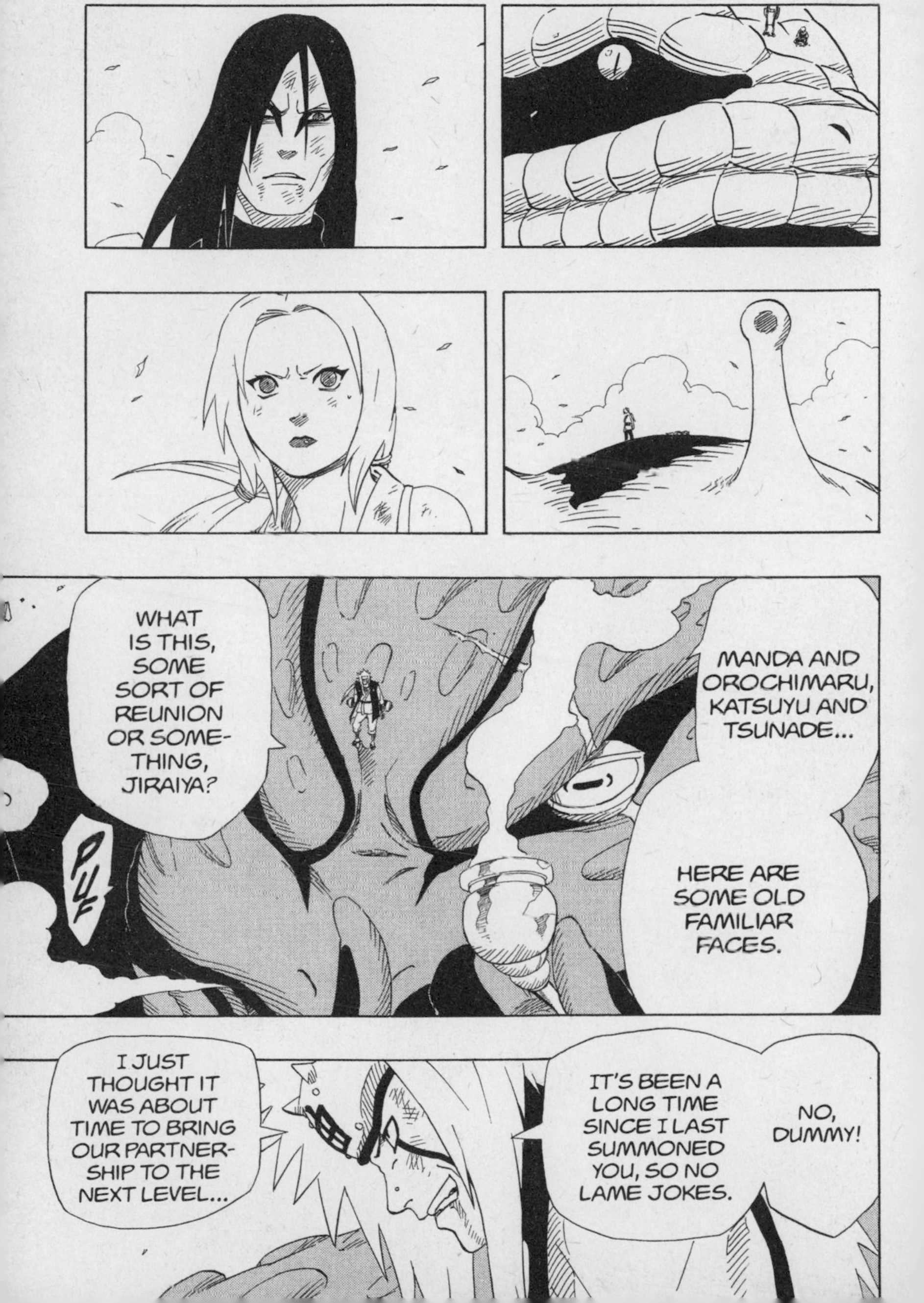
MANDA AND OROCHIMARU, KATSUYU AND TSUNADE...
HERE ARE SOME OLD FAMILIAR FACES.
WHAT IS THIS, SOME SORT OF REUNION OR SOME-THING, JIRAIYA?
PUF
NO, DUMMY!
IT'S BEEN A LONG TIME SINCE I LAST SUMMONED YOU, SO NO LAME JOKES.
I JUST THOUGHT IT WAS ABOUT TIME TO BRING OUR PARTNER-SHIP TO THE NEXT LEVEL...

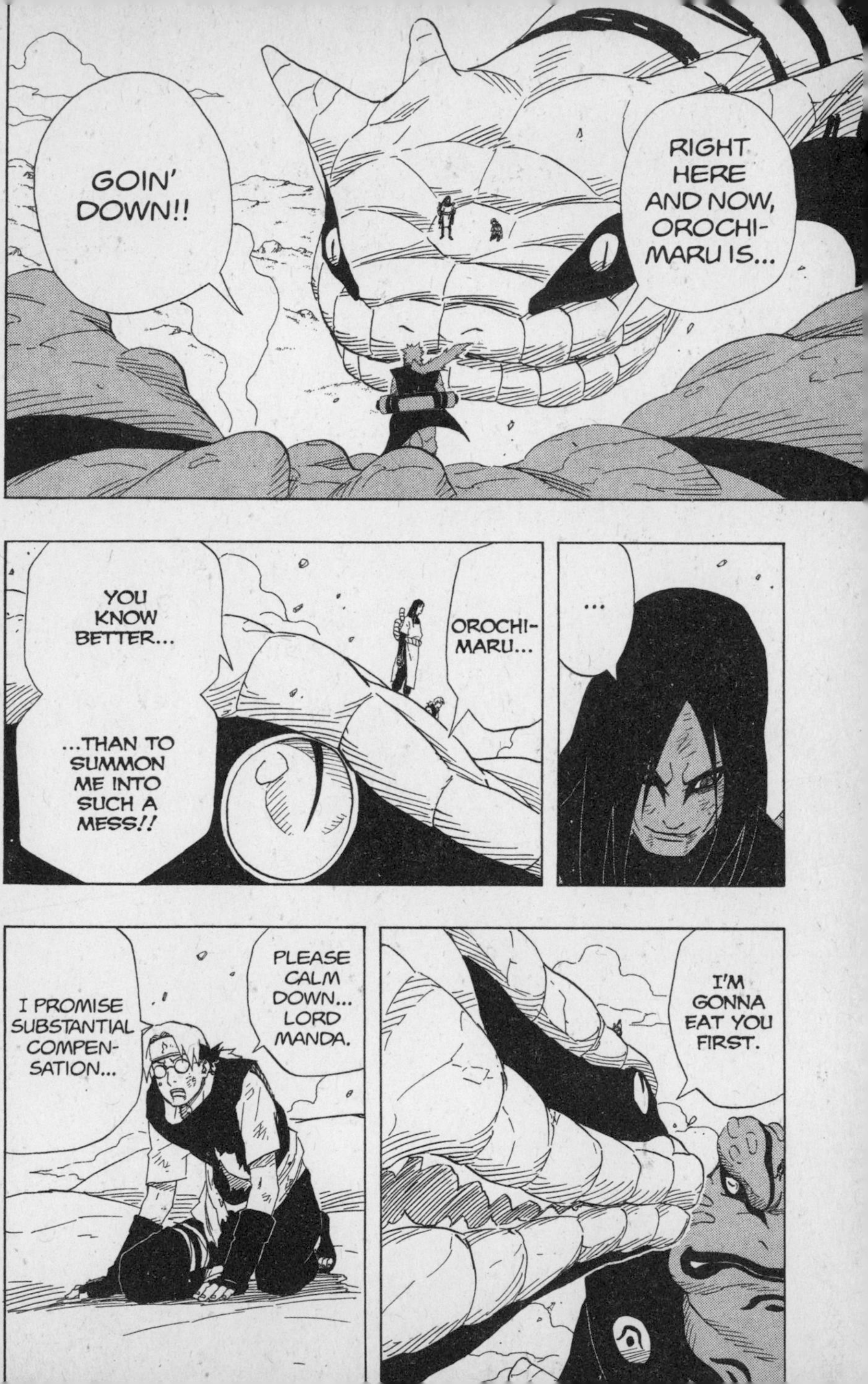
RIGHT HERE AND NOW, OROCHI-MARU IS...
GOIN' DOWN!!
...
OROCHI-MARU...
YOU KNOW BETTER...
...THAN TO SUMMON ME INTO SUCH A MESS!!
I'M GONNA EAT YOU FIRST.
PLEASE CALM DOWN... LORD MANDA.
I PROMISE SUBSTANTIAL COMPEN-SATION...

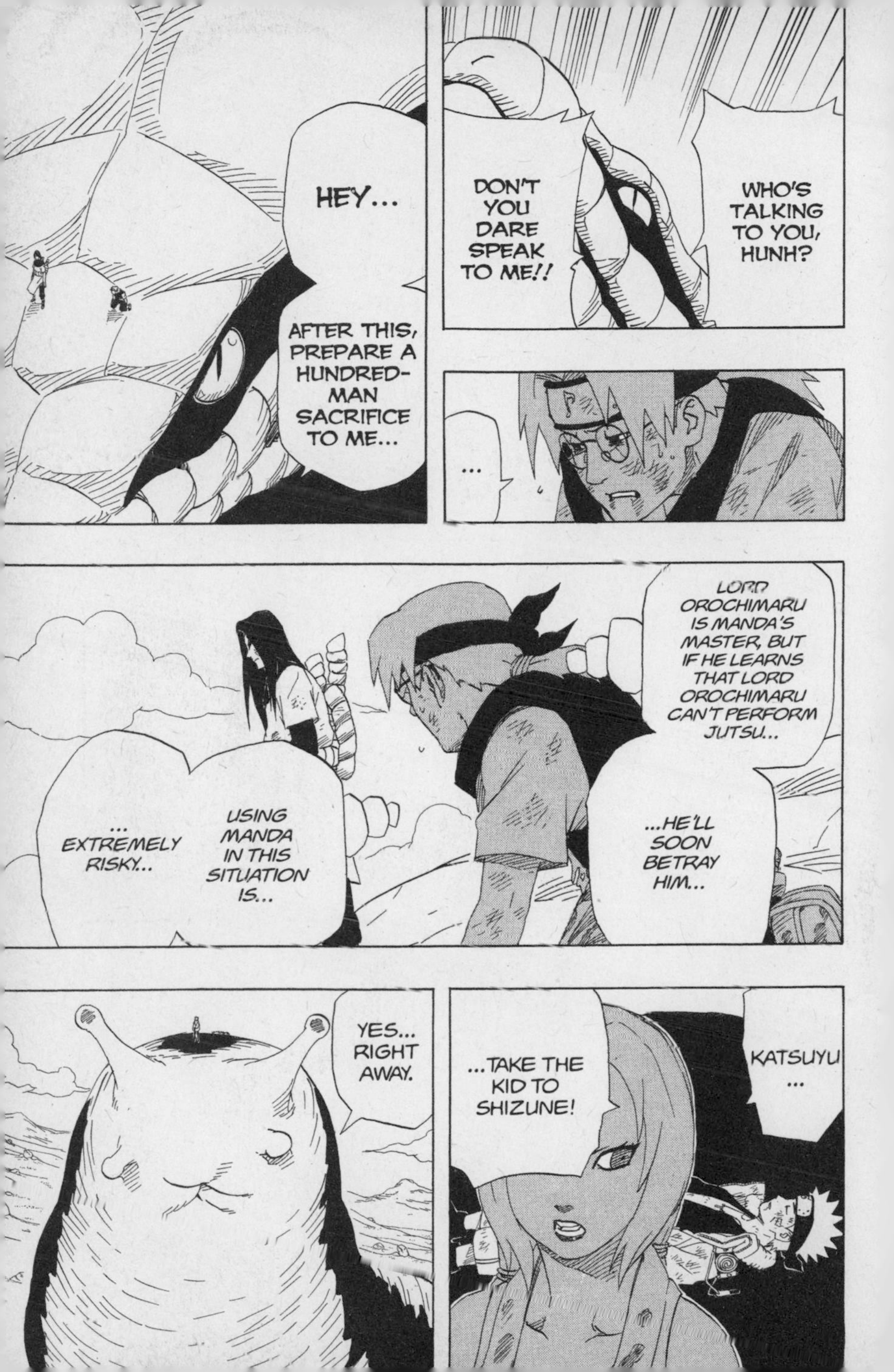

WHO'S TALKING TO YOU, HUNH?
DON'T YOU DARE SPEAK TO ME!!
...
HEY...
AFTER THIS, PREPARE A HUNDRED-MAN SACRIFICE TO ME...
LORD OROCHIMARU IS MANDA'S MASTER, BUT IF HE LEARNS THAT LORD OROCHIMARU CAN'T PERFORM JUTSU...
...HE'LL SOON BETRAY HIM...
USING MANDA IN THIS SITUATION IS...
...EXTREMELY RISKY...
KATSUYU...
...TAKE THE KID TO SHIZUNE!
YES... RIGHT AWAY.

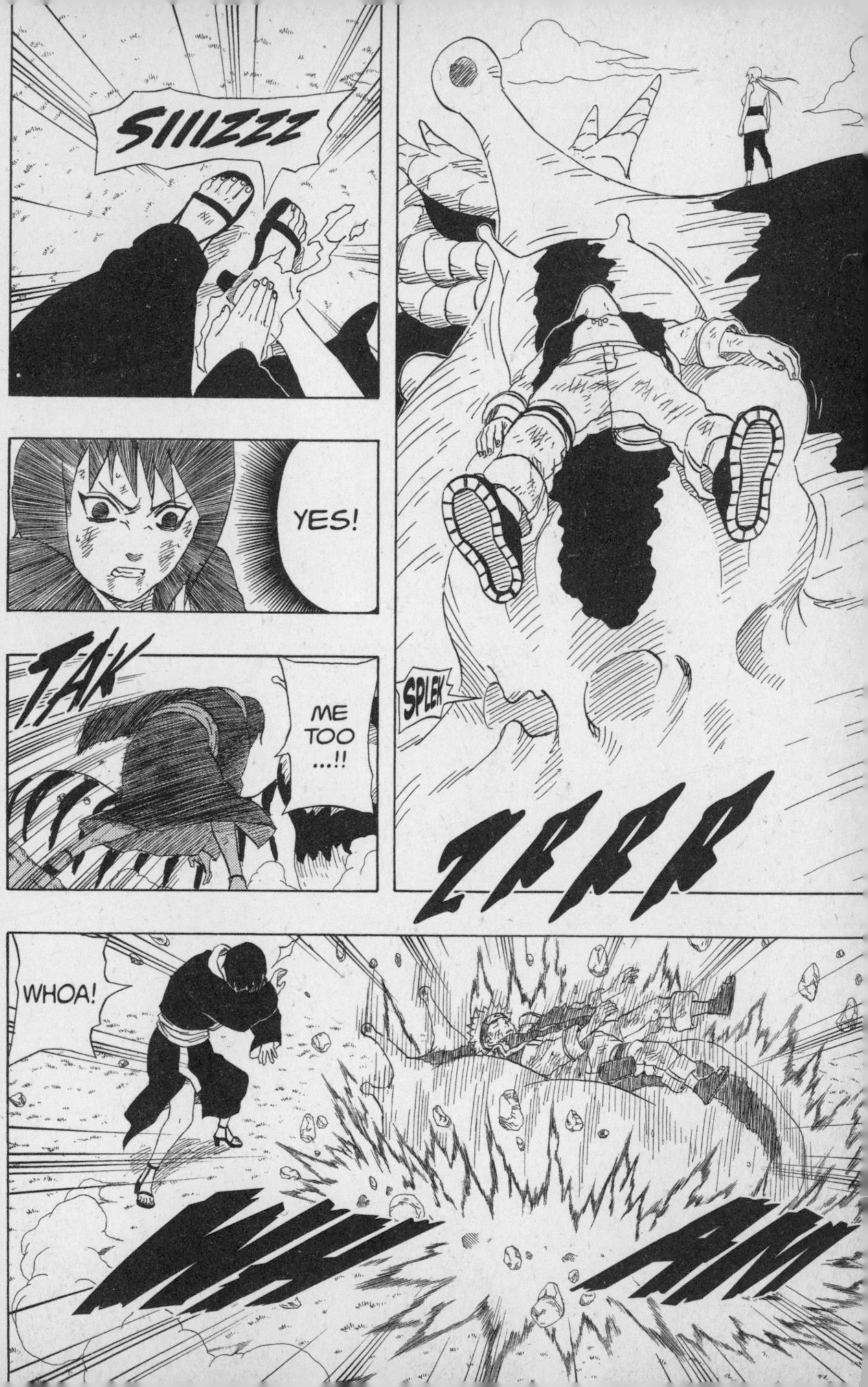
SPLEK
ZRRR
SIIIZZZ
YES!
ME TOO ...!!
TAK
WHOA!
WHAM

READ THIS WAY

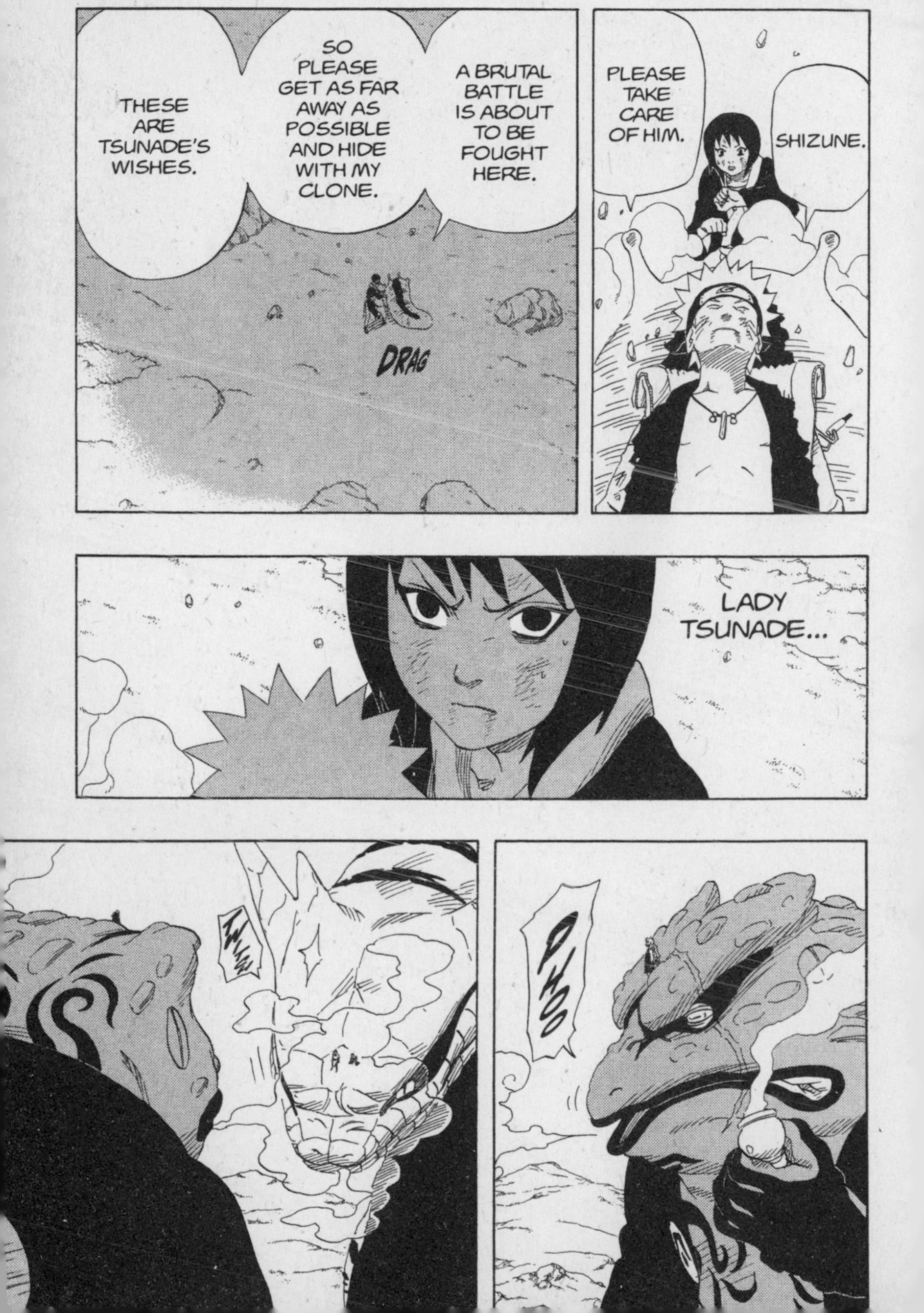
SHIZUNE.
PLEASE TAKE CARE OF HIM.
A BRUTAL BATTLE IS ABOUT TO BE FOUGHT HERE.
SO PLEASE GET AS FAR AWAY AS POSSIBLE AND HIDE WITH MY CLONE.
THESE ARE TSUNADE'S WISHES.
DRAG
LADY TSUNADE...

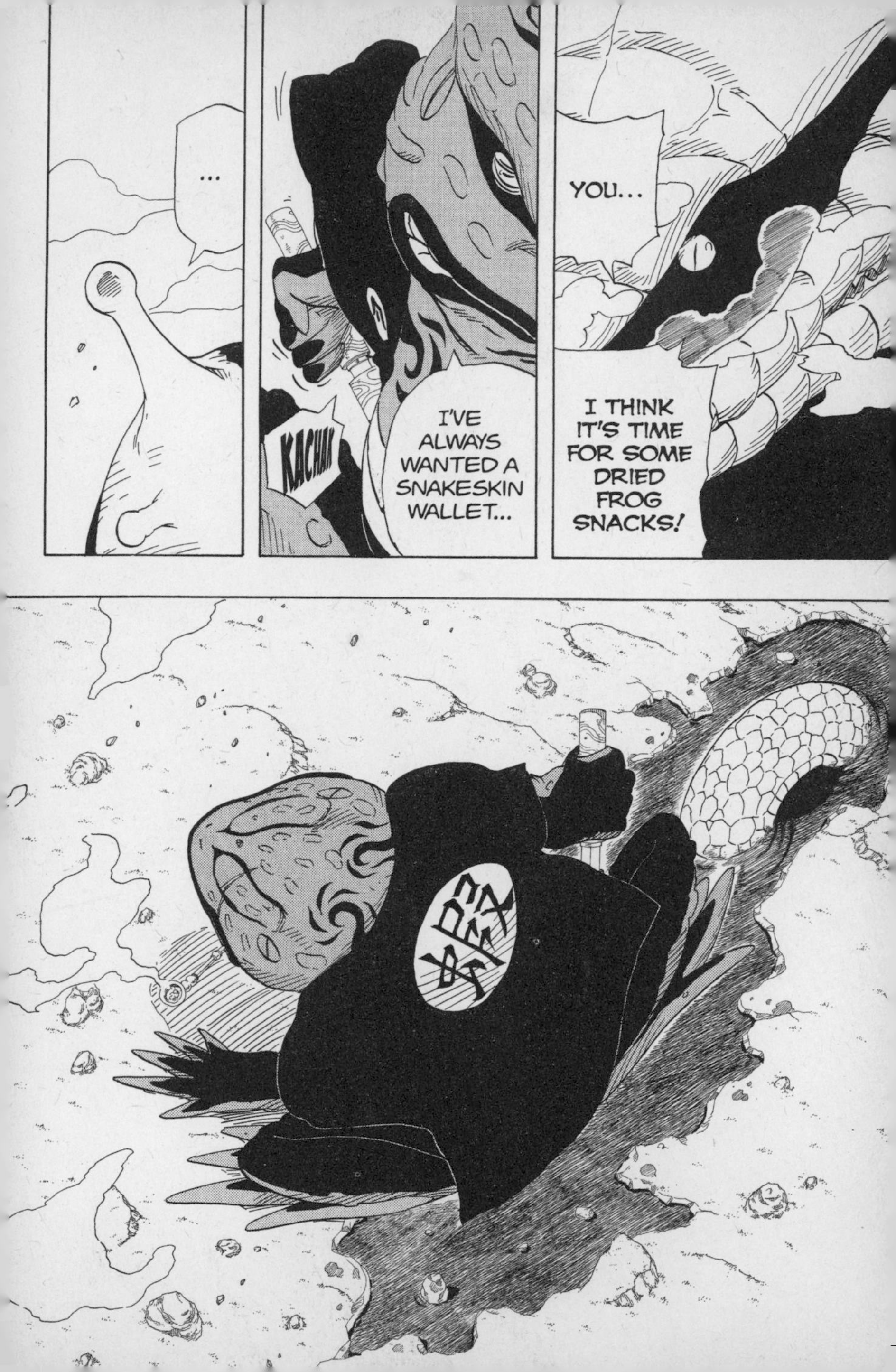
YOU...
I THINK IT'S TIME FOR SOME DRIED FROG SNACKS!
KACHAK
I'VE ALWAYS WANTED A SNAKESKIN WALLET...
...

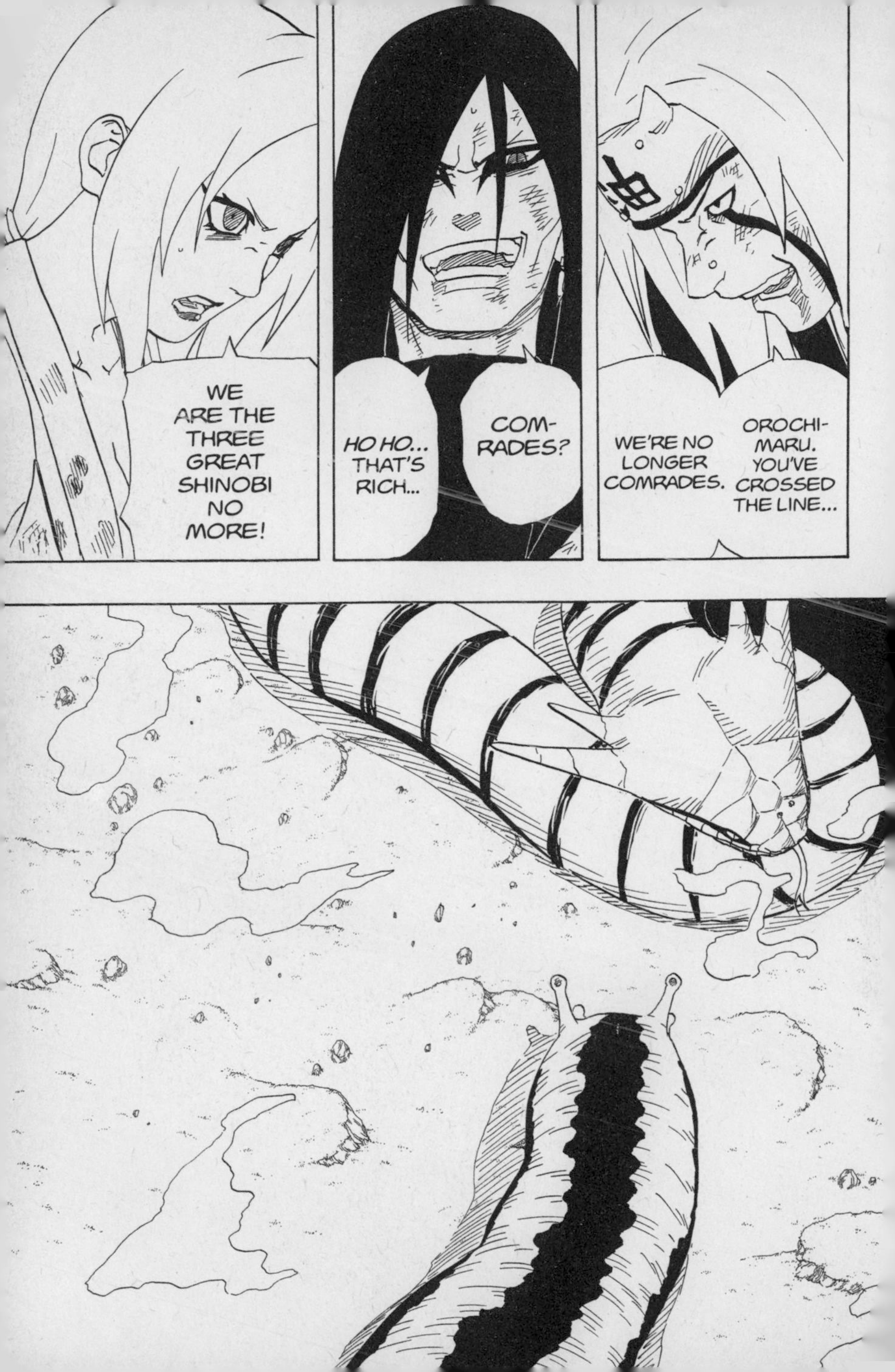
OROCHIMARU. YOU'VE CROSSED THE LINE...
WE'RE NO LONGER COMRADES.
COMRADES?
HO HO... THAT'S RICH...
WE ARE THE THREE GREAT SHINOBI NO MORE!

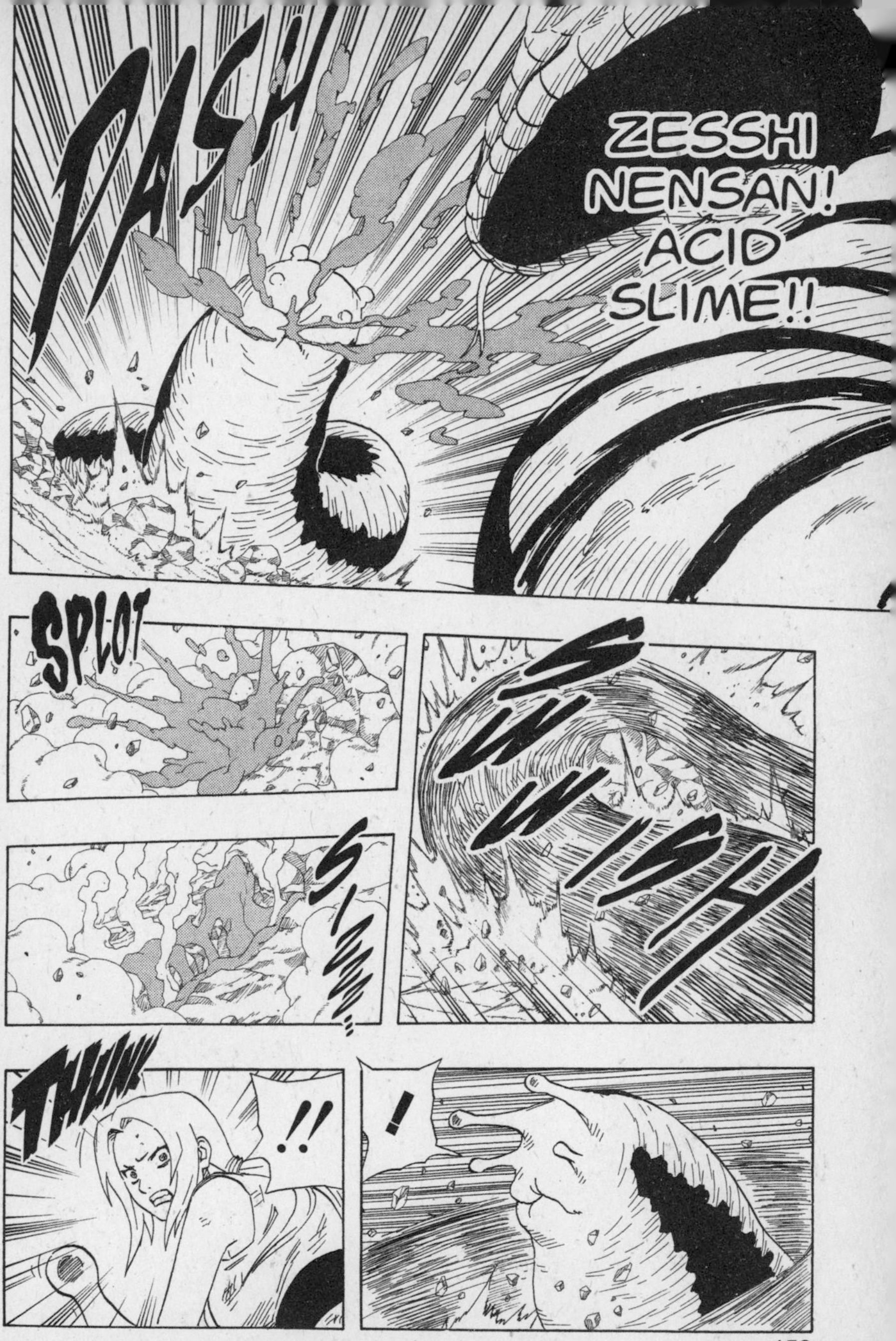
ZESSHI NENSAN! ACID SLIME!!
DASH
SWISH
SPLOT
!
!!
THUNK

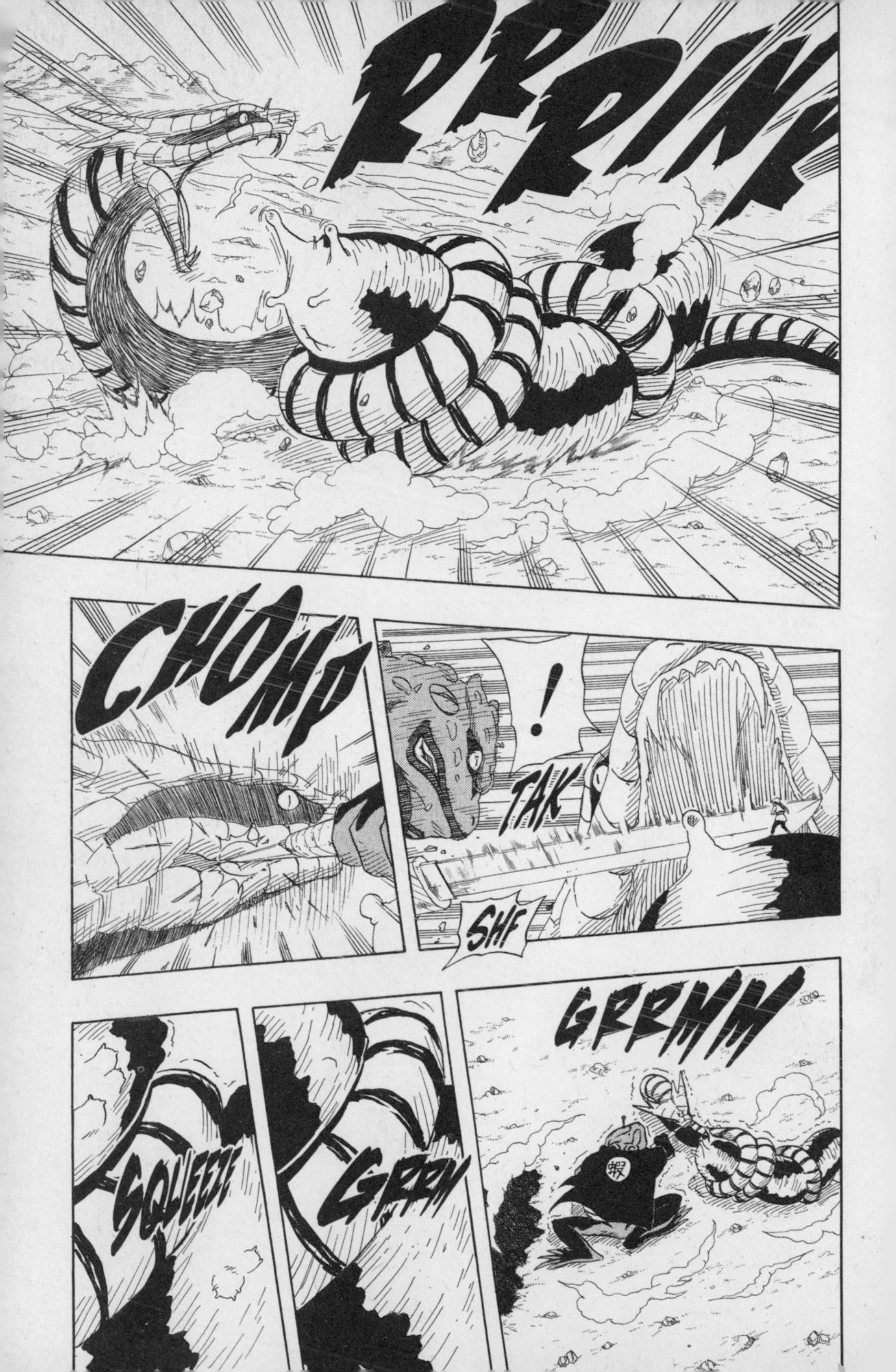
PRRIN
!
TAK
SHF
CHOMP
GRRMM
GRRM
SQUEEEZE

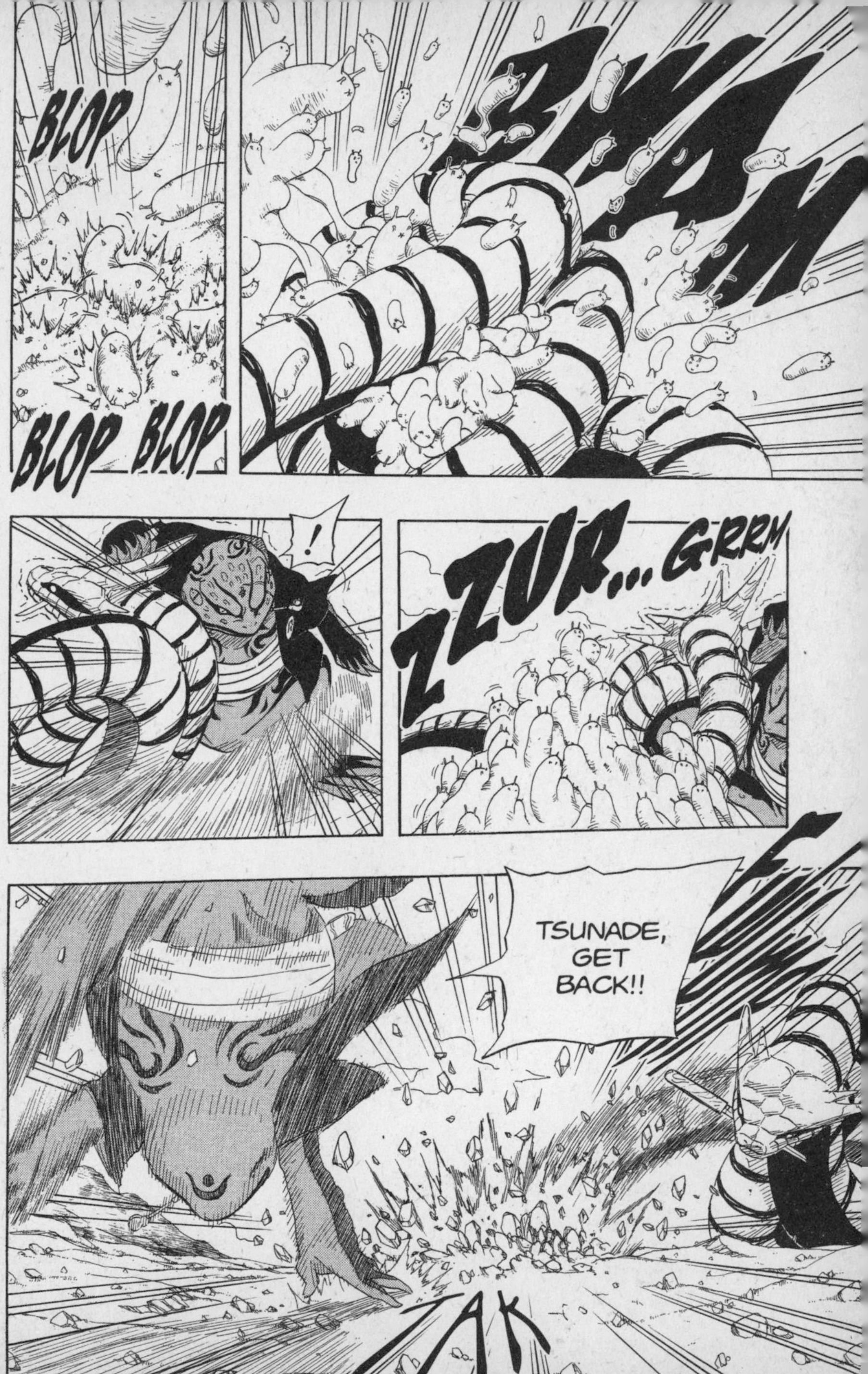
BLOP
BLOP
BLOP
ZZZUR... GRRM
!
TSUNADE, GET BACK!!
ZAK

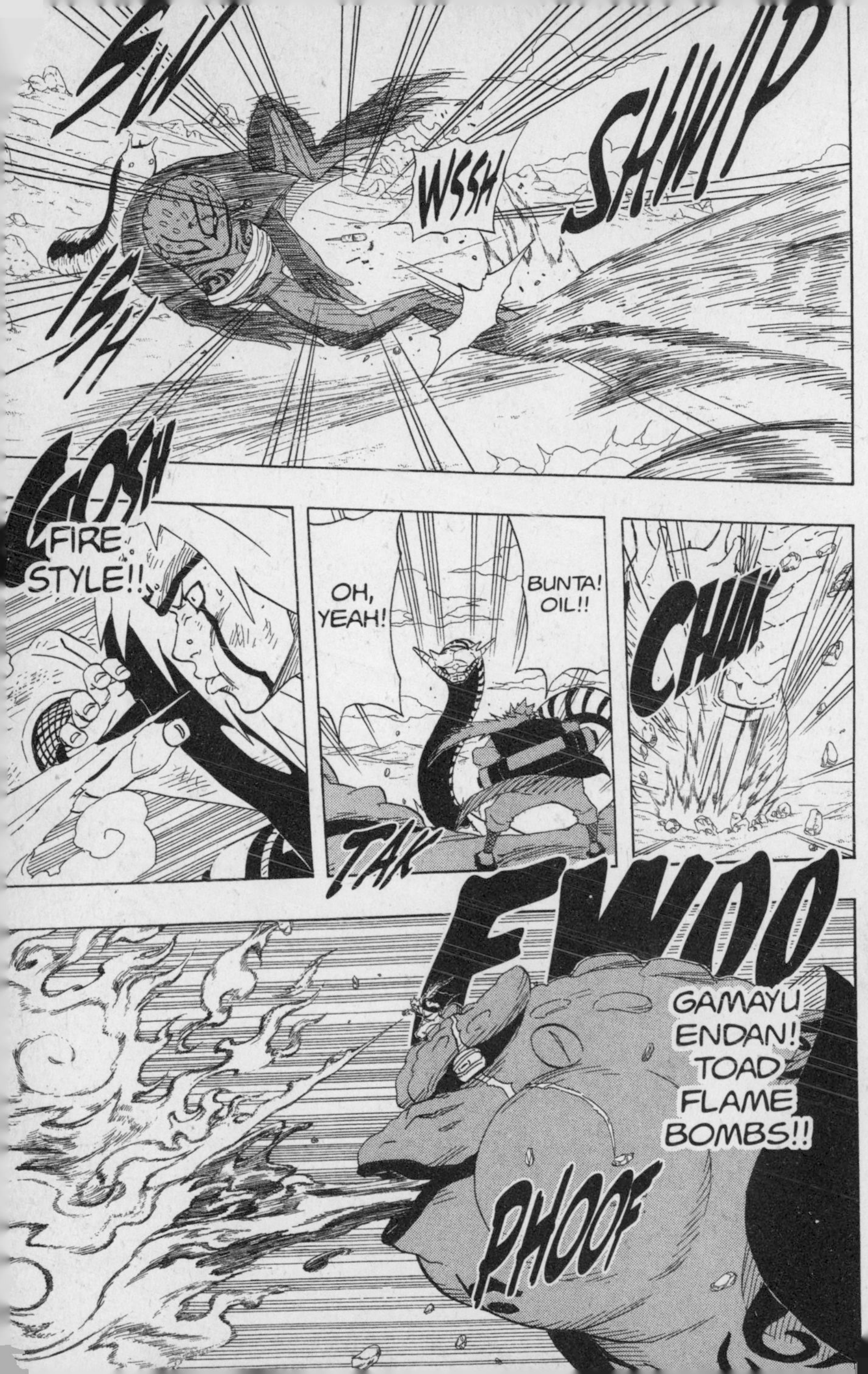
SHWIP
WSSH
SWISH
CHUN
BUNTA! OIL!!
OH, YEAH!
TAK
GOSH
FIRE STYLE!!
FWOO
GAMAYU ENDAN! TOAD FLAME BOMBS!!
PHOOF

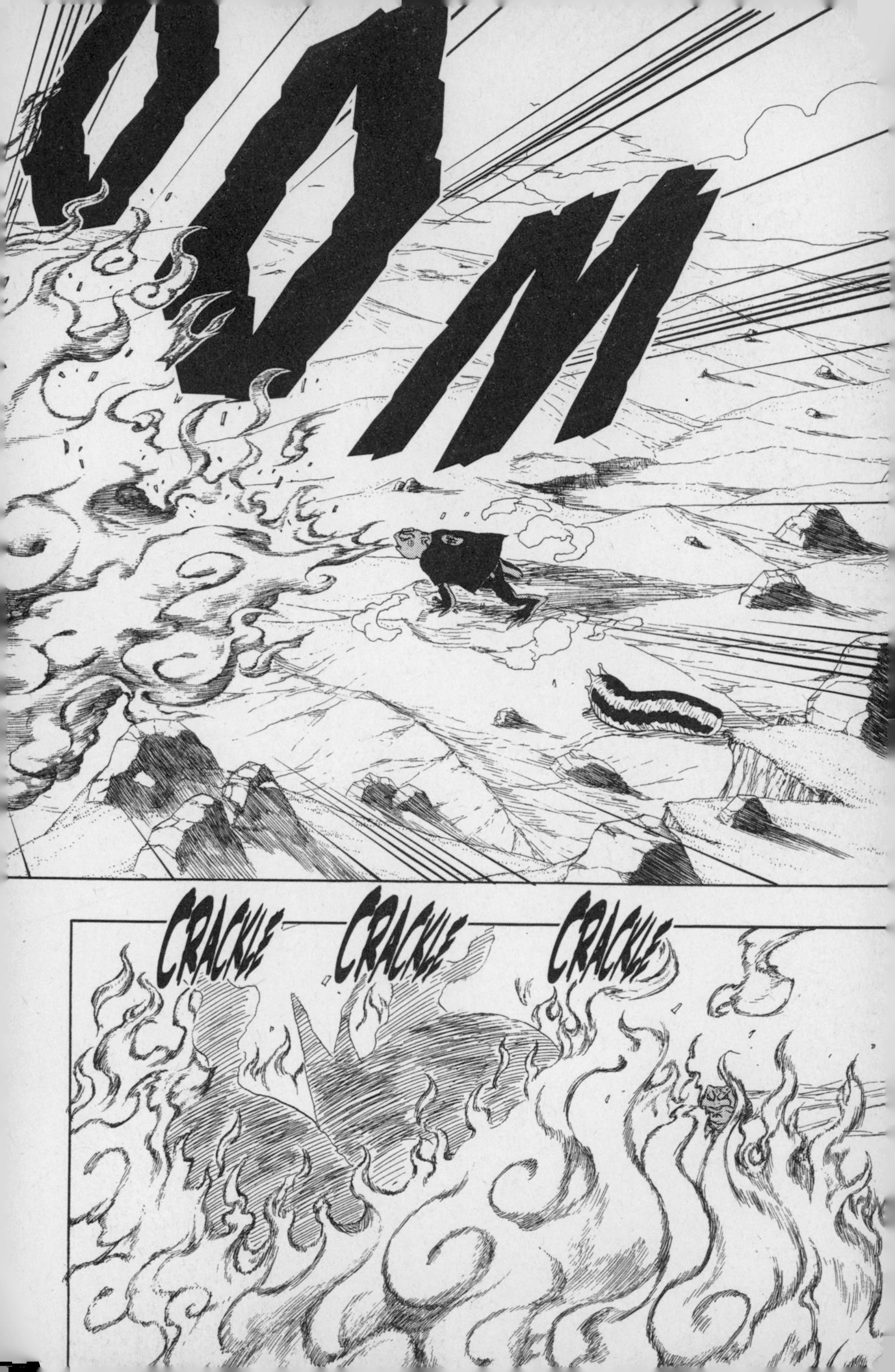
OOM
CRACKLE CRACKLE CRACKLE

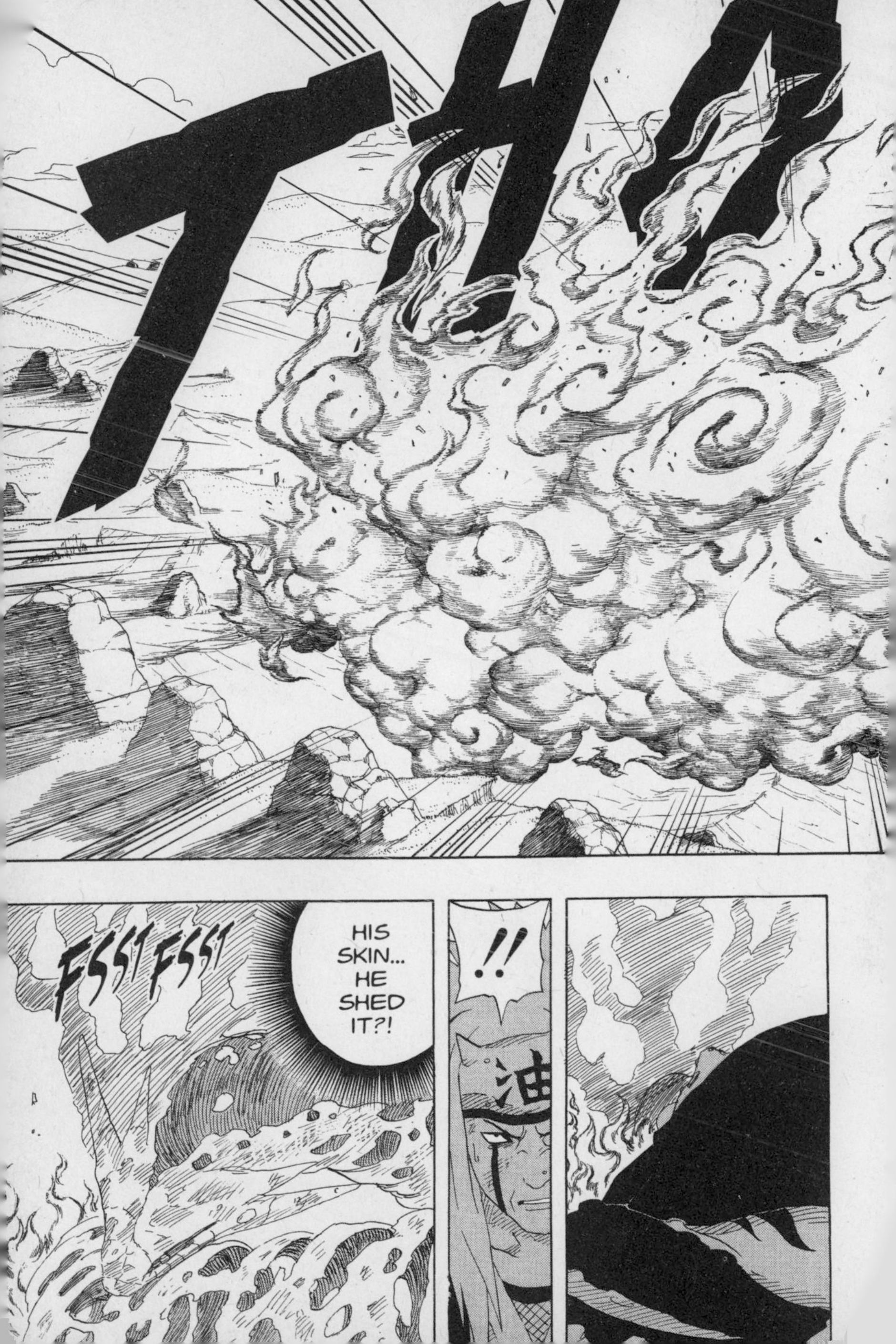
!!
HIS SKIN... HE SHED IT?!
FSST FSST

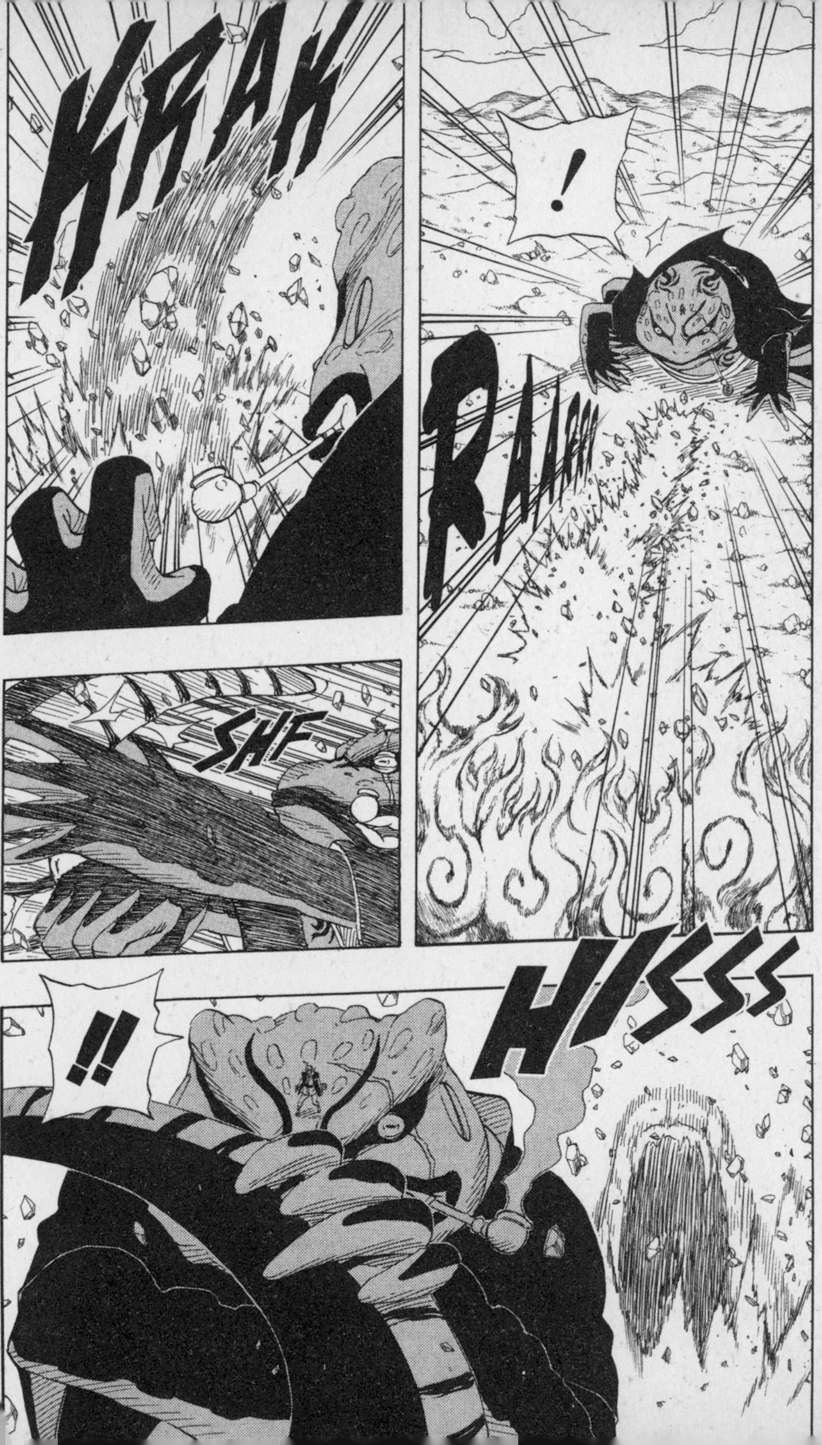
!
RAARR
KRAK
SHF
!!
HISSS

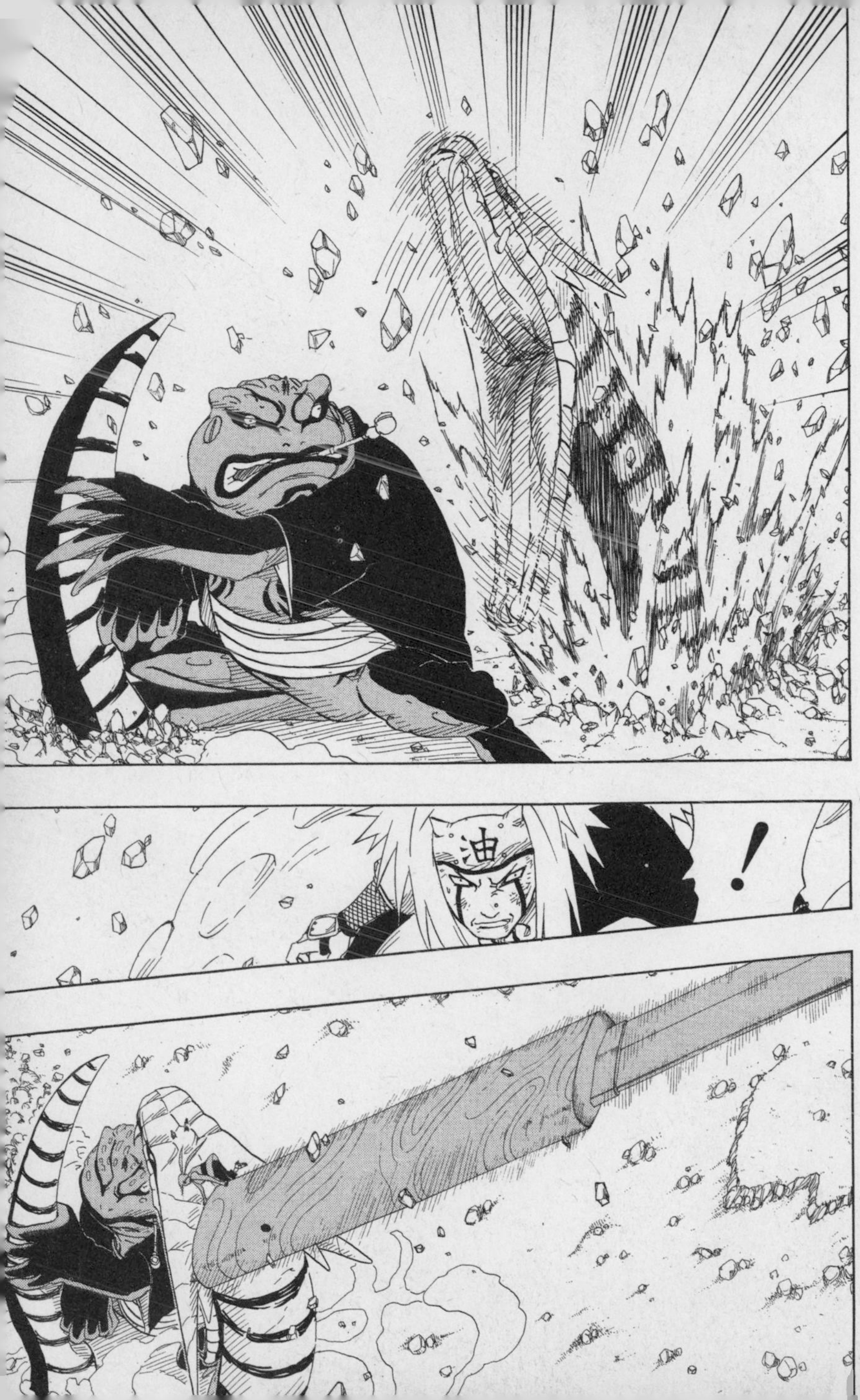
!
油

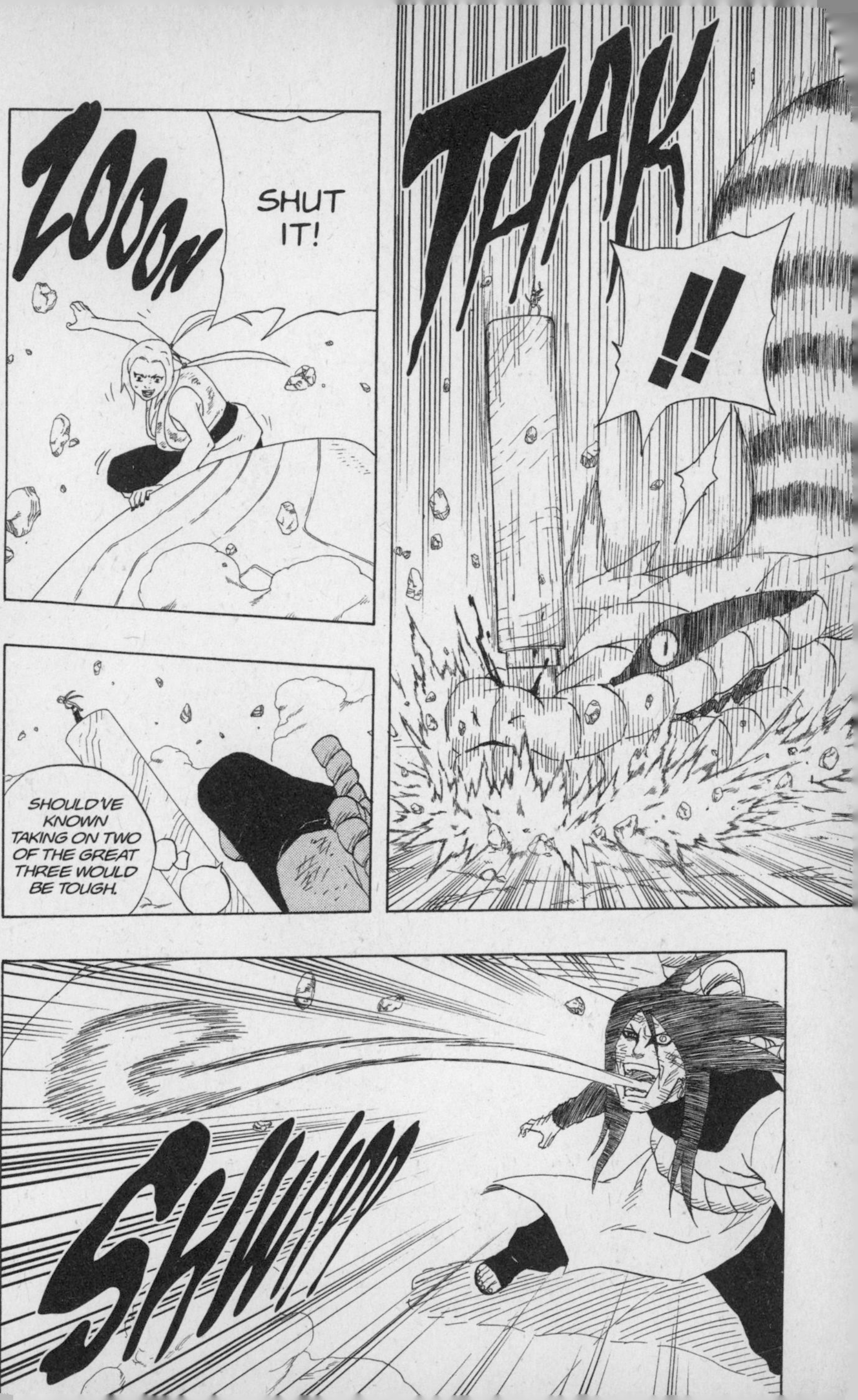
THAK
!!
ZOOOM
SHUT IT!
SHOULD'VE KNOWN TAKING ON TWO OF THE GREAT THREE WOULD BE TOUGH.
SHWIPP

READ THIS WAY

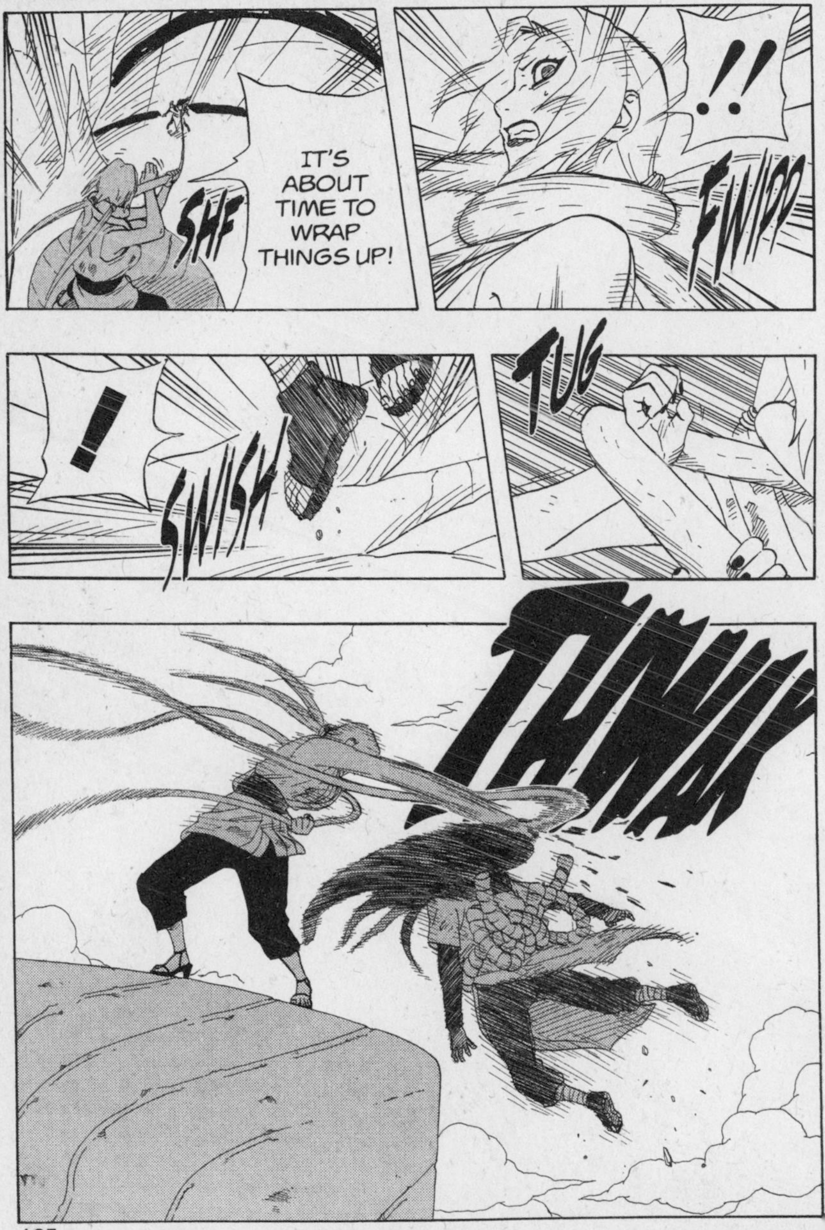
!!
FWIPP
IT'S ABOUT TIME TO WRAP THINGS UP!
SHF
TUG
!
SWISH
THWAK

THE WORLD OF KISHIMOTO MASASHI
MY PERSONAL HISTORY, PART 30: NO.4

DURING THE TWO LONG AND BITTER YEARS AFTER COLLEGE, WHICH WERE STILL ENJOYABLE BECAUSE I COULD FEEL MYSELF IMPROVING, I ORGANIZED MY OWN METHOD OF MANGA WRITING IN A NOTEBOOK. THIS IS THE TOP SECRET KISHIMOTO MASASHI NOTEBOOK. IT'S A MASTER PLAN I CAN'T SHOW ANYBODY!

IN THESE TWO YEARS, I GAINED A LOT OF CONFIDENCE. SO, WITHOUT FURTHER DELAY I SET ABOUT WRITING MANGA USING MY CONFIDENTIAL NOTEBOOK. MY THEME WAS BASEBALL! AND THE TITLE WAS *YAKYU-OH*, BASEBALL KING!

AFTER A SHORT TIME, I FINISHED THE SCRIPT AND SHOWED IT TO MY EDITOR, MR. YAHAGI. "IT'S INTERESTING, BUT...I THINK IT'S A BIT DARK," HE SAID. "BUT I DIDN'T KNOW YOU COULD WRITE THIS STYLE OF MANGA... YOU'VE IMPROVED." I WAS DELIGHTED TO HEAR THOSE WORDS. ALTHOUGH *YAKYU-OH* PASSED MR. YAHAGI'S CHECK, A HIGHER COMMITTEE DECIDED THAT THE CONTENT WAS TOO SERIOUS FOR A BOYS' MAGAZINE... IN SHORT, IT WAS TURNED DOWN.

STILL, *YAKYU-OH* WAS MY TURNING POINT. THOUGH IT WAS NOT PUBLISHED, MR. YAHAGI SAID, "INTERESTING! THIS MANGA IS DEFINITELY INTERESTING! IT WOULD'VE BEEN TOTALLY FINE FOR A YOUNG ADULT MAGAZINE..." THIS MANGA WAS THE FIRST WORK OF MINE TO RECEIVE SUBSTANTIAL PRAISE FROM MR. YAHAGI. I FELT MY TWO YEARS OF WORK HAD SURE PAID OFF.

FOUR MONTHS LATER, I WROTE A MANGA SCRIPT FOR ANOTHER BOYS' MAGAZINE AND SHOWED IT TO MR. YAHAGI. MR. YAHAGI SAID, "IT'S PERFECT! SOME MINOR PARTS WILL HAVE TO BE REVISED, THOUGH!" IN THOSE TWO YEARS, I WAS ABLE TO CHANGE MYSELF A LITTLE BIT. WHAT'S MORE, I MANAGED TO START A SERIES WITH THAT STORYBOARD.

Number 171: Successor

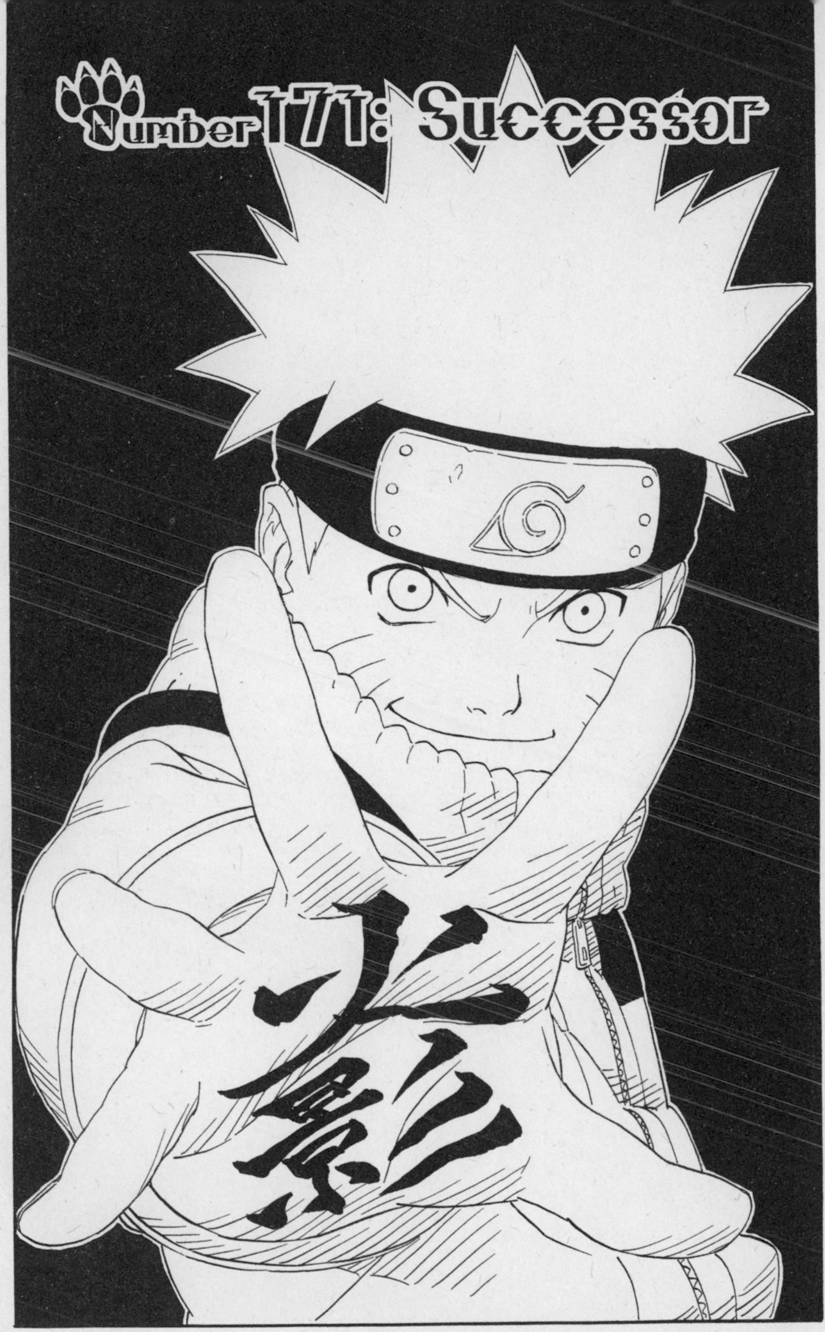
火影

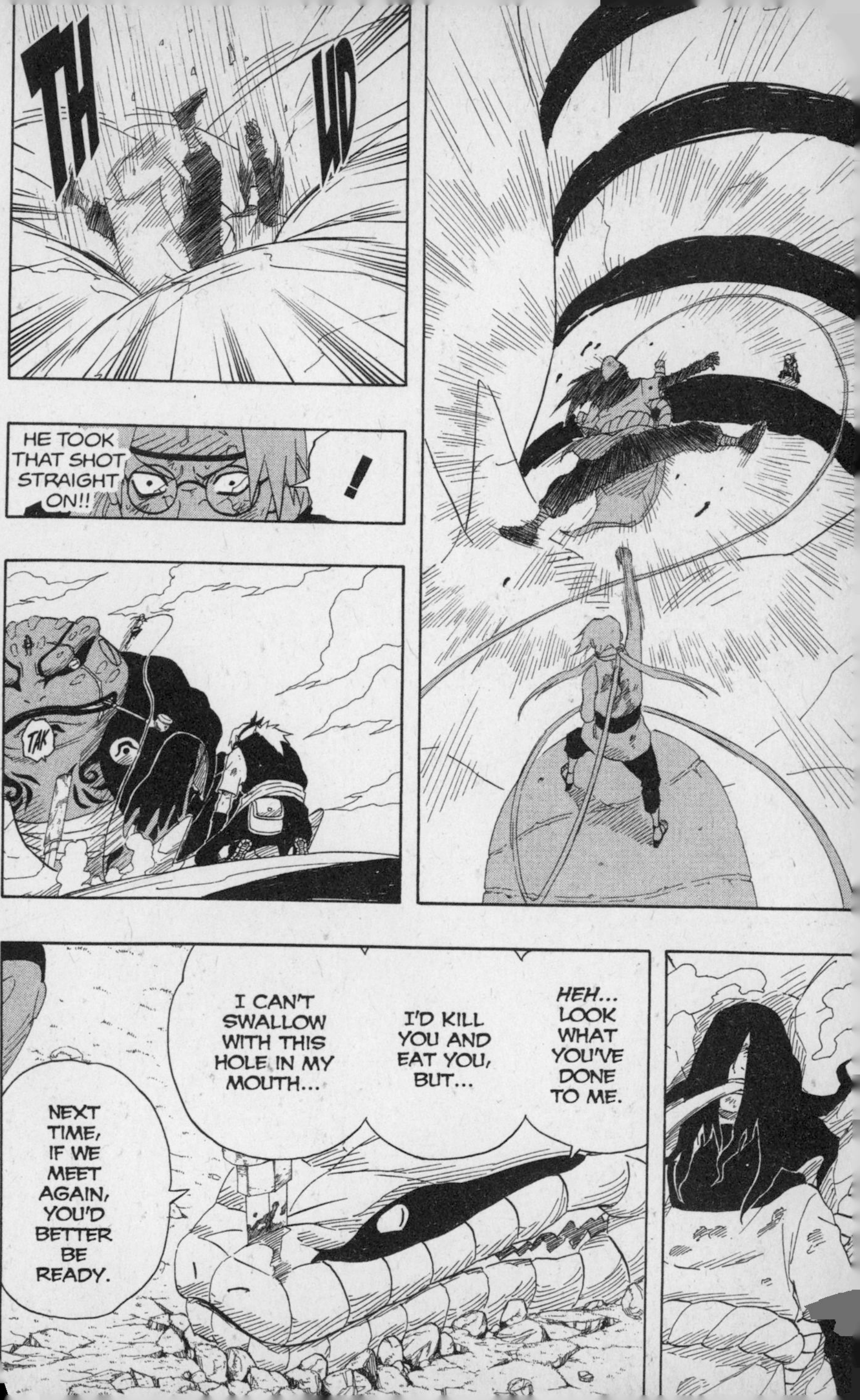
THUD
HE TOOK THAT SHOT STRAIGHT ON!!
!
TAK
HEH... LOOK WHAT YOU'VE DONE TO ME.
I'D KILL YOU AND EAT YOU, BUT...
I CAN'T SWALLOW WITH THIS HOLE IN MY MOUTH...
NEXT TIME, IF WE MEET AGAIN, YOU'D BETTER BE READY.

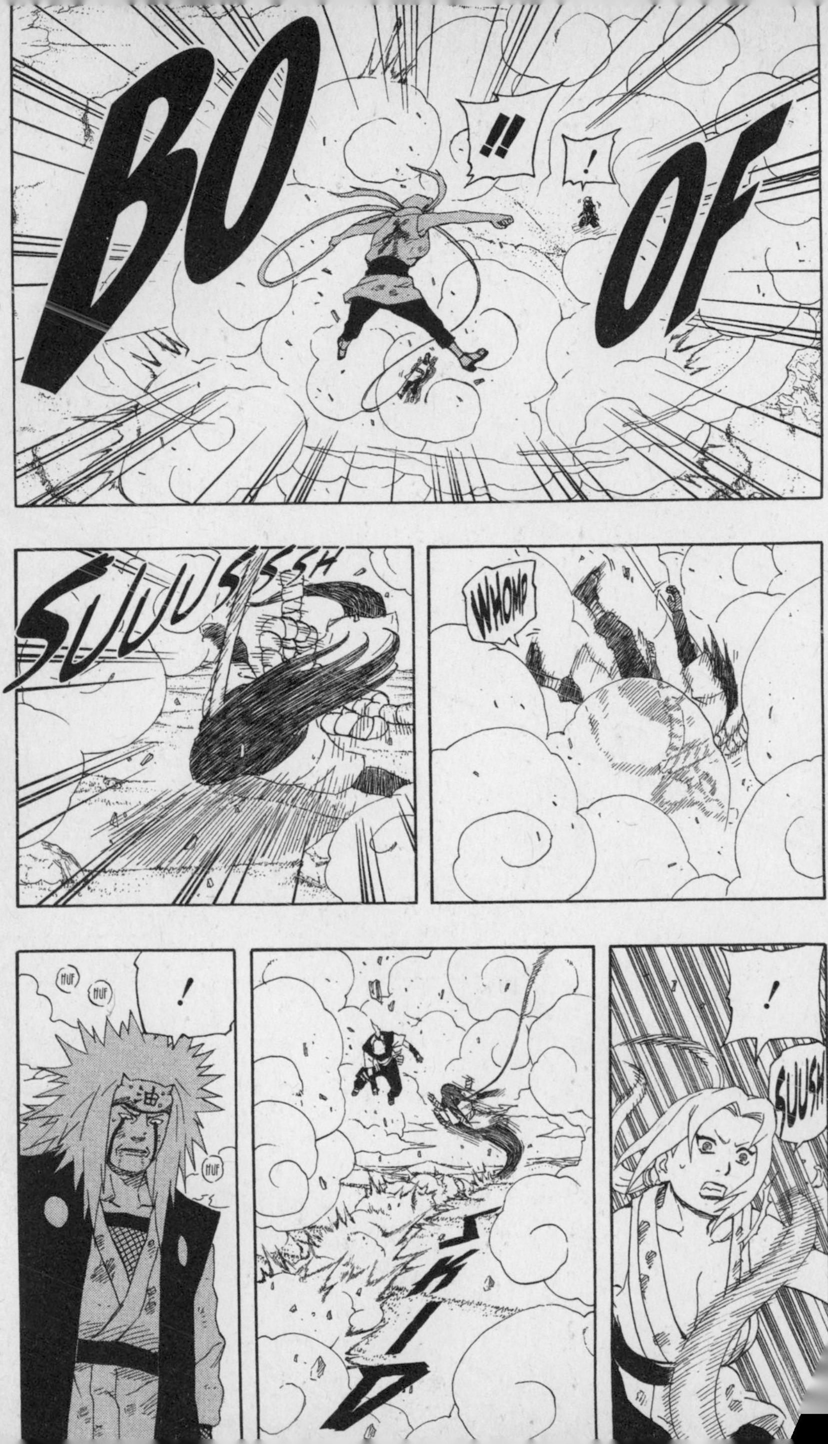
BOOF
!
!!
WHOMP
SUUUSSSH
!
SUUSH
HUF
HUF
!
HUF

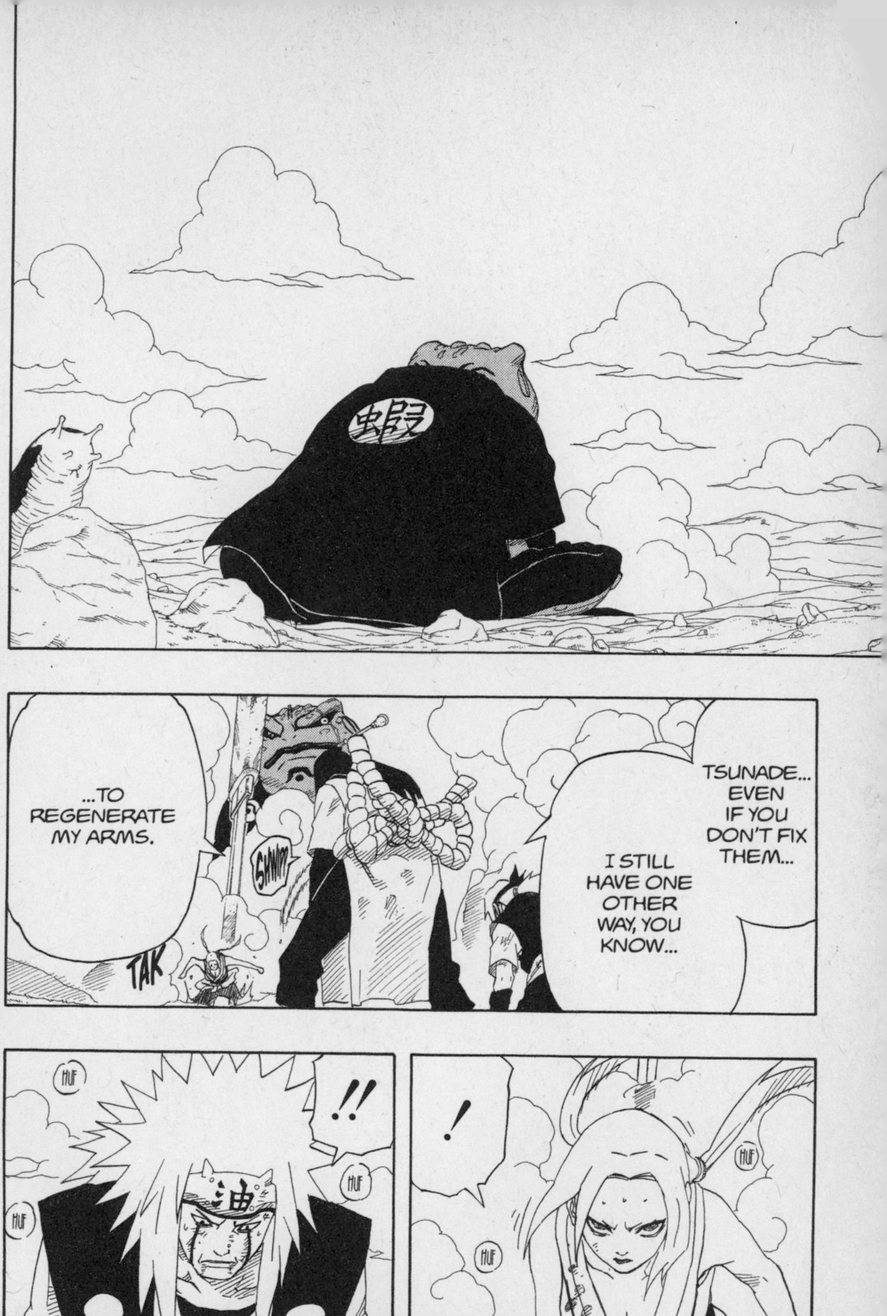
TSUNADE... EVEN IF YOU DON'T FIX THEM...
I STILL HAVE ONE OTHER WAY, YOU KNOW...
...TO REGENERATE MY ARMS.
SHWIP
TAK
!
HUF
HUF
!!
HUF
HUF
HUF

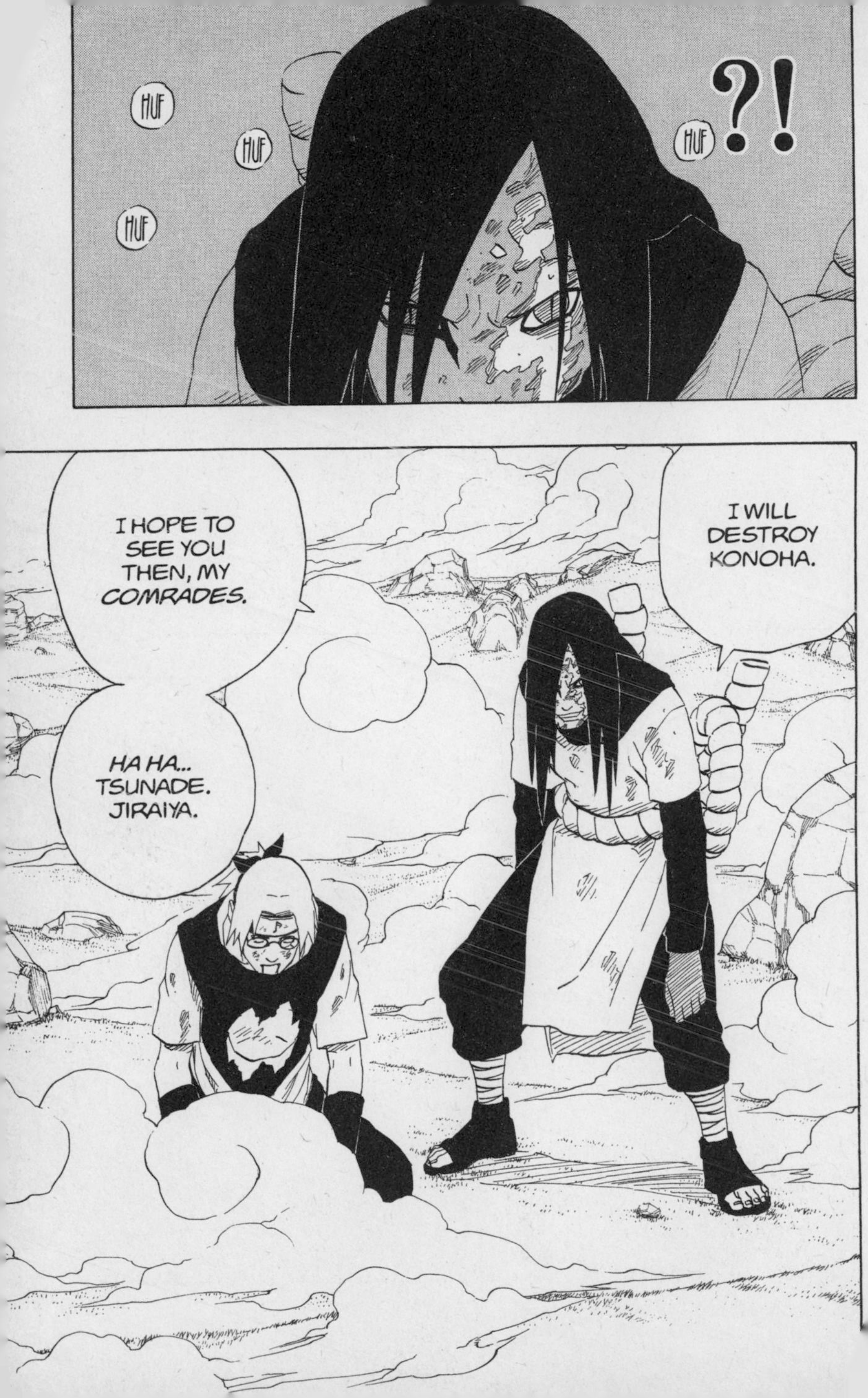
?!
HUF
HUF
HUF
HUF
I WILL DESTROY KONOHA.
I HOPE TO SEE YOU THEN, MY *COMRADES.*
HA HA... TSUNADE. JIRAIYA.

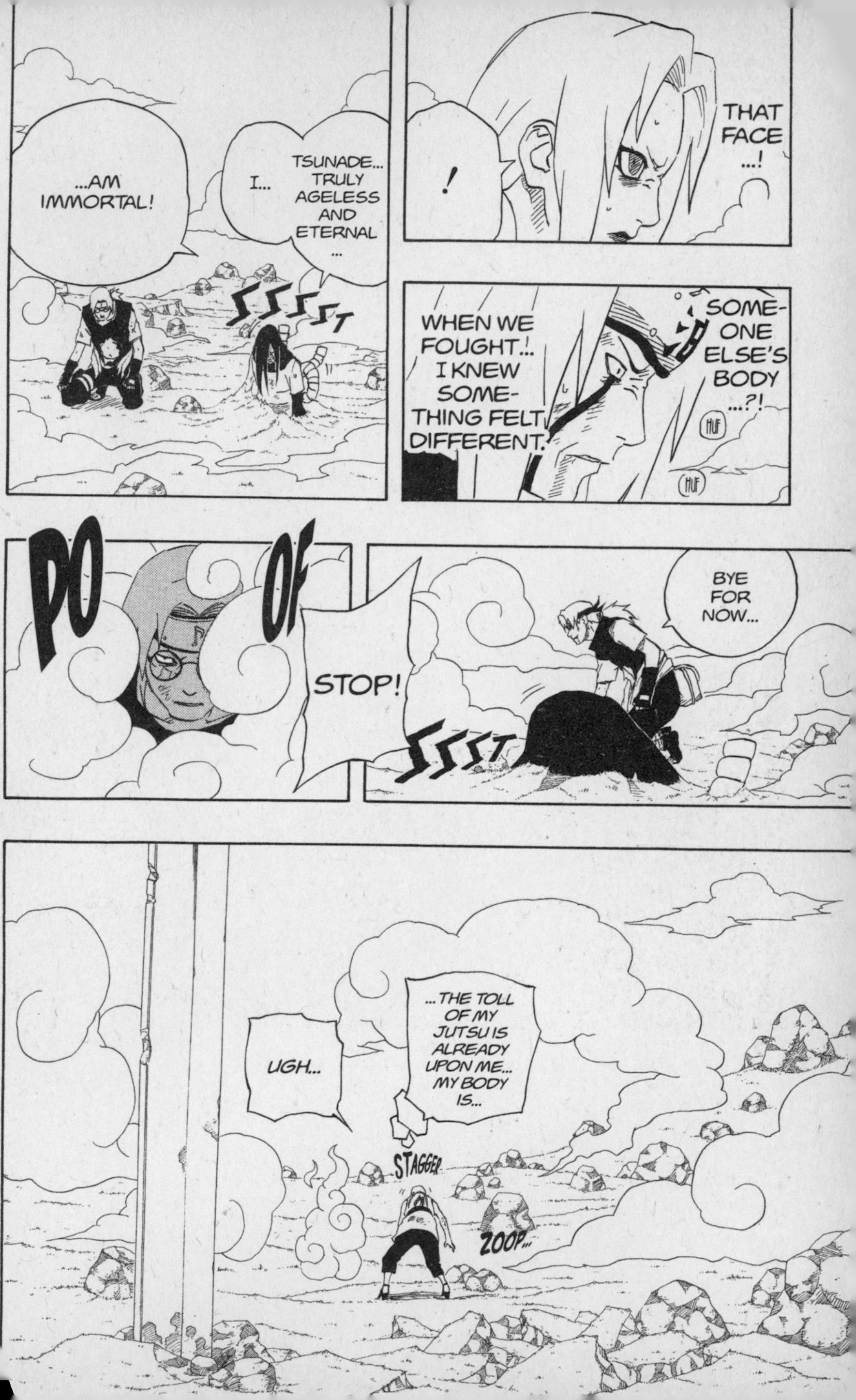
!
THAT FACE ...!
SOME-ONE ELSE'S BODY ...?!
HUF
HUF
WHEN WE FOUGHT... I KNEW SOME-THING FELT DIFFERENT.
TSUNADE... TRULY AGELESS AND ETERNAL ... I...
...AM IMMORTAL!
SSSST
BYE FOR NOW...
SSST
STOP!
POOF
...THE TOLL OF MY JUTSU IS ALREADY UPON ME... MY BODY IS...
UGH...
STAGGER
ZOOP...

READ THIS WAY

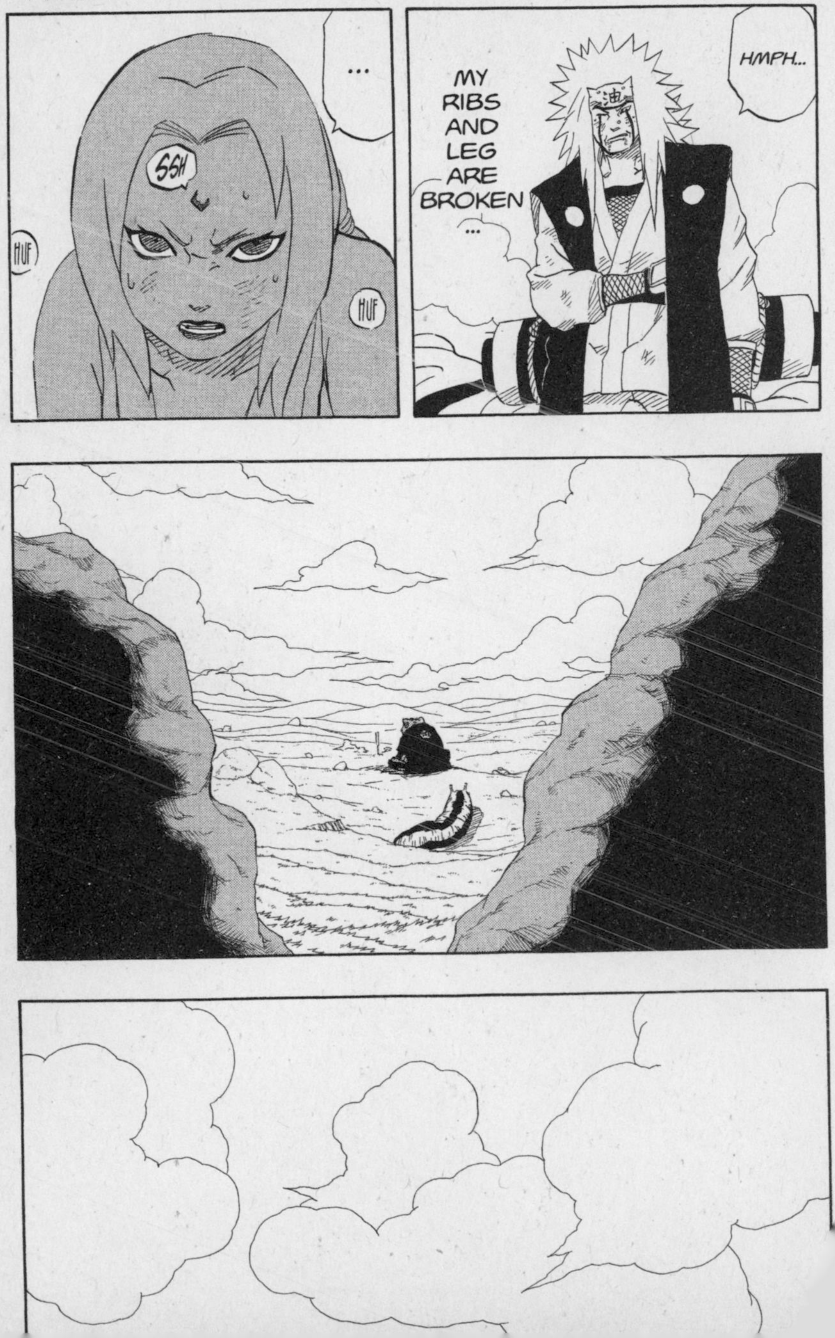
HMPH...
MY RIBS AND LEG ARE BROKEN ...
...
SSH
HUF
HUF

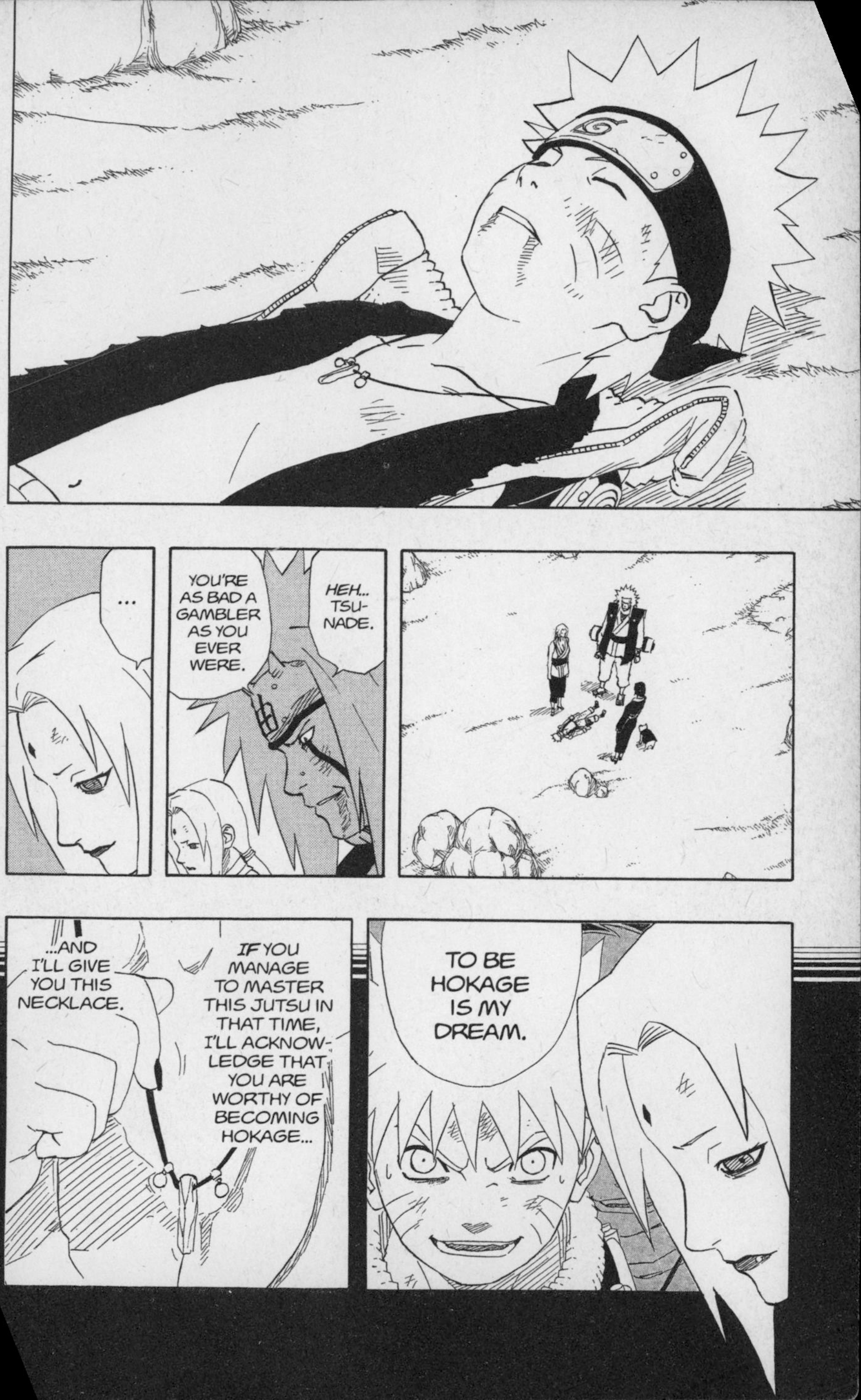
HEH... TSU-NADE.
YOU'RE AS BAD A GAMBLER AS YOU EVER WERE.
...
TO BE HOKAGE IS MY DREAM.
IF YOU MANAGE TO MASTER THIS JUTSU IN THAT TIME, I'LL ACKNOW-LEDGE THAT YOU ARE WORTHY OF BECOMING HOKAGE...
...AND I'LL GIVE YOU THIS NECKLACE.

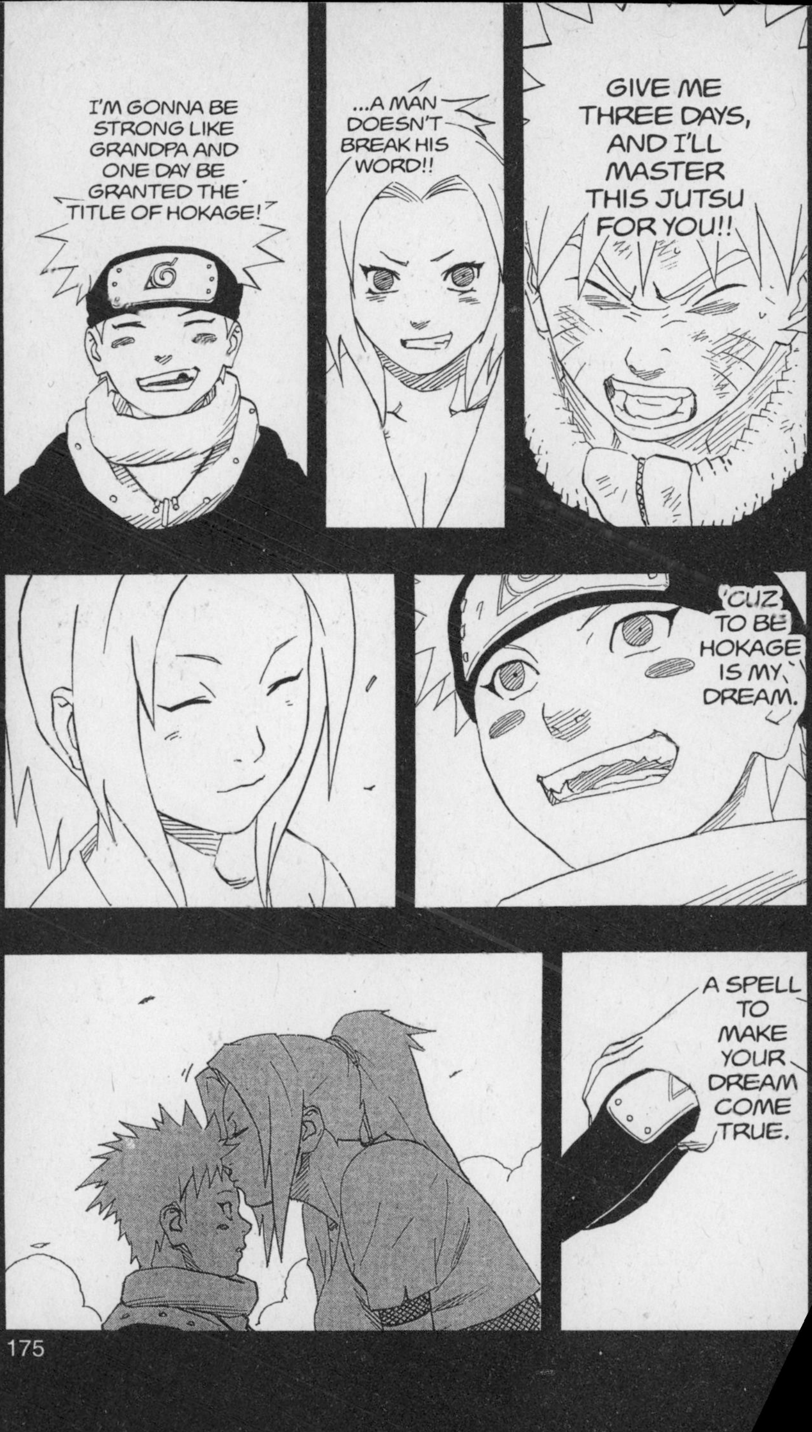
GIVE ME THREE DAYS, AND I'LL MASTER THIS JUTSU FOR YOU!!
...A MAN DOESN'T BREAK HIS WORD!!
I'M GONNA BE STRONG LIKE GRANDPA AND ONE DAY BE GRANTED THE TITLE OF HOKAGE!
'CUZ TO BE HOKAGE IS MY DREAM.
A SPELL TO MAKE YOUR DREAM COME TRUE.

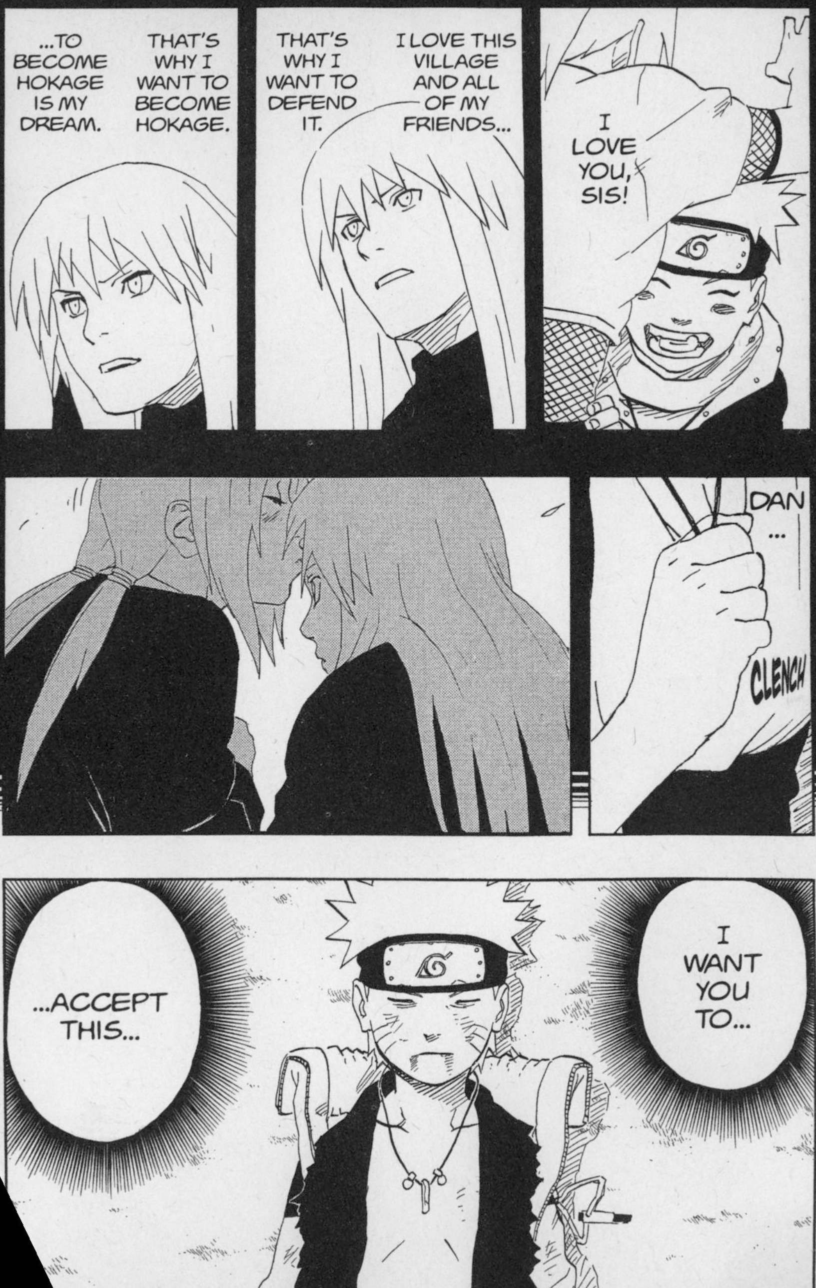
I LOVE YOU, SIS!
I LOVE THIS VILLAGE AND ALL OF MY FRIENDS...
THAT'S WHY I WANT TO DEFEND IT.
THAT'S WHY I WANT TO BECOME HOKAGE.
...TO BECOME HOKAGE IS MY DREAM.
DAN...
CLENCH
I WANT YOU TO...
...ACCEPT THIS...

READ THIS WAY

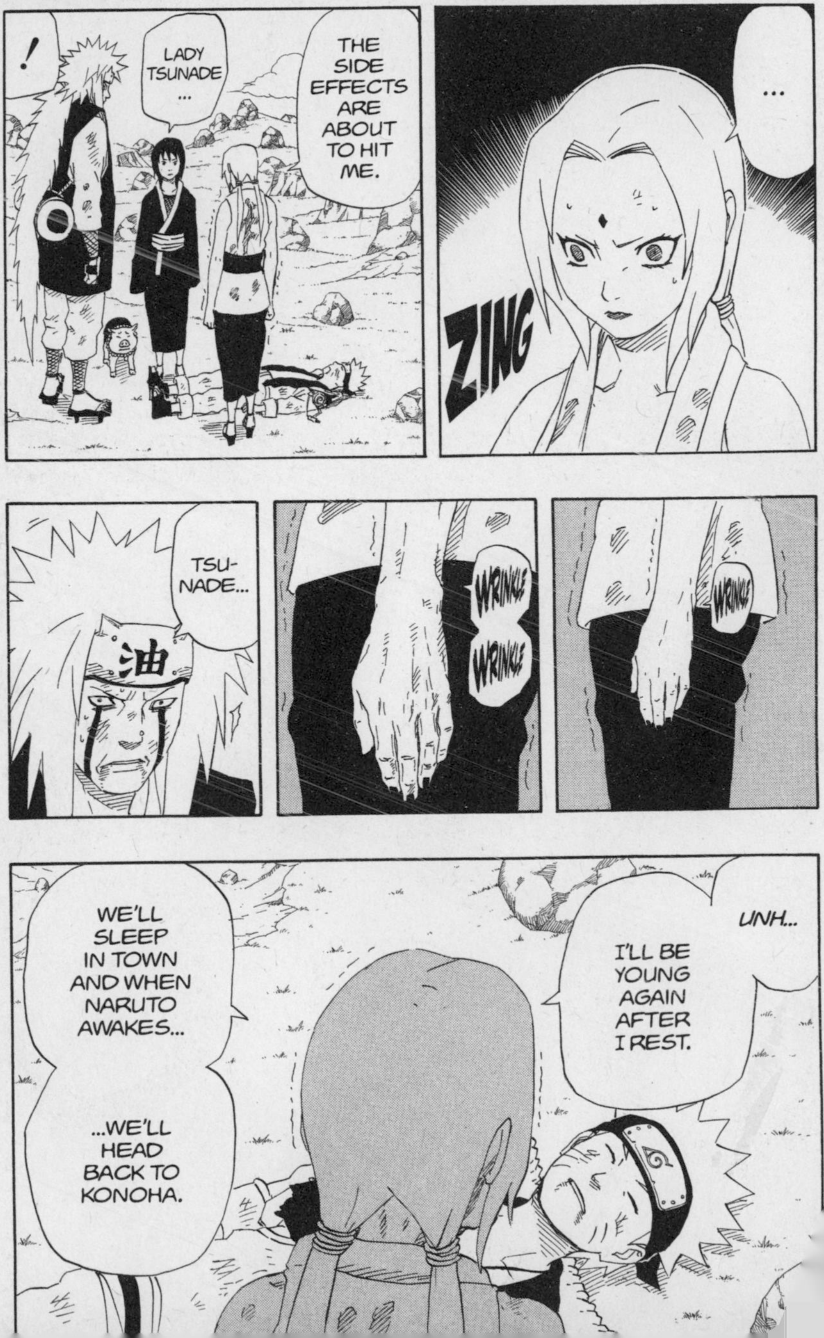
...
ZING
THE SIDE EFFECTS ARE ABOUT TO HIT ME.
LADY TSUNADE ...
!
WRINKLE
WRINKLE
WRINKLE
TSU-NADE...
UNH...
I'LL BE YOUNG AGAIN AFTER I REST.
WE'LL SLEEP IN TOWN AND WHEN NARUTO AWAKES...
...WE'LL HEAD BACK TO KONOHA.

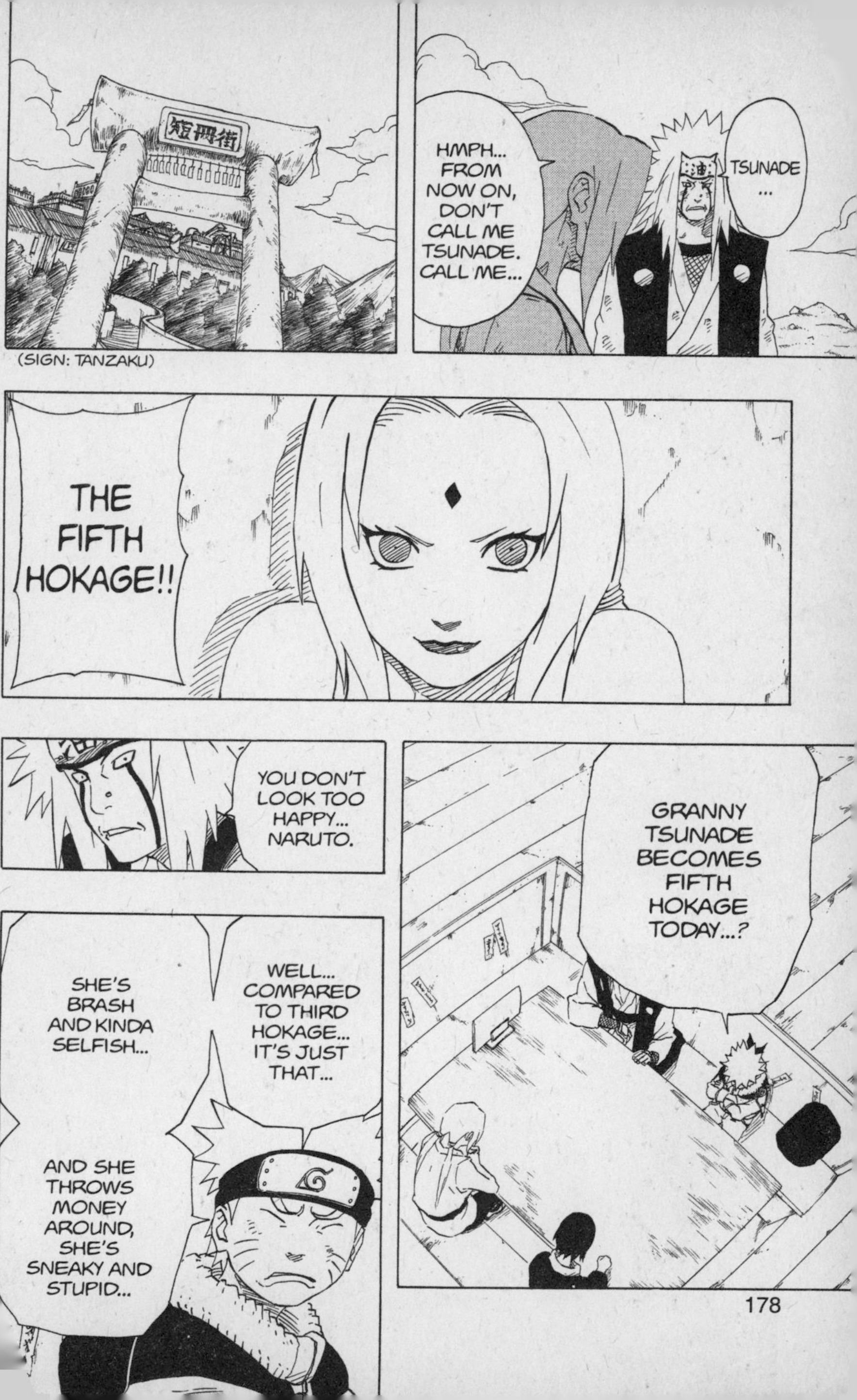
TSUNADE ...
HMPH... FROM NOW ON, DON'T CALL ME TSUNADE. CALL ME...
短冊街
(SIGN: TANZAKU)
THE FIFTH HOKAGE!!
GRANNY TSUNADE BECOMES FIFTH HOKAGE TODAY...?
YOU DON'T LOOK TOO HAPPY... NARUTO.
WELL... COMPARED TO THIRD HOKAGE... IT'S JUST THAT...
SHE'S BRASH AND KINDA SELFISH...
AND SHE THROWS MONEY AROUND, SHE'S SNEAKY AND STUPID...

READ THIS WAY

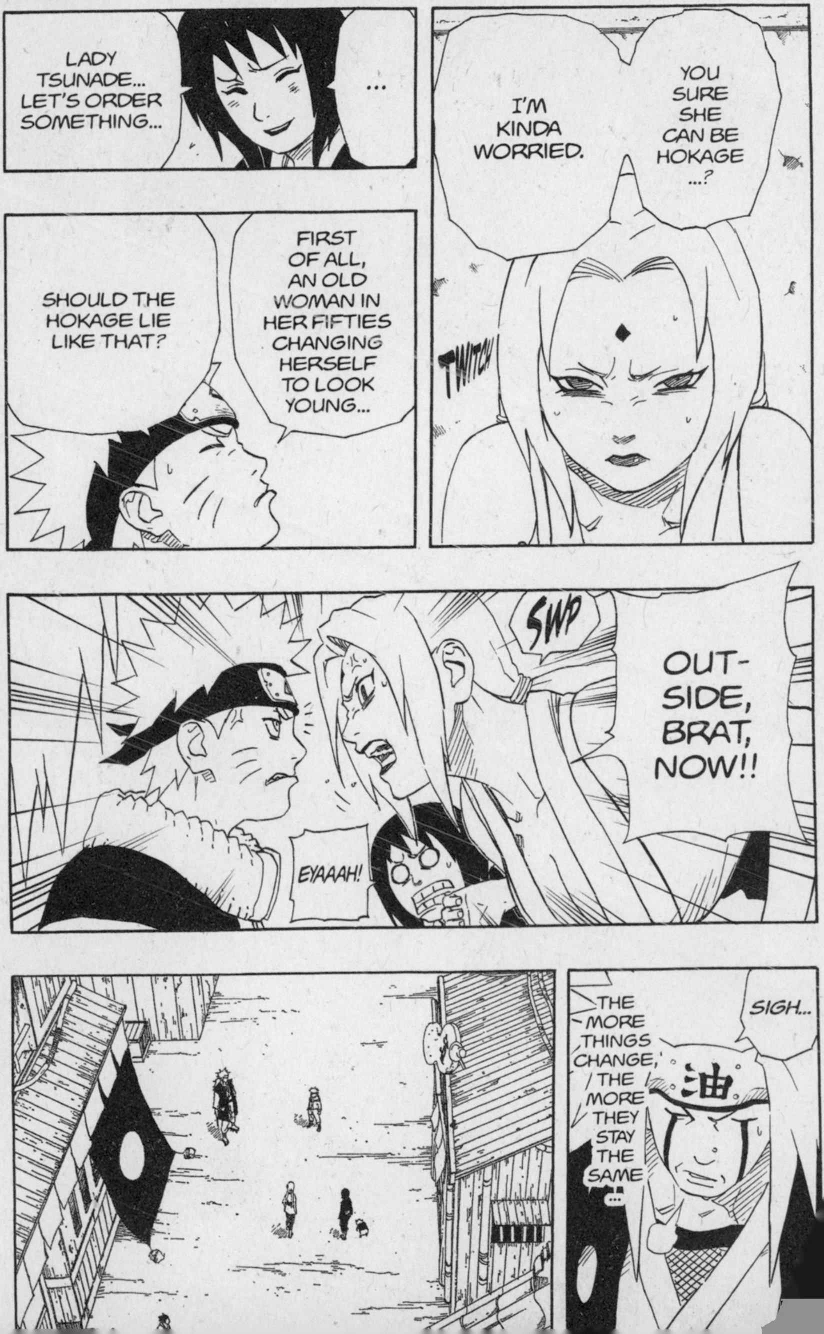
YOU SURE SHE CAN BE HOKAGE ...?
I'M KINDA WORRIED.
TWITCH
...
LADY TSUNADE... LET'S ORDER SOMETHING...
FIRST OF ALL, AN OLD WOMAN IN HER FIFTIES CHANGING HERSELF TO LOOK YOUNG...
SHOULD THE HOKAGE LIE LIKE THAT?
SWP
OUT-SIDE, BRAT, NOW!!
EYAAAH!
SIGH...
THE MORE THINGS CHANGE, THE MORE THEY STAY THE SAME ...
油

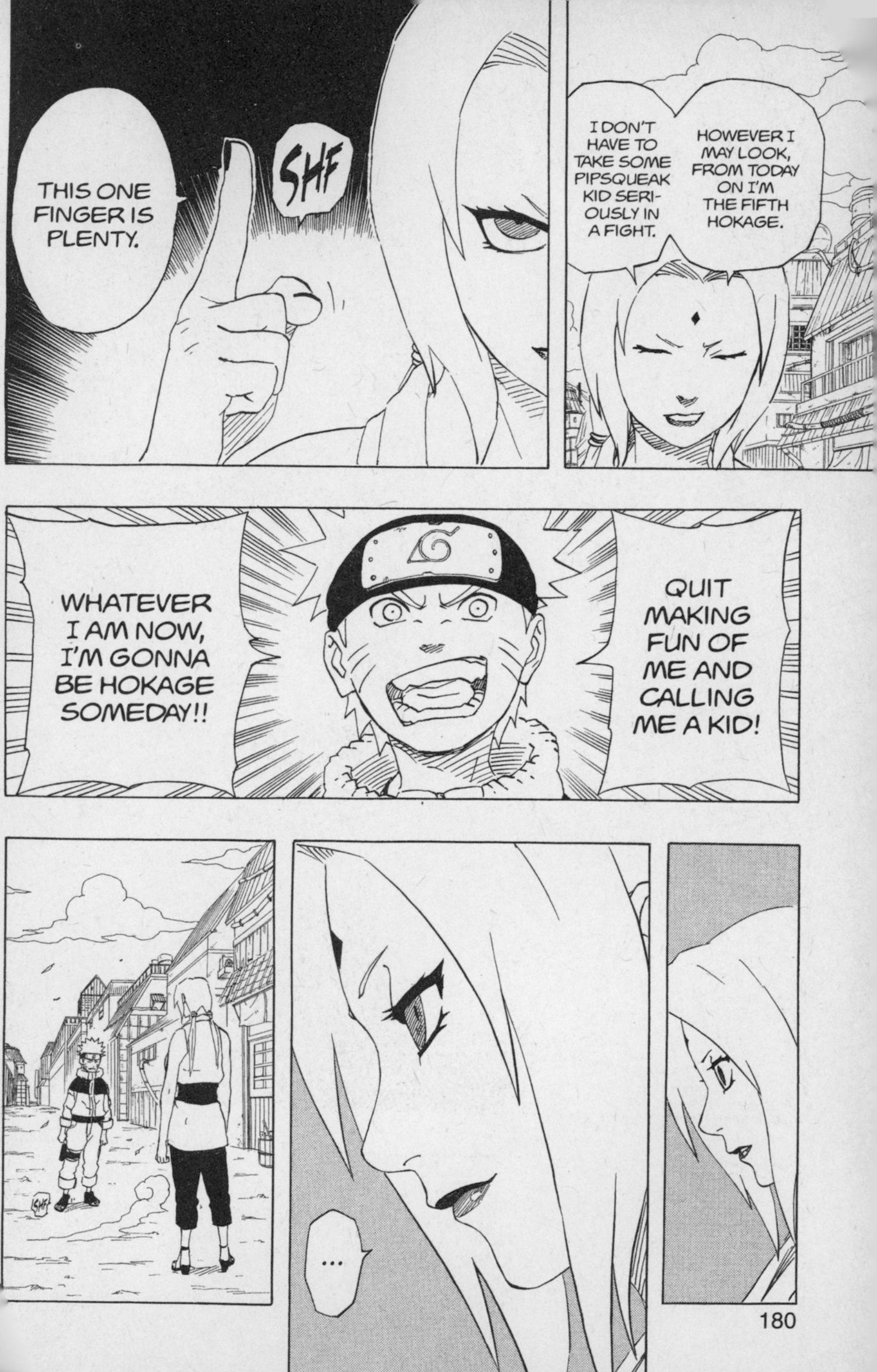
HOWEVER I MAY LOOK, FROM TODAY ON I'M THE FIFTH HOKAGE.
I DON'T HAVE TO TAKE SOME PIPSQUEAK KID SERI-OUSLY IN A FIGHT.
SHF
THIS ONE FINGER IS PLENTY.
QUIT MAKING FUN OF ME AND CALLING ME A KID!
WHATEVER I AM NOW, I'M GONNA BE HOKAGE SOMEDAY!!
...
SHF

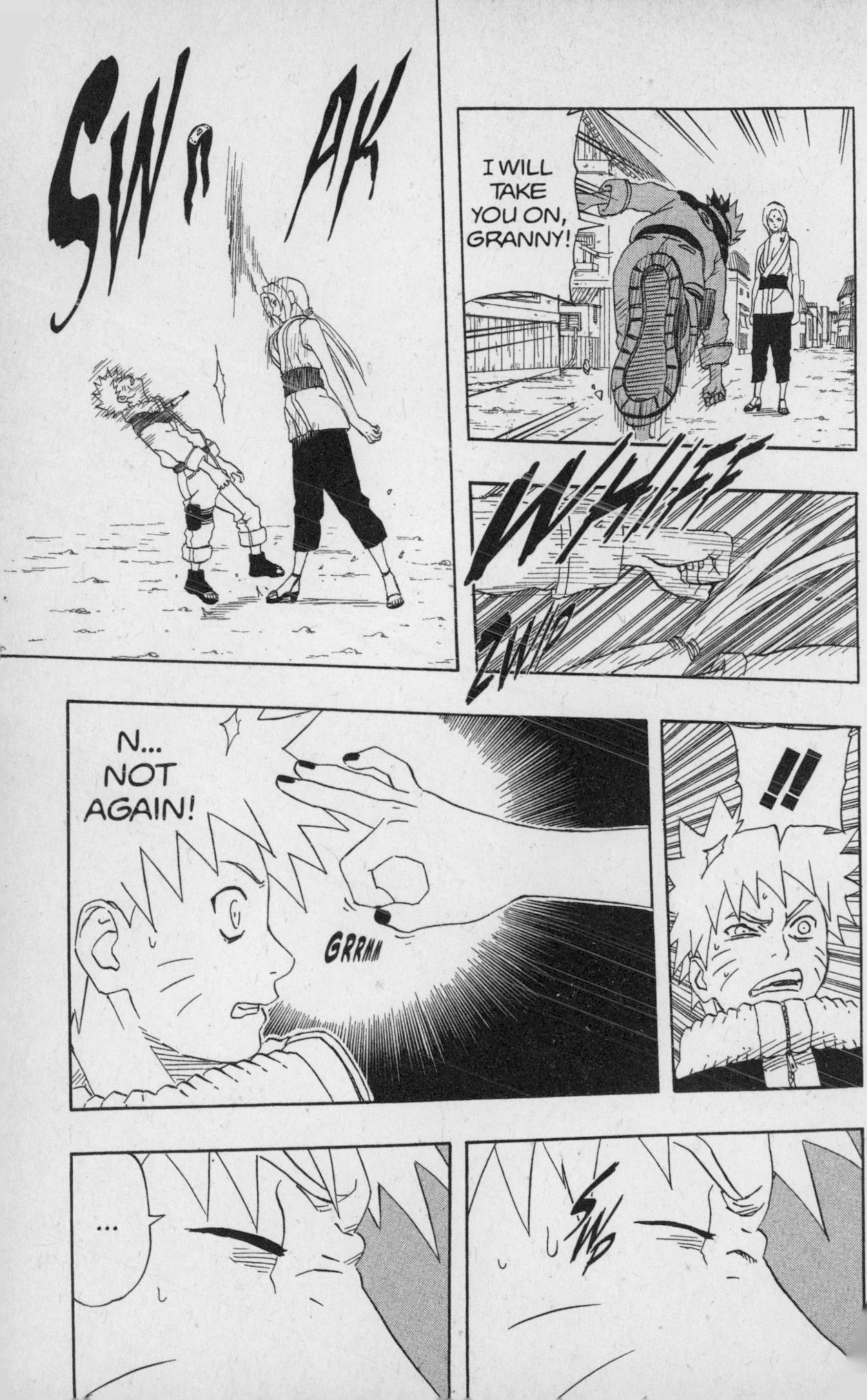
I WILL TAKE YOU ON, GRANNY!
WHIFF
ZWIP
SWAK
!!
N... NOT AGAIN!
GRRMM
SWD
...

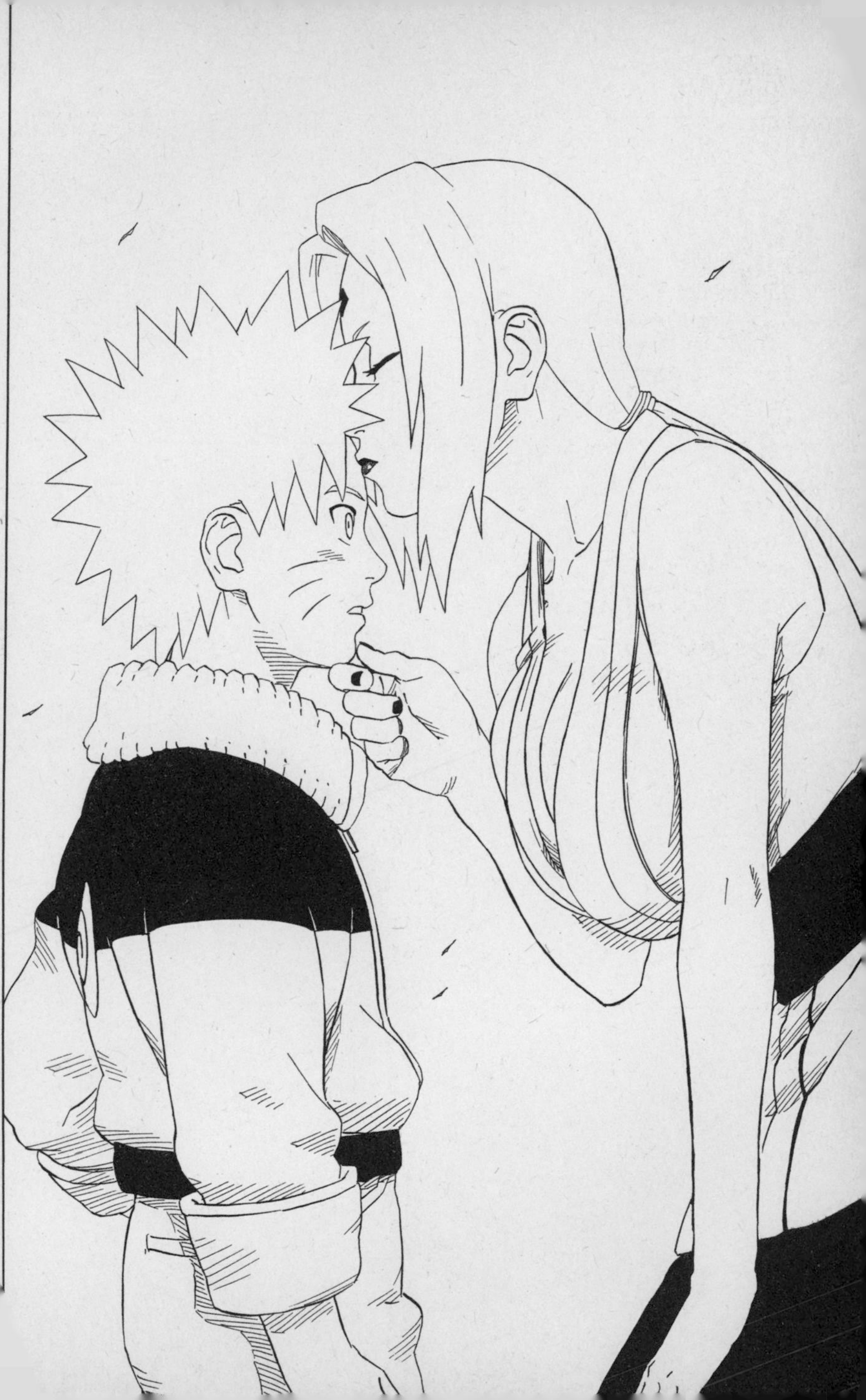

READ THIS WAY

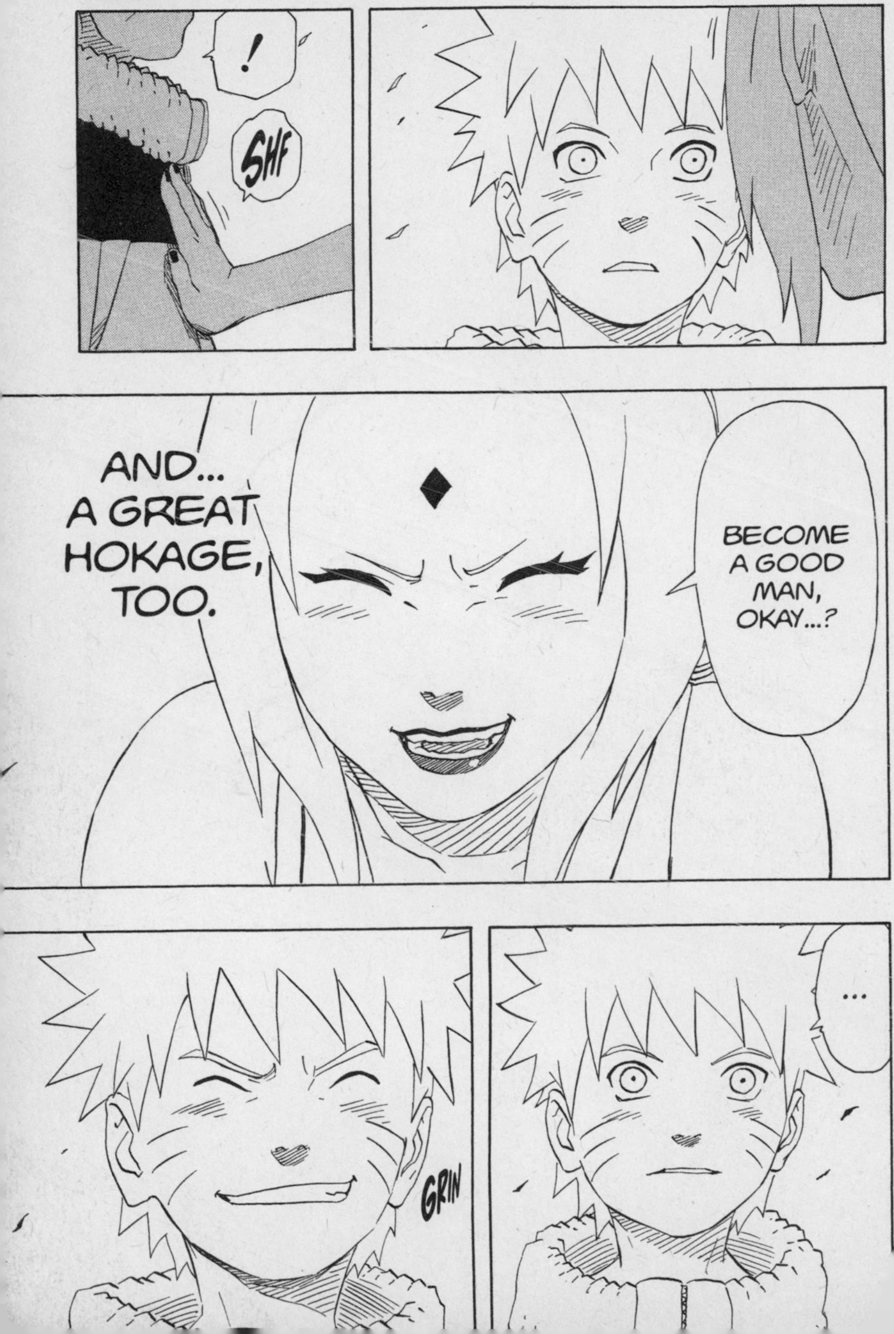
!
SHF
BECOME A GOOD MAN, OKAY...?
AND... A GREAT HOKAGE, TOO.
...
GRIN

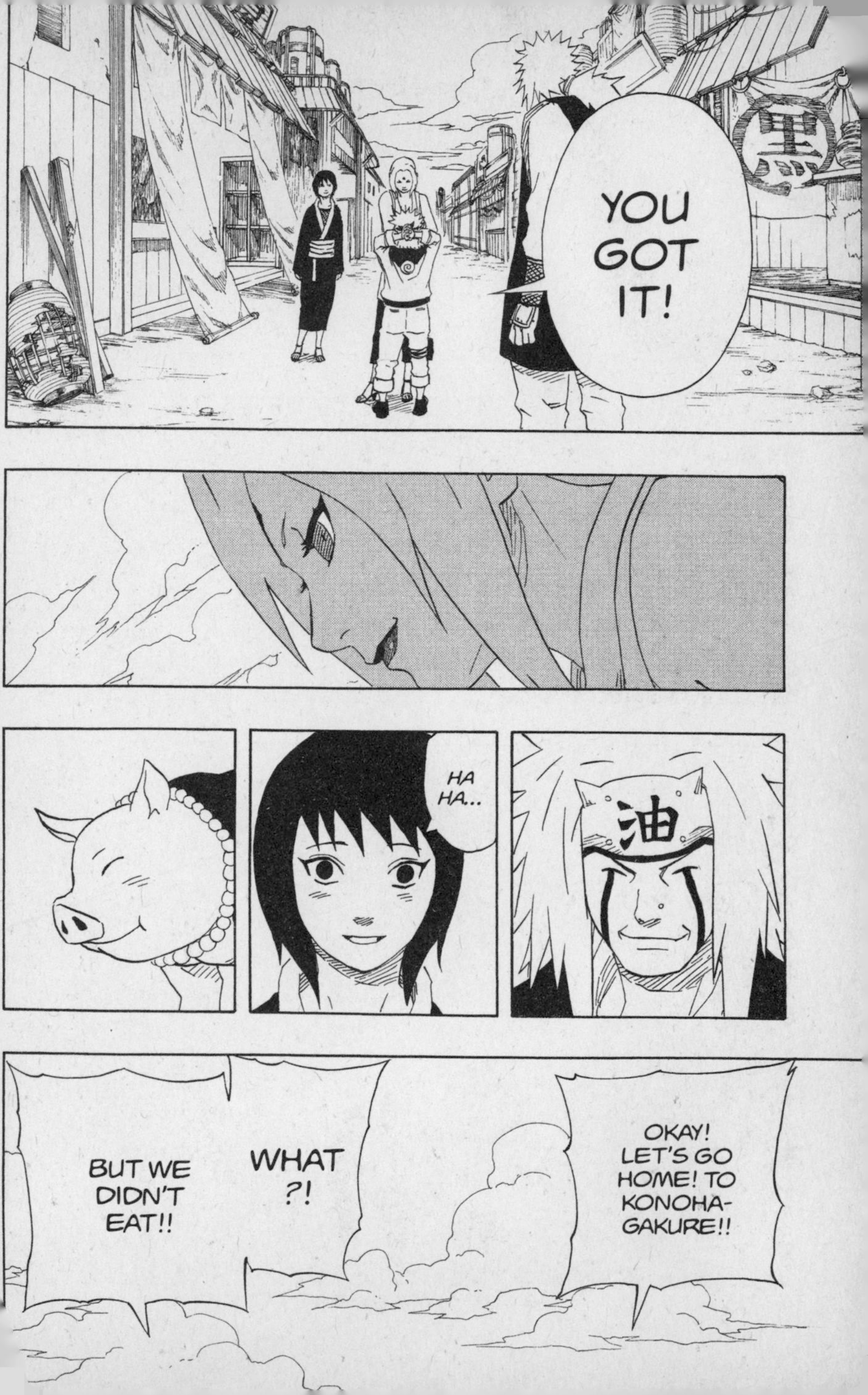
YOU GOT IT!
油
HA HA...
OKAY! LET'S GO HOME! TO KONOHA-GAKURE!!
WHAT ?!
BUT WE DIDN'T EAT!!

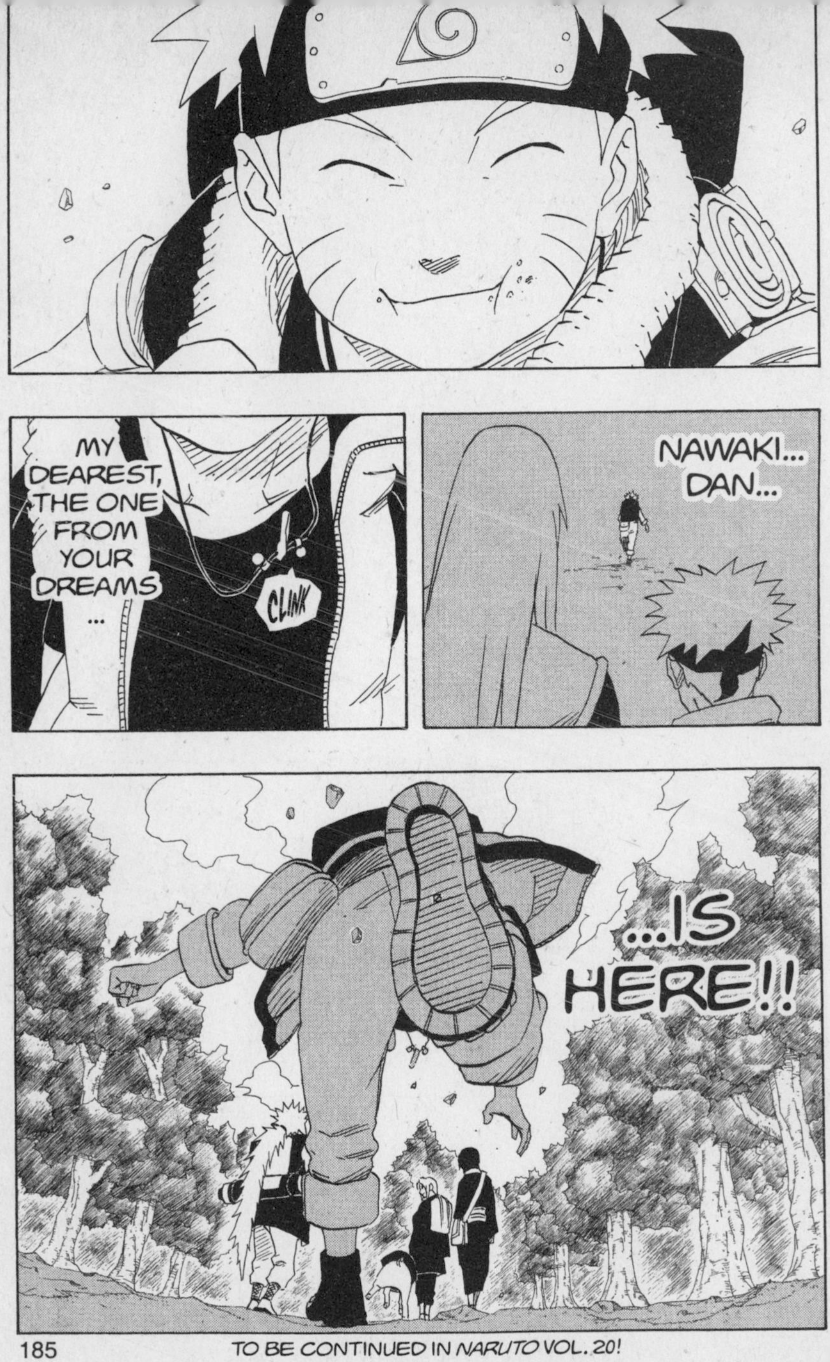
NAWAKI... DAN...
MY DEAREST, THE ONE FROM YOUR DREAMS ...
CLINK
...IS HERE!!

TO BE CONTINUED IN *NARUTO* VOL. 20!

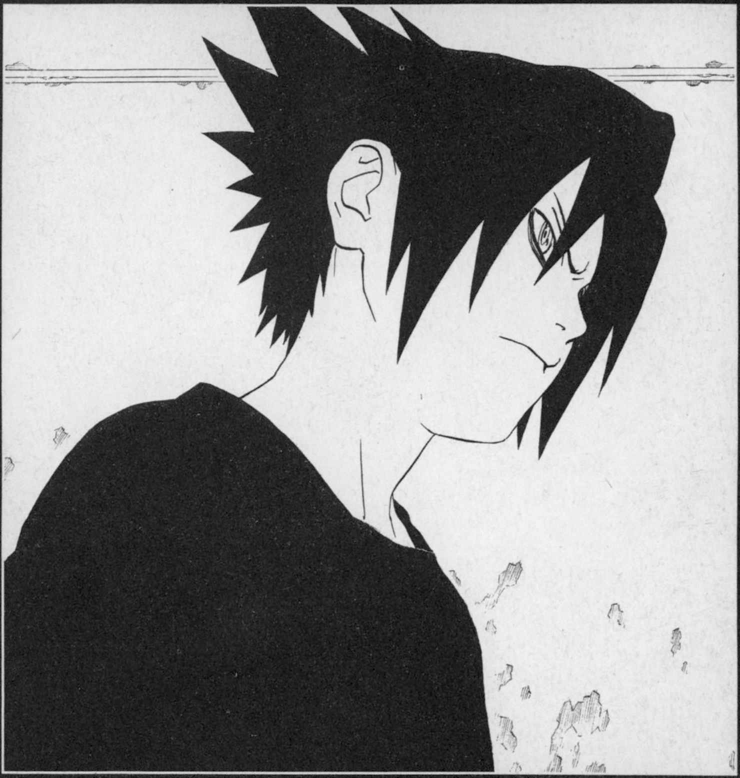

IN THE NEXT VOLUME...

NARUTO VS. SASUKE

It's ninja vs. ninja, with Sakura caught in the middle. Egos are bruised, and some alliances strengthened while others are weakened. With the Sound Four looming close, all three friends speed toward an uncertain future and find that growing up sometimes means growing apart.

AVAILABLE OCTOBER 2007!

SERVING JUSTICE TO EVIL SPIRITS IS THEIR SPECIALTY! SJ

Muhyo & Roji's
Bureau of Supernatural Investigation BSI

MANGA SERIES ON SALE NOW!

$7.99

Muhyo & Roji's
Bureau of Supernatural Investigation
BSI
By Yoshiyuki Nishi

SHONEN JUMP
THE WORLD'S MOST POPULAR MANGA

On sale at:
www.shonenjump.com
Also available at your local bookstore and comic store.

RATED TEEN
ratings.viz.com

VIZ media
www.viz.com

MUHYO TO ROZY NO MAHORITSU SODAN JIMUSHO © 2004 by Yoshiyuki Nishi/SHUEISHA Inc.

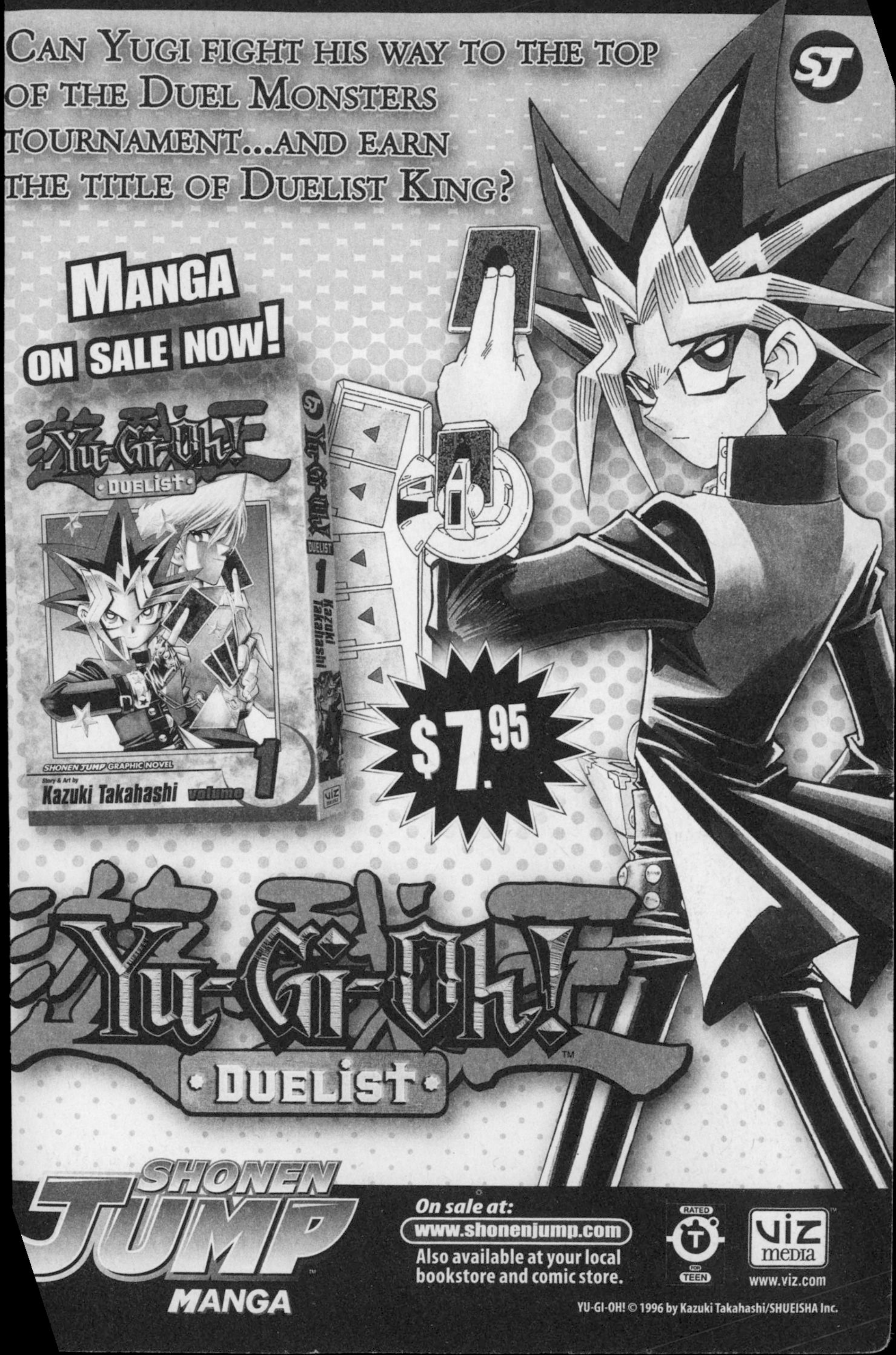
CAN YUGI FIGHT HIS WAY TO THE TOP OF THE DUEL MONSTERS TOURNAMENT...AND EARN THE TITLE OF DUELIST KING?
SJ
MANGA ON SALE NOW!
YU-GI-OH! DUELIST
SHONEN JUMP GRAPHIC NOVEL
Story & Art by
Kazuki Takahashi volume 1
$7.95
YU-GI-OH!™ DUELIST
SHONEN JUMP™ MANGA
On sale at:
www.shonenjump.com
Also available at your local bookstore and comic store.
RATED T FOR TEEN
VIZ media
www.viz.com
YU-GI-OH! © 1996 by Kazuki Takahashi/SHUEISHA Inc.

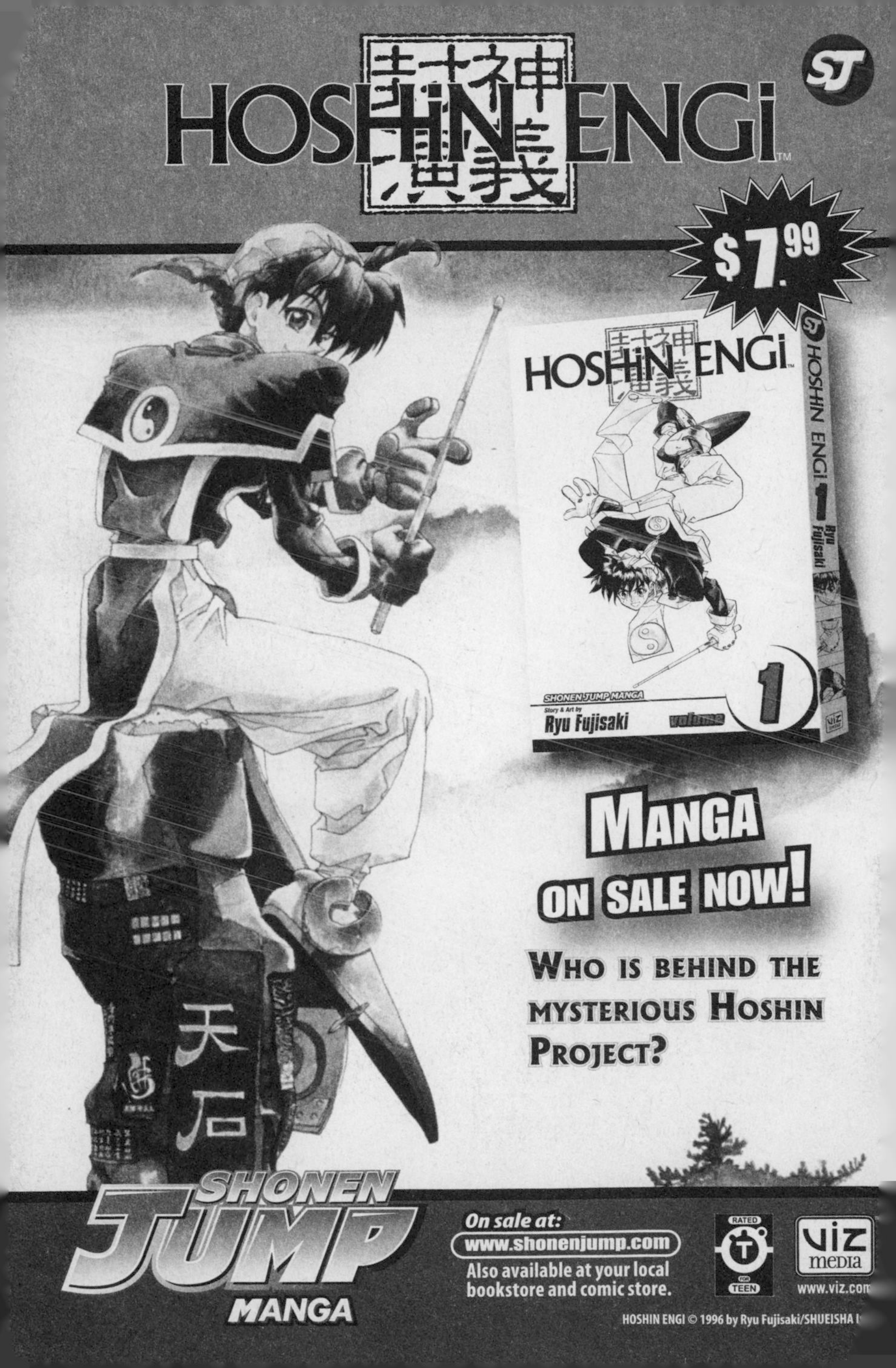
HOSHIN ENGI™
SJ
$7.99
HOSHIN ENGI™
SHONEN JUMP MANGA
Story & Art by
Ryu Fujisaki
volume 1
MANGA
ON SALE NOW!
WHO IS BEHIND THE
MYSTERIOUS HOSHIN
PROJECT?
SHONEN JUMP
MANGA
On sale at:
www.shonenjump.com
Also available at your local
bookstore and comic store.
RATED T FOR TEEN
VIZ media
www.viz.com
HOSHIN ENGI © 1996 by Ryu Fujisaki/SHUEISHA I

Tell us what you think about SHONEN JUMP manga!

Our survey is now available online.
Go to: www.*SHONENJUMP*.com/mangasurvey

Help us make our product offering better!

THE REAL ACTION STARTS IN...

THE WORLD'S MOST POPULAR MANGA
www.shonenjump.com

ST
ADVANCED

ST

VIZ
MEDIA

BLEACH © 2001 by Tite Kubo/SHUEISHA Inc. NARUTO © 1999 by Masashi Kishimoto/SHUEISHA Inc.
DEATH NOTE © 2003 by Tsugumi Ohba, Takeshi Obata/SHUEISHA Inc. ONE PIECE © 1997 by Eiichiro Oda/SHUEISHA Inc.

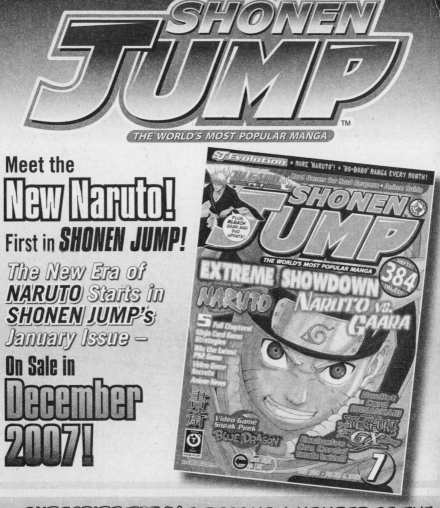

SHONEN JUMP

THE WORLD'S MOST POPULAR MANGA

Meet the
New Naruto!
First in SHONEN JUMP!

The New Era of NARUTO Starts in SHONEN JUMP's January Issue –

On Sale in December 2007!

SUBSCRIBE TODAY & BECOME A MEMBER OF THE SHONEN JUMP SUBSCRIBER CLUB...

You'll Get:
- ➡ Access to EXCLUSIVE Online Content!
- ➡ 50% Savings Off the Newsstand Price!
- ➡ EXCLUSIVE Premiums!

All this available **ONLY** to SUBSCRIBERS!

FILL OUT THE **SUBSCRIPTION CARD** ON THE OTHER SIDE, OR **SUBSCRIBE ONLINE** AT: **WWW.SHONENJUMP.COM**

Save **50%** off the newsstand price!

SHONEN JUMP
THE WORLD'S MOST POPULAR MANGA

SUBSCRIBE TODAY and SAVE 50% OFF the cover price PLUS enjoy all the benefits of the SHONEN JUMP SUBSCRIBER CLUB, exclusive online content and special gifts ONLY AVAILABLE to SUBSCRIBERS!

Only **$29⁹⁵!**

☑ **YES!** Please enter my 1 year subscription (12 issues) to *SHONEN JUMP* at the INCREDIBLY LOW SUBSCRIPTION RATE of $29.95 and sign me up for the SHONEN JUMP Subscriber Club!

NAME

ADDRESS

CITY   STATE   ZIP

EMAIL ADDRESS   P7NAGN

☐ MY CHECK IS ENCLOSED   ☐ BILL ME LATER

CREDIT CARD: ☐ VISA   ☐ MASTERCARD

ACCOUNT #   EXP. DATE

SIGNATURE

CLIP AND MAIL TO ➤

SHONEN JUMP
Subscriptions Service Dept.
P.O. Box 515
Mount Morris, IL 61054-0515

Make checks payable to: **SHONEN JUMP**. Canada price: $41.95 USD, including GST, HST and QST. US/CAN orders only. Credit card payments made SECURE & EASY at www.shonenjump.com. Allow 6-8 weeks for delivery.
NARUTO © 1999 by Masashi Kishimoto/SHUEISHA Inc.

RATED
FOR
TEEN
ratings.viz.com